AF697156

WITHDRAWN

THE EXERCISE OF JUDICIAL POWER 1789 - 1864

DAVID MARSHALL BILLIKOPF

VANTAGE PRESS

New York Washington Hollywood

FIRST EDITION

All rights reserved, including the right of reproduction in whole or in part in any form.

Copyright © 1973 by David Marshall Billikopf

Published by Vantage Press, Inc.
516 West 34th Street, New York, New York 10001

Manufactured in the United States of America

Standard Book No. 533-00755-0

For Louis Marshall

without whom

this book would not have been written

PREFACE

When I was in the sixth grade at school I counted among my personal possessions nine ordinary pencils of various colors, lengths, and states of health, each with its own personality and name. I would be hard put at this late date to give a detailed description of each member of this collection, but a little judicious research has enabled me to reconstruct a list of the names. My pencils were: Charles Evans Hughes, Willis Van Devanter, James Clark McReynolds, Louis D. Brandeis, George Sutherland, Pierce Butler, Harlan Fiske Stone, Owen J. Roberts and Benjamin N. Cardozo. It was 1937 and Roosevelt's court-packing plan was the topic of the day. Of more immediate influence was the fact that on two occasions when my father had taken me on visits to Washington I had met two of my future pencils, Cardozo and Brandeis, the first of whom is reputed to have told me that if I wanted to see the Supreme Court in agreement it would be necessary to watch the members file into the courtroom together, as that was the only thing they did in unison. It is no wonder then that my pencils were usually lined up on opposite sides of the desk in five to four or six to three arrangements.

Childhood games when once put aside are usually put aside forever. However, during the spring of 1966, by which time all of my pencils were long since dead, it occurred to me that reading the reports of the United States Supreme Court might be an entertaining way of spending the coming winter (I was then living in South America). Therefore, believing that the most appropriate place to begin was at the beginning, I acquired the Curtis-Miller twenty-five volume edition of the Supreme Court reports which conveniently took me up to 1864 and the death of Taney. I found the reading far more entertaining and educational than I had suspected, and before long I was taking notes on everything which struck me as interesting. Having had no legal training, what struck me as interesting was everything which might be of interest to the layman, specifically constitutional law and the role of the court in American history. Two years later I supplemented my diet with the equally stimulating thirty-volume collection of federal cases, which included all available reports of the lower federal courts up to the year 1881. Here I discovered another world of information which forms an integral part of the development of American Constitutional law. I realized then that I must choose between spending the remainder of my life reading the more than three hundred volumes of Supreme Court reports which have appeared since the Civil War, as well as an even greater number emanating from the lower courts, or confining myself to some topical or chronological division of the entire subject in the hopes of producing a book.

The final choice was the judicial power of the United States during the period 1789-1864, a topic which has never received the thorough treatment which has been given to other portions of the Constitution, such as the contract or commerce clauses. Curtis and Miller supplied the original motive for deciding on the cut-off point in time; however, there were other good and more substantial reasons. The year 1864 marked the death of Chief Justice Taney and the period which may be called the Marshall-Taney era; one year later the Civil War came to an end which, along with the Thirteenth and Fourteenth Amendments, ratified soon after, marked the beginning of a new period in American history. The greater part of the cases arising out of the Civil War itself, however, were commenced or continued beyond 1864 and are therefore not included in this study.

Strictly speaking, every case brought before a judge involves—implicitly or explicitly—the jurisdiction and power of the court. In the majority of adjudged cases neither jurisdiction nor judicial power are discussed; they are assumed, either on the basis of previous decisions or because there is no question as to the court's authority to proceed with the substance or merits of the suit. But there is another range of cases where the judges are obligated to examine conscientiously the very foundation of their own authority;

these are the cases in which the jurisdiction or powers of the court are challenged, either by the contending parties or the judges themselves. This study of the exercise of judicial power is deliberately confined to the examination of these latter cases, in which the judiciary turned inward in order to determine its own limits and role under the Constitution and laws, as well as its relationships with the other branches of government. It is for this reason that so many leading constitutional cases of the period have been omitted except insofar as they fall within the discussion of the Third Article of the Constitution.

This study has gone beyond the usual limits of constitutional law, especially in the discussion of the Judiciary Act of 1789. It is not possible to understand the manner in which the power and jurisdiction of the federal courts developed without constant and recurring reference to this early and basic law. Thus there is no pretense of confining this work to "constitutional law" in the strictest sense. Further, it is perhaps necessary to justify the length at which the admiralty and maritime jurisdiction of the United States is discussed. Strictly speaking, anything to be determined under this heading is a Constitutional question; but even if it were not, the subject was of such importance during the early decades of American history—an importance equalled only by that of the commerce clause in the years which followed—that the author feels justified in making up for the almost total neglect into which the topic has fallen by devoting an entire chapter to it.

As for the citation of opinions of the lower federal courts, these have been generally ignored in treatises on Constitutional law, except perhaps in specialized studies and biographies of the justices. They are, however, of the utmost importance: first, because the lower court opinions often anticipated the final decisions handed down by the Supreme Court in the same or similar cases; secondly, because the judgments of these lower courts were often final; if not forever, at least for long periods of time. And, like the decisions of the higher court, they were authoritative, even if in a more limited geographical scope.

It is *because* these opinions are authoritative that they

possess so much value. They are not mere speculations of political philosophers or historians, but binding rules and interpretations as to the meaning of the Constitution. They not only possess validity in themselves but constitute the foundation on which later generations of judges were to build. It is because the words of the jurists rather than any summaries were authoritative that a more than generous use of quotations has been made. It is hoped, however, that the threads employed by the author to string these citations together in orderly fashion will convert this book from a simple anthology into a logical treatment of the development of ideas.

It is perhaps proper at this point to say a few words about a deliberate omission. Most studies of constitutional law have been written in terms of the historical and political setting which gave rise to or were the results of the leading cases decided by the court[1], or with special emphasis on the political, economic or personal bias of the justices. In such an approach, motives have often been considered more important than the abstract principles of jurisprudence underlying the decisions of the court, to the extreme, at times, of questioning the very existence of principle. Moreover, this "following the election returns" interpretation of Constitutional law fails to do justice to the intrinsic merits of the opinions (and dissents) of the court and tends to undermine both the validity and the authority of the court's decisions.

It is the opinion of this author that it is the final result reached by the court and handed down to us in the form of opinions that counts, far more than the motives underlying those opinions or the historical context which gave rise to them. Just as the written product of the Constitutional Convention rather than the debates and commentaries constitutes the authoritative Constitution of the United States, it is the published reports of the Supreme Court rather than the factors which motivated the decisions which constitute the authoritative interpretation of the Constitution. No matter how much a decision may be explained away, it is the opinion and not the explanation which stands and is inherited by future generations. Further, no matter how we may feel personally about the members of the court at any given time, the decisions of the court as a collective body, transcending the individuals which compose it, continue to constitute the final constitutional authority in spite of attempts to whittle away at their validity by impugning the motives of their authors. It is for this reason that the present study chooses to stand on the opinions of the court and the opinions and dissents of its individual members.

Constitutionally speaking, the court is more than the sum of its individual members, and only an opinion supported by a majority may be considered *authoritative.* Nevertheless, the concurring opinions and dissents deserve and are given special attention in this study: first, in order to follow the contributions made to constitutional thought by the individual justices; second, because by contrasting with the majority opinion they aid us in understanding just what was decided by the court; and finally, because they play an essential role in the evolution of constitutional exegesis.

(*Note:* Some of the footnotes at the end of each chapter, in addition to serving as reference notes, will further explain some of the thinking which entered into many Supreme Court decisions.)

[1] The best short introduction to constitutional law is, perhaps, Benjamin F. Wright's *The Growth of American Constitutional Law.* There are doubtless many excellent books which go beyond the published opinions and enhance the understanding of the reader by delving further behind the scene, without undermining respect for the integrity of the court. Among these are Charles Warren's gossipy *The Supreme Court in United States History* and Charles G. Haines' *The Role of the Supreme Court in American Government and Politics, 1789-1835* and its sequel, co-authored by Foster Sherwood, covering the period 1835-1864.

CONTENTS

THE EXERCISE OF JUDICIAL POWER 1789 - 1864

CHAPTER ONE

THE COURTS OF THE UNITED STATES

One of the great achievements of the Constitutional Convention of 1787 was the establishment of a judicial system for the new nation which would be independent of the states and the existing state judiciaries. The new courts, which were created to exercise the judicial power of the United States, owed their existence to three sources: the Constitution, the Congress, and the President of the United States. The first created them in theory, the second created them in fact, and the third created their membership. They owed their power not only to the Constitution and the Congress but to one additional source: themselves.

Succinctly but adequately, the Constitution vested the judicial power of the United States "in one Supreme Court, and in such inferior courts as the Congress may from time to time ordain and establish."[1] The limits of jurisdiction were given in the subsequent section.[2] In Article II, the President was given the power to nominate and appoint, with the advice and consent of the Senate, the judges of the Supreme Court and the inferior courts.[3] Tenure for life, or during good behavior, was guaranteed the judges by the second sentence of Article III, Section 1.

If the Constitution itself was the *sine qua non* of the judicial power of the United States, the Judiciary Act of September 24, 1789, was the blueprint and enabling act without which the Supreme Court and the lower courts would not have come into being.[4] Section 1 stipulated that, "The Supreme Court of the United States shall consist of a chief justice and five associate justices,"[5] and proceeded to fix the time for the court's sessions. Sections 2, 3, 4 and 5 brought to life district courts, district judges[6] and circuit courts. Sections 9, 10 and 11 spelled out the jurisdiction of the district and circuit courts. Section 12 provided for the removal of causes from the state courts to the federal courts under certain conditions. Section 13 described the exclusive and the original but not exclusive jurisdiction of the Supreme Court, authorized its appellate jurisdiction, and enumerated certain of its powers. Section 14 referred to the writs which both the Supreme Court and the lower courts could issue. Section 16 prohibited suits in equity where remedy at law was available. Section 22 outlined the procedure for appeals within the federal system, while Section 25 provided for examination by the Supreme Court of the judgments of the highest courts of the states where federal questions were involved. Finally, Section 34 specified that the laws of the states should be regarded as rules of decision in trials in the courts of the United States.

1. The Supreme Court

The first justices to serve on the Supreme Court reflected a geographical distribution which was to prevail for at least the first seventy years of the court's history. This is so evident that it is safe to speak of the New England seat, the New York seat, the Virginia seat, etc. Chief Justice John Jay, co-author of *The Federalist*, was from New York; William Cushing was from Massachusetts; James Wilson, signer of the Delaration of Independence and member of the Constitutional Convention, from Pennsylvania; John Blair and John Rutledge[7], from Virginia and South Carolina, respectively, also members of the Constitutional Convention, and James Iredell, from North Carolina. The first meetings of the court took place in New York City in February, 1790, and again in August of the same year.

During the following decade in which the court met in Philadelphia, a number of changes took place in its membership. Rutledge was replaced by Thomas Johnson of Maryland who in turn was succeeded by William Paterson of New Jersey. When John Jay resigned in 1795 his place was given to Rutledge, who managed to serve one term before his nomination was rejected by the Senate. Oliver Ellsworth of

Connecticut became the next chief justice, to serve only for four years. Blair was replaced by Samuel Chase of Maryland; Wilson by Bushrod Washington (who was from Virginia but represented the "Pennsylvania" seat); and Iredell by Alfred Moore of North Carolina.

It is difficult to attribute any lasting important contribution to constitutional law or to the evolution of the powers of the court to any of the judges whose term expired before the turn of the century, though Justice Iredell has been cited for his dissenting opinion in *Chisholm v. Georgia*, which agreed with the subsequently adopted Eleventh Amendment.

In 1801, when John Marshall took his seat as Chief Justice of the Supreme Court, which henceforth would meet in Washington, only William Cushing remained of the original appointees. But six different states were still represented on the court, if Bushrod Washington is considered in terms of his Pennsylvania Circuit. The period between Marshall's accession to the court and the outbreak of the Civil War is perhaps the period of greatest stability on the court in terms of its membership. Only twenty-one new justices took office during those sixty years, and for one period of eleven years (1812-1823) no change at all took place on the court. It is revealing that during this period of stability some of the court's most important decisions were handed down, in contrast to the first ten years of continual rotation.

John Marshall served for 34 years, while William Johnson of South Carolina, Jefferson's first appointee to the court, in replacement of Moore, served for 30 years, as did Bushrod Washington, who had joined the court only two years before Marshall. Other justices to serve long terms during the Marshall-Taney period were: Joseph Story, 33 years; John McLean, 31 years; John Catron, 28 years; and Roger Taney, also 28 years. James Wayne, Samuel Nelson and Robert Grier, averaging 29 years on the court, continued to serve until after the Civil War. Longevity is no guarantee of creative ability or substantial achievement, but there is no doubt that among the ten justices listed above, Marshall, Johnson, Story and Taney earned permanent niches in the history of the court, while Washington and McLean were not without their important contributions in their own fields.

In 1807 a new associate judgeship was created by an act of Congress, bringing the total number of justices to seven. The new "Western" post was first filled by Thomas Todd of Kentucky. In the same year Brockholst Livingston of New York was named to replace Paterson, while in 1812 Joseph Story joined the court following the death of Cushing. Gabriel Duval's appointment to the Maryland seat rounded out the membership of the court during the middle period of the Marshall era.

Smith Thompson of New York succeeded to Livingston's seat in 1823, and in turn was replaced by Samuel Nelson in 1843. Robert Trimble of Kentucky served only long enough to take part in *Ogden v. Saunders* and a few other cases before the new seat, which he had inherited from Todd, was turned over to John McLean of Ohio, a "minor" justice whose outspoken ideas were felt in all fields of law. In 1830 Henry Baldwin of Pennsylvania replaced Bushrod Washington, and although Baldwin's personality has been described as erratic, his unique and close reasoning in cases ranging from admiralty to appellate jurisdiction is well worth studying. Another important appointment to the court—and one might say a solid one—was that of James Moore Wayne of Georgia who, to his credit, was more Unionist than Southerner, at a time when his state followed another course.

By chance the elderly Gabriel Duval of Maryland resigned in the same year that Marshall of Virginia died. Thus President Jackson was able to preserve the Virginia and Maryland seats, even if the new chief justice, Roger Taney, represented Maryland while the new associate justice, Philip Barbour, was the representative of Virginia. Two years later, in 1837, a new Act of the Congress created two new positions on the court, which were filled by John Catron of Tennessee and John McKinley of Alabama.

Only a few changes took place during the remaining years before the Civil War. Peter V. Daniel, arch-conservative and unyielding opponent of the extension of federal jurisdiction,[8] replaced the short-lived Barbour in 1841. In 1845-1846, Samuel Nelson of New York replaced Thompson; Levi Woodbury of New Hampshire succeeded to Story's seat;

and Robert Grier followed Baldwin in Pennsylvania. Of these three, Woodbury proved to be the most outstanding, albeit prolix; unfortunately death terminated his term on the court only five years later. He was succeeded, in turn, by the equally capable and equally prolix Benjamin R. Curtis of Massachusetts, whose term was also cut short, by resignation rather than by death. Nathan Clifford of Maine completed the roster of New England justices. The only other change was the accession of John A. Campbell of Alabama to McKinley's seat.

During the final years of the Taney period and following the outbreak of the Civil War, President Lincoln made four appointments: Noah H. Swayne of Ohio to replace McLean; Samuel F. Miller of Iowa and David Davis of Illinois to fill the vacant seats of two Southerners, Daniel (who died on the eve of the war) and Campbell (who submitted his resignation when the war broke out). When Congress added a tenth justice to the court in 1863, the seat was filled by Stephen J. Field of California.[9] [10]

2. The Lower Federal Courts

The original Judiciary Act of 1789 created eleven district courts to coincide with each of the states which had by that date ratified the Constitution. Each district court was presided over by a district judge. These districts were in turn grouped into three circuits: Eastern, Middle and Southern. Two justices of the Supreme Court were assigned to each circuit on a permanent basis. In addition to fulfilling their duties on the Supreme Court, the two justices were directed to hold court twice a year in each district within their circuit, in company with the district judge. The court so held was known as the Circuit Court for the District of (name of state).[11] Though the name and duties of these circuit courts differed from those of either of the other courts, the membership of the former was drawn entirely from the district and Supreme Courts. Thus there were no circuit judges as such, only circuit courts.

Whereas independent districts were established in Maine

and Kentucky, during 1790 and 1791 the newly created District Courts of Rhode Island and Vermont were added to the Eastern District while North Carolina became a part of the Southern District. Thus by 1792 there were fourteen district courts within the three circuits and two district courts without. Already the burden on the Supreme Court justices of holding so many sessions and of doing so much circuit riding became the subject of a letter of complaint from the justices to President Washington. The following year, therefore, the Congress passed an Act (March 2, 1793) providing that the circuit courts would henceforth be composed of but one justice and the district judge, thus eliminating an unnecessary duplication and reducing by half the circuit duties of each justice. The justices were to be assigned to different circuits each year instead of being confined to a fixed circuit as originally provided.

Although the measure offered some relief, it was still considered unsatisfactory by the justices and the Attorney General as well as many members of Congress.[12] An attempt to divorce the district courts from state boundaries and to relieve the justices of circuit duty was defeated in 1800, but in the following year, on the eve of Jefferson's accession to the presidency, the Federalist-controlled Congress passed the Circuit Court Act of February 13, 1801. This law effectively relieved the Supreme Court justices of all circuit court duties, at the same time creating a total of six circuit courts (First to Sixth) and sixteen separate circuit judgeships which were promptly filled by President Adams in his last days of office.

Whether or not such an organization of the courts would have prospered at a period free of party passion, the change was poorly timed insofar as its ultimate success was concerned, for virtually the first effort made by the victorious anti-Federalists was to repeal the Act of 1801, mostly as a legal means of undoing the appointment of sixteen Federalist judges,[13] and only partly as a result of the conviction that it was unwise to separate the Supreme Court justices from their duties on the local benches.

The Repeal Act of March 8, 1802 was immediately followed by the Act of April 29th, which borrowed from the

Circuit Court Act (just repealed) the division of the courts into six circuits and assigned one Supreme Court justice to each circuit on a permanent basis. The circuit courts were to be composed of one justice and the district judge, and two annual sessions were to be held each year in each district.[14] The territories of the circuits were by this time rearranged in such a way that no circuit included more than four districts. (Between 1791 and 1801, the Eastern Circuit comprehended six districts.) The repeal of the 1801 Act and the operation of the Act of April 29th went into effect on July 1st, 1802.

No substantial changes in the organization of the Federal courts were made until after the close of the Civil War, although in 1844 the justices were relieved from attending more than one term of circuit court within each district in any year. In 1807 the Seventh Circuit was created and a seventh justice was added to the Supreme Court. Also in 1837, an eighth and ninth circuit with two new seats on the Supreme Court bench were created. Finally in 1855 a California circuit was added, headed by a specially appointed circuit judge who did not have a seat on the bench of the High Court. (For three brief years, 1863-1866, a Tenth Circuit existed with a tenth member of the Supreme Court. This expansion was short-lived.)

It was only in 1869 that Congress enacted a law (Act of April 10th) drastically curtailing circuit riding; another two decades passed before a system of circuit courts of appeal, similar to that provided for in the Act of 1801, was established (Act of March 3, 1891). As late as 1923, however, Supreme Court justices were still sitting occasionally on circuit courts.[15]

3. Circuit Duty of Supreme Court Justices

No sooner had the Judiciary Act of 1789 gone into effect than the circuit duties of the Supreme Court justices came under fire in a debate which was to continue for over eighty years. The initial attack was three-pronged: the Congress did not possess the constitutional power to impose circuit duty on the justices; the justices did not have time to fulfill both duties; the hardships and physical risks of travel were excessive.

As early as 1790, Chief Justice Jay raised the constitutional issue in a complaint to President Washington. The justices, however, acquiesced to the statute requiring performance of circuit duty, and the issue did not arise again until Marshall succeeded to the bench and faced the requirements of the new Act of 1802. His own opinion was that "the Constitution requires distinct appointments and commissions for the Judges of the inferior Courts from those of the Supreme Court",[16] but he deferred to the opinion of his associates for a final determination of the matter. Paterson, Cushing and Washington considered that the question of constitutionality must be regarded as settled, while Chase inclined to Marshall's point of view. In March, 1803, the Court, speaking through Paterson, put the Constitutional question to rest in *Stuart v. Laird:* "Practice and acquiescence. . .for a period of years, commencing with the organization of the judicial system, affords an irresistible answer, and has indeed fixed the construction. It is a contemporary interpretation of the most forcible nature. This practical exposition is too strong and obstinate to be shaken or controlled. Of course, the question is at rest, and ought not now to be disturbed."[17]

Fourteen years later, in *United States v. Jacobson,*[18] a capital case in the Circuit Court for New York, presided over by Justice Livingston, involving the willful destruction of his ship by a master with intent to commit fraud. Before sentencing, the defendant's counsel pleaded the unconstitutionality of that part of the Act of 1802 assigning Justices of the Supreme Court to hold circuit courts. Livingston replied that he was "decidedly in favor of the objection. The Act of Congress directing the justices of the Supreme Court to hold circuit courts was unconstitutional, and not binding on the judges." After stating his arguments against such circuit duty, Livingston acknowledged that:

". . .it is unnecessary to pursue this inquiry further; for

although this be my own opinion, which I have thought it my duty to express, it will be remembered that the question came before the Supreme Court in 1803, when the judges, waiving any opinion on the constitutionality of this act, were pleased to consider the practice of a few years under it as precluding all arguments on the subject. Whether, if the question shall ever come before that court, it will consider such acquiescence as putting at rest this great constitutional question I cannot say, as it has never received a decision on its merits. It is not yet too late, in my opinion, to review the one which has taken place; but until that be done in its proper place, this court is bound by it. . ."

Whereupon the judge sentenced the prisoner to be executed, thus laying to rest both the constitutional objections to circuit duty and the master of the ship *Aristides.* (No appeal from a decision of a circuit court in a criminal case was available unless the circuit court was divided.)

Another early and more enduring argument was that put forth by Attorney General Edmund Randolph in a report to the Congress at the end of 1790: the justices would not find time to fulfill both duties. Furthermore, the work of the Supreme Court demanded the entire energy and talent of the judges. The only effective reply to this argument was an attempt to demonstrate that the volume of business did not yet justify an increase in the number of judicial posts, a contention which soon became obsolete.

To the third argument that circuit duty involved excessive hardship and physical risk, no reply was attempted. The physical labor of travel over great distances with scanty means of transportation was vividly depicted. The justices were often unable to attend circuits due to illness or bad weather.[19] Livingston pointed out that, "It is a fact that the labor of holding circuit courts has become much more burdensome to the judges of the Supreme Court than the discharge of their regular, appropriate, and constitutional functions in the court for which they are commissioned. It may be added, for so the fact is, that the business of the Supreme Court is much impeded by the attention of the judges to their circuit duties."[20]

Furthermore, as the nation moved westward there were even greater distances to travel. In 1835, the thought of creating but one Western circuit to cover the independent districts which had been established since the Seventh Circuit had been created in 1807, prompted Senator Benton of Missouri to protest against "this perfect monstrosity. . .which extended from the Gulf of Mexico to Lake Michigan, from the torrid to the frigid zone" and to wonder whether it wouldn't be more prudent to wait "till we have arrived at a greater art in aerial navigation," unless it was possible for the circuit justice to attach himself "to one of those flights of wild geese which periodically emigrate from the North." [21]

In 1838, it was estimated that the distance travelled by the justices on circuit duty varied from 438 miles for Taney to 10,000 for McKinley in Alabama, Louisiana, Mississippi and Arkansas.[22]

Two further arguments contrary to circuit duty were put forward: that it would be extremely unlikely that the justices, when hearing appeals on the Supreme bench, would change the opinions they had emitted on the circuit court (an objection that became virtually irrelevant once the number of justices sitting in any one case at circuit was reduced from two to one and as the total number of justices increased); and that an excessive increase in the number of justices would result from an increase in the number of circuits needed to cover the nation.[23]

On the other side there were also three principal arguments in favor of maintaining the existing organization of the courts: the need for the justices to keep in close contact with the nation; fear of the influence of Washington, D.C., and fear of the increasing Executive patronage which would result from the naming of a new set of judges to preside over the circuits.

A genuine fear existed that, as the result of the abolition of circuit duty, the justices would lose contact with the local bar and other judges and become only book-men, overly insulated; that they would become alienated from the people and the needs of the states; that they would not be versed in local laws.[24]

Further, it was felt that the justices should preside over jury trials, which was practical only on the circuits and, as Daniel Webster pointed out in 1826, it was necessary for them to "see in practice the operation and effect of their own decisions" to "prevent theory from running too far."[25]

As the counterpart of this argument, it was pointed out that the justices were to serve as educative agencies and symbols of a new nation.[26] Thus they were to carry the message of federalism or nationalism from Washington to the provinces. (Ironically, it was the Federalists who principally opposed circuit duty and the anti-Federalists who favored it.)

The fear lest the justices would become "completely cloistered within the city of Washington"[27] and that they would succumb to its "polluted" atmosphere (at that time the problem was exclusively moral) was accompanied by the claim that the Court would end by swallowing the Executive or that the Executive would end by swallowing the Court.

Of a practical nature and therefore of more weight than the theoretical arguments was the opposition to the establishment of new circuit judgeships due to the fear of increasing Executive patronage. Several times, when it appeared possible that a change in the system would be made, Congressional members of the opposition party held back in order to deprive the President of the opportunity to fill the new judicial posts which would have been created. That this fear was justified may be best illustrated by President Adams' last-minute nomination of sixteen new circuit judges in 1801 "chosen practically from members of his own party."[28]

But, finally, the increase in federal jurisdiction and the growing litigation created a case load which no longer allowed time for the justices to perform circuit duty. This practical fact was decisive and was recognized after the Civil War, when relief was finally if not completely granted.

Footnotes:

CHAPTER ONE:

[1] Article III, Section 1.

[2] Chapters Five, Six, Seven and parts of other chapters deal with the subject of jurisdiction.

[3] "All other officers of the United States whose appointments are not herein otherwise provided for, and which shall be established by law."

[4] The Supreme Court was created by the Constitution and some of its powers and jurisdiction were given, but the nature of its composition—one judge? thirteen judges?—not to mention its manner of proceeding, depended on Congressional action. See Robert Jennings Harris, *The Judicial Power of the United States*, p. 89: "The debates in Congress over the judiciary bill are significant. . .because they reveal that Congress, at least, entertained no delusions concerning. . .the self-executing nature of the grant of judicial power."

[5] The compensation of the judges was fixed by a law enacted the preceding day: Chief Justice, $4,000; associate justices, $3,500. Compare these salaries with that of the President: $25,000.

[6] The salaries of the district judges ranged from $800 (Delaware) to $1,800 (Virginia and South Carolina).

[7] Rutledge never attended court as an associate justice.

[8] One of this author's "favorite" justices.

[9] No attempt is made here to assess any of these post-1860 appointees or Clifford, all of whom more properly belong to a subsequent era.

[10] This brief listing of names with briefer evaluations is intended to be just that. There is no reference to political affiliations as this is not a political history. See Warren, *The Supreme Court in United States History, passim,* for more information on the appointment of justices and the political setting. See also *Justices of the U.S. Supreme Court, 1789-1969*, edited by Leon Friedman and Fred L. Israel, Vols. I and II, for recent biographical sketches of the members of the court during the period 1789-1864.

[11] For the locations of the first Circuit Courts, see Section 5 of the Act of September 24, 1789.

[12] For the history of legislation concerning the circuit duty of the Justices, see "Circuit Courts" in the index of Warren, *op. cit.*, II, 771, and Frankfurter, *The Business of the Supreme Court, passim.* For arguments pro and con, see "Circuit Duty of Supreme Court Justices."

[13] Only two ever entered the Federal judiciary again: Dominick Augustine Hall became District Judge for New Orleans and later Louisiana (1804-1813; 1813-1820); while Henry Potter served as District Judge for North Carolina from 1802 until his death at the age of 92 in 1857. Two of the other "short-lived" circuit judges became Chief Justices of their own states: Jeremiah Smith (New Hampshire) and William Tilghman (Pennsylvania).

[14] The first Circuit Justices were: William Cushing (First); William Paterson (Second); Bushrod Washington (Third); Samuel Chase (Fourth); Chief Justice John Marshall (Fifth); and Alfred Moore (Sixth).

[15] Frankfurter, 79.

[16] Warren, I, 270.

[17] I Cranch 299; 309.

[18] 26 FC 567 (1817).

[19] In February 1811, only three Justices showed up in Washington and no term was held that year. In February 1812, Cranch reported that "The Chief Justice did not attend until Thursday, February 18th. He received an injury by the oversetting of the stagecoach on his journey from Richmond." (7 Cranch 1).

[20] 26 FC 567 (1817).

[21] Warren, I, 801.

[22] In 1849, Howard reported that "Mr. Justice McKinley did not attend the court during this term, having been engaged in holding an important session of the United States circuit court at New Orleans." (8 Howard 1).

[23] Story's reaction in 1838 to the expansion of the Court to nine members was: "Many men of many minds require a great deal of discussion to compel them to come to definite results; and we found ourselves often involved in long and very tedious debate. I verily believe, if there were twelve Judges, we should do no business at all, or at least very little." Warren, II, 42.

[24] To this last contention, Gouverneur Morris replied in the Senate in 1802: "I am not quite convinced that riding rapidly from one end of the country to another is the best way to study law." Frankfurter, 17.

[25] Warren, I, 678.

[26] Frankfurter, 19.

[27] Warren, I, 672.

[28] Warren, I, 188.

CHAPTER TWO:

JUDICIAL POWER IN GENERAL

1. 1790-1821

When Chief Justice John Jay and his three associates met for the first time in New York in February, 1790, to organize the Supreme Court of the United States, they faced an empty docket. Although the previous year had witnessed both the passage of the first Judiciary Act and the appointment of the judges to the Court, the new government was less than a year old and there were no cases or controversies to be decided. The docket remained empty throughout 1790 and until August of the following year when the Court, now meeting in Philadelphia, dismissed the first case which was presented to it. It was not until August, 1793, that the Court first handed down a final decision, in *Chisholm v. Georgia.*

This slow start is understandable when we recall that each of the thirteen states had its own judicial system which existed anterior and parallel to the new federal courts. Although the jurisdiction of the national courts as outlined in the Constitution was most ample, there were as yet few laws or treaties to interpret, no constitutional conflicts, and only a handful of controversies arising out of diversity of citizenship. The Supreme Court was not created to give gratuitous opinions or to announce general theories regarding the law or the Constitution; thus it must wait patiently to hear and decide concrete cases, in law and equity, of admiralty and maritime jurisdiction, which were brought before it.

Although members of the Court had little to do, other

than in the fulfillment of their circuit court obligations, they conscientiously limited the exercise of their duties by refusing to act in their official capacity as commissioners under an act of Congress designating them to pass on pension claims arising out of the Revolutionary War. While thus placing a limit on their constitutional duties, at the same time they strengthened the power and the independence of the judiciary. Although the Supreme Court as such did not rule on the subject, the members of the Court, in their separate circuits, made statements of their views which, though extra-judicial in nature, amounted to a binding rule of conduct. A portion of the opinion of the Circuit Court for the District of New York summarizes the views of the Justices. That Court agreed:

"That by the Constitution of the United States, the government thereof is divided into three distinct and independent branches, and that it is the duty of each to abstain from, and to oppose encroachments on either.

"That neither the Legislative nor the Executive branches can, constitutionally, assign to the Judicial any duties but such as are properly judicial, and to be performed in a judicial manner.

"That the duties assigned to the Circuit Courts by this act are not of that description, and that the act itself does not appear to contemplate them as such, inasmuch as it subjects the decisions of these courts, made pursuant to those duties, first to the consideration and suspension of the Secretary at War, and then to the revision of the Legislature; *whereas by the Constitution, neither the Secretary at War, nor any other Executive officer, nor even the Legislature, are authorized to sit as a Court of Errors on the judicial acts or opinions of this Court.*"[1]

The Circuit Court for the District of Pennsylvania reiterated this view, stating that "such revision and control we deemed radically inconsistent with the independence of that judicial power which is vested in the courts;"[2] while in North Carolina, Justice Iredell observed, "*that no decision of any court of the United States can, under any circumstances, in our opinion, agreeable to the Constitution, be liable to a reversion, or even suspension, by the Legislature itself,* in whom no judicial power of any kind appears to be vested, but the important one relative to impeachments." [3]

These early opinions of the Supreme Court Justices were doubly important. Not only did the Judges explicitly deny to the Legislature and the Executive the right to revise the decisions of the courts, but tacitly they assumed the right to pass judgment on the validity of an act of Congress. Referring to these pension claim cases sixty years later, Chief Justice Roger Taney, in a note to a case of a similar nature, stated:

"The result of the opinions expressed by the judges of the Supreme Court of that day in the note to Hayburn's case, and in the case of the *United States v. Todd*, is this:

"1. That the power to be conferred on the circuit courts of the United States by the act of 1792 was not judicial power within the meaning of the Constitution, and was, therefore, unconstitutional, and could not lawfully be exercised by the courts."[4]

Thus, before any case had been finally decided by the Supreme Court, the Justices were already concerned with the threefold problem of judicial duty, judicial independence, and judicial review. If the first of these related subjects was relatively clear, the second generally acceptable but still debatable, the third was highly controversial. But the controversy was yet to begin, for it was certainly not the opinions of the circuit courts on the invalid pensioners' cases that ignited the flame.

The first case in which the Supreme Court handed down a final decision was that of *Chisholm v. Georgia,*[5] in August, 1793. The question was whether, in accordance with the constitutional provision that "the judicial power shall extend to controversies between a state and citizens of another state," the Supreme Court could exercise jurisdiction in a suit initiated by a citizen of South Carolina against the State of Georgia. All but one of the justices held that the judicial power did extend to such controversies. But this first decision of the court was also the first one which was directly overruled by an amendment to the Constitution, for no sooner had the judgment been given than the Eleventh

Amendment was proposed and adopted. Confirming the interpretation of the sole dissenter, Justice Iredell, the amendment stated that: "The judicial power of the United States shall not be construed to extend to any suit in law or equity, commenced or prosecuted against one of the United States by citizens of another state, or by citizens or subjects of any foreign state." The ease and rapidity with which this amendment was adopted pointed the path to those who, in the future, were to express their discontent with constitutional rulings and decisions of the court and who favored the process of amendment as the solution. But with counted exceptions the path was not to be repeated with similar success, and henceforth the decisions of the court were to stand until modified by the court itself.

Meanwhile, the circuit courts began to assume an almost revolutionary power which was nowhere explicitly granted to them, either by the Constitution or by law—the right to pass on the constitutionality of state statutes. As early as May, 1791, the Circuit Court for the First Circuit was confronted with a conflict between a statute law of the State of Connecticut and the treaty of peace with Great Britain. The judges of the court came to the conclusion that the state law infringed the provisions of the treaty and was therefore invalid.[6] Similar decisions were made in the two following years in the circuit courts meeting in Savannah and Charleston, where Judge Iredell and Judge Paterson, respectively, came to the same conclusion reached in the Connecticut case.[7]

At the same time, in Rhode Island, the circuit court, for the first time, held that a state law was invalid because it was in conflict with a provision of the Constitution of the United States. In *Champion v. Casey* (1792), the court held that a state law exempting an individual from arrest and his estate from attachment for private debt was "clearly a law impairing the obligation of contracts, and therefore contrary to the Constitution of the United States."[8]

Three years later Judge Paterson, sitting in the Circuit Court for the District of Pennsylvania, held a state statute to be void under the Constitution of Pennsylvania and unconstitutional under the contract clause of the United

States Constitution. Here, in *Vanhorne's Lessee v. Dorrance* (1795), in Paterson's charge to the jury, for the first time in an authoritative court opinion we find a general discussion of the concept of constitutionality and judicial review which goes beyond the immediate issue involved.

"In England, from whence most of our legal principles and legislative notions are derived," the judge points out, "the authority of the Parliament is transcendent and has no bounds."

After quoting a passage from Coke on Parliament, Paterson proceeds with an essay which is worth quoting in its entirety, considering its clear, forceful and early presentation of what was to become a fundamental tenet of American constitutional law:

"From this passage it is evident, that, in England, the authority of the Parliament runs without limits, and rises above control. It is difficult to say what the Constitution of England is because, not being reduced to written certainty and precision, it lies entirely at the mercy of the Parliament. It bends to every governmental exigency; it varies and is blown about by every breeze of legislative humor or political caprice. Some of the judges in England have had the boldness to assert that an act of Parliament, made against natural equity, is void; but this opinion contravenes the general position, that the validity of an act cannot be drawn into question by the judicial department. It cannot be disputed and must be obeyed. The power of Parliament is absolute and transcendant; it is omnipotent in the scale of political existence. Besides, in England there is no written Constitution, no fundamental law, nothing visible, nothing real, nothing certain, by which a statute can be tested. In America the case is widely different: Every state in the Union has its Constitution reduced to written exactitude and precision.

"What is a Constitution? It is the form of government, delineated by the mighty hand of the people, in which certain first principles of fundamental laws are established. The Constitution is certain and fixed; it contains the permanent will of the people and is the supreme law of the land, it is paramount to the power of the Legislature, and can be revoked or altered only by the authority that made it. The life-giving principle and the death-doing stroke must proceed from the same hand. What are legislatures? Creatures of the Constitution; they owe their existence to the Constitution; they derive their powers from the Constitution; it is their commission, and therefore all their acts must be conformable to it, or else they will be void. The Constitution is the work or will of the people themselves, in their original, sovereign, and unlimited capacity. Law is the work or will of the Legislature in their derivative subordinate capacity. The one is the work of the Creator, and the other of the Creature. The Constitution fixes limits to the exercise of legislative authority, and prescribes the orbit within which it must move. In short, gentlemen, the Constitution is the sum of the political system, around which all legislative, executive and judicial bodies must revolve. Whatever may be the case in other countries, yet in this there can be no doubt, that every Act of the Legislature repugnant to the Constitution is absolutely void. . .

"I take it to be a clear position; that if a legislative act oppugns a constitutional principle, the former must give way and be rejected on the score of repugnance. I hold it to be a position equally clear and sound that in such case it will be the duty of the Court to adhere to the Constitution, and to declare the act null and void. The Constitution is the basis of legislative authority; it lies at the foundation of all law and is a rule and commission by which both legislator and judges are to proceed. It is an important principle which, in the discussions of the present kind, ought never to be lost sight of—that the judiciary in this country is not a subordinate but a coordinate branch of the government."[9]

If Paterson presented the first judicial defense of the court's power to pass on the constitutionality of laws, the Supreme Court as a whole adopted his position the following year when in the case of *Ware v. Hylton* it held void, for the first time, a state law in conflict with a treaty. In the words of Justice Chase: "A treaty cannot be the supreme law of the land, that is, of the United States, if any act of a state legislature can stand in its way. If the Constitution of a State. . .must give way to a treaty, and fall before it, can it be questioned whether the less power—an act of the state legislation—must not be prostrate?. . .It is the declared duty of the state judges to determine any constitution or laws of any state contrary to that treaty, or any other, made under the authority of the United States, null and void. National or federal judges are bound by duty and oath to the same conduct."[10]

At the same session of the court the question of the constitutionality of an act of Congress was raised. In reaching a decision in *Hylton v. United States* the court did not find it necessary to pass on this question. However, Justice Chase, in a dictum, anticipated the rule which was to prevail during the entire first period of court history: "It is unnecessary at this time for me to determine whether this court constitutionally possesses the power to declare an act of Congress void, on the ground of its being made contrary to, and in violation of, the Constitution; but if the court has such power, I am free to declare that I will never exercise it but in a very clear case."[11]

The preceding cases were ones which were decided in the lower federal courts or had originated there and had been brought before the Supreme Court on appeal. In *Olney v. Arnold*, in a case brought before the Supreme Court on a writ of error to the Superior Court of Rhode Island under Section 25 of the Judiciary Act, the court, for the first time, reversed the judgment of a state court. The case involved the construction and validity of an act of Congress; the state court had given judgment against the party who pleaded the act of Congress in his defense. This power, exercised under a clear legislative grant, was only later to become the subject of dispute in a running battle between the national judiciary and the advocates of state sovereignty. For the time being, just as in the early cases settled by the circuit courts in which the power to void state laws was assumed, there was general acquiescence in the decision.[12]

Two years later, in *Calder v. Bull*, we find Justice Iredell confirming the warning given by Chase in the Hylton case: "If any act of Congress, or of the legislature of a state violates those constitutional provisions, it is unquestionably void; though, I admit, that as the authority to declare it void is of a delicate and awful nature, the court will never resort to that authority but in a clear and urgent case."[13]

But Iredell does not stop there. Aware that "some speculative jurists have held that a legislative act against natural justice must in itself be void," Iredell meets this argument head on and rejects it: "If. . .the legislature of the union, or the legislature of any member of the union, shall pass a law within the general scope of their constitutional power, the court cannot pronounce it to be void merely because it is, in their judgment, contrary to the principles of natural justice. The ideas of natural justice are regulated by no fixed standard; the ablest and the purest men have differed upon the subject; and all that the court could properly say in such an event would be that the legislature, possessed of an equal right of opinion, had passed an act which, in the opinion of the judges, was inconsistent with the abstract principles of natural justice."[14]

In the same year, on circuit, Iredell explores this thesis further: "Two principles appear to me to be clear: If an act be unconstitutional, it is void. If it be constitutional, it is valid. In the latter case it must be admitted that the legislature have exercised a trust confided to them by the people. In doing so they necessarily are left to their own discretion, and it is to be presumed they will have a due regard to justice in all their conduct. It is, however, I conceive, left to them so far without control; and if they abuse their trust in the exercise of an acknowledged power, they are indeed responsible in the only way in which a legislature can be responsible, for not exercising their authority properly; but still, having exercised an authority confided to them, their act is legal in the same manner as a judgment given by this court would be, in a case confessedly within its jurisdiction, however erroneous the principles may be on which the court decided. The words 'against natural justice' are very loose terms, upon which very wise and upright members of the legislature and judges might differ in opinion. If they did, whose opinion is properly to be regarded—those to whom the authority of passing such an act is given, or a court to whom no authority, in this respect, necessarily results? This case is surely different from an unconstitutional act which the courts must certainly declare to be void, because it was passed without any authority whatever. The Constitution, by saying that the legislature shall have authority in certain cases but shall not have in others, as plainly declares everything valid done in pursuance of the first provision, as everything void that is done in contradiction of the last; and it may surely be inferred that if, in addition to other restrictions on the legislative power, such a restriction as that in question was intended, so as to leave it to the courts, in all instances, to say whether an act was agreeable to natural justice or not, this restriction would have been inserted, together with others. . .I am of opinion that no court has authority to say the act is void because in their opinion it is not agreeable to the principles of natural justice."[15]

This brief but strong declaration in favor of judicial restraint, this cautious approach to the question of constitutionality, this skeptical attitude toward the confusion of higher law with the written Constitution, is to run through the entire history of the court. In this early period we see the standard passed down from Iredell to William Johnson and from Johnson to Peter Daniel. It is a lawyer's point of view but not an excessively legalistic one; it is the point of view of the non-doctrinaire common lawyer who believes in common sense and the common man's use of words.

Again in 1798, still another aspect of judicial restraint was emphasized by Justice Chase in defining the jurisdiction of the federal courts over the punishment of common law offenses. "Upon the whole," he wrote, "it may be a defect in our political institutions, it may be an inconvenience in the administration of justice that the common law authority, relating to crimes and punishments, has not been conferred upon the government of the United States, which is a government in other respects also of a limited jurisdiction; but judges cannot remedy political imperfections, nor supply any legislative omission."[16]

Two years later, approaching the close of the pre-Marshall period, we find additional references to the power of the court to decide on the constitutionality of acts of Congress. While in the *Case of Fries*, Justice Chase clearly states that the federal courts do possess "complete authority to decide whether any law is contrary to the Constitution,"[17] in *Cooper v. Telfair* he points out that there has been "no adjudication of the supreme court itself upon the point."[18]

In this same case, both Washington and Paterson reiterate the warnings given earlier by Iredell and Chase. While the first of these judges says, "The presumption, indeed, must always be in favor of the validity of laws, if the contrary is not clearly demonstrated;" the second states. "To authorize this court to pronounce any law void, it must be a clear and unequivocal breach of the Constitution, not a doubtful and argumentative application."[19]

Thus, before *Marbury v. Madison*, there was already a unanimous acceptance of the power of the court to decide on the constitutionality of legislation; there was also a unanimous reluctance to exercise that power.

Finally, in *United States v. Callender*, Justice Chase once more returned to the emerging doctrine of judicial supremacy. Although it was his purpose to refute counsel's contention that it was within the power of the jury to pass on the constitutionality of an act of Congress, the effect of Chase's opinion was to firmly locate that power in the judiciary. Citing the declaration in Article Six that the Constitution shall be the supreme law of the land and Article Three's vesting of the judicial power of the United States in the courts, Chase concludes "that the judicial power of the United States is the only proper and competent authority to decide whether any statute made by Congress (or any of the state legislatures) is contrary to, or in violation of, the federal Constitution."[20]

Marbury v. Madison is commonly considered the case in which the judicial supremacy of the Supreme Court was firmly established. In a technical sense that is true, since it is the first time that the Supreme Court itself held an act of Congress unconstitutional and, in so doing, established its power. But, as we have seen, the doctrine, if not previously established, had been frequently asserted. Thus as an authoritative statement the importance of the case cannot be underestimated; as a constitutional concept it was little more than the summing up of earlier opinions.

Marshall, faced with the question of whether an act repugnant to the Constitution can become the law of the land, acknowledges that the principles on which the issue is to be decided have been "long and well-established." He reiterates Paterson's summary of the distinction between a government in which Parliament is supreme and one in which a written Constitution is paramount.

"The powers of the legislature are defined and limited; and that those limits may not be mistaken, or forgotten, the Constitution is written. To what purpose are powers limited, and to what purpose is that limitation committed to writing, if these limits may, at any time, be passed by those intended to be restrained? The distinction between a government with limited and unlimited powers is abolished, if those limits do not confine the persons on whom they are imposed, and if acts prohibited and acts allowed, are of equal obligation.

"Certainly all those who framed written constitutions," the Chief Justice continues, "contemplate them as forming the fundamental and paramount law of the nation, and, consequently, the theory of every such government must be, that an act of the legislature, repugnant to the Constitution, is void."

Marshall then proceeds to demonstrate that a void law is not binding on the courts. "It is emphatically the province and duty of the judicial department to say what the law is. . .If two laws conflict with each other, the courts must decide on the operation of each.

"So if a law be in opposition to the Constitution; if both the law and the Constitution apply to a particular case, so that the court must either decide that case conformably to the law, disregarding the Constitution, or conformably to the Constitution, disregarding the law, the court must determine which of these conflicting rules governs the case. This is of the very essence of judicial duty.

"If, then, the courts are to regard the Constitution, and the Constitution is superior to any ordinary act of the legislature, the Constitution, and not such ordinary act, must govern the case to which both apply."

Not satisfied to rest his argument on general principles, Marshall refers to the Sixth Article of the Constitution: "It is also not unworthy of observation, that in declaring what shall be the supreme law of the land, the Constitution itself is first mentioned; and not the laws of the United States generally, but those only which shall be made in pursuance of the Constitution have that rank.

"Thus, the particular phraseology of the Constitution of the United States confirms and strengthens the principle, supposed to be essential to all written constitutions, that a law repugnant to the Constitution is void; and that courts, as well as other departments, are bound by that instrument." [21]

Thus the Supreme Court, in ruling on the validity of a rather technical matter—the original jurisdiction of the Court as granted by the Constitution on the one hand and legislated by the Congress on the other—in effect established a principle of transcendental importance: that the Supreme Court possessed the power to decide when the limits of the Constitution had been exceeded and to hold void any law which so exceeded those limits. Though it was more than fifty years before the Court was to hold unconstitutional another law of Congress, the establishment of this rule of judicial supremacy could not have failed to exercise a controlling influence over the future acts of the executive and legislative departments. The debate over judicial prerogatives was not over but it was already won.

Five years later a case came before the District Court of Massachusetts in which the constitutionality of the Embargo Acts was challenged. Independently of *Marbury v. Madison* (referred to but briefly by the judge in a belated footnote), Judge Davis held that it was the duty of the national courts to regard as void any acts of Congress which were repugnant to exceptions or restrictions to the legislative authority or to affirmative provisions of the Constitution. But here was a law which counsel for the defendant held to be unconstitutional for want of conformity to the constitutional powers vested in the legislature; because, in short, "the act in question is not authorized by any of these powers."

The immediate question was: Does the Congress have the

power or authority by the Constitution to prohibit commercial intercourse with foreign nations? The general question was: "Is a mere exceeding of the powers of Congress, in legislation, without a repugnancy to express provisions of the Constitution, among the proper objects of cognizance in the federal judiciary?"

Reviewing previous cases involving the judicial determination of the constitutionality of Congressional acts, Judge Davis could find no decision or opinion in which an act of Congress had been held void for a defect of constitutional power. The judge, therefore, turned to the 78th number of *The Federalist* where he found support for the following conclusion: "It is evident, that the judicial authority, is precisely limited, in regard to deciding on the validity of legislative acts; and that the power to declare them void exists, only, in cases of contravention, opposition or repugnancy, to some express restrictions or provisions contained in the Constitution. The examples and the argument apply only to cases of legislative action which their powers forbid; not to those, which their powers may be supposed not to authorize."

Interferences of the judiciary with the legislature, Judge Davis continued, should be limited to cases, "easily to be understood," in which the will of the people who established the Constitution is "clearly and peremptorily expressed. To extend this censorial power further. . .would be found extremely difficult, if not impracticable, in execution. To determine where the legitimate exercise of discretion ends, and usurpation begins, would be a task most delicate and arduous. . .Before a court can determine, whether a given act of Congress, bearing relation to a power with which it is vested, be a legitimate exercise of that power, or transcend it, the degree of legislative discretion, admissible in the case, must first be determined. Legal discretion is limited. . .Political discretion has a far wider range. It embraces, combines and considers, all circumstances, events and projects, foreign or domestic, that can affect the national interests. Legal discretion has not the means of ascertaining the grounds, on which political discretion may have proceeded. It seems admitted, that necessity might justify the acts in question.

But how shall legal discussion determine, that political discretion, surveying the vast concerns committed to its trust, and the movements of conflicting nations, has not perceived such necessity to exist? Considerations of this nature have induced a doubt of the competency, or constitutional authority of the court, to decide an act invalid, in a case of this description."

Applying this principle of judicial deference to an act of Congress which "bears relation to a power with which it is vested" (in this case, the relationship which exists between the regulation and the prohibition of commerce), Davis holds that the Embargo Acts are within the power of Congress under the commerce clause, even if the act in question is not explicitly authorized by the Constitution. He concluded with a personal observation—it must be remembered that Davis was a Federalist appointed by President Adams in 1801—that we will discover in many future opinions: "I say nothing of the policy of the expedient. It is not within my province. But, on the abstract question of constitutional power, I see nothing to prohibit or restrain the measure."[22]

Justice Story, who argued in favor of the constitutionality of the Embargo Acts before he became a member of the Supreme Court, afterwards wrote: "I have ever considered the Embargo a measure which went to the utmost limits of constructive power under the Constitution; it stands on the extreme verge of the Constitution."[23]

In referring to this opinion, Warren wrote: "On October 3, 1808, Judge Davis rendered his opinion, sustaining in the broadest terms the legal validity of the statute, and construing the constitutional powers of Congress in respect to it as broadly as Marshall himself at his zenith could have done."[24]

The real question which must be asked, then, as now, is: Did the court adhere to a loose construction of the constitutional powers of Congress or did the court assume a strict construction of the constitutional powers of the judiciary? It is, of course, impossible to deny that both elements were involved in the position, since the roles of Congress and the judiciary were obviously reciprocal, so much so that the greater the self-restraint exercised by the courts, the greater the power left in the hands of Congress. Thus it is clear from the beginning—as in this case—that the terms "loose construction" and "strict construction" are meaningless unless the terms of reference are stated. To attribute to Judge Davis, for instance, a loose construction in upholding the validity of the Embargo Acts is to lose sight of the judge's more fundamental argument—that the judiciary is incompetent to resolve cases of this description. His refusal to invalidate the act is not an explicit approval of what Congress has done but a denial of the power of the judiciary to encroach on the power of Congress where no clear constitutional repugnancy exists. If this be "loose construction," it is at the same time the strictest of "strict construction."

It is worthwhile noting that the restraint exercised by Judge Davis ("To determine where the legitimate exercise of discretion ends and usurpation begins would be a task most delicate and arduous") parallels that suggested by Justice Iredell in refusing to apply the principles of natural justice to the determination of constitutionality ("The words 'against natural justice' are very loose terms. . .").

In the same year that Judge Davis handed down his opinion, acquiesced in by the interested parties, the Supreme Court, through Chief Justice Marshall, emphasized another aspect of judicial restraint when it declared that the court must defer to the executive department in political questions, such as the recognition of foreign governments. After the colony of Santo Domingo had declared its independence from France, the claim was made that the court should now recognize that colony as a sovereign state. The court, however, ruled: "It is for governments to decide whether they will consider Santo Domingo as an independent nation, and until such decision shall be made, or France shall relinquish her claim, courts of justice must consider the ancient state of things as remaining unaltered, and the sovereign power of France over that colony as still subsisting."[25]

A doctrine which was to prove to be of greater importance and a subject of much future controversy was that laid down by Marshall in the case of *United States v. Peters.* The first of many cases in which the authority of the state legislature was to clash with the power of the national courts, the State of Pennsylvania had authorized the governor of that state to protect certain of its citizens against any process issued out of any federal court to obtain possession of funds which had been in controversy since the time of the Revolution. In rejecting this state challenge to its authority and in awarding a *mandamus* directing Federal Judge Peters to execute his own earlier decree, the court declared: "If the legislatures of the several states may, at will, annul the judgments of the courts of the United States, and destroy the rights acquired under these judgments, the Constitution itself becomes a solemn mockery; and the nation is deprived of the means of enforcing its laws by the instrumentality of its own tribunals."[26]

Up until 1810 the decisions of both the Supreme Court and the lower federal courts seem to be clear and unidirectional, each opinion borrowing from and building on rules laid down in previous cases. In *Fletcher v. Peck* the court continues this process, inasmuch as it holds void the act of a state legislature for being in conflict with a provision of the Constitution, in this case, the contract clause. Marshall reiterates the cautious approach of his predecessors when he says: "The question, whether a law be void for its repugnancy to the Constitution is, at all times, a question of much delicacy, which ought seldom, if ever, to be decided in the affirmative, in a doubtful case. The court, when impelled by duty to render such a judgment, would be unworthy of its station, could it be unmindful of the solemn obligations which that station imposes. But it is not on slight implication and vague conjecture that the legislature is to be pronounced to have transcended its powers, and its acts to be considered as void. The opposition between the Constitution and the law should be such that the judge feels a clear and strong conviction of their incompatibility with each other."

Here, Marshall finds a clear incompatibility between the rescinding act of the State of Georgia and the constitutional provision prohibiting the passage of any law impairing the obligation of contracts. But not content to rest his decision on the constitutional conflict, Marshall adds: "There are certain great principles of justice, whose authority is universally acknowledged, that ought not to be entirely disregarded," and thereupon cites those "general principles which are common to our free institutions" as a reason for voiding the state law. Thus we find a clear rejection of Justice Iredell's thesis that legislative acts may not be held unconstitutional for being in conflict with principles of natural justice.[27]

Justice Johnson goes even further than Marshall (it might even be asked whether Marshall included the alternative of "general principles" in order to obtain the unanimous approval of the court in this case), when he rejects resorting to the contract clause as a reason for holding the state law void and states: "I do not hesitate to declare that a state does not possess the power of revoking its own grants. But I do it on a general principle, on the reason and nature of things: a principle which will impose laws even on the Deity."[28]

The importance usually given to the case of *Fletcher v. Peck* in American Constitutional law is the resort to the contract clause and the fact that this marks the first time that the Supreme Court itself holds void a state law for being in conflict with the Constitution. But of equal importance is the concept of natural justice, or higher law, brought into the opinions of both Marshall and Johnson.

According to Donald G. Morgan, author of *Justice William Johnson*, this appeal of Johnson to natural law was an exception, based on the fact that he rejected Marshall's resort to the contract clause, yet was hostile to the retrospective character of the state action. In the future, he relied on his own interpretation of the *ex post facto* clause rather than on an appeal to the principles of natural justice.[29]

As for Marshall, Robert McCloskey, in his *The American Supreme Court*, writes: "Marshall may have been toying with the idea of claiming for the Court the power to overthrow laws which violated such agreements on the basis of natural law or 'right reason' without reference to any specific constitutional clause. This idea was abroad in the land at the time, and hints of it keep turning up in Supreme Court opinions for many years to come. At first glance it might seem that this carte blanche for judicial governance would be very appealing to Marshall, for it would supply him with a roving commission to invalidate any law he disapproved, subject only to the proviso that the incantations of the natural law tradition must be recited. But he surely realized that the Court's future lay with the tangible Constitution itself rather than its invisible and most disputable higher law background, that a Court which claimed the power to go beyond the Constitution would be dispensing with its most valuable support and might end by possessing no power at all. In the long run, therefore, he preferred to moor his arguments in the language of the Constitution."[30]

In his *The Role of the Supreme Court: 1789-1835*, Haines has this comment to make: "It was assumed, therefore, that the Rescinding Act was invalid because it violated some of the fundamental or natural law principles which surround and control the exercise of legislative powers. And, even if a state may be conceded to have authority to judge its own case, yet 'there are certain great principles of justice that ought not to be entirely disregarded.' "

Haines goes on to say: "But it is apparent, not only from the opinion itself, but also from Marshall's political ideas and faith, that the argument predicated on general principles and on implied limitations on legislative powers was the primary and fundamental part of his opinion and that the reasoning founded on the constitutional inhibition was secondary. In the *Bank of the United States v. Deveaux*, Marshall noted that the Constitution deals in general terms, not in detail, and that since the framers could not perceive the minute distinctions which arise in the progress of the nation, they had therefore confined its language 'to the establishment of broad and general principles.' These broad and general principles were now being interpreted to carry into effect one of the most important purposes of Federalism—the preservation of the sacredness of contractual rights against legislative interference. It is obvious that such rights were to be preserved whether or not constitutional provisions so declared."[31]

Beveridge confirms this conclusion: "Thus, at first, Marshall rested his opinion on elementary 'principles of justice,' rather than on the Constitution. . .Again Marshall founds his reasoning, not on the Constitution but on fundamental principles;" yet seems to undermine its importance when he states: "Marshall finally came to the conclusion that the Constitution plainly covered the case."[32]

Finally, B. F. Wright recalls an opinion given in 1796 by Hamilton on the validity of the land titles: "Without pretending to judge the original merits or demerits of the purchasers, it may be safely said to be a contravention of the first principles of natural justice and social policy." However, Hamilton also considers the law contrary to the contract clause of the Constitution.

Wright claims that, "Marshall, like the parties to the suit, desired to have a judicial determination of the validity of the repeal act, and he wished to base that decision on the contract clause, or at least partially on that clause, for he followed Hamilton in hesitating to decide on that ground alone. . .It was principally indicative that [Marshall] was uncertain as to precisely why the repeal act was invalid, although he was very sure that it was invalid."[33]

In his *The Growth of American Constitutional Law*, Wright again takes up the case and concludes: "It is apparent from his opinion, and especially from his concluding paragraph, that he was not entirely certain whether the Constitution alone could sustain this interpretation [based on the contract clause]. The 'general principles' of society and of government are brought in for support, even as Hamilton had employed them. The Hamilton-Marshall theory of natural law was, to this extent, written into the Constitution."[34]

Thus we find a considerable amount of speculation based on a few phrases supporting a line of reasoning which was, as Donald Morgan pointed out, an exception rather than a rule. Nevertheless the strong position taken earlier by Justice Iredell can no longer be said to be a self-evident premise, and we shall henceforth be on the lookout for extra-constitutional standards brought to apply in cases where discretion is at a premium.

Whatever doubts the court may have entertained as to its power to invalidate state laws under the contract clause of the Constitution, were dispelled by the court's rulings in *New Jersey v. Wilson*[35] and *Sturges v. Crowninshield.*[36] In the first of these cases the court held void a state act which was limited to the repeal of an earlier contract law; in the latter, the court ruled unconstitutional a general law of the state. In neither of these decisions was there any reference to general principles.

In the same decade that these cases were decided, the question of appellate power over the judgments of state courts was aired before the Supreme Court. As we have seen, as early as 1796, in *Olney v. Arnold*, the court exercised its power under the 25th Section of the Judiciary Act of 1789 to revise the judgment of the higher court of a state. However, in the case of *Martin v. Hunter's Lessee*, the culmination of a legal dispute which had been before the courts virtually from the time of the Revolution, the State of Virginia challenged a previous judgment of the Supreme Court overruling its own, and refused to obey the mandate of the higher court. In a strong opinion, Justice Story upheld the exercise of its appellate power and the constitutionality of Section 25.[37]

Following a lengthy explanation of the significance of the third article vesting the judicial power of the United States,[38] Story points out that the Constitution contemplated and provided for the exercise of this power over cases originating before state tribunals. To the argument that "such an appellate jurisdiction over state courts is inconsistent with the genius of our governments, and the spirit of the Constitution," Story replies that the Constitution was "designed to operate upon states, in their corporate capacities," as well as upon the people.

"The courts of the United States," the opinion continues, "can, without question, revise the proceedings of the executive and legislative authorities of the states, and if they are found to be contrary to the Constitution may declare them to be of no legal validity. Surely the exercise of the same right over judicial tribunals is not a higher or more dangerous act of sovereign power.

"Nor can such a right be deemed to impair the independence of state judges. It is assuming the very ground in controversy to assert that they possess an absolute independence of the United States. In respect to the powers granted to the United States, they are not independent; they are expressly bound to obedience by the letter of the Constitution; and if they should unintentionally transcend their authority, or misconstrue the Constitution, there is no more reason for giving their judgments an absolute and irresistible force than for giving it to the acts of the other coordinate departments of state sovereignty.

"The argument urged from the possibility of the abuse of the revising power, is equally unsatisfactory. It is always a doubtful course to argue against the use or existence of a power, from the possibility of its abuse. It is still more difficult, by such an argument, to ingraft upon a general power, a restriction which is not to be found in the terms in which it is given. From the very nature of things, *the absolute right of decision, in the last resort, must rest somewhere*—wherever it may be vested it is susceptible of abuse. In all questions of jurisdiction the inferior or appellate court must pronounce the final judgment; and common sense, as well as legal reasoning, has conferred it upon the latter."

Turning to the motives which induced the framers of the Constitution to grant to the Supreme Court appellate power over the decisions of the state tribunals, Story stresses the importance and necessity of a uniformity of decisions throughout the whole United States. "If there were no revising authority to control these jarring and discordant judgments and harmonize them into uniformity, the laws, the treaties, and the Constitution of the United States would be different in different states, and might perhaps never have precisely the same construction, obligation, or efficacy in any two states. The public mischiefs that would attend such a state of things would be truly deplorable; and it cannot be believed that they could have escaped the enlightened convention which formed the Constitution. What, indeed, might then have been only prophecy has now become fact; and the appellate jurisdiction must continue to be the only adequate remedy for such evils."

After pointing out that this final revising power is but a corollary of the power of removal of cases from the state to the federal courts, Story turns to the accepted practice of the past twenty years and affirms: "It is an historical fact that the Supreme Court of the United States has, from time to time, sustained this appellate jurisdiction in a great variety of cases, brought from the tribunals of many of the most important states in the union, and that no state tribunal has ever breathed a judicial doubt on the subject, or declined to obey the mandate of the Supreme Court, until the present occasion. This weight of contemporaneous exposition by all parties, this acquiescence of enlightened state courts, and these judicial decisions of the Supreme Court through so long a period, do, as we think, place the doctrine upon a foundation of authority which cannot be shaken, without delivering over the subject to perpetual and irremediable doubts."[39]

In a curious concurring opinion, Justice Johnson reveals his mixed feelings concerning this monumental conflict between state sovereignty and judicial power. Concerned not to offend the state tribunal by any direct showdown, and wary lest "the state sovereignties shall be prostrated at the feet of the general government," the judge from South Carolina expresses a desire to "borrow the language of a celebrated orator, and exclaim, 'I rejoice that Virginia has resisted.' "

Nevertheless, and in spite of a lengthy discussion of the most diplomatic *modus operandi* for avoiding a direct clash, Johnson, in unambiguous terms, deplores the state court's lack of moderation in disobeying the higher court's mandate, and rejects the thesis that the judgment of the Supreme Court can be subsequently reviewed by another. Referring to the doctrine of judicial comity, Johnson writes: "Ours is the superior claim upon the comity of the state tribunals." [40]

Five years later, Chief Justice Marshall pursued the position taken by Story (Marshall himself did not write the opinion in the earlier case as he had an indirect interest in the outcome) when he rejected "the mischievous consequences of the construction contended for on the part of Virginia" which would "prostrate the government and its laws at the feet of every state in the union.

"What power of the government could be executed by its own means, in any state disposed to resist its execution by individuals acting within the several states. If these individuals may be exposed to penalties, and if the courts of the Union cannot correct the judgments by which these penalties may be enforced, the course of the government may be, at any time, arrested by the will of one of its members.

"A constitution is framed for ages to come," Marshall continues, "and is designed to approach immortality as nearly as human institutions can approach it. . .No government ought to be so defective in its organization, as not to contain within itself the means of securing the execution of its own laws against other dangers than those which occur every day. Courts of justice are the means most usually employed; and it is reasonable to expect that a government should repose on its own courts, rather than on others."[41]

Thus, in the twenty-five years between 1796 and 1821, the Supreme Court had exercised the power to declare unconstitutional both state statutes and laws of Congress; to revise the judgments of state tribunals when in conflict with the Constitution, laws or treaties of the United States; and to enforce its own mandates or those of the lower federal courts against resistance on the part of the states. Some of these powers were granted to the court by Congress, while others were assumed as implicit in the Constitution and the nature of government. The common denominator underlying all these instances of judicial prerogative was the thesis that the Supreme Court was to be supreme not only within the judicial system of the United States, but in its relations with the legislative and executive departments of the federal government as well as in its confrontations with the states.

At the same time, this bold display of power was cautiously hedged with voluntary (for who else but the court could place limits upon its own power once the doctrine of judicial supremacy had been established?) and prudent (the judges were not unaware that they too were responsible to the Constitution and to the people) self-restrictions. The right to hold a statute unconstitutional was not to be exercised except in a clear case; the judges were not to examine statutes in the light of their own conceptions of natural justice but in accordance with the letter and spirit of the Constitution. (Eventually these two approaches were to be fused or confused.) Finally, the court must defer to the executive and legislative branches on questions of a political nature.

2. 1821-1835

Pursuing the line of judicial deference to the executive in foreign affairs, previously adopted by the court in *Rose v. Himely* and *Gelston v. Hoyt*, a majority of the Supreme Court insisted on judicial restraint in the interpretation of treaties. In a case involving the question of whether or not the terms of a treaty had been literally complied with, Story, speaking for the majority, said: "This court does not possess any treaty-making power. That power belongs, by the Constitution, to another department of the government, and to alter, amend, or add to any treaty, by inserting any clause, whether small or great, important or trivial, would be on our part an usurpation of power, and not an exercise of judicial functions. It would be to make and not to construe a treaty. Neither can this court supply a *casus omissus* in a treaty, any more than a law."[42]

Justice Johnson, in this as in other cases, showing his independent spirit, dissented from the majority, arguing in favor of the obligation to execute treaties "in a spirit not only of good faith, but of liberality." He contended that it was sufficient that the terms of the treaty were "substantially" complied with and, "Whether it is substantially complied with or not, must be a question for the courts of the contracting parties."[43]

Again, in *Foster v. Neilson*, the Court ruled that the judiciary must defer to the legislature with respect to a political question, such as the location of boundaries of nations. "It is the province of the court to conform its decisions to the will of the legislature," wrote Marshall, "if that will has been clearly expressed. The judiciary is not that department of the government to which the assertion of its interests against foreign powers is confided and its duty, commonly, is to decide upon individual rights according to those principles which the political departments of the nation have established." It was not, said Marshall, for the courts to pronounce the course followed by the legislature erroneous.[44]

The important case of *Ogden v. Saunders*, which has been too often neglected, brings us once more to the court's role in deciding on the constitutionality of state legislation. A majority of five opposed a strong minority, represented by the Chief Justice, in upholding the constitutionality of a state insolvent law insofar as it applied to contracts entered into after the statute had gone into effect. The majority, in separate opinions which reached the same conclusion, assumed that the framers of the Constitution intended to prohibit only retrospective laws which impaired the obligation of contracts and did not have in mind a sweeping prohibition against state laws with a forward-looking application. The constitutional provision was not explicit on this point and so it was only natural that the court should determine its meaning and define its range. Marshall, in keeping with his conservative ideas concerning state interference in debtor-creditor relationships, virtually denied to the states the right to relieve debtors of their contractual debts; for him, the constitutional provision was an absolute in both directions—retrospective and prospective. But to other members of the court the provision was at best ambiguous. In such a case, as Justice Washington said, "It is but a decent respect due to the wisdom, the integrity, and the patriotism of the legislative body by which any law is passed, to presume in favor of its validity until its violation of the Constitution is proved *beyond all reasonable doubt.*" [45]

Seconding this judicial philosophy of "innocent until proven guilty," Thompson stated that this area, in which there arose potential conflict between a department of the federal government and a state government, was "the point upon which the harmony of our system is most exposed to interruption." Citing the rule laid down in *Fletcher v. Peck*, calling for caution and reluctance as the authority by which this issue was to be governed, the justice from New York was "certainly not prepared to say that it is not, at least, a doubtful case," or that he was clearly convinced that the law in question was incompatible with the Constitution. Under those circumstances the law was valid.[46] [47]

In another case which came before the Court during the same year, Thompson, dissenting, again upheld a state law which to him was not clearly in conflict with the Constitution of the United States. Marshall, this time speaking for the majority, admitted that, "It has been truly said that the presumption is in favor of every legislative act, and that the whole burden of proof lies on him who denies its constitutionality," but in this case, Marshall concluded, the unconstitutionality had been proven.[48]

Taking up this point of doubtful cases, Johnson, in the following year, dissented from a court decision invalidating a law of the State of Missouri as repugnant to the constitutional prohibition of state bills of credit. Considering certain certificates issued by the state as "of a truly amphibious character," he concluded that, "as it is a doubtful case, for that reason we are bound to pronounce it innocent. It does, indeed, approach as near to a violation of the Constitution as it can well go without violating its prohibition, but it is in the exercise of an unquestionable right, although in rather a questionable form." Then Johnson adds a novel criterion for the solution of questions of constitutionality: "And I am bound to believe that *it was done in good faith*, until the contrary should more clearly appear."[49]

Johnson, who was now serving his last years on the Court, was supported in his deference to state legislatures by Judge McLean, whose position a few years later was to become that of the majority of the court in a similar case.[50] "If the act of Missouri conferred benefits upon the people of the State, and was guarded in its provisions as to protect them from all possible evil, no court could feel inclined to declare it to be unconstitutional and void, unless it was directly opposed to the letter and spirit of the Constitution. As the spirit of that provision was to protect the citizens of the States against the evils of a debased currency; and as the act under consideration, so far as it operated upon the people of Missouri, had no tendency to produce this evil, but to relieve against it, the spirit of the Constitution was not violated."[51]

Thus we see the emergence of three new criteria: good faith, the spirit of the Constitution, and the conferment of benefits upon the people, as allies of the states and checks on the power of the judiciary to invalidate laws. Marshall, who was so imaginative when it came to enlarging the powers of the court and the national government, became a literalist when it came to such matters as state powers and debtor-creditor relationships. For Marshall, the question of the good faith of the states and the conferment of benefits was an irrelevant begging of the question. For Johnson, on the other hand, the Constitution was to be interpreted generously not only in favor of the judiciary and the central government but vis-a-vis the states as well.

We have seen how many years earlier Iredell spoke up strongly against deciding constitutional questions on abstract principles of natural justice. Justice Baldwin now expressed his support for this thesis and issued an even stronger warning in a case involving the Constitution and the laws of the State of New Jersey. In upholding a state fisheries law, Baldwin, concluding that the constitutional powers of the state were plenary and unrestrained on the subject, wrote: "We may think the powers conferred by the Constitution of this state too great, or dangerous to the rights of the people, and that limitations are necessary, but we cannot affix them, or act on cases arising under state laws *as if* boundaries had been affixed by the Constitution previously. We cannot declare a legislative act void because it conflicts with our opinions of policy, expediency or justice. We are not the guardians of the rights of the people of a state unless they are secured by some constitutional provision which comes within our judicial cognizance."

Were the federal courts to adopt the general principles put forward by the counsel, continued Baldwin, the court would "submit state laws to a test as fallible and uncertain as all rules must be which have not their sources in some certain and definite standard, which varies neither with times, circumstances, or opinions. . .There is no paramount and supreme law which defines the law of nature, or settles those great principles of legislation which are said to control state legislatures in the exercise of the powers conferred on them by the people in the Constitution. If it is once admitted that there exists in this court a power to declare a state law void, which conflicts with no constitutional provision—*if we assume the right to annul them for their supposed injustice, or oppressive operation, we become the makers and not the expounders of Constitutions*—our opinion will not be a judgment on what was the pre-existing law of the case, but on what it is after we shall have so amended and modified it as to meet our ideas of justice, policy and wise legislation, by a direct usurpation of legislative power, and a flagrant violation of the duty enjoined on us by the judiciary act."

For Baldwin, "the remedy for unwise or oppressive legislation, within constitutional bounds, is by an appeal to the justice and patriotism of the representatives of the people. If this fails, the people in their sovereign capacity can correct the evil; but courts cannot assume their rights."[52]

In rejecting recourse to abstract principles of natural justice and the intromission of personal opinions concerning policy, Baldwin spelled out the clear rule by which legislation was to be measured—certain and definite constitutional standards which vary neither with times, circumstances or opinions. For the judge from Pennsylvania, the meaning of constitutional provisions was fixed and certain. The duty of the court was to apply these standards to the cases which came before it, not to enlarge or restrict the standards themselves. Thus, for Baldwin, the Constitution and its meaning was rigid and unchanging; changes, if needed or desired, were to be carried out by constitutional amendments, not by judicial legislation. This doctrine of judicial deference was to have its ups and downs throughout the history of the court. For the moment it had its strong advocates.

But if Baldwin here supported the doctrine of judicial deference, in another case he jealously defended the right of the judiciary to decide on the constitutionality of an act of

Congress, independently of the views of the President as expressed in a veto message. "The judicial power cannot be exercised on the reasons which have governed the exercise of the veto power," he stated in his charge to the jury. "We cannot look to the construction given to the Constitution by the executive department as a guide to our judgment; for no appellate or supervisory power over our proceedings has been confided to that department." It was to the judgment of the Supreme Court that the circuit judge and the members of the jury must look and not to the opinion of the President.[53]

In a case before the Supreme Court, however, Baldwin, dissenting from the majority opinion, reiterated his cautious approach to judicial power, when he warned against that court's assumption of the prerogative powers of the English Court of King's Bench, where no law had clearly granted such powers.[54]

Meanwhile, Johnson once more had an opportunity to comment on judicial power and the relations of the court to the President. In his concurring opinion in *Cherokee Nation v. Georgia*, as an additional reason for denying jurisdiction in the case, he warned against permitting a situation in which the judicial department might clash head on with the executive department in the interpretation and application of treaty rights. Where the President had refused to act on a petition on the part of the Cherokee Nation, Johnson considered it improper for the court to take a position which would compel the executive to pursue a course of policy contrary to his own idea of what should be done. "Courts of justice are properly excluded from all considerations of policy," concluded Johnson, "and therefore are very unfit instruments to control the action [of the executive branch]."[55]

One more opinion given before the year 1835 is worth noting. In the case of *Worcester v. Georgia*, Justice McLean upheld the power of the court to declare state legislature void, pointing out, as had Paterson in the case of *Vanhorne v. Dorrance*, that if the court lacked that power there would ensue "the destruction of all constitutions; and the will of the legislature, like the acts of the Parliament of Great Britain, must be the supreme, and only law of the land.

"The powers of this court," he continued, "are expressly, not constructively, given by the Constitution, and within this delegation of power, this court is the Supreme Court of the people of the United States. . .and are equally, within their powers, the supreme court of the people of each State."[56]

Looking back over the period of the Marshall Court, it is worth noting that outside of *Marbury v. Madison* it was not the Chief Justice himself who had most to say on the powers of the judiciary, and what he did say, as we have seen, was in the nature of an official approval of previously stated opinions. It was Marshall's colleagues—especially Johnson, Story, Baldwin and McLean—who had the most to contribute to this field of thought, and several of them, as we shall see, remained on the court long enough to make further contributions.

3. 1836-1864

In 1836, a case arose involving the verification of deeds in which one of the parties asked the court to construe the state law in such a way as to embrace proofs not provided for by the state legislation. Acknowledging that there was no reason for the legislators to have omitted the means of proof employed by the interested party, Justice McLean, speaking for the court, refused to give the desired construction to the law: "It is not for the court to say, where the language of the statute is clear, that it shall be so construed as to embrace cases, because no good reason can be assigned as to why they were excluded from its provisions. . .The legislature having made a distinction, whether it was intentional or not, reasonable or unreasonable, the court is bound by the clearly expressed language of the act."[57]

In the following year the much-debated case of the Charles River Bridge came before the court. The resolution of the case depended on whether a constitutionally protected contract could be read into a legislative act, granting the plaintiff the right to construct a bridge. The new chief justice, Taney, speaking for a divided court, rejected the idea that the court, "acting upon its own views of what justice required, and the parties ought to have done," could create such a contract in the absence of any explicit words on the part of the state legislature. Story, on the other hand, insisted that the implication was "natural, necessary and indispensable" and arose out of the very nature and object of the grant of the bridge franchise; that it was not for the court to deny the contractual nature of the grant where the legislature itself had not done so expressly and in so many words. Despite Taney's warning, it was inevitable that the court must act upon its own views of what justice required, the question here being whether justice required liberality or parsimony in interpreting the words and intentions of the legislature; and if liberality, whether toward the public which granted the franchise or toward the bridge company which was the recipient. Whatever else may be said of the case, here was a situation which demanded judicial discretion; deference to the legislature was no solution when the legislation itself was not clear.[58]

Bank of Augusta v. Earle offered another complicated challenge to the court's ability to establish the correct policy in the interpretation of state laws. Once again, a state had neither expressly authorized out-of-state corporations to carry on business within the state nor explicitly prohibited them from doing so. What was to be the role of the court in such a case? The Chief Justice took the position that it was not for the courts to forestall the state's decision in advance of legislation on the subject by assuming a state prohibition; McKinley, on the other hand, took the position that by upholding the validity of the contract in the absence of an explicit law of the state authorizing it, the majority of the court "maintain a power in the federal government, and in the judicial department of it, to do that which, in my judgment, belongs exclusively to the state governments; and to be exercised by the legislative and not the judicial departments thereof."[59] Thus, for the one, it was an abuse of judicial power to read into the law a prohibition which did not exist; for the other, it was an abuse to assume an approval which was not there.

In the case of *Williams v. The Suffolk Insurance Company*, the Supreme Court once more confirmed the rule laid down thirty years earlier in *Rose v. Himely* that the judiciary must defer to the executive department on political questions. The decision of the executive branch regarding the sovereignty of an island or a country is conclusive on the judicial department, "whether the executive be right or wrong." This rule prevails in order to "avoid irreconcilable differences between the executive and judicial departments. By one of these departments, a foreign island or country might be considered as at peace with the United States; whilst the other would consider it in a state of war. No well-regulated government has ever sanctioned a principle so unwise, and so destructive of national character."[60]

In another case involving a matter of minor importance but a principle which was to be repeated time after time, the court ruled that a law of the State of Maryland embraced all illegitimate children and did not exclude the offspring of an incestuous relationship. "The expediency and moral tendency of this new law," said Taney, "is a question for the legislature of Maryland, and not for this court."[61]

No authoritative decision was given by the court in *Holmes v. Jennison*, a case involving a conflict between the treaty power of the national government and the police power of the State of Vermont. Holmes, a fugitive wanted by the Canadian authorities, was arrested by Vermont officials. To avoid being turned over to Canada, he appeared before the state court of Vermont under *habeas corpus* proceedings, claiming that under the Constitution and laws of the United States the State of Vermont had no authority to extradite him. The immediate question was whether the Supreme Court had jurisdiction to review the state court's dismissal of his petition. The judges were divided on the issue. Both Thompson and Baldwin pointed out, among the reasons given for denying jurisdiction, that it was not in the power of the Supreme Court to enforce its judgment in such a case. Both judges admitted that were the jurisdiction clear, the court could proceed to the ultimate consequences—the issuance of a peremptory *mandamus* to the state judges and fine and imprisonment if they were to disobey the mandate. But, they argued, since this course of action was so extreme, it should be employed only where the authority of the court was absolutely certain and not in a case of doubtful construction of its appellate power. Thus, in a circular fashion, the measures involved in carrying out a decision were to become a consideration in reaching that decision.[62] This approach echoes that suggested by Johnson in the *Cherokee Nation* case, where he argued backwards from the inconveniences of clashing with the executive department.

If the court, or certain members of it, was wary of showdowns of power, there was no shyness when it came to the mere interpretation of a law. Although the construction given by a department of the government deserved the respect of the judiciary, "still, however, if it is not in conformity to the true intendment and provisions of the law, it cannot be permitted to conclude the judgment of a court of justice. The construction given to the laws by any department of the executive government is necessarily *ex parte*, without the benefit of an opposing argument, in a suit where the very matter is in controversy. The judicial department has imposed upon it by the Constitution," continued Story, "the duty of interpreting the laws and deciding in the last resort, however disagreeable it may be, to differ from the judgment of executive functionaries."[63]

We now turn to a problem which the court faced for the first time. The rule of *stare decisis*, or standing on decisions previously made, was one of the fundamental principles of the common law and one which the court had hitherto applied unhesitantly to many questions involving its own jurisdiction. In 1844, however, a case came before the court involving the citizenship of corporations. This problem had been solved many years before during (and, in part, before) the early period of the Marshall court. The court had then chosen to restrict jurisdiction in cases involving diversity of citizenship to suits in which all the parties on one side were citizens of one state and all other parties citizens of another. This rule, in effect, made it impossible to take jurisdiction in cases where one of the parties (or both) was a corporation and the members of the corporation were citizens of various states.

But, as Justice Wayne pointed out, this solution was neither satisfactory to the bar, the court or the public.

Finally the court had an opportunity to re-examine its position in the case of *Louisville Railroad Company v. Letson.* Here it unanimously overruled the previous leading cases on the subject and established a completely new rule (which we will examine under a subsequent heading). Facing up to the principle of *stare decisis,* Wayne wrote:

"And now we are called upon in the most imposing way to give our best judgments to the subject, yielding to decided cases everything that can be claimed for them on the score of authority, except the surrender of conscience. . .Upon our maturest deliberation we do not think that the cases relied upon for a doctrine contrary to that which this court will here announce, are sustained by a sound and comprehensive course on professional reasoning. Fortunately, a departure from them involves no change in a rule of property. Our conclusion, too, if it shall not have universal acquiescence, will be admitted by all to be coincident with the policy of the Constitution and the condition of our country."[64]

Here, then, we have a novel exercise of the judicial power—the power of the court to overrule itself. Especially noteworthy in Wayne's position are three elements: first, conscience takes priority over precedent; second, departures which do not involve changes in rules of property are privileged; and third, "the condition of our country" becomes a necessary measurement. The first of these elements is undoubtedly acceptable to all; the second is more debatable since, as we will see when studying problems in jurisdiction, jurisdictional limits previously established are of utmost importance to the legal profession; while the third, "the condition of our country," was to become the crux of a bitter and unending debate between conservative constitutionalists and creative jurists.[65]

At the same time that the Supreme Court was overruling itself, Judge Betts of the District Court of New York was emphasizing the importance of adhering to the doctrine of acquiescence. "The Supreme Court," he wrote, "regards it as a circumstance of deserved weight in support of the constitutionality and validity of an act of Congress, that there has been a uniform course of action, or a partial acquiescence for a long period of time in consonance with the power exercised under the act."

Elsewhere in this same opinion, Betts reiterated the often expressed doctrine that "the collision between the Constitution and statute, or the defect of power in Congress to pass the law, must be of the most plain and indisputable character to justify in any tribunal a refusal to recognize its validity. . .The presumption is always to be in favor of the validity of statutes, until the contrary is clearly demonstrated. Full effect will be given by every judicatory to a statute, unless its opposition to the Constitution is of that nature that the court feels a clear and strong conviction of their incompatibility. . .Unless the discrepancy between the Constitution and the act in question is palpable and irreconcilable, this court must acquiesce in the authority of Congress to pass it."

Doubt, concludes Betts, works in support of the validity of a law, not against it.[66]

In another lower court decision, Justice McLean, an outspoken opponent of slavery, overruling the argument that the constitutional provision concerning fugitive slaves was inapplicable to states other than the original thirteen, also insisted that the policy or impolicy of the constitutional provision was not a subject for the court to decide. The court would not discuss the origins of slavery or the declaration of the natural rights of man as expressed in the Declaration of Independence but would look only to the law as it stands. "If the Constitution is less perfect than the parties, on either side, would have it," he said, "we are not the less bound by its provisions. If an alteration in the instrument be desirable, let it be made, or attempted to be made, in the mode provided."[67]

It was one thing to advocate acquiescence, judicial deference and a "hands-off" policy on political questions; it was another to insist on the subordination of the judicial power to that of the legislature. Justice Daniel was perhaps the foremost proponent of this doctrine. In the case of *Cary v. Curtis* he reveals his philosophy concerning the proper place of the judiciary in the scheme of government:

"The judicial power of the United States, although it has its origin in the Constitution, is—except in enumerated instances applicable exclusively to this court—dependent for its distribution and organization, and for the modes of its exercise, entirely upon the action of Congress." The Congress, points out Daniel, possesses the sole power of creating the lower courts, of investing them with jurisdiction, or of withholding jurisdiction. "To deny this position would be to elevate the judicial over the legislative branch of the government, and to give to the former powers limited by its own discretion merely."[68]

This was by no means Daniel's final word on the subject of judicial subordination. We shall come across more of his observations, especially as we study the question of jurisdiction, as his position matured and became more self-assured.

While Daniel was reminding the court of its dependence on Congress, his colleague, Justice Woodbury, attempted to combat the idea that changing conditions of the country justified the court in extending its own jurisdiction. Dissenting from the majority in *Waring v. Clarke*,[69] Woodbury, whose service on the court was limited to an all too short period of years, argued that "in case of supposed improvements or increased convenience by changes of the law, it is an imperative duty on us to let them be made by representatives of the people and the states, through acts of Congress, rather than by judicial legislation."

Addressing himself to the problem of admiralty jurisdiction, Woodbury concedes that new exigencies in society and different stages of business and civilization necessitate improvements in the law and jurisdiction over navigable waters. "But," he asks, "does this court possess that legislative power?. . .It certainly seems much wiser in doubtful cases to let Congress extend our power, than to do it ourselves by construction or analogy."[70]

As a corollary, in a subsequent case Woodbury declared the general principle that the state legislatures "must be presumed to act from public considerations, being in a high public trust; and when their measures relate to matters of general interest, and can be vindicated under express or justly implied powers, and more especially when they appear intended for improvements, made in the true spirit of the age, or for salutary reforms in abuses, the disposition of the judiciary should be strong to uphold them."[71] Thus the conservative reply to the problem of change.

At the same time, Justice Daniel, dissenting in *New Jersey Steam Navigation Co. v. Merchants' Bank*, picked up where Woodbury had left off the preceding year in *Waring v. Clarke.* Distinguishing between the advantages of permitting the admiralty jurisdiction to encroach on the province of the common law (which he denied) and the power of the court to authorize this encroachment, Daniel pointed out:

"An argument in favor of power founded upon calculations of advantage, in a government of strictly delegated powers, is scarcely legitimate when addressed to the legislature; addressed to the judiciary, it seems to be especially out of place. . .If a restricted admiralty jurisdiction, though ever so impotent for good or prolific of inconvenience, has been imposed by the Constitution, either or both these evils must be of far less magnitude than would be attempts to remedy them by means subversive of the Constitution itself, by unwarranted legislative assumption, or by violent judicial constructions."[72]

For Daniel, as for all his fellow conservatives, the solution of the problem, if the necessity for change were sufficiently pressing, was to amend the Constitution by means of the modes provided rather than by direct judicial modification.

While certain members of the court were shying away from judicial activism, the Chief Justice was willing to commit himself and his colleagues to a course in which they would play a greater role as arbiters in the federal system. In his opinion in the *License Cases* (one of many), Taney, pointing out the difficulty of drawing a line between foreign and domestic commerce, denied to both Congress and the state legislatures the authority to define these limits, since neither could enlarge its own powers or restrict those of the other. Since the Constitution itself does not draw the line, he concluded, "the question is necessarily one for judicial decision."[73] This was but one of a growing number of opinions which was to expand the role and power of the court, first in the field of commerce, eventually wherever certain and definite lines were not drawn by the

Constitution.

One of the now forgotten events of American history provided the court with yet another opportunity to define the position of the federal judiciary in political affairs. In the early 1840's Thomas Dorr led an unsuccessful attempt to replace the charter government of Rhode Island with a new government under a new constitution. The authorities under the old charter government, including the state courts, denied any validity to the proceedings under the new constitution and declared all acts performed under it illegal. When Dorr, elected governor under the new constitution, prepared to assert the authority of the new government by force, the old government declared the state to be under martial law and called out the militia, which, among other things, broke into the house of a Mr. Luther, one of Dorr's supporters. Luther, claiming the validity of the new constitutional government, brought suit against Borden, the militia officer, in the Circuit Court of the United States, and when that court upheld the charter government, appeal was made to the Supreme Court.

Although Justice Woodbury dissented from the majority in the final disposition of the case—he contended that the statute establishing martial law was unconstitutional under the charter government—the court was unanimous in ruling that the question of which of the two contending governments, the charter or the constitutional, was the legitimate one, was not a question for the judiciary to decide.

Taney, speaking for the court, declared that the power of determining that a state government had been lawfully established when the courts of the state held otherwise was not one of the powers of the federal courts. Further, he said, "It is no part of the judicial functions of any court of the United States to prescribe the qualifications of voters in a state, giving the right to those to whom it is denied by the written and established Constitution and laws of the state, or taking it away from those to whom it is given."

As for the constitutional provision guaranteeing a republican form of government for every State, again it was not for the judiciary to determine this question but one in which they were to follow the lead of other departments of government. Nor were the courts to decide when the federal government should intervene in cases of domestic violence. Nor could the courts inquire whether the decision of the President to call out the militia was correct, for, "If the judicial power extends so far, the guarantee contained in the Constitution of the United States is a guarantee of anarchy, not of order."

Then, in closing, the Chief Justice attempted to place his idea of the role of the court in proper focus:

"Much of the argument on the part of the plaintiff turned upon political rights and political questions, upon which the court has been urged to express an opinion. We decline doing so. The high power has been conferred on this court, of passing judgment upon the acts of the state sovereignties, and of the legislative and executive branches of the federal government, and of determining whether they are beyond the limits of power marked out for them respectively by the Constitution of the United States. This tribunal, therefore, should be the last to overstep the boundaries which limit its jurisdiction. And while it should always be ready to meet any question confided to it by the Constitution, it is equally its duty not to pass beyond its appropriate sphere of action, and to take care not to involve itself in discussions which properly belong to other forums."[74]

To this part of the court's opinion, Woodbury assented: "This court can never with propriety be called on officially to be the umpire in questions merely political." The line between political and judicial functions was to be drawn by allowing the people to make and unmake constitutions and by allowing their representatives to make and unmake laws, "without our interference as to their principles or policy in doing it. . .When constitutions and laws are made and put in force by others, then the courts, as empowered by the states or the Union, commence their functions. . .Our power begins after theirs ends."

Political questions are to be decided by political tribunals, continues Woodbury, and not by "a class of men who are so far removed from [the people] as the judiciary; a class, also, who might decide them erroneously as well as right; and if in the former way, the consequences might not be able to be averted except by a revolution, while a wrong decision by a political forum can often be peacefully corrected by new elections or instructions in a single month. And if the people, in the distribution of powers under the Constitution, should ever think of making judges supreme arbiters in political controversies, when not selected by nor frequently amenable to them, nor at liberty to follow such various considerations in their judgments as belong to mere political questions, they will dethrone themselves and lose one of their own invaluable birthrights; building up in this way—slowly but surely—a new sovereign power in the republic, in most respects irresponsible and unchangeable for life, and one more dangerous, in theory at least, than the worst elective oligarchy in the worst of times."

A more skeptical attitude toward the Supreme Court than this presented by one of its own members is hard to imagine.

Again: "The judiciary, by its mode of appointment, long duration in office, and slight accountability, is rather fitted to check legislative power than political, and enforce what the political authorities have manifestly ordained. These last authorities are, by their pursuits and interests, better suited to make rules; we, to expound and enforce them, after made."

Applying the rule laid down earlier by the court concerning the recognition of foreign sovereignties, Woodbury reiterates that the judiciary must conform to the political decisions of the executive or legislative branches of the government.

The conservative judge then concludes with this not-so-conservative advice to those who recur to the judiciary for redress and find the door closed:

"If it be asked what redress have the people, if wronged in these matters, unless by resorting to the judiciary, the answer is, they have the same as in all other political matters. In those, they go to the ballot boxes, to the legislature or the executive, for the redress of such grievances as are within the jurisdiction of each, and, for such as are not, to conventions and amendments of constitutions. And when the former fail, and these last are forbidden by statutes, all that is left in extreme cases, where the suffering is intolerable and the prospect is good for relief by action of the people without the forms of law, is to do as did Hampden and Washington, and venture action without those forms, and abide the consequences."[75]

One cannot help but think of the years which followed the Dred Scott decision and. . .the consequences.

We must also ask in this and in many other similar cases whether the court was shirking its legitimate duty by denying itself the power or jurisdiction to settle the more difficult problems which arose in the nation, or whether it was sincere in deferring to the judgment of the political branches of government; whether, in short, the judges or the people, directly or indirectly, were to have the last say on the burning issues. If we look either to the Constitution or to the Judiciary Act we will find no answer. It is no wonder then that this debate has been going on since the question was first posed and continues to our day.

We have seen how in the *License Cases* Taney contended that it was for the court to draw the line where domestic commerce ended and foreign commerce began. But when it came to the question of state regulation of immigration, the Chief Justice, dissenting from the majority of the court, insisted on deferring to the judgment of the states. The majority held, in effect, that the states could not prohibit the immigration of foreigners in general, although they implied that paupers and diseased persons could be kept out. Taney argued that it was not for the court to draw such a line, but that it was within the discretionary power of the states to establish the requirements they deemed appropriate in accordance with their police power. "Most evidently," he wrote, "this court cannot supervise the exercise of such a power by the state, nor control or regulate it, nor determine whether the occasion called for it, nor whether the funds raised here have been properly administered. This would be substituting the discretion of the court for the discretionary power reserved to the states. Moreover, if this court should undertake to exercise this supervisory power, it would take upon itself a duty which it is utterly incapable of discharging."[76]

It is interesting to note that although Taney's general rule in these two cases undergoes a complete reversal—in the case of imported merchandise the question of whether interstate or domestic commerce is involved is necessarily one for judicial decision; in the case of regulating the immigration of persons there is "no ground for the exercise of this power by the government of the United States or any of its tribunals"—the practical results he reaches are identical: both of the state regulatory measures are constitutional. But in determining the philosophy of the members of the court, it is the *dicta*—the general ideas, the underlying premises—which interest us more than the actual decisions, and in this case it is difficult to reconcile Taney's discrimination between the judicial treatment of persons and things.

As for *dicta*, in the *Passenger Cases* the Chief Justice digresses to give his opinion on the revision of previous interpretations of the Constitution:

"I do not, however, object to the revision of [the construction of the Constitution], and am quite willing that it be regarded as the law of this court, that its opinion upon the construction of the Constitution is always open to discussion when it is supposed to have been founded in error, and that its judicial authority should hereafter depend altogether on the force of the reasoning by which it is supported."[77]

This rule of revision echoes the idea underlying Wayne's opinion in the Letson case. It is the principle that sound reasoning takes precedence over *stare decisis* when there is conflict between the two.

But then Taney adds this important warning to those who might feel tempted to attribute a meaning to words in the Constitution which was not in the minds of the framers:

"The members of the convention unquestionably used the words they inserted in the Constitution in the same sense in which they used them in their debates. It is their object to be understood, and not to mislead, and *they ought not to be supposed to have used familiar words in a new or unusual sense.* And there is no reason to suppose that they did not use the word 'imports,' when they inserted it in the Constitution, in the sense in which it had been familiarly used for ages, and in which it was daily used by themselves. *If in this court we are at liberty to give old words new meanings when we find them in the Constitution, there is no power which may not, by this mode of construction, be conferred on the general government and denied to the states.*"[78]

Although this was a mere *dictum* in a dissenting opinion, the importance of these remarks of Taney are not to be underestimated. The liberty to give old words new meanings is not only a means to enlarge the powers of government by judicial fiat, it is also a means to deprive the government of powers. In short, it is a mode by which the court, for better or for worse, rewrites the Constitution and creates new relationships never dreamed of by the founding fathers nor desired by the people. It is to go beyond the judicial revision envisioned by Marshall and to create the government by the judiciary which Justices Woodbury and Daniel so much feared.

As is wont to occur within any long-lived institution whose membership changes from time to time, once again more than one justice of the Supreme Court troubled himself to repeat doctrines laid down in an earlier period in order to emphasize their enduring validity. Both Justices Grier and Daniel returned to the problem of determining the constitutionality of state legislation.

Dissenting from a court decision which had held a state law to be in conflict with the contract clause and therefore unconstitutional, Grier (joined by Daniel and Catron) wrote: "There is no portion of the power and jurisdiction committed to this court which demands so much caution in its exercise, as that of declaring the legislation of a state to be null and void, because it comes in conflict with the Constitution of the United States."[79]

As for Daniel himself, who was becoming more articulate as his role as the principal conservative spokesman grew, he added, in another case decided in the same year: "It has been repeatedly said by this court that to pronounce a law of one of the sovereign states of this Union to be a violation of the Constitution is a solemn function, demanding the gravest and most deliberate consideration; and that a law of one of the states should never be so denominated, if it can upon any other principle be correctly explained. Indeed, it would seem that, if there could be any course of proceeding more than all others calculated to excite dissatisfaction, to awaken a natural jealousy on the part of the states, and to estrange them from the federal government, it would be the practice, for slight and insufficient causes, of calling on those states to justify, before tribunals in some sense foreign to themselves, their acts of general legislation."[80]

The first time that the Supreme Court overruled one of its own decisions was in the case of *Louisville Railroad Company v. Letson.* Eight years later the court did the same in *Genesee Chief v. Fitzhugh.* The Chief Justice, speaking for the majority, found two justifications for the new position taken by the court: first, conditions had changed; second, the decision involved a question of jurisdiction only and not a rule of property.

Acknowledging "the great weight" to which the earlier decision in the case of *The Thomas Jefferson* was entitled, Taney continued: "If we follow it, we follow an erroneous decision into which the court fell, when the great importance of the question as it now presents itself could not be foreseen. . .The decision was made in 1825 when the commerce on the rivers of the west and on the lakes was in its infancy, and of little importance, and but little regarded compared with that of the present day."

Further, he said, the doctrine of *stare decisis* is relative; that is, where rules of property are involved, the doctrine should be adhered to; but where there is a question of jurisdiction only, the court is free to expand its jurisdiction by its own initiative, despite previous decisions of a more restrictive nature. "As we are convinced that the former decision was founded in error, and if not corrected, must produce serious public as well as private inconvenience and loss, it becomes our duty not to perpetuate it."[81]

The medula of this position is that the Constitution must be reinterpreted in accordance with changing circumstances, that economic and pragmatic considerations are to be given high priority, and that rules of the court which were formerly valid cannot bind posterity.

To this radical assumption of judicial power, Justice Daniel dissented vigorously: "The doctrine at present promulged by this court, is based upon assumptions still more irregular in my view, still more dangerous than that above adverted to, because it claims for this court, wholly irrespective either of the Constitution or the legislation of Congress, powers to be assumed and carried into execution by some rule which in the judgment of this court is to be applied according to its own opinions of convenience or necessity. . .Now it is insisted that. . .the Constitution may, nay must be altered by the same process, and must be enlarged not by amendment in the modes provided, but according to the opinions of the judiciary, entertained upon their views of expediency and necessity."[82]

The reasoning of the judicial mind is fine and subtle. Just as one believes he has grasped the underlying philosophy of a judge, that same judge issues a new opinion which does not fit in with the general rule which one has tentatively proposed. Thereupon preliminary classifications must be revised and generalizations must be modified. In part, this practice results from a natural tendency to over-simplify; in part, because we all too often accept as a true description of one position that presented by an opponent. Thus, from a picture formed from reading Justice Daniel's dissents added to a few general words taken from the opinions of the Chief Justice, we are led to expect that we will forever find these two judges in opposite camps when matters concerning judicial power are involved.

Yet in the same year that Taney and Daniel were at odds over the power of the court to extend the admiralty jurisdiction, we find them together in dissenting from the majority over the right of the court to substitute its own opinion for that of Congress in deciding whether or not a bridge over the Ohio River is an unlawful obstruction of commerce. Here the Chief Justice joined his conservative colleague from Virginia in denying to the court the power to exercise its discretion in a matter which was one for the legislature.

In an equity suit brought directly before the Supreme Court by the State of Pennsylvania, the majority decided that the Wheeling Bridge Company had constructed a bridge which unlawfully obstructed the right of free navigation on the Ohio River. The court therefore ruled that the obstruction must be removed, either by raising the height of the bridge, opening an alternative channel or dismantling the bridge entirely.

This power Taney denied to the court. If the bridge was an obstruction, it was for Congress to correct the evil. "But if Congress has not thought proper, or does not think proper, to exercise this power, and public mischief has arisen, or may arise from it, *it does not follow that the judicial power of the United States may step in and supply what the legislative authority has omitted to perform.* It does not by any means follow that the judicial power may declare an obstruction in or over a navigable stream, an offense against the United States, before the legislative power has forbidden it, and conferred authority upon the courts to punish or remove it."

To the implication that Congress' power to regulate commerce somehow authorized the courts to prohibit what Congress had not explicitly authorized, Taney replied: "I cannot perceive how the mere grant to the legislative department of the government to regulate commerce, can give to the judicial branch of the government the power to declare what shall and what shall not be regarded as an unlawful obstruction." Further, to Taney, the "broad and undefinable discretion" which must be exercised in making such a determination "appears to me much more appropriately to belong to the legislature than to the judiciary."[83]

How Taney could advocate the court's assumption of power to determine the limits of the admiralty jurisdiction without any guidelines from Congress or the Constitution itself, while denying to the court the right to settle a case in equity because Congress had not spoken on the subject, is, indeed, difficult to understand, especially when virtually all the other members of the court were for the active judicial role in both cases. Perhaps the solution is that Taney's underlying premise was not of a judicial nature but was economic. For here, as in the earlier *Charles River Bridge* case, we find Taney taking a position which favored the prosperity of the country: in the one case, against bridge monopolies; in the other, favorable to railroad transportation whose growing importance Taney recognized early. When we reconsider the Chief Justice's position in the case of the *Genesee Chief* we see that he is motivated more by the effects of his decision on the control of inland waterways transportation (greater uniformity and swifter justice) than by any theoretical notions as to the ideal exercise of judicial power.

But if consistency is found in these opinions of Taney by resorting to a common practical denominator, Daniel's consistency is discovered within the confines of his philosophy of the role of the judiciary. For the judge who was alarmed at the court's extension of its own jurisdiction and power, it was only natural to inveigh against the majority decision in the *Wheeling Bridge* case:

"I ask upon what foundation the courts of the United States, limited and circumscribed as they are by the Constitution, and by the laws which have created them and defined their jurisdiction, can, upon any speculations of public policy, assume to themselves the authority and functions of the legislative department of the government, alone clothed with those functions by the Constitution and laws, *and undertake of their mere will, to supply the omissions of that department?* Is it either in the language or theory of the Constitution, that this court shall exercise such an auxiliary or rather guardian and paramount authority? Cannot the legislative department of the government be intrusted with the fulfillment of its peculiar duties? Such an act as this court has been called upon to perform; such an act as it has just announced as its own, is, in my opinion, virtually an act of legislation, or, in stricter propriety, (I say it not in an offensive sense), an act of usurpation."[84]

We have seen how, in order to expand the jurisdiction of the federal courts, both Taney and Wayne found it necessary to overrule previous decisions, justifying their position by pointing out the relativity of *stare decisis.* But once the court had given a new meaning to the constitutional provisions concerning admiralty jurisdiction and cases involving corporations, it was for the majority to take the conservative position and for Justice Daniel to question the force of the recent rulings. To the argument that the diversity of citizenship clause authorized the court to take jurisdiction over corporations and that the matter was no longer open to discussion, Daniel replied, "that this is a matter involving a construction of the Constitution, and that wherever the construction or the integrity of that sacred instrument is involved, I can hold myself trammelled by no precedent or number of precedents. That instrument is above all precedents, and its integrity every one is bound to vindicate against any number of precedents, if believed to trench upon its supremacy."[85]

The following year the court answered Daniel. Forgetting that only ten years earlier in the Letson case the court had rejected the principle of *stare decisis* in arriving at its assumption of jurisdiction over corporations, Justice Grier, speaking for the court, now insisted on "adherence to the maxim of *stare decisis.*" Pointing out that since 1844 the interpretation in the Letson case had been accepted without dissent, and that great numbers of cases involving corporations had been decided by the federal courts, Grier continued: "If we should now declare these judgments to have been entered without jurisdiction or authority, we should inflict a great and irreparable evil on the community. There are no cases, where an adherence to the maxim of *stare decisis* is so absolutely necessary to the peace of society, as those which affect retroactively the jurisdiction of courts.[86] For this reason alone, even if the court was now of the opinion that the principles affirmed in the case just mentioned, and that of *The Bank v. Deveaux*, were not founded on right reason, we should not be justified in overruling them."[87]

Daniel once more delivered a vigorous dissent. Stating that, "it would have been thought *a priori* that the very last aid to be invoked in support [of this new doctrine] would be the maxim *stare decisis,*" he reiterated his belief that the doctrine of *stare decisis* was relative. Those who uphold "the iron rule of *stare decisis,*" he wrote, "are saying the abuse has been already put in practice; it has by practice, merely, become sanctified; and may therefore be repeated at pleasure."[88]

Justice Campbell, also dissenting, invoked the rule of *stare decisis* in order to justify the same conclusion reached by Daniel, namely that the court did not have jurisdiction over corporations under the diversity of citizenship clause. Whereas Daniel was ready to reject the rule of the court laid down in the Letson case, Campbell merely ignored its importance and rested his argument on "the ancient landmarks of the court" which long preceded the Letson decision.[89]

The case of *Marshall v. Baltimore and Ohio Railroad Co.* is a perfect example of how one rule may be used (or abused) in so many different ways to arrive at conflicting conclusions or to justify those conclusions. It would certainly give us grounds for being wary of arguments based on precedent and general rules.

Two more cases confirm the court's long-standing reluctance to interfere in questions which they considered strictly political. In *Kennett v. Chambers* the court held that it was for the executive branch to determine at what time Texas had become an independent state, "And if we undertook to inquire whether she had not in fact become an independent sovereign state before she was recognized as such by the treaty-making power, we should take upon ourselves the exercise of political authority, for which a judicial tribunal is wholly unfit, and which the constitution has conferred exclusively upon another department."[90]

In the second case, *Doe v. Braden*,[91] the court held that it could not look beyond a treaty in order to determine whether it had been properly ratified by a foreign nation, as this was a political and not a judicial question, which belonged exclusively to the executive department of the government.

A more important decision handed down in 1854 was that of *Piqua Branch v. Knoop*, where the court insisted on reserving to itself the power in the last resort of deciding whether or not a constitutionally privileged contract was involved in an act of the State legislature. As a rule, the court acknowledged, the construction given to state statutes by the courts of the state was to be followed; but where there was a question as to whether the state law was in conflict with the Constitution of the United States, it was the Supreme Court and not that of the state which was to make the final determination. "The decision of the Supreme Court of the State is before us for revision, and if their construction of the contract in question impairs its obligation, we are required to reverse their judgment. To follow the construction of a State court in such a case, would be to surrender one of the most important provisions in the federal Constitution."[92]

The above case, in laying down the rule that the Supreme Court "has reserved to itself the final authority to determine whether a contract existed, the nature of its obligations, and whether a State law has impaired these obligations,"[93] by the same token vastly expanded its power under the contract clause, just as earlier, in the *License Cases*, Taney had claimed for the court the inescapable role of arbiter under the commerce clause.

In the following year the court was called upon to order the Secretary of the Treasury to pay the salary to a territorial judge for the remainder of his appointed term after he had been removed from his post by order of the President. The majority, however, denied the petition, holding that the territorial judges were subject to removal by the executive and therefore not entitled to any salary beyond the date of removal.

Justice McLean dissented in a lengthy opinion in which he equated the territorial judges with all others appointed by the President and pointed out the dire effects of control of the judiciary by the executive power: "Whenever any portion of the judicial power shall become subject to the executive, there will be an end of its independence and purity. It will become the register of executive decrees and of a party policy. What would create a deeper degradation than to see any branch of the judiciary, which stands between the executive power and the rights of the citizen, become the mere instrument of that power?"[94]

This plea for the independence of the judiciary is interesting not so much in itself (the majority did not even refer to this issue) as for the fact that it is the rare exception in which a judge found it necessary to put forward an argument which was long since universally accepted; for with this exception (if it may be considered one), the question of judicial independence was not an issue in American history.

In *Taylor v. Morton,*[95] a case decided by the Circuit Court, the question arose as to whether a treaty of the United States was paramount to an act of Congress where there was a conflict between the two. Justice Curtis held that this was not a question to be decided by the judiciary but by the executive and legislative departments. It was not for the court to invalidate a law applying duties to imports which an existing treaty declared should not be levied; the remedy of the injured party was to complain to those who had made and enforced the law.

In *Murray's Lessee v. Hoboken Land & Improvement Co.*, the court decided two important points: first, that due process of law was obtainable outside of the courts; and second, that not all inquiries into the existence of facts and the application to them of rules of law were matters exclusively for the judicial power. An act of Congress authorizing the Treasury Department to issue a distress warrant against the property of a revenue officer for amounts found due in adjusting his account was held to be constitutional. "Though partaking of the nature of judicial power in some respects," the court held, "it is a power long exercised by the executive department in England and in the States, and is not prohibited by the division of executive and judicial powers in the federal Constitution.[96]

"It is not sufficient to bring such matters under the judicial power," wrote Curtis, "that they involve the exercise of judgment upon law and fact. It is necessary to go further, and show not only that the adjustment of the balances due from accounting officers may be, but from their nature must be, controversies to which the United States is a party, within the meaning of the second section of the third article of the Constitution."[97]

The gist of Justice Curtis' decision is that it was necessary for Congress to give jurisdiction to the court over such disputes in order for them to be considered judicial controversies.

If the exercise of judicial power was subject in the last resort to the consent of Congress, it was at least in no way subordinate to the power of the states. Not since *Martin v.*

Hunter's Lessee and Cohens v. Virginia did the court deliver such a strong argument in favor of its own supremacy as arbiter of the Constitution as in the opinion of Justice Wayne in *Dodge v. Woolsey.* As in the case of *Piqua Branch v. Knoop*, the question was whether it was for the state courts or the Supreme Court of the United States to decide finally whether or not a state law was in the nature of a constitutionally privileged contract. In the Piqua Branch case the State of Ohio had passed a law increasing the rate of taxation on a State-chartered bank whose charter guaranteed the bank against additional levies; in *Dodge v. Woolsey*, the state law increasing the tax rate was explicitly authorized by a provision in the new state constitution, adopted by the people of the state after the charter was granted.

Over a strong dissent by Justice Campbell (joined by Catron and Daniel)[98], the court held on the principal point at issue that changing the constitution of the state could not validate an act otherwise contrary to the Constitution of the United States.[99] But Justice Wayne, speaking for the court, went beyond the immediate controversy to speak of the role of the Supreme Court.

That there might be interferences on the part of the state legislatures, either with the Constitution or between their enactments and those of Congress, "suggested the necessity, or rather made it obvious, that our national union would be incomplete and altogether insufficient for the great end contemplated, unless a constitutional arbiter was provided to give certainty and uniformity, in all of the states, to the interpretation of the Constitution and the legislation of Congress; with powers also to declare judicially what acts of the legislature of the States might be in conflict with either."

"The foundation of the right of citizens of different states to sue each other in the courts of the United States," continued Wayne, "is not an unworthy jealousy of the impartiality of the state tribunals. It has a higher aim and purpose. It is to make the people think and feel, though residing in different states of the Union, that their relations to each other were protected by the strictest justice, administered in courts independent of all local control or connection with the subject matter of the controversy between the parties to a suit."

Further: "Without such a court the citizens of each state could not have enjoyed all the privileges and immunities of citizens in the several states, as they were intended to be secured by the second section of the fourth article of the Constitution. Nor would the judicial power have been extended in fact to [all the cases provided in Article Three of the Constitution].

"Without the Supreme Court, as it has been constitutionally and legislatively constituted, neither the Constitution nor the laws of Congress passed in pursuance of it, nor treaties, would be in practice or in fact the supreme law of the land, and the injunction that the judges in every state should be bound thereby, anything in the Constitution or laws of any state to the contrary notwithstanding, would be useless, if the judges of the state courts, in any one of the states, could finally determine what was the meaning and operation of the Constitution and laws of Congress, or the extent of the obligation of treaties."

Again: "As it was thought that [Congress] and the state legislatures might pass laws conflicting with the letter or spirit of the Constitution under which they legislated, it became necessary to make a judicial department for the United States, with a jurisdiction best suited to preserve harmony between the states, severally and collectively, with the national government, and which would give the people of all of the states that confidence and security under it anticipated by them [in the preamble to the Constitution]. Without a judicial department, just such as it is, neither the powers of the Constitution nor the purposes for which they were given could have been attained."

In conclusion, Wayne wrote: "Without such a judicial tribunal there are no means provided by which the conflicting legislation of the states with the Constitution and the laws of Congress may be terminated, so as to give to either a national operation in each of the states. To such an event no means have been provided for an amicable accommodation, none for a compromise; none for mediation; none for arbitration; none for a congress of the states as a mode of conciliation. The consequence [of which] would be a permanent diversity of the operation of the Constitution in the states, as well in matters exclusively of public concern as in those which secure individual rights. Fortunately it is not so. A supreme tribunal has been provided, which has hitherto, by its decisions, settled all differences which have arisen between the authorities of the states and those of the United States. The legislation under which its appellate powers is exercised has been of sixty-seven years' duration, without any countenanced attempt to repeal it. It is rather late to question it; and in continuing to exercise it, this court complies with the decisions of its predecessors, believing, after the fullest examination, that its appellate jurisdiction is given in conformity with the Constitution."[100]

Wayne's opinion may appear to us to be gratuitous, but when we examine the dissent of Campbell we will understand why it was necessary for the judge from Georgia to revive once more the question of the supremacy of the Supreme Court.

Campbell, indignant that the court should lay down the doctrine that a state was hamstrung by the Constitution of the United States in carrying out its own policy of internal taxation, lashed out against the power of the court iself:

"As to the claim made for the court to be the final arbiter of these questions of political power, I can imagine no pretension more likely to be fatal to the Constitution or the court itself. If this court is to have an office so transcendent as to decide finally the powers of the people over persons and things within the state, a much closer connection and a much more direct responsibility of its members to the people is a necessary condition for the safety of the popular rights. . .

"The inquiry recurs: have the people of Ohio deposited with this tribunal the authority to overrule their own judgment upon the extent of their own powers over institutions created by their own government and commorant within the state? The fundamental principle of American constitutions, it seems to me, is that to the people of the several states belongs the resolution of all questions, whether of regulation, compact, or positive justice, arising out of the action of their municipal government upon their citizens, or depending upon their constitution and laws, and are judges of the validity of all acts done by their municipal authorities in the exercise of their sovereign rights, in either case without responsibility or control from any department of the federal government."

To the query of who, in the United States, is to resolve the conflicts of the sort arising in this case, Campbell replies: "The true principle. . .would seem to be, that if there was any conflict in the tax laws of the state, and a supposed contract of its legislative or executive agents with one of its citizens, it would be for the state to harmonize the two upon principles of general equity; but in no condition of facts for the judiciary department to interfere with state affairs by writs of replevin or injunction. The acknowledgement of such a power would be to establish the alarming doctrine that the empire of Ohio, and the remaining states of the Union, over their revenues, is not to be found in their people, but in the numerical majority of the judges of this court."

In conclusion, Campbell states that the provision of the constitution of Ohio, for whatever motives the people of that state may have seen fit to incorporate it, "is above and beyond the supervision or control of the judiciary department of this government."[101]

It is worthwhile to observe that whereas in the earlier cases in which the court asserted its supremacy over the decisions of the state courts it was unanimous, here, after sixty-seven years, three of the nine justices openly rejected this philosophy as incompatible with the sovereignty of the states. This was but one demonstration of a growing reaction to the power of the central government, especially noteworthy in that it came from men who represented that government.

Four years after handing down its order in *Pennsylvania v. Wheeling Bridge Co.*, the court was faced with another problem arising out of the case. Six months after the court had issued its decreee, Congress passed a statute declaring the bridge to be a lawful structure and not an obstruction to navigation. Subsequently the bridge collapsed, whereupon the State of Pennsylvania applied to Justice Grier for an injunction prohibiting the bridge company from reconstructing the bridge. Notwithstanding the injunction and on the authority of the act of Congress, the bridge was rebuilt.

In 1856 the case came before the Supreme Court once more on motions to enforce the original decree, and for attachment against the officials of the bridge company for disobeying the injunction of Justice Grier. The court held, first, that the act of Congress was valid; second, that following the act of Congress the decree directing the alteration or abatement of the bridge could not be carried into execution; and third, that no attachment for contempt could issue.

On the principal point the court held that if the case had been an action at law and a judgment had been rendered in favor of the plaintiff for damages, the award would have been beyond the reach of Congress; but insofar as the decree was limited to enjoining a structure which it considered an obstacle to navigation, it could no longer be enforced now that Congress had ruled that the bridge was not an obstruction.[102]

This deference to the superior right of Congress to decide the issue by no means met with the unanimous approval of the court. Justices McLean, Grier and Wayne each filed separate dissents.

"The decree in the Wheeling Bridge case," wrote McLean, "was the result of a judicial investigation, founded upon facts ascertained in the course of the hearing. It was strictly a judicial question. The complaint was an obstruction of commerce, by the bridge, to the injury of the complainant, and the court found the fact to be as alleged in the bill. It was said by Chief Justice Marshall, many years ago, that Congress could do many things, but that it could not alter a fact. This it has attempted to do in the above act."

"The Congress and the court constitute coordinate branches of the government; their duties are distinct and of a different character. The judicial power cannot legislate, nor can the legislative power act judicially. The Constitution has declared, that the judicial power shall extend to all cases in law and equity arising under the Constitution, the laws of the United States, and treaties, etc. All legislative powers are vested in Congress. While these functionaries are limited to their appropriate duties as vested, there can be little or no conflict of jurisdiction.

"From the organization of the legislative power, it is unfitted for the discharge of judicial duties; and the same may be said of this court in regard to legislation. It may therefore happen that, when either trenches upon the appropriate powers of the other, their acts are inoperative and void.

"The judicial power is exercised in the decision of cases; the legislative, in making general regulations by the enactment of laws. The latter acts from considerations of public policy; the former by the pleadings and evidence in a case. From this view it is at once seen, that Congress could not undertake to hear the complaint of Pennsylvania in this case, take testimony, or cause it to be taken, examine the surveys and reports of engineers, decide the questions of law which arise on the admission of the testimony, and give the proper and legal effect to the evidence in the final decree. To do this is the appropriate duty of the judicial power. And this is what was done by this court, before the above act of Congress was passed. The court held that the bridge obstructed the navigation of the Ohio River, and that, consequently, it was a nuisance. The act declared the bridge to be a legal structure, and, consequently, that it was not a nuisance. Now, is this a legislative or a judicial act? Whether it be a nuisance or not, depends upon the fact of obstruction; and this would seem to be strictly a judicial question, to be decided on evidence produced by the parties in a case."

McLean went further and held that under the commerce clause Congress did not have the power to legalize a bridge over navigable waters; that "the act of Congress declaring the bridge to be a legal structure, being the exercise of a judicial and an appellate power, is unconstitutional, and consequently inoperative. It is what it purports to be, a reversal of the decree of this court, in effect, if not in terms."[103]

Justice Grier concurred with McLean that "Congress cannot annul or vacate any decree of this court; that the assumption of such a power is without precedent, and, as a precedent for the future, it is a dangerous example."[104]

Wayne, also agreeing with McLean, rejected the decision of the majority that the act of 1852 relieved the defendants from the operation of the judgment of the court: "I know of no power in Congress to interfere with such a judgment, under the pretence of a power to legalize the structure of bridges over the public navigable rivers of the United States. . .or under the commercial power of Congress to regulate commerce among the states."[105] [106]

This lengthy debate over the destiny of a bridge was in reality a three-way discussion as to who was to decide on the merits of Pennsylvania's complaint. In the original case, the majority held that the Supreme Court sitting in equity was the constitutionally designated and legally correct body to make the decision, while both Taney and Daniel vigorously insisted that it was a matter for a jury to determine. In the second round, only three justices remained firm in their insistence on the ultimate right of the court to make such a decision, while the majority (including Taney and Daniel) expressed their willingness to defer to Congress, even if their own previous decision was thereby overruled. Whether or not Congress succeeded in altering a fact, it succeeded in placing the court in a dubious position. At least the partisans of the court could console themselves that the court itself acquiesced in this reversal.

In the celebrated Dred Scott case,[107] six of the judges of the court decided that the Act of 1820, prohibiting slavery in the territories north of 36° 30′, was unconstitutional. Although this was the first time since *Marbury v. Madison*, fifty-four years earlier, that the court found an act of Congress unconstitutional, there was no general discussion here, as in the former case, of a power which by now was taken for granted.

It is interesting to note that various grounds were put forward for finding the Act of 1820 unconstitutional. Taney (with Wayne in agreement) contended that the act was in conflict with the due process clause of the Fifth Amendment protecting property rights; Catron claimed that it was in violation of both the privileges and immunities clause and the Treaty of 1803; Daniel and Campbell simply stated that

Congress did not have the power; while Grier does not give any explicit reason. Nelson avoided this question completely and did not pass judgment on the act. McLean and Curtis both held the Missouri Compromise to be a constitutional law.

Whether the decision of the court on this point was authoritative or mere *obiter dicta* has been an issue ever since the opinions were initially delivered. McLean and Curtis both contended in their dissents that nothing said by the court which did not have a direct bearing on the jurisdiction of the court could be considered as authority. This position has been defended by many writers. However, without entering into the details of the issue, we are inclined to agree with Benjamin Wright's assessment, that, "It is not so certain as many writers have assumed that the part of the opinion asserting the unconstitutionality of the Missouri Compromise was *obiter dicta.*"[108]

Taney (joined by Wayne) certainly considered the question of constitutionality an integral part of the decision; Daniel considered it proper but not necessary to make such a determination; Nelson, Grier, Campbell and Catron were silent on the point; only McLean and Curtis were explicit in treating the majority point of view as *dicta.*

Beyond the question of the constitutionality of the Missouri Compromise, two of the justices who composed the majority took pains to examine the constitutional provision empowering Congress to make rules and regulations for the territories of the United States.[109] Both Taney and Campbell contended that this grant was limited; that the term "rules and regulations" was to be understood in a narrow sense and not as synonomous with general powers of legislation; and that, consequently, the Congress was not empowered by it to make laws concerning property in the territories.

With this interpretation, Curtis dissented: "Rules and regulations must be needful. But undoubtedly the question whether a particular rule or regulation be needful, must be finally determined by Congress itself. Whether a law be needful, is a legislative or political, not a judicial question. Whatever Congress deems needful is so, under the grant of power."

Referring to three different and opposite views concerning the power of Congress over slavery in the territories, Curtis continued: "With the weight of either of these considerations, when presented to Congress to influence its action, this court has no concern. One or the other may be justly entitled to guide or control the legislative judgment upon what is a needful regulation. The question here is, whether they are sufficient to authorize this court to insert into this clause of the Constitution an exception of the exclusion or allowance of slavery, not found therein, nor in any other part of that instrument. To engraft on any instrument a substantive exception not found in it, must be admitted to be a matter attended with great difficulty. And the difficulty increases with the importance of the instrument, and the magnitude and complexity of the interests involved in its construction. To allow this to be done with the Constitution, upon reasons purely political, renders its judicial interpretation impossible—*because judicial tribunals, as such, cannot decide upon political considerations.* Political reasons have not the requisite certainty to afford rules of judicial interpretation. They are different in different men. They are different in the same men at different times. *And when a strict interpretation of the Constitution, according to the fixed rules which govern the interpretation of laws, is abandoned, and the theoretical opinions of individuals are allowed to control its meaning, we have no longer a Constitution;* we are under the government of individual men, who for the time being have power to declare what the Constitution is, according to their own views of what it ought to mean. When such a method of interpretation of the Constitution obtains, in place of a republican government with limited and defined powers, we have a government which is merely an exponent of the will of Congress; or what, in my opinion, would not be preferable, an exponent of the individual political opinions of the members of this court."[110]

To Justice Catron's opinion that property in slaves in the Louisiana Territory was protected by provisions of the Treaty of 1803, and that said treaty could not be repealed by

Congress, Curtis replied: "If it were admitted that the treaty between the United States and France did contain an express stipulation that the United States would not exclude slavery from so much of the ceded territory as is now in question, this court could not declare that an act of Congress excluding it was void by force of the treaty. Whether or no a case existed sufficient to justify a refusal to execute such a stipulation, would not be a judicial but a political and legislative question, wholly beyond the authority of this court to try and determine."[111]

Finally, it was Curtis' contention that the court had no business passing judgment on Congressional legislation over the territory. That region was acquired for the equal benefit of every individual citizen "to be administered justly and impartially according to the best judgment and discretion of Congress; to whose power, as the legislature of the nation which acquired it, the people of the United States have committed its administration. Whatever individual claims may be founded on local circumstances, or sectional differences of condition, cannot, in my opinion, be recognized in this court, without arrogating to the judicial branch of the government powers not committed to it; and which, with all the unaffected respect I feel for it, when acting in its proper sphere, I do not think it fitted to wield."[112]

Ever since the decision in *Waring v. Clarke* in 1847, a minority of the court resisted the expanded admiralty jurisdiction assumed by the majority. Both Woodbury and Daniel filed strong dissents on several occasions. In *Jackson v. James* ("The Steamboat Magnolia"), Daniel once more found an opportunity to criticize the doctrine that the judiciary must interpret or reinterpret the Constitution to meet the exigencies of changing conditions. In a belated postscript to his dissent in *Genesee Chief v. Fitzhugh*, decided six years earlier, Daniel called attention to "the disregard manifested, in the reasoning of the court, to this great fundamental principle of republican government, that if the Constitution was, at the period of its adoption, or has since, by the mutations of time and events, become inadequate to accomplish the objects of its creation, it belongs exclusively to those who formed it, and in whom resides the right to alter or abolish it, to remedy its defects. No such power can exist with those who are the creatures of the Constitution, clothed with the humbler office of executing the provisions of that instrument."

Then Daniel asks: "If the system was thus limited, and was known to be so by the framers of the Constitution, and if this instrument was designed to be applicable to the existing state of things, and was complete in itself, in all its delegations of and restrictions upon power, where is to be sought the right or power to enlarge or to diminish the effect or meaning of the instrument to make it commensurate with a predicament or state of things not merely *not existing* when the Constitution was framed, but which was not even within the contemplation of those by whom it was created?"

For Daniel, the argument of the court that the admiralty jurisdiction had to be enlarged, because the United States now had thousands of miles of public navigable waters which were not included within the limits of the original thirteen States in 1787, amounts to this: "The Constitution, which at its adoption suited perfectly well the situation of the country, and which *then* was unquestionably of supreme authority, we now adjudge to have become unequal to the exigencies of the times; it must therefore be substituted by something more efficient; and as the people, and the states, and the federal legislature, are tardy or delinquent in making the substitution, the duty or the credit of this beneficient work must be devolved upon the judiciary."[113]

In a separate dissent Campbell, joined by Catron, argued that had a collision taken place at this same place in 1789, no one would have admitted the existence of an admiralty jurisdiction over the case; and that, "Such being the facts. . .no change in the opinion of men, nor in the condition of the country, nor any apparent expediency, can render that constitutional which those who made the Constitution did not design to be so."[114]

Here, in these dissents, we find the medula of the conservative position: the total rejection of the idea that it is for the judiciary to amend the Constitution. For Justice Daniel, both the Constitution and its meaning were fixed for all time at the moment the former was framed and ratified. The role of the court was to apply the Constitution in accordance with what it meant in 1789. It was not a flexible instrument, whose terms and provisions were constantly undergoing re-examination, but a rigid document which could be altered only by the people who made it, in accordance with the procedures provided therein. What was constitutional remained constitutional and what was not constitutional could not now become constitutional by judicial fiat.

This interpretation, however, was not that of the majority of the court. Those whom Daniel attacked were not yet guilty of the charges levied against them. They were, perhaps, not as articulate in presenting their judicial philosophy, but it is clear that they did not conceive of themselves as radicals, amending the Consitution at will and in defiance of the Constitution itself; they were merely fulfilling their duty to interpret the Constitution correctly and to rectify errors committed by their predecessors. They rejected the dead weight of *stare decisis* (even Justice Daniel concurred with them here) as well as the idea that the meaning of the Constitution was clear from the beginning and for all time; but their deference to the legislature on political issues clearly exempts them from being labelled activists in the modern sense of the word.

We certainly must not permit Daniel's hyperbole to cloud our judgment. Yet we must credit this conservative judge with an early warning against tendencies which were eventually to dominate the court: particularly, the employment of words in a sense not dreamed of by the framers of the Constitution nor, in most cases, desired by the people; and the notion that the court must step in to play an active role where the people and the other branches of government remain silent.

Only one year after the Wheeling Bridge case was aired in the Supreme Court, a similar dispute came before the Circuit Court for New York. The plaintiffs, owners of vessels employed in the navigation of the Hudson River, applied to the court for an injunction restraining the defendant bridge company from erecting a state-authorized bridge over the

Hudson at Albany.[115] When the case came before the court again two years later on a final hearing, the two members of the court were divided in opinion. Nelson favored the granting of a permanent injunction but gave no opinion. District Judge Hall, however, decided that the court had no authority to annul the legislation of the state by the restraining process of injunction. As the result of this division of opinion and a further division within the Supreme Court when the case went up on appeal, the plaintiffs' bill was finally dismissed.[116] Under the circumstances, it is doubtful how authoritative the opinion of the District Judge should be considered; nonetheless, in view of the fact that it was not overruled by the higher court, it is interesting to note his arguments.

Hall pointed out that it had not been the policy of Congress and should not be the policy of the courts to encourage suits in equity and injunctions in preference to ordinary common law remedies; and that this was not a proper case for an injunction. The question of the relative rights of river and bridge travel was one which must be decided, but not by the courts. "It would seem to be necessary that some department of government should have the power to decide between these conflicting interests, to give preference to the one or the other, or to provide for the simultaneous exercise of rights which the public interest must require to be accorded to each. I do not doubt that such a power exists, but, in my judgment, it is a legislative and not a judicial power. The courts cannot make or change the law applicable to either of these cases. They can only administer the existing law, and they must leave to the legislature the duty of modifying it, as the changes in the condition and course of the business of the country and the ever varying interests of trade, commerce and navigation may require."

Since Congress, which possesses the paramount right to legislate on this subject, had not acted on this matter, Hall argued that "the law of the state must furnish the rule for our decisions." The settlement of the conflicting claims of the owners of vessels and the users of the bridge "is the appropriate business of the legislature, while it is not within the legitimate province of the judicial department of the state or of the national government.

"If the state legislature assumes to authorize what Congress, in the legitimate exercise of its delegated powers, has prohibited, the courts of the United States may declare the state legislation which contravenes that of the nation to be void, and that the proper authority of the United States shall be upheld; but, until the legislation of the state conflicts with that of Congress, or with the Constitution of the United States, this court has no authority to annul the legislation of the state, by the restraining process of injunction."[117]

It is interesting to note that the district judge rejected the decision in the first Wheeling Bridge case as authority to issue an injunction. Although Hall did not allude to the matter explicitly, it might have been that his opinion was influenced by the proceedings in Congress "overruling" the decree in the former case, and legalizing the bridge which the court had ordered to be altered or abated. The history of that case would certainly have given the judge good reason for hesitancy and caution. It is unfortunate that no opinions were given in the Supreme Court on this question on the two occasions that the case came before it on appeal.

After seventy years, during which the court had so many times successfully demonstrated that it was the constitutionally designated arbiter in conflicts with the states, it would seem unnecessary for the members of the court to write any additional vindications of their power. But this is exactly what Taney did in 1859 in the case of *Ableman v. Booth.* Perhaps because the greatest danger to the Union was the growing doctrine of state sovereignty, perhaps because his judicial career was coming to a close, the Chief Justice summarized his thoughts on the role of the court.

"The supremacy conferred on this government could not peacefully be maintained, unless it was clothed with judicial power, equally paramount in authority to carry it into execution; for if left to the courts of justice of the several states, conflicting decisions would unavoidably take place, and the local tribunals could hardly be expected to be always free from the local influences of which we have spoken. And the Constitution and laws and treaties of the United States, and the powers granted to the federal government, would soon receive different interpretations in different states, and the government of the United States would soon become one thing in one state and another thing in another. It was essential, therefore, to its very existence as a government, that it should have the power of establishing courts of justice, altogether independent of state power, to carry into effect its own laws; and that a tribunal should be established in which all cases which might arise under the Constitution and laws and treaties of the United States, whether in a state court or a court of the United States, should be finally and conclusively decided. Without such a tribunal, it is obvious that there would be no uniformity of judicial decision; and that the supremacy, (which is but another name for independence), so carefully provided in the clause of the Constitution above referred to, could not possibly be maintained peacefully, unless it was associated with this paramount judicial authority.

"It is manifest that this ultimate appellate power in a tribunal created by the Constitution itself was deemed essential to secure the independence and supremacy of the general government in the sphere of action assigned to it; to make the Constitution and laws of the United States uniform and the same in every state; and to guard against evils which would inevitably arise from conflicting opinions between the courts of a state and of the United States, if there was no common arbiter authorized to decide between them."

Taney continued: "As the courts of a state and the courts of the United States might, and indeed certainly would often differ as to the extent of the powers conferred by the general government, it was manifest that serious controversies would arise between the authorities of the United States and of the states which must be settled by force of arms, unless some tribunal was created to decide between them finally and without appeal.

"The Constitution has accordingly provided, as far as human foresight could provide, against this danger, and in conferring judicial power upon the federal government, it declares that the jurisdiction of its courts shall extend to all cases arising under this Constitution and the laws of the

United States. . .The judicial power covers every legislative act of Congress, whether it be made within the limits of its delegated powers, or be an assumption of power beyond the grants in the Constitution.

"This judicial power was justly regarded as indispensable, not merely to maintain the supremacy of the laws of the United States, *but also to guard the states from any encroachment upon their reserved rights by the general government.* And as the Constitution is the fundamental and supreme law, *if it appears that an act of Congress is not pursuant to and within the limits of the power assigned to the federal government, it is the duty of the courts of the United States to declare it unconstitutional and void.* The grant of judicial power is not confined to the administration of laws passed in pursuance to the provisions of the Constitution, nor confined to the interpretation of such laws; but, by the very terms of the grant, the Constitution is under their view when any act of Congress is brought before them, and it is their duty to declare the law void and refuse to execute it, if it is not pursuant to the legislative powers conferred upon Congress. And as the final appellate power in all such questions is given to this court, controversies as to the respective powers of the United States and the states, instead of being determined by military and physical force, are heard, investigated, and finally settled with the calmness and deliberation of judicial inquiry. And no one could fail to see that if such an arbiter had not been provided in our complicated system of government, internal tranquility could not have been preserved; and if such controversies were left to arbitrament of physical force, our government, state and national, would soon cease to be governments of laws, and revolutions by force of arms would take the place of courts of justice and judicial decisions.

"So long, therefore, as this Constitution shall endure," wrote Taney, in conclusion, "this tribunal must exist with it, deciding in the peaceful forms of judicial proceeding the angry and irritating controversies between sovereignties, which in other countries have been determined by the arbitrament of force."[118]

The tragic irony of this opinion is that the Supreme Court

was not, in the last resort, capable of resolving the most important controversy of all, for only two years later there came to pass what Marshall had feared forty years earlier when he wrote, in *Cohens v. Virginia:* "The framers of the Constitution were, indeed, unable to make any provisions which should protect that instrument against a general combination of states, or of the people, for its destruction; and, conscious of this inability, they have not made the attempt."[119]

There are those who attribute the failure of the court to avoid the Civil War to the "hands-off" decision in the Dred Scott case. Perhaps had Curtis and McLean been able to convince a majority to their point of view, history would have pursued a different course. But the issues which divided the country went deeper than the standing of slaves or former slaves in the federal courts or their access to freedom in exceptional cases. Further, as we have noted continuously during the survey of this period, the court was philosophically opposed to resolving political questions, and, to expect of them the resolution of the slavery question was, under the circumstances, to expect the impossible. It was for a later court to assume an active role on political issues, perhaps, in part, because of the pre-war court's failure to do so.

One more case arose in the court which gave the Chief Justice an opportunity to speak of relations between the court and the state authorities. In *Kentucky v. Dennison*, decided on the eve of the Civil War,[120] the court backed away from a showdown with a state governor. As in so many of the conflicts between the courts and the states, this one also involved a Northern state. Dennison, the Governor of Ohio, had refused to discharge his legal duty to arrest a fugitive from justice and surrender him to the authorities of the State of Kentucky. The State of Kentucky brought suit against the governor for this failure.

The Supreme Court refused to issue the requested *mandamus*, ordering the governor to perform his duty. It held unanimously that the words, "It shall be the duty," used in the Act of Congress of February 12, 1793, declaring that it shall be the duty of the governor of the State to cause a fugitive from justice to be arrested and to be given up to the properly authorized agent of the state making the demand, are not used in a mandatory sense, but are expressive merely of the moral obligation of the state executive to obey the Constitution of the United States on that subject. The duty rested solely on the sense of honor and good faith of the states. Hence, if the governor of any state refused to discharge this duty, "there is no power delegated to the general government, either through the judicial department or any other department, to use any coercive means to compel him."[121]

Again, we may speculate on the effects which might have been produced in the South had the Supreme Court found its way to issue the *mandamus* to the governor. Would they have thought twice about defying the authority of a national government represented by a strong court? Or would the governor, in keeping with the spirit of the times, have defied the court, providing further fuel for the advocates of rebellion? We may once more fault the court for avoiding a direct collison, even if no worthwhile practical effect would have resulted, but, as we observed about the Dred Scott case, we would thereby be requiring an attitude which had not yet come to birth.

CHAPTER TWO:

Footnotes:

[1] Quoted in 2 Dallas 410 (1792), as footnote to Hayburn's Case. Italics by author.

[2] *Ibid.*

[3] *Ibid.*

[4] Note to *United States v. Ferreira,* 13 Howard 53 (1851).

[5] 2 Dallas 419 (1793).

[6] Warren, I, p. 65. Name of case is not given.

[7] *Brailsford v. Spalding* (1792); *Higginson v. Greenwood* (1793).

[8] Warren, I, 65-69.

[9] *Vanhorne v. Dorrance,* Case 16,857, 28 FC 1012 (1795), Circuit Court Pennsylvania, Paterson.

[10] *Ware v. Hylton,* 3 Dallas 199; 236-237 (1796) It is interesting to note that John Marshall, counsel for the debtors who defended themselves under the state law, in this, his sole appearance as counsel before the Supreme Court, argued against the binding force of the treaty over the law of the State.

[11] *Hylton v. United States,* 3 Dallas 171; 175 (1796).

[12] *Olney v. Arnold,* 3 Dallas 308 (1796).

[13] *Calder v. Bull,* 3 Dallas 386; 399 (1798).

[14] *Ibid.* 399.

[15] *Minge v. Gilmour,* Case 9,361, 17 FC 440; 443-444 (1798), Circuit Court North Carolina.

[16] *United States v. Worrall,* Case 16,766, 28 FC 774; 779-780 (1798) Circuit Court Pennsylvania. District Judge Peters dissented, claiming that, "The power to punish misdemeanours. . .might have been exercised by Congress in the form of a legislative act; but it may also, in my opinion, be enforced in a course of judicial proceeding." Chase's thesis was the one eventually adopted by the Supreme Court on this particular issue; the more important question of judicial remedy of legislative omissions is still open.

[17] *Case of Fries,* Case 5,127, 9 FC 924; 932 (1800) Circuit Court Pennsylvania.

[18] *Cooper v. Telfair,* 4 Dallas 14; 19 (1800).

[19] *Idem* p. 18; p. 19.

[20] *United States v. Callender,* Case 14,709, 25 FC 239; 256-257 (1800) Circuit Court Virginia.

[21] *Marbury v. Madison,* 1 Cranch 137; 176-178; 180 (1803).

[22] *United States v. The William,* Case 16,700, 28 FC 614; 615-620 (1803), District Court Massachusetts.

[23] Quoted in Warren, I, p. 344.

[24] Warren, I, p. 345.

[25] *Rose v. Himely*, 4 Cranch 241; 272 (1808). See also, *Gelston v. Hoyt*, 3 Wheaton 246-324 (1818).

[26] *United States v. Peters*, 5 Cranch 115; 136 (1809).

[27] *Fletcher v. Peck*, 6 Cranch 87; 128; 133 (1810).

[28] Concurring opinion of Johnson, 6 Cranch 143.

[29] Morgan, p. 210-213.

[30] McCloskey, p. 51.

[31] Haines, 317-319.

[32] Beveridge, III, p. 588.

[33] Wright, *The Contract Clause*, 21-22; 31; 34.

[34] Wright, *The Growth of American Constitutional Law*, 42-43, For another example of the double-barrelled treatment of a void law, compare Marshall's treatment of the New York statute in *Gibbons v. Ogden*, 9 Wheaton 1. The alternative bases for decision are different but the uncertainty remains.

[35] 7 Cranch 164 (1812).

[36] 4 Wheaton 122 (1819).

[37] *Martin v. Hunter's Lessee*, 1 Wheaton 304 (1816).

[38] See under "Jurisdiction" for further discussion of this case.

[39] *Idem* pp. 338-362. Italics added.

[40] Concurring opinion of Johnson in *Martin v. Hunter's Lessee*, 1 Wheaton 362-382.

[41] *Cohens v. Virginia*, 6 Wheaton 264; 387-388 (1821).

[42] *The Amiable Isabelle*, 6 Wheaton 1; 71 (1821).

[43] Dissent of Johnson, *idem*, pp. 85 and 94.

[44] 2 Peters 253; 307 (1829).

[45] *Ogden v. Saunders*, 12 Wheaton 213; 270 (1827).

[46] *Idem*, p. 294.

[47]It has been observed that this was the only case involving the interpretation of the Constitution in which Marshall dissented from the majority. Of more importance, the outcome of the case was to legitimize state bankrupt laws and usher in a new era of business ethics. Had Marshall been able to convince only one of the majority to his point of view, the states would have been completely eliminated from the field of bankruptcy legislation and debtors would have had to wait for relief until the national legislature had acted in this area. One has the feeling that Marshall would have invalidated any national legislation on this point as well, so strong were his views on this issue, had such a case come before him for decision. He would have had no constitutional provision to resort to, but it is not impossible that he might have once more recurred to the principles of natural justice. This is mere conjecture, but what is clear is that if it had been up to Marshall to frame the pertinent constitutional provision, he would have incorporated an absolute prohibition against exempting the future acquisitions of bankrupts from liability for prior debts. It is interesting to speculate on how this would have affected an increasingly credit-minded society.

[48] *Brown v. Maryland,* 12 Wheaton 419; 436 (1827).

[49] Dissent of Johnson, *Craig v. Missouri,* 4 Peters 444 (1830). (Italics added.)

[50] *Briscoe v. Bank of Kentucky,* 11 Peters 257 (1837).

[51] Dissent of McLean, *Craig v. Missouri,* 4 Peters 457.

[52] *Bennett v. Boggs,* Case 1,319, 3 FC 221; 227-228 (1830), Circuit Court New Jersey.

[53] *United States v. Shive,* Case 16,278, 27 FC 1065; 1067 (1832), Circuit Court Pennsylvania.

[54] Dissent of Baldwin, *Ex parte Crane,* 5 Peters 190; 222-223 (1831).

[55] Concurring opinion of Johnson, 5 Peters 1; 30 (1831).

[56] Concurring opinion of McLean, 6 Peters 572 (1832).

[57] *Denn v. Reid,* 10 Peters 524; 527 (1836).

[58] *Charles River Bridge v. Warren Bridge,* 11 Peters 420 (1837).

[59] *Bank of Augusta v. Earle,* 13 Peters 519; 594; 601 (1839).

[60] 13 Peters 415; 420 (1839), McLean, affirming a circuit court

decision (and opinion) of Story of the same tenor.

[61] *Brewer's Lessee v. Blougher,* 14 Peters 178; 198 (1840).

[62] *Holmes v. Jennison,* 14 Peters 540; 584; 632-633 (1840). See more under "Jurisdiction."

[63] *United States v. Dickson,* 15 Peters 141; 161-162 (1841).

[64] 2 Howard 497; 555-556 (1844).

[65] See particularly the later opinions of Justice Daniel on this same subject and the opinions of Justice Woodbury on Admiralty Jurisdiction.

[66] *United States v. MacKenzie,* Case 18,313, 30 FC 1160; 1166; 1162; 1164 (c. 1843, exact date not given), District Court S.D. New York.

[67] *Vaughan v. Williams,* Case 16,903, 28 FC 1115; 1116 (1845), Circuit Court Indiana. See also *Miller v. McQuerry,* Case 9,583, 17 FC 335; 339 (1853), Circuit Court Ohio.

[68] *Cary v. Curtis,* 3 Howard 236; 245 (1845).

[69] See under "Admiralty Jurisdiction" for additional treatment.

[70] 5 Howard 441; 468; 475-476; 496 (1847).

[71] *Planters' Bank v. Sharp,* 6 Howard 301; 319 (1848). However, in this case the court held that the state law was in conflict with the contract clause and therefore void.

[72] 6 Howard 344; 410 (1848).

[73] *License Cases,* 5 Howard 574 (1847).

[74] *Luther v. Borden,* 7 Howard 1; 40-41; 42-43; 46-47 (1849).

[75] 7 Howard 51; 52-53; 56-57; 54-55.

[76] *Passenger Cases,* 7 Howard 283; 469-470 (1849).

[77] *Idem,* 7 Howard 470.

[78] *Idem,* 7 Howard 477-478 (italics added).

[79] Dissent of Grier in *Woodruff v. Trapnall,* 10 Howard 190; 209 (1851).

[80] *Butler v. Pennsylvania,* 10 Howard 402; 415-416 (1851).

[81] *Genesee Chief v. Fitzhugh,* 12 Howard 443; 456; 458-459 (1852).

[82] *Idem,* 12 Howard 464-465.

[83] Dissent of Taney, *Pennsylvania v. Wheeling Bridge Co.,* 13 Howard 581-582; 587 (1852). (Italics added.)

[84] Dissent of Daniel, *idem,* 13 Howard 599. (Italics added.) It is worth noting that the Taney-Daniel position in this case was, in a sense, vindicated when Congress shortly thereafter passed a law holding the bridge at Wheeling to be legal. The act, however, did not settle the controversy as to the court's power to intervene in such a case in the absence of legislation.

[85] Dissent of Daniel, *Rundle v. Delaware & Raritan Canal Co.,* 14 Howard 80; 98-99 (1853).

[86] Compare Wayne in *Letson* and Taney in *The Genesee Chief,* above.

[87] *Marshall v. Baltimore & Ohio Railroad Co.,* 16 Howard 314; 325-326 (1854).

[88] *Idem,* dissent of Daniel, 16 Howard 343-344; 347.

[89] *Idem,* dissent of Campbell, 16 Howard 351.

[90] 14 Howard 38; 50-51 (1853), Taney.

[91] 16 Howard 635; 657 (1854), Taney.

[92] 16 Howard 369; 391-392 (1854), McLean.

[93] B.F. Wright, *The Contract Clause,* p. 80.

[94] Dissent of McLean, *United States v. Guthrie,* 17 Howard 284; 310 (1855).

[95] Case 13,799, 23 FC 784 (1855), Circuit Court Massachusetts.

[96] 18 Howard 272 (1856).

[97] *Idem,* 18 Howard 280-281. See more under "Jurisdiction."

[98] Campbell interpreted the prohibition against impairment of the obligation of contracts to be limited in its application to acts of the state legislature; for him there was no such prohibition if an impairment

was effected directly by the sovereign people of the State through their constitution. (18 Howard 379).

[99] See B.F. Wright, *The Contract Clause,* p. 74.

[100] *Dodge v. Woolsey,* 18 Howard 331; 350; 354-355; 355-356; 358 (1856).

[101] *Idem,* dissent of Campbell, 18 Howard 373-374; 375-376; 377.

[102] *Pennsylvania v. Wheeling Bridge Co.,* 18 Howard 421 (1856).

[103] *Idem,* dissent of McLean, 18 Howard 439; 440-441; 443.

[104] *Idem,* dissent of Grier, 18 Howard 449.

[105] *Idem,* dissent of Wayne, 18 Howard 450.

[106] On the question of contempt for disobeying the injunction, Nelson and Curtis joined Grier and Wayne in supporting the attachment, notwithstanding the act of Congress. McLean, however, parted ways with the two latter colleagues and held that "the law was unconstitutional and void, and yet I consider it as excusing the defendants' contempt. I cannot punish defendants, by fine or imprisonment, for doing that which the law authorized them to do." (18 Howard 449). Thus the court held 5-4 to deny the motion for attachment for contempt.

[107] *Dred Scott v. Sandford,* 19 Howard 393 (1857).

[108] B.F. Wright, *The Growth of American Constitutional Law,* p. 76.

[109] Art. IV, Section 3 (2): "The Congress shall have power to dispose of and make all needful rules and regulations respecting the territory or other property belonging to the United States."

[110] *Dred Scott v. Sandford,* 19 Howard 614-615; 619-621, dissent of Curtis.

[111] *Idem,* 19 Howard 629-630. In Curtis' opinion the Treaty of 1803 had no bearing on the present question.

[112] *Idem,* 19 Howard 626.

[113] Dissent of Daniel, *Jackson v. James,* 20 Howard 296; 317-319 (1858)

[114] *Idem,* dissent of Campbell, 20 Howard 334.

[115] *Silliman v. Hudson River Bridge Co.*, Case 12,851, 22 FC 116 (1857).

[116] The Supreme Court, 1 Black 582 (1862) was equally divided on the question of the jurisdiction of the Circuit Court; no opinions were given. The Circuit Court then dismissed the bill, Case 2,983, 6 FC 62 (1862). On appeal, the Supreme Court was once more divided, 2 Wallace 403 (1865).

[117] Opinion of Hall, *Silliman v. Hudson River Bridge Co.*, Case 12,852, 22 FC 120 (1859), Circuit Court N.D. New York.

[118] *Ableman v. Booth*, 21 Howard 506; 517-521 (1859). Italics added. See also Chapter Four, pp. 156-157

[119] 6 Wheaton 390 (1821).

[120] March 14, 1861.

[121] *Kentucky v. Dennison*, 24 Howard 66; 110 (1861), Taney.

CHAPTER THREE:

THE WRIT OF *MANDAMUS*—THE POWER TO COMPEL

One of the powers granted to the courts of the United States by the Judiciary Act of 1789 was that of issuing writs of *mandamus* under certain specified conditions. The writ of *mandamus* was a common-law prerogative writ, issued in England by the King's Bench, directing some person or inferior court to perform a specified official act or duty where there was no other adequate remedy. By the thirteenth section of the Judiciary Act, the Supreme Court was given the power "to issue writs of *mandamus* in cases warranted by the principles and usages of law, to any courts appointed, or persons holding office, under the authority of the United States." By the fourteenth section, all the courts of the United States were given the power to issue "all. . .writs not specially provided for by statute, which may be necessary for the exercise of their respective jurisdictions, and agreeable to the principles and usages of law."

Although strictly speaking this was not a constitutional issue, the exposition and application of these legislative grants was an important problem, inasmuch as the writ of *mandamus* brought the courts into conflict with other departments of government and with the state authorities. As was the case with so many clauses of Article III and the Act of 1789, the Supreme Court worked out an interpretation only after the course of several decades.

The first case to appear before the Supreme Court involving the writ of *mandamus* was that of *United States v. Judge Lawrence*, in which the higher court held that it could not compel a district court judge to issue a warrant if he deemed the evidence insufficient. The government's motion for a *mandamus* to the district judge was refused because the Supreme Court had no power to compel the judge to decide according to the dictates of any judgment other than his own.[1]

Marbury v. Madison, otherwise known as the *mandamus* case, was the first full discussion of the writ. Here the motion was for a *mandamus* to issue, requiring Madison, the Secretary of State, to deliver to Marbury his commission as a justice of the peace for Washington County in the District of Columbia, the position to which he had been appointed by the outgoing President Adams. This was not an internal matter affecting the relationship between the courts but a conflict between the judicial and the executive departments.

Unfortunately for Mr. Marbury, he presented his motion to the wrong court. The motion was made directly to the Supreme Court, which was obliged to refuse jurisdiction because, notwithstanding Section 13 of the Judiciary Act, the case was not one in which—by the terms of the Constitution—the Supreme Court could take original jurisdiction.[2] Nonetheless, Chief Justice Marshall took the opportunity to deliver a lengthy *obiter dicta* on the relations between the judiciary and the executive and the use of the writ of *mandamus*.

Distinguishing between ministerial acts and those of a discretionary nature, Marshall contends that the delivery of the commission to the judge was a duty of the Secretary of State, prescribed by law, and not dependent on the will of the President: "It is a ministerial act which the law enjoins on a particular officer for a particular purpose. . .To withhold his commission, therefore, is an act deemed by the court not warranted by law, but violative of a vested legal right." The discretionary portion of the act was terminated when the appointment was made.

The court then took up the question of whether the legality of an act of the head of a department was examinable in a court of justice. Acts of a political character, in which the President or his officers are to use discretion, cannot be controlled by the courts. "But when the legislature proceeds to impose on that officer other duties; when he is directed peremptorily to perform certain acts; when the rights of individuals are dependent on the performance of those acts; he is so far the officer of the law [and] is amenable to the laws for his conduct. . .

"The conclusion from this reasoning," Marshall continues, "is that where the heads of departments are the political or confidential agents of the executive, merely to execute the will of the President, or rather to act in cases in which the executive possesses a constitutional or legal discretion, nothing can be more perfectly clear than that their acts are only politically examinable. But where a specific duty is assigned by law, and individual rights depend upon the performance of that duty, it seems equally clear that the individual who considers himself injured has a right to resort to the laws of his country for a remedy."

Again: "The question of whether a right has vested or not is, in its nature, judicial, and must be tried by the judicial authority."

Proceeding to examine the nature of the writ of *mandamus*, Marshall refers to the English rule that the writ may be granted only when the person applying for it "has no other specific legal remedy" or "where the law has established no specific remedy."

Once more Marshall states his position: "It is not by the office of the person to whom the writ is directed, but the nature of the thing to be done, that the propriety or impropriety of issuing a *mandamus* is to be determined. Where the head of a department acts in a case in which executive discretion is to be exercised, in which he is the mere organ of executive will, it is again repeated that any application to a court to control, in any respect, his conduct, would be rejected without hesitation.

"But where he is directed by law to do a certain act affecting the absolute rights of individuals, in the performance of which he is not placed under the particular direction of the President, and the performance of which the President cannot lawfully forbid, and therefore is never presumed to have forbidden;. . .in such cases, it is not perceived on what ground the courts of the country are further excused from the duty of giving judgment that right be done to an injured individual, than if the same services were to be performed by a person not the head of a department."

However, although it is clear that this was a case for the issuance of a *mandamus*, the Chief Justice noted one more indispensable condition: "To enable this court. . .to issue a *mandamus*, it must be shown to be an exercise of appellate jurisdiction, to be necessary to enable them to exercise appellate jurisdiction." As this was clearly an original action and not one necessary to enable the court to exercise its appellate jurisdiction, the court could not take jurisdiction of the case, Section 13 notwithstanding.[3]

Although this part of the decision was not authoritative, it presented the important distinction between discretionary and ministerial acts, and the rule of "no other specific legal remedy" as guidance to future cases involving the writ of *mandamus*.

In 1808, Justice Johnson of the Circuit Court of South Carolina was faced with a problem which was particularly difficult for him. At the time that the Embargo Act was in effect, the owner of a domestic vessel was denied permission by the Collector of the Port of Charleston to engage in a northbound voyage. The ground for the refusal was a letter of instructions sent out by the President of the United States rather than the terms of the law itself. The owner applied to the Circuit Court for a writ of *mandamus* to issue, commanding the collector of the port to grant the clearance of the ship. Concluding that the act of Congress did not authorize the detention of the vessel, Johnson issued the desired *mandamus*, directed to the collector.[4]

The Attorney General of the United States, C.A. Rodney, was not content to let the decision stand without further comment and wrote an open letter to President Jefferson, giving his own opinion on the matter. Rodney contended that only the Supreme Court could possess such a power as that just exercised by the Circuit Court, and the fact that by virtue of *Marbury v. Madison* the Supreme Court could not act in a case of original jurisdiction was no ground for the lower court's assumption of the power. Only the King's Bench in England possessed the power to issue a *mandamus*, argued Rodney, and there was no possible analogy between that court and the circuit courts of the United States.

In addition, the Attorney General objected that the *mandamus* is not issued to a ministerial officer to compel him to do his duty; that the decision of the collector was discretionary; and that the *mandamus* should not be granted when parties possess a legal remedy against the officer.

"It might perhaps with propriety be added," continued Rodney, "that there does not appear in the Constitution of the United States anything which favors an indefinite extension of the jurisdiction of the courts over the ministerial officer within the executive department. On the contrary, the careful discrimination which is marked between the several departments should dictate great circumspection to each, in the exercise of powers having any relation to the other." Admitting that parties might have legal redress for wrongs committed by ministerial officers, Rodney insisted that, "The redress is to be administered by due and legal process in the ordinary way," and not by the interposition of a mandatory writ.

"Writs of this kind, if made applicable to officers indiscriminately," the Attorney General warned, "would necessarily have the effect of transferring the powers vested in one department to another department. If, in a case like the present, where the law vests a duty and a discretion in an executive officer, a court can not only administer redress against the misuse of the authority, but previously direct the use to be made of it, it would seem that under the name of judicial power, an executive function is necessarily assumed, and that part of the Constitution perhaps defeated, which makes it the duty of the President to take care that the laws be faithfully executed. I do not see any clear limitation to this doctrine, which would prevent the courts from compelling by *mandamus* all the executive officers, all subordinate to the President at least, whether charged with legal duties in the treasury or other departments, and to execute the same, according to the opinion of the judiciary and contrary to that of the executive."[5]

To this letter, Johnson replied with an exposition of his ideas on the use of the *mandamus.* Although these remarks did not form a part of the opinion in the *Gilchrist* case, Johnson justified their publication on the ground that when the case came before the court, the question of jurisdiction was not raised; if it had been raised there, he said, the grounds upon which it was assumed would have been made public.

Johnson denied that the power to issue the writ of *mandamus* is analogous to the prerogative power of the King's Bench in England; it is a power given by Congress, an exercise of jurisdiction within the judicial powers of the United States. The *mandamus* was the appropriate procedure in a case such as this and the only one which provided the desired remedy. Johnson denied that the collector had discretion or that his judgment was controlled by the President.

To the charge that through the indiscriminate use of the *mandamus* the judiciary would exercise executive functions, Johnson replied: "The courts do not pretend to impose any restraint upon any officer of government, but what results from a just construction of the laws of the United States. Of these laws the courts are the constitutional expositors, and every department of government must submit to their exposition, for laws have no legal meaning but what is given them by the courts to whose exposition they are submitted. It is against the law, therefore, and not the courts, that the executive should urge the charge of usurpation and restraint—a restraint which may at times be productive of inconveniences, but which is certainly very consistent with the nature of our government."[6]

The assumption of jurisdiction in the *Gilchrist* case, justified by Johnson's subsequent exposition, was a tentative position. Only five years later the Supreme Court was faced with the problem of determining the extent of the circuit courts' power to issue the writ of *mandamus.* In *McIntire v. Wood*, Johnson took a closer look at the Judiciary Act and spoke for a unanimous court in ruling that the power of the circuit courts to issue the writ of *mandamus* was confined exclusively to those cases in which it might be necessary to the exercise of their jurisdiction. In the *Gilchrist* case Johnson assumed that by virtue of the constitutional grant the circuit court possessed jurisdiction over all cases arising under the laws of the United States and that, since the case before him arose under a law of the United States, the issuance of the writ of *mandamus* was in order. But now, having examined the matter more thoroughly, Johnson pointed out that, "although the judicial power of the United States extends to cases arising under the laws of the United States, the legislature has not thought proper to delegate the exercise of that power to its circuit courts, except in certain specified cases." The jurisdiction of the circuit court was defined by Section 11 of the Judiciary Act, and unless the circuit court possessed jurisdiction under that section, it could not assume it independently in order to issue a *mandamus*. Since the case of *McIntire v. Wood*, a motion for a *mandamus* to be directed to the register of the land office, was not in itself a case in which the circuit court possessed jurisdiction under Section 11, it did not possess the power to issue the *mandamus*.[7]

Johnson refers to the earlier case of *Gilchrist* and admits that the *mandamus* to the collector was issued "upon a supposition inconsistent with the decision in this case." He states that the *mandamus* was awarded because the collector consented to the jurisdiction. This explanation left much to be desired, in light of the general rule of the courts[8] that consent could not give jurisdiction and, more explicitly, in view of Johnson's posterior justification of jurisdiction when challenged by the Attorney General. *McIntire v. Wood*, in short, overruled the assumption of jurisdiction in the *Gilchrist* case though it left intact the other portions of Johnson's exposition on the writ of *mandamus*.

When a similar motion came before the Supreme Court in 1817 and again in 1821, the court ruled that it had no jurisdiction to issue a writ of *mandamus* to the register of a land office of the United States, when the *mandamus* had been refused by the Supreme Court of the State of Ohio. In the first case the motion was denied without opinion.[9] In the second case, Justice Johnson, speaking for a unanimous court, held that neither the courts of the United States nor the State Court of Ohio had jurisdiction over the case. Again Johnson reiterated that it was within the judicial power of the United States to award *mandamus*, but not within the legal power, since no law authorized its use in such a case: "The 14th section [of the Judiciary Act] could only have been intended to vest the power now contended for in cases where the jurisdiction already exists, and not where it is to be courted or acquired, by means of the writ proposed to be sued out." Interestingly enough, in view of Johnson's exposition in the *Gilchrist* case, he declared "that parties should be referred to the ordinary mode of obtaining justice, instead of resorting to the extraordinary and unprecedented mode of trying such questions on a motion for a *mandamus.*"[10]

In other cases brought before the courts during the Marshall period, the writ of *mandamus* had a checkered career. In *Spraggins v. County Court of Humphries*, the Circuit Court of Tennessee held that a *mandamus* may issue from the circuit court to a state court in order to remove a cause to the federal courts when the state court refused an application for removal. "It is a legal privilege which the defendant possesses to have his cause tried here," said District Judge McNairy, "but if the state court illegally and unjustifiably refuses the transmission of the suit, and this court refuses by *mandamus* to aid the applicant, will he not be remediless? And no principle is clearer than that where the law has given a clear right, and no remedy exists, the respective courts will interfere by *mandamus*, and see that justice and law is administered." Here the court held that to maintain the jurisdiction of the court, it was necessary to issue the writ.[11]

When it came to the supervision of the higher courts over those below, the court followed no general rule. In *Smith v. Jackson*, Justice Thompson denied to the Circuit Court of New York the power to issue a *mandamus* to the District Court to disallow certain amendments in the cause which were necessary for acquiring jurisdiction. Thompson stated that if the district court should refuse to give judgment, there would be a proper case for the circuit court to issue a *mandamus* to compel it to proceed to judgment, but such was not the circumstance. "This court," wrote Thompson, "has not the like superintending authority over the district courts, as the King's Bench in England, and the Supreme Court of this state over inferior tribunals. Many cases therefore which have arisen in those courts where writs of *mandamus* have been issued, are not applicable here."[12]

Likewise, the Supreme Court held that it would not grant a *mandamus* to revise the proceedings of a Circuit Court as to the pleadings, which could be done only by a writ of error after a final judgment. The reason for this rule was to avoid delays and multiple presentations of causes before the Supreme Court.[13]

On the other hand, the court held, over the dissent of Baldwin, that it had the power to issue a writ of *mandamus* to a judge of a circuit court, commanding him to sign a bill of exceptions so that the case could come before the Supreme Court for revision. "A *mandamus* to an officer is held to be the exercise of original jurisdiction," said Chief Justice Marshall, referring to the earlier decisions of the court, "but a *mandamus* to an inferior court of the United States is in the nature of appellate jurisdiction." Although the motion was denied in this case, the court held that the power to issue the writ of *mandamus* existed.[14]

Baldwin took issue with the court's decision that it possessed the power to issue the writ of *mandamus* in such a case. "A *mandamus* being a writ to compel the performance of a ministerial act by a judicial officer, is not, and cannot be a subject matter for the cognizance of an appellate court," he contended. Neither Section 13 nor Section 14 of the Judiciary Act authorized the Supreme Court to issue the writ, in his opinion.[15] Even if it were admitted that the *mandamus* was included in the writs referred to in Section 14, Baldwin objected that it was not warranted by the principles and usages of law. "It is," he said, "a prerogative writ issuing from the court of King's Bench, by virtue of its general and supervising powers, on motion, and for cause shown. This is a court of special jurisdiction, limited in the exercise of its powers to specified cases; it has no prerogative powers, and can issue no prerogative writs; it possesses no supervisory powers over inferior tribunals, and can in no case grant a *mandamus* on its inherent authority. . .This, then, is not a court which by the principles and usages of the common law can issue a *mandamus.*"[16] Johnson, who had by now completely abandoned the position he had taken in *Gilchrist*, concurred with Baldwin's opinion.

The case of *Ex parte Bradstreet* demonstrated as well as any the complexities and inconveniences arising from the use of the *mandamus.* In 1832, the court granted a rule to show cause why a *mandamus* should not issue, where it was shown that a district court judge had neglected or refused to enter a judgment.[17] The following year the court awarded the writ, ordering the judge to reinstate the case and proceed to try it.[18] But when the case came before the court once again, the Chief Justice held that a *mandamus* could not issue, after all, ordering a judgment to be entered on a verdict, it appearing that a motion for a new trial was under advisement. "We have only to say," said Marshall, "that a judge must exercise his discretion in those intermediate proceedings which take place between the institution and trial of a suit; and if in the performance of this duty he acts oppressively, it is not to this court that application is to be made."[19]

At the same term, the court directed that a *mandamus* be issued, directing the district judge to sign a judgment which his predecessor had failed to sign prior to his death. Here the court held that the plaintiffs had no other remedy than to obtain the signature, without which further proceedings were impossible. "On a *mandamus,*" wrote McLean, "a superior court will never direct in what manner the discretion of an inferior tribunal shall be exercised; but they will, in a proper case, require the inferior court to decide."[20] But the court pointed out very clearly when the same case arose the following year that it could not and would not compel the district judge by *mandamus* to extend the earlier judgment to subjects not comprehended within it. "This court is asked to decide that the merits of the cause are with the plaintiffs and to command the district court to render judgment in their favor," said Marshall. "It is an attempt to introduce the supervising power of this court into a cause while depending on an inferior court, and presumably to decide it. In addition to the obvious unfitness of such a procedure, its direct repugnance to the spirit and letter of our whole judicial system of jurisprudence." In the previous case, the court had ordered the performance of a mere ministerial act; in this case the court had been asked to direct the manner in which the district court should exercise its discretion.[21]

Thus, by 1835, the court had declared its authority to issue the writ of *mandamus* as part of its legitimate appellate jurisdiction, but had shown considerable reluctance to exercise the power. While the majority of cases involved internal matters within the judicial department, these cases had helped the court underline the important distinction between ministerial and discretionary acts.

The most important and most controversial case involving *mandamus* was that of *Stokes v. Kendall.* Stokes was a mail contractor to whom the government owed large sums of money. Having unsuccessfully attempted to obtain payment from the Postmaster General, who strongly objected to the accounts, Stokes and his partners succeeded in inducing Congress to pass a special act for their relief, requiring the Solicitor of the Treasury of the United States to award the correct amount. The award was duly made but the payment was not forthcoming. Thereupon, Stokes petitioned the Circuit Court of the District of Columbia to issue a writ of *mandamus*, commanding Kendall, the Postmaster General, to credit the petitioners with the amount awarded.

The Attorney General of the United States advised the Postmaster General that the Circuit Court of the District of Columbia lacked jurisdiction to issue a writ of *mandamus* in such a case, contending that the decision in *McIntire v. Wood* applied equally to the District of Columbia Court and the Circuit Courts in the States. The first question, then, was whether the Court of the District of Columbia possessed a jurisdiction different from that of the other circuit courts. Only after that point had been decided was it possible to examine the propriety of issuing a *mandamus.*

The circuit court decided, against the opinion of the Attorney General, that it possessed jurisdiction in all cases arising under the Constitution and laws of the United States, if either of the parties is a resident or is found within the District of Columbia. It had, unlike the other circuit courts, all the judicial power of the United States, unrestrained by the limitations of Section 11 of the Judiciary Act.[22] Having determined that it possessed this unique jurisdiction, the court ruled that it had the authority to issue a *mandamus* to an officer of the United States Government, commanding him to perform a ministerial duty required by an act of Congress, where the right of an individual is concerned, if that right was clear, and he had no other specific legal remedy.

Judge Cranch began his opinion by demonstrating that *McIntire v. Wood*, rather than an obstacle to the use of the *mandamus* as the Attorney General contended, was an invitation to its employment. In that case, Justice Johnson had said: "Had the eleventh section of the Judiciary Act covered the whole ground of the Constitution, there would be much reason for exercising this power in many cases wherein some ministerial act is necessary to the completion of an individual right arising under laws of the United States, and the fourteenth section of the same act would sanction the issuing of the writ for such a purpose."[23] The Circuit Court of the District of Columbia, said Cranch, was in the condition to which Johnson referred.[24]

As if in reply to Johnson's argument in *McClung v. Silliman*, Cranch stated that the issuance of a writ of *mandamus* did not create a jurisdiction which did not exist before, but was the exercise of a necessary power in the court in a cause where jurisdiction already existed, in this case by virtue of the fact that the case arose under a law of the United States.

Turning to the propriety of issuing the *mandamus*, Cranch wrote: "Here is a case in which a ministerial act is necessary to the completion of an individual right under the laws of the United States. The right of the relators,[25] and the obligation of the Postmaster General are clear and absolute. It is a case in law; and the only appropriate remedy is a writ of *mandamus*. This is the only judicial tribunal which can take original cognizance of the case and apply the proper remedy. How, then, can this court refuse it? To refuse it would be a denial of justice."

To the argument of inconvenience and judicial interference with the executive department, Cranch replied:

"If it should be said that if every neglect of duty by a public officer, by which an individual suffers an injury, is to be the subject of a *mandamus*, it will become the common mode of redress in such cases, and the officers of government may be harassed; we answer that every public officer who neglects or refuses to perform a mere ministerial duty, whereby an individual is injured, is legally responsible to that individual in some form or other; and a *mandamus* is one of the mildest forms of action which can be used, as it supposes that the duty may still be performed, and as it does not subject the officer to pecuniary damages, and is one of the best forms in which the right of the supposed injured party may be tried. As it can be used only in cases where a duty is to be performed, and where it is still in the power of the officer to perform it, the cases cannot be very numerous, and the officers will be less harassed by this form of action than by the other usual forms of action which are generally commenced by the severe process of personal arrest."

The court then ordered the Postmaster General to show cause why a *mandamus* should not issue in the case. Kendall submitted his own arguments and those of the Attorney General,[26] but they did not convince the court which issued a peremptory *mandamus*, commanding the Postmaster General to proceed to credit the amount previously awarded.

Cranch once more submitted the opinion of the court. He denied at the outset that the Postmaster General had discretion under the act; the act was obligatory and gave no appellate jurisdiction to the Postmaster General.

"The discretion which is claimed by the Postmaster General," said Cranch, "is no other than that discretion which every man has in regard to his own actions. Every man is a free agent. He has the power to do or not to do a particular act; and he decides upon his own responsibility. Neither his discretion nor his decision makes the act lawful or unlawful. . .We are of opinion, therefore, that the Postmaster

General had not such a discretion over the duty enjoined by the statute, as renders it improper that a *mandamus* should issue in this case."

Cranch denies that the writ of *mandamus* gives the judiciary control of executive officers in the exercise of their discretionary functions: "A *mandamus* is a simple command to a person to do an act which he is bound by law to do, and which he has no lawful right to refuse to do. In the present case, the *mandamus* asked for is a writ commanding the Postmaster General to do an act which a statute positively requires him to do; which he cannot lawfully refuse to do; and in regard to the doing of which he is not bound to act according to the will of any superior officer; the court therefore, in issuing the *mandamus*, does not attempt to control him in his executive functions. . .The abstract proposition arising upon the case is that this court has power to issue a *mandamus* to an executive officer of the United States, commanding him to do a ministerial official act which he is positively required by law to do, over which he has no discretion, and in regard to which he is not bound, by law, to act according to the will of another, and by his refusal to do which an individual has sustained, or will sustain injury."

The question, said Cranch, was whether the court could issue a *mandamus* commanding an executive officer to perform a certain act rather than issue a warrant for his arrest for his failure to do so, a proceeding, as Justice Johnson had pointed out as early as the *Gilchrist* case, which did not furnish a remedy to the petitioner's right.

Taking up the Attorney General's argument that when a *mandamus* issues from the judiciary to an executive ministerial officer, the judges "attempt to control the executive power, to assume the functions of the President, and to make themselves the executive in the last resort," Cranch examines the relationship between the executive and the judicial departments of the government:

"The three great departments of this government are only branches of the sovereign power of the nation, each exercising its functions in the name and under the authority of that sovereign power. When the President does an act in virtue of his office, it is the act of the sovereign power. So when the judiciary does a judicial act, it is still the act of the same sovereign power. When a *mandamus* is sent by a court to an executive officer, it is not the court that commands, but the sovereign power. All commands from the court are issued in the name and by the authority of the United States. In each case, it is the whole sovereign power acting by its appropriate organ. The executive and judicial departments are not rivals. They must unite their functions, or the laws cannot be exercised. The President is as dependent on the judiciary to enable him to see that the laws be faithfully executed, as the judiciary is on him to enforce its judgments."

Finally, he rejects the argument that the court has no power to issue the writ because the President could defeat its execution by dismissing the marshal who comes to serve an attachment, or by dismissing the officer to whom the *mandamus* is issued, in order to prevent the execution of the lawful judgment of the court. The power of the President to defeat the execution of the court in a case in which the court has jurisdiction, Cranch affirms, "is no evidence of the want of jurisdiction in the court."[27]

Not surprisingly, the decision was appealed to the Supreme Court, where the judgment of the court below was affirmed by a 6-3 division in which three separate dissents were filed.

Justice Thompson, speaking for the majority, held that the act required by the law to be done by the Postmaster General was a purely ministerial one, in which there was no discretion whatsoever. To the argument that the executive officers were under the exclusive control of the President, Thompson answered:

"It was urged at the bar that the Postmaster General was alone subject to the direction and control of the President, with respect to the execution of the duty imposed upon him by this law; and this right of the President is claimed, as growing out of the obligation imposed upon him by the Constitution, to take care that the laws be faithfully executed. This is a doctrine that cannot receive the sanction of this court. It would be vesting in the President a dispensing power which has no countenance for its support in any part of the Constitution; and is asserting a principle which, if carried out in its results, to all cases falling within it, would be clothing the President with a power entirely to control the legislation of Congress, and paralyze the administration of justice. To contend that the obligation imposed on the President to see the laws faithfully executed implies a power to forbid their execution, is a novel construction of the Constitution, and entirely inadmissible."

The court then proceeded to uphold the writ of *mandamus* in this case as both fit and appropriate; fit because the Circuit Court of the District of Columbia had acquired Maryland's common-law right to employ this prerogative writ; appropriate because it was the only remedy available under the circumstances.

"There can be no doubt but that, in the State of Maryland, a writ of *mandamus* might be issued to an executive officer, commanding him to perform a ministerial act required of him by law," said Thompson, "and if it would lie in that state, there can be no good reason why it should not lie in this district, in analogous cases. But the writ of *mandamus*, as it is used in the courts of the United States, other than the Circuit Court of this District, cannot, in any just sense, be said to be a prerogative writ, according to the principles of the common law." Thus the court clearly distinguishes the special powers of the Circuit Court of the District of Columbia from those of the other circuit courts and the Supreme Court itself.

Thompson confirms Cranch's conclusion that the Circuit Court of the District possessed jurisdiction in all cases arising under the Constitution and laws of the United States, free of the limitations contained in Section 11 of the Judiciary Act. Thus the wide jurisdiction of the Court of the District of Columbia, equivalent to the constitutional grant of judicial power, combined with that court's powers acquired from the common-law powers of the State of Maryland, gave the court in question an authority to issue the writ of *mandamus* which no other court of the United States possessed.[28] [29]

This ruling of the court was especially important as it was

precisely within the District of Columbia, the seat of the national government, where it was most likely that motions for the issuance of *mandamus* would be made. Independent of any inherent merit in the position of Cranch and the majority of the Supreme Court, it was an extremely practical means of getting around the prohibitions arising from the earlier rulings of *McIntire v. Wood* and *McClung v. Silliman*. But the decision was by no means readily accepted. Chief Justice Taney, who had only recently been a cabinet officer himself, was the first to dissent.

Taney agreed that the duty enjoined upon the Postmaster General was ministerial rather than discretionary and that this was a proper case for a *mandamus*, provided the Circuit Court of the District of Columbia possessed the prerogative jurisdiction and powers attributed to it by the majority. But this proposition the Chief Justice denied.

"As no reason of policy or public convenience can be assigned for giving to the circuit court here a jurisdiction on this subject, which has been denied to the other circuit courts," he wrote, "those who maintain that it has been given ought to show us words which distinctly give it, or from which it can be plainly inferred."

Only the General Court of Maryland received the prerogative right of issuing the writ of *mandamus* within Maryland, said Taney, who was a native of that state. The Circuit Court of the District of Columbia, he continued, was not comparable to the King's Bench, but was the equivalent of a county court of the state, which did not possess the power to issue the writ of *mandamus* at the time the Circuit Court of the District was established.

Secondly, argued Taney, if the Circuit Court of the District of Columbia had cognizance of "all cases in law and equity," it did not thereby acquire the power to issue a *mandamus*, because this process was not a case in law or equity. Finally, the Chief Justice contended, the acts of Congress did not give the Circuit Court of the District the wider jurisdiction claimed for it by Cranch.

"It is difficult to believe that Congress meant to have given the high prerogative power in so many places and yet, in every one of them, [they] have left it, at best, so ambiguous and doubtful," said Taney in conclusion. "And if we now sanction its exercise, we shall give to the court, by remote inferences and implications, a delicate and important power which I feel persuaded Congress never intended to intrust to its hands."[30]

Justice Barbour devoted his dissent to demonstrating that the circuit courts of the United States did not have the power to issue the writ of *mandamus* and that the powers of the Circuit Court of the District of Columbia were the same as those of the other circuit courts.[31]

Catron's dissent was of the same tenor as that of Taney and Barbour. He added: "The truth is that Congress has been unwilling to expose the action of the government in the administration of its vast and complicated affairs, and its officers, who have charge of their management, to the danger and indignity of being coerced and controlled by the writ of *mandamus.*"[32]

In his annual message to Congress in December, 1838, President Van Buren criticized the decision; a bill to repeal the power of the Circuit Court of the District to issue writs of *mandamus* was passed in the Senate the following year but did not become law.[33] [34]

The next case to come before the court was that of *Decatur v. Paulding.* The widow of Stephen Decatur had petitioned the Circuit Court of the District of Columbia to issue a *mandamus* ordering the Secretary of the Navy to pay her an $18,600 pension to which she claimed to be legally entitled. In keeping with the decision in *Kendall v. United States,* the Circuit Court entertained jurisdiction in the case but refused to award the writ. Mrs. Decatur appealed to the Supreme Court, which held that the duty of the Secretary of the Navy in this matter was not merely ministerial but required the exercise of judgment and discretion, and that therefore the writ of *mandamus* could not be issued by the circuit court.

The majority of the Supreme Court did not take up the question of whether it could revise the judgment of the circuit court, but merely assumed that right. They looked, instead, into the powers of the circuit court and held that a writ of *mandamus* could not be issued by the circuit court for the District of Columbia to compel the Secretary to perform a discretionary executive act involving the exercise of judgment. The circuit court, they held, had no power, either by appeal from the Secretary's decision or by *mandamus*, to control the judgment or discretion of the head of an executive department. "The interference of the courts with the performance of the ordinary duties of the executive departments of the government," said the Chief Justice, speaking for the court, "would be productive of nothing but mischief, and we are quite satisfied that such a power was never intended to be given to them."[35]

Justice Baldwin, rather than examine the nature of the Secretary's duty and the correctness of the circuit court's decision, immediately considered the question of the Supreme Court's jurisdiction over the case. He held that the latter court could not revise the circuit court's judgment to award or to refuse to award a writ of *mandamus* because the Judiciary Act did not make provision for appellate proceedings over such a judgment.[36]

Justice Catron, going beyond the legal arguments which he had submitted in the Kendall case, devoted his concurring opinion to a criticism of judicial interference with the executive branch. He felt that the court had assumed an almost unlimited discretion to determine in each case the nature of executive duties, whether ministerial or discretionary.

"The court-assumed jurisdiction," he observed, "compelled the United States, through the Secretary of the Navy, to file a long answer, and in a tedious lawsuit to defend the United States. That he did so successfully is of little consequence; the evil lies not in the loss of $18,600 to the government, but in the concession by this court that the Circuit Court of the District has the power to sit in judgment on the Secretary's decision; to reverse the same at its pleasure, and to order the money to be paid out of the treasury, contrary to his will.

"The conflict between the executive and judiciary departments could not well be more direct, nor more dangerous," continued Catron. "The idea that they are distinct and their duties separate is confounded, if the jurisdiction of the court below is sustained; placing the executive power at its mercy, in case of all contested claims. . .

"And here it may be safely asked, whether the Secretary and President, the latter elected by the nation, and responsible to the people directly, and to their representatives in Congress, each exercising an undoubtedly legitimate authority, were not the safest and best to decide on the rights of the nation, and of the petitioner seeking justice at its hands?. . .What guarantee have the people of this country that the Circuit Court of the District will as faithfully perform the functions they have assumed, when dealing out the public money to satisfy rejected claims, as the heads of the departments? The court is wholly irresponsible to the people for its acts; is unknown to them; the judges hold appointments of an ordinary judicial character, and are accidentally exercising jurisdiction over the territory where the treasury and public officers are located."[37]

Echoes of this extra-legal argument against the pretensions of the judiciary to the exercise of discretion over the acts of the executive department have been heard ever since and, as in this case, the real argument is not the letter of the Judiciary Act but the philosophy of government: whether the executive branch is to be as independent of the judicial power as the judiciary is to be of the executive. It is interesting to note, in light of Catron's strong objection to interference via the writ of *mandamus*, that the Supreme Court did not again uphold the use of that writ in a case such as *United States v. Kendall* or *Decatur v. Paulding* during the remainder of Taney's years on the court.

During the next decade a variety of petititions for *mandamus* were turned down by the courts. In *Ex parte Schamburg*, the Circuit Court of the District of Columbia refused to issue a *mandamus* to the Secretary of War, ordering him to reinstate the petitioner in the Army, on the ground that his removal was a completely discretionary act of the executive department.[38] In *Ladd v. Taylor*, the Circuit Court of Massachusetts would not issue a *mandamus* to a state court to remove a cause to the federal court, not only because the requisites for removal were not met, according to the criterion of the state judge, but because it was questionable whether the federal court possessed the authority to employ a *mandamus* in such a case.[39] In *Brashear v. Mason*, the Supreme Court upheld the circuit court's refusal to issue a *mandamus* compelling the Secretary of Navy to pay arrearages to a Navy officer, both because it was a matter of judgment and discretion and because no appropriation had been made by Congress for the purpose.[40]

This last position was again taken in *Reeside v. Walker*, where the court held that, "Though a *mandamus* may sometimes lie against a ministerial officer to do some ministerial act connected with the liabilities of the government, yet it must be where the government itself is liable, and the officer himself has improperly refused to act." Where there was no appropriation, there could be no *mandamus.*[41]

Nor, held the Supreme Court, could the circuit court grant a *mandamus* to compel the Superintendent of Public Printing of the Houses of Congress to place a document in the hands of the printer of the Senate instead of in the hands of the printer of the House, since the Superintendent was obliged to use his discretion before he acted. Speaking for the court, the Chief Justice stated: "Nor is there any reason of public policy or individual right which requires that this remedy should be extended beyond its legitimate bounds, in order to embrace cases of this description; for it would embarrass the operations of the legislative and executive departments of the government if the court of this district was authorized to interfere, by this summary process, in controversies between officers in their respective employments, whenever differences of opinion as to their respective rights may arise."[42]

Only in *United States ex rel. Goodrich v. Guthrie* was some dissatisfaction shown on the court with the restrictive use of the *mandamus* and then only by one judge, McLean. While eight justices upheld the decision of the Circuit Court of the District refusing to issue a *mandamus* commanding the Secretary of the Treasury to pay a territorial judge his salary for the unexpired term of office from which he had been removed by the President, McLean held that the writ was both legal and appropriate in the case. An appropriation had been made by Congress and the payment of the salary was merely a ministerial act, contended McLean. The majority replied that on the one hand the President had the right to remove the territorial judge,[43] which automatically would terminate his right to a salary, and on the other hand the petitioner must show a legally determined right to the salary before a *mandamus* could issue, since a writ of *mandamus* was not the proper procedure for trying that right.[44]

It was not until 1861 that the court again upheld the use of a *mandamus* by one of the circuit courts. In *Aspinwall v. County Commissioners*, the Circuit Court of Indiana granted a peremptory *mandamus* ordering the Board of Commissioners of Knox County to levy a tax to raise the funds necessary to pay the interest on county bonds, after the petitioner had won a judgment for interest in the federal court and the county had failed to comply with the judgment. Here the issue was as delicate as that between the federal judiciary and the executive department; indeed more so, since the conflict involved a state governmental unit. Judge Huntington pointed out that the court had previously decided that it had the power to issue this prerogative writ in order to sustain its jurisdiction and enforce its judgment. "Indeed, to deny this power is to deny the jurisdiction of the court," he wrote, "for it would be a farce to say that this court has the power to give a judgment without the power to enforce it. The board has a mere ministerial duty to perform," Huntington continued, "and it contumaciously refuses to perform it, and we know of no other mode in which it can be enforced than by this prerogative writ."[45]

The Board of Commissioners appealed to the Supreme Court, which upheld the authority of the lower court under the 14th Section of the Judiciary Act to issue the *mandamus* when necessary to its jurisdiction. Here the jurisdiction of the circuit court existed prior to the *mandamus* proceedings and was not disputed. "It is 'necessary' to an efficient exercise of this jurisdiction," said Justice Grier, "that the court have authority to compel the exercise of a ministerial duty by the corporation, which by law they are bound to perform."[46]

At the same term the Supreme Court was enfronted with a motion to grant a *mandamus* in the exercise of its original jurisdiction. Here, for the first time, the 13th Section of the Judiciary Act was appropriately and constitutionally resorted to, the case being one in which a state was a party. The Commonwealth of Kentucky had applied to the court to issue the *mandamus* to compel the Governor of the State of Ohio to deliver up a fugitive from justice.

Before deciding on the motion, the Chief Justice referred to the writ itself. "It is. . .well settled," he said, "that a *mandamus* is nothing more than an action at law between the parties, and is not now regarded as a prerogative writ. It undoubtedly came into use by virtue of the prerogative power of the English crown, and was subject to regulations and rules which have long since been disused. But the right to the writ, and the power to issue it, has ceased to depend upon any prerogative power, and it is now regarded as an ordinary process in cases to which it is applicable. . .The writ of *mandamus* does not issue from or by any prerogative power, and is nothing more than the ordinary process of a court of justice, to which every one is entitled, where it is the appropriate process for asserting the right he claims."

Having declared the right of the court to issue the writ, Taney then examined the nature of the act which the Governor was called upon to perform and concluded that it was merely ministerial. The motion, however, was denied because the duty of the Governor to deliver the fugitive, though clear, was only "morally" binding, for the act of Congress had provided no means to compel the execution of the duty and no power had been delegated to the general government, either through the judicial department or any other, to use any coercive means to compel him. Going beyond the Act of 1793 which governed the return of fugitives from justice, Taney, referring to the use of the *mandamus* in a case such as this, stated: "Indeed, such a power would place every state under the control and dominion of the general government, even in the administration of its internal concerns and reserved rights. And we think it clear that the federal government, under the Constitution, has no power to impose on a state officer, as such, any duty whatever, and compel him to perform it."[47] Thus once again the court stepped away from the use of this special power and, without denying their authority to use the *mandamus*, made it clear that its use was a matter of discretion.

In *Evans v. Pittsburgh*, a case similar to that of *Aspinwall*, Justice Grier of the Circuit Court of Pennsylvania issued the requested *mandamus.*[48] But in *United States ex rel. Learned v. Burlington*, the *mandamus* was refused when it was shown that the city could not be compelled to levy the necessary tax because it would thereby exceed its legal taxing powers, which had already been used to their fullest extent.[49] Thus the *mandamus* could not be used to give a remedy which was not a legal remedy.

The last case involving the *mandamus* prior to 1865 was similar in nature but opposed in outcome to one of the earliest cases. In *Spraggins v. County Court of Humphries*, the Circuit Court of Tennessee had asserted the authority to issue a *mandamus* to a state court in order to remove a cause pending in that court.[50] In *Hough v. Western Transportation Co.*, however, the Circuit Court of Illinois held that a United States circuit court had no such power. The remedy, it held, was by appeal to the State Supreme Court and thence by writ of error to the United States Supreme Court, rather than by summary process as claimed in the earlier decision. "The Congress of the United States has not seen fit to give this summary remedy by writ of *mandamus*, if it was competent for them to do it," said Judge Drummond, "and until they have done that, either by express language or by necessary implication, I do not think that this court ought to exercise a doubtful power. The application will therefore be dismissed."[51]

After seventy-five years, then, the courts had made some headway in defining the circumstances in which the writ of *mandamus* could be employed. The power of the judiciary to control the executive department by means of this writ, after first being restricted by *McIntire v. Wood*, then enlarged by *Kendall v. United States*, fell into disuse. Its application in cases involving states and state governmental units was limited, and used on so few occasions that it was hardly of any importance. The writ of *mandamus* was more than anything else a writ "which might have been."

CHAPTER THREE:

Footnotes:

[1] 3 Dallas 42 (1795).

[2] See Chapter Two, p. 39 ff.

[3] *Marbury v. Madison*, 1 Cranch 137 (1803).

[4] *Gilchrist v. The Collector of Charleston*, Case 5,420, 10 FC 355 (1808).

[5] Letter from Attorney General C.A. Rodney to President Jefferson, July 15, 1808, 10 FC 357-359.

[6] Exposition of Johnson in reply to letter of Attorney General to President Jefferson, 10 FC 359-366 (1808).

[7] *McIntire v. Wood*, 7 Cranch 504 (1813).

[8] This rule was explicitly stated by the Supreme Court many years later in *Cutler v. Rae*, 7 Howard 729; 731 (1849), but was not of recent origin.

[9] *McClung v. Silliman*, 2 Wheaton 369 (1817).

[10] *McClung v. Silliman, 6 Wheaton 598 (1821).*

[11] *Case 13,246, 22 FC 955 (1812).*

[12] *Case 13,064, 22 FC 575 (1825).*

[13] *Bank of Columbia v. Sweeney*, 1 Peters 567 (1828).

[14] *Ex parte Crane*, 5 Peters 190 (1831).

[15] His argument was that Section 14 referred to "writs not specially provided for by statute"; that the *mandamus* was referred to in the previous section; but that in accordance with *Marbury v. Madison*, Section 13 was inoperative.

[16] Dissent of Baldwin, *Ex parte Crane*, 5 Peters 200-223 (1831).

[17] 6 Peters 774 (1832).

[18] 7 Peters 634 (1833).

[19] 8 Peters 588 (1834).

[20] *Life & Fire Insurance Co. of New York v. Wilson's Heirs*, 8 Peters 291 (1834).

[21] *Life & Fire Insurance Co. of New York v. Adams*, 9 Peters 571 (1835).

[22] See Chapter Five, pp. 218-220 for discussion of this point.

[23] *McIntire v. Wood*, 7 Cranch 504 (1813).

[24] It would also seem that Cranch attributed the Circuit Court's power to issue a *mandamus* to its common-law powers received from the States of Maryland and Virginia when the court was instituted, powers which remained in force.

[25] Stokes and his partners.

[26] The Attorney General contended, among other things, that the President was responsible for the faithful execution of the laws and for the official acts of all the officers of the executive department; that it is within the province of the President to instruct and command or to remove the officer, a responsibility not to be interfered with by the courts.

[27] *United States ex. rel. Stokes v. Kendall,* Case 15,517, 26 FC 702 (1837).

[28] *Kendall v. United States ex. rel. Stokes,* 12 Peters 524 (1838). Thompson was joined by Story, McLean, Wayne, McKinley and Baldwin.

[29] See Chapter Five, pp. 218-220 for further discussion of jurisdiction.

[30] *Idem,* dissent of Taney, 12 Peters 626-641.

[31] *Idem,* dissent of Barbour, 12 Peters 641-653.

[32] *Idem,* dissent of Catron, 13 Peters 607-612 (originally published in Appendix to Volume 13).

[33] Warren, II, pp. 48-49.

[34] The balance of the award was credited to the account of Stokes and his partners following the decision. Nonetheless, they sued Kendall for damages for the delay in entering the credit on the books. A jury allowed them damages of $11,000. [Case 13,479, 27 FC 140 (1840)] The Supreme Court reversed the judgment awarding damages, holding that an application by a private person for a writ of *mandamus* proceeds upon the ground that he has no other adequate remedy, that therefore the damage suit was untenable. [3 Howard 87 (1845)] McLean dissented, affirming the judgment of the lower court.

[35] 14 Peters 497 (1840).

[36] *Idem,* concurring opinion of Baldwin, 14 Peters 599-613. It is difficult to reconcile this position of Baldwin's with his tacit concurrence in *Kendall v. United States,* where the Supreme Court also entertained jurisdiction over a Circuit Court decision involving a *mandamus.* See Baldwin's opinion on the revision of the writ of *habeas corpus* in *Holmes v. Jennison,* Chapter Six, pp. 281-283, below.

[37] 14 Peters 518-523.

[38] Case 12,441, 21 FC 654 (1846

[39] Case 7,975, 14 FC 923 (1847).

[40] 6 Howard 92 (1848).

[41] 11 Howard 272 (1851).

[42] 17 Howard 225 (1855).

[43] McLean protested that the President had no such right.

[44] 17 Howard 284 (1855).

[45] Case 593, 2 FC 67 (1859).

[46] *Board of Commissioners of Knox County v. Aspinwall,* 24 Howard 376 (1861).

[47] *Commonwealth of Kentucky v. Dennison,* 24 Howard 66 (1861). See Chapter Two, pp. 97-98.

[48] Case 4,567, 8 FC 878 (1862). (However, the following year the judge set aside the writ as irregular and void because issued to the wrong persons.)

[49] Case 14,687, 24 FC 1302 (1863), Circuit Court, Iowa.

[50] See this chapter, p.113, above.

[51] Case 6,724, 12 FC 581 (1864).

CHAPTER FOUR:

THE FEDERAL COURTS AND THE STATES

We have previously examined one of the areas in which the federal courts displayed their superior power, that involving conflicts with state governments and state courts. In *Martin v. Hunter's Lessee*[1] the Supreme Court firmly established its supervisory role over state tribunals in cases involving the constitutionality of state court decisions. Again in *Ableman v. Booth*[2], the court reiterated its right to exercise the final appellate power in a controversy involving the respective powers of the United States and the states. However, in other points of contact between the federal courts and the states, there was no one easy and simple rule or role to control their relationships. Rather, a series of specific solutions evolved, or were given by statute, to resolve the specific problems which arose. The principal areas of friction were: revision of state court judgments and removal of causes; general conflicts of jurisdiction; conflicts with the admiralty jurisdiction; cases in which a state was defendant, and rules regarding the interpretation of state laws.

1. Section 25 of the Judiciary Act.

The authors of the Constitution must undoubtedly have realized that conflicts would arise between the judicial system created by them and the existing state judiciaries. By extending the judicial power of the United States to all cases in law and equity arising under the Constitution, laws and treaties, and by establishing the Constitution and the laws made under it as the supreme law of the land, "anything in the Constitution or laws of any state to the contrary notwithstanding," the Third and Sixth Articles presupposed certain inevitable conflicts. But the Constitution itself did not provide any explicit mechanism by which these differences might be resolved.

The courts were not left entirely to their own devices in working out a *modus operandi*, even if the general assumption of power stemmed from the very nature of the constitutional provisions. In Section 25 of the Judiciary Act, the First Congress supplied the procedure by which the implied constitutional mandate was to be implemented. That section authorized the Supreme Court to re-examine and reverse or affirm, "a *final judgment* or decree in *any suit*, in the highest court of law or equity of a state in which a decision in the suit could be had, where is drawn in question the validity of a treaty or statute of, or an authority exercised under the United States, and the decision is against their validity; or where is drawn in question the validity of a statute of, or an authority exercised under any state, on the ground of their being repugnant to the Constitution, treaties or laws of the United States, and the decision is in favor of such their validity; or where is drawn in question the construction of any clause of the Constitution, or of a treaty, or statute of, or commission held under the United States, and the decision is against the title, right, privilege or exemption specially set up or claimed by either party, under such clause of the said Constitution, treaty, statute or commission. . ."[3]

Another potential source of conflict was the constitutional grant of jurisdiction over controversies between citizens of different states, for it was only to be expected that suits would often be prosecuted in state courts against citizens of other states, who would prefer to exercise their right to defend themselves in the newly established federal courts. Therefore, Section 12 of the Judiciary Act was included, to provide alien and out-of-state defendants in suits before the state courts involving more than $500, the right to have their causes removed for trial to the next United

States circuit court to be held in the district. Although the operations and purposes of Section 12 and 25 were entirely different, they will be treated together here inasmuch as they both affect the mode by which federal courts assumed jurisdiction over cases originating in the state courts.

The first case brought before the Supreme Court on appeal[4] under the twenty-fifth section of the Judiciary Act was that of *Olney v. Arnold*, in 1796. The only question concerning Section 25 on which the court ruled was whether the Superior Court of Rhode Island was the highest court of law in that state or was subordinate to the General Assembly. The court ruled that the court mentioned was the highest court since the General Assembly could only set aside but not make a judicial decision. As to the merits of the case, the Supreme Court reversed the judgment of the state court, thus exercising its rights under the latter part of Section 25 and establishing a precedent for future action.[5]

In the following year, on a writ of error to the High Court of Appeals of Maryland, the Supreme Court reversed the judgment of the state court and held a state law as to British debts invalid for coming in conflict with a treaty.[6] No interpretation of Section 25 itself was given in this case or in the subsequent one of *Calder v. Bull*, where, for the first time, the constitutionality of a state law was called in question. The case, having come up from the Supreme Court of Errors of Connecticut, involved the interpretation of the *ex post facto* clause, and the Supreme Court affirmed the decree of the state court.[7] Nor was there any discussion of Section 25 in the fourth case to come before the Supreme Court under this section. This case involved the interpretation of an act of Congress, and the judgment was affirmed.[8]

The following year the court, for the first time, dismissed a writ of error under Section 25 for want of jurisdiction. In this case the conditions which permitted recourse to Section 25 were not fulfilled; the decision of the state court was favorable to and not against the privilege claimed under the statute of the United States.[9]

It was not until 1812 that the Supreme Court reversed the judgment of a state court on the constitutionality of a state law. In *State of New Jersey v. Wilson*, the highest court of the State of New Jersey upheld a state law repealing an earlier act of the legislature. The plaintiff (Wilson) brought the case before the Supreme Court, on a writ of error under Section 25, on the ground that the repealing act was repugnant to the contract clause of the Constitution of the United States. The Supreme Court agreed with the claim of the plaintiff.[10]

In *Otis v. Bacon*, a case involving the construction of an act of Congress, the Supreme Court affirmed the judgment of the state court. When exceptions were taken to the rejection by the state court of certain evidence offered by the appellant, Justice Washington replied: "This court has no authority, under the law which authorizes this appeal, to notice any error except such as appears on the face of the record and immediately respects the questions of validity of the Constitution, treaties, statutes, commissions, or authorities in dispute. The opinions of the court below, in relation to the evidence offered by the appellant, even if erroneous, which we neither affirm nor deny, have nothing to do with the construction of any statute of the United States; and therefore they cannot be regarded by this court."[11] The court thus announced that it had no intention of going beyond its statutory powers in the exercise of its supervision over state court judgments.

In the same year, the case of *Fairfax's Devisee v. Hunter's Lessee* came before the Supreme Court on a writ of error to the Court of Appeals of Virginia, in an action of ejectment involving the construction of the treaties between Great Britain and the United States, the judgment of the state court having been against the right claimed under those treaties. The Supreme Court reversed the judgment of the highest state court and affirmed the judgment of the inferior district court of the State of Virginia.[12]

When the Court of Appeals of Virginia refused to obey the mandate of the Supreme Court requiring its judgment to be carried into execution, the plaintiff in error again had recourse to the Supreme Court under Section 25 of the Judiciary Act. The first question to be resolved was the constitutionality of Section 25 itself, for the Court of

Appeals had said, in refusing to carry out the judgment of the Supreme Court: "The court is unanimously of the opinion that the appellate power of the Supreme Court of the United States does not extend to this court, under a sound construction of the Constitution of the United States; that so much of the 25th section of the Act of Congress to establish the judicial courts of the United States, as extends the appellate jurisdiction of the Supreme Court to this court, is not in pursuance of the Constitution of the United States; that the writ of error in this cause was improvidently allowed under the authority of that act; that the proceedings thereon in the Supreme Court were *coram non judice*, in relation to this court, and that obedience to its mandate be declined by the court."

Justice Story's reply concerning the power and the jurisdiction of the United States Supreme Court has been taken up in Chapters Two and Five, respectively.[13] It is sufficient to mention here Story's arguments in defense of Section 25. First, there was the need for harmony and uniformity throughout the country in the interpretation of statutes, treaties and the Constitution itself. Second, "The Constitution of the United States was designed for the common and equal benefit of all the people of the United States. The judicial power was granted for the same benign and salutary purposes. It was not to be exercised exclusively for the benefit of parties who might be plaintiffs, and would elect the national forum, but also for the protection of defendants who might be entitled to try their rights or assert their privileges before the same forum. Yet, if the construction contended for be correct, it will follow, that as the plaintiff may always elect the state court, the defendant may be deprived of all the security which the Constitution intended in aid of his rights. Such a state of things can, in no respect, be considered as giving equal rights.

"To obviate this difficulty, we are referred to the power which it is admitted Congress possesses to remove suits from state courts to the national courts; and this forms the second ground upon which the argument we are considering has been attempted to be sustained. This power of removal is not to be found in express terms in any part of the Constitution; if it be given, it is only given by implication, as a power necessary and proper to carry into effect some express power."

Story proceeds to show that the power of removal presupposes an exercise of original jurisdiction to have attached elsewhere. The power of removal itself is the exercise of an appellate power. "If, then," he continues, "the right of removal be included in the appellate jurisdiction, it is only because it is one mode of exercising that power, and as Congress is not limited by the Constitution to any particular mode, or time of exercising it, it may authorize a removal either before or after judgment. The time, the process, and the manner, must be subject to its absolute legislative control. A writ of error is, indeed, but a process which removes the record of one court to the possession of another court, and enables the latter to inspect the proceedings, and give such judgment as its own opinion of the law and justice of the case may warrant. There is nothing in the nature of the process which forbids it from being applied, by the legislature, to interlocutory as well as final judgments. And if the right of removal from state courts exists before judgment, because it is included in the appellate power, it must, for the same reason, exist after judgment.

"On the whole," concludes Story, "the court is of the opinion that the appellate power of the United States does extend to cases pending in the state courts; and that the twenty-fifth section of the Judiciary Act, which authorizes the exercise of this jurisdiction in the specified cases, by a writ of error, is supported by the letter and spirit of the Constitution."

Denying that the record of the preceding case (7 Cranch 603) was before the court, nonetheless Story devoted several pages of his opinion to demonstrating that the court possessed jurisdiction to decide the former as well as the present case under Section 25. The *Fairfax's Devisee* case "was strictly a suit where was drawn in question the construction of a treaty, and the decision was against the title specially set up or claimed by the defendant. It would fall, then, within the very terms of the act."

The defendant in error, however, contended that the court could not inquire into the title but only into the correctness of the construction put upon the treaty by the State Court of Appeals. Story rejected this narrow construction of Section 25 and held that the Supreme Court could examine the title and its legal validity as well as the abstract construction of the treaty itself.[14] [15]

Once the Supreme Court had definitively upheld the constitutionality of Section 25, it still had work to do interpreting its many clauses. Thus, in *Inglee v. Coolidge*, the court held that there must be something apparent on the record to justify bringing the case before the court;[16] in *Houston v. Moore* the writ of error was dismissed because the judgment of the state court was not a final one;[17] and in *Miller v. Nicholls*, the court ruled that it could acquire appellate jurisdiction if the record showed that an act of Congress was applicable to the case, even if it was not drawn in question.[18]

In the years following *Martin v. Hunter's Lessee*, Section 25 was the means by which some of the most important cases to be decided by the court came before it: *McCulloch v. Maryland*,[19] *Trustees of Dartmouth College v. Woodward*,[20] *Houston v. Moore*,[21] *Cohens v. Virginia*[22], *Gibbons v. Ogden*[23] and *Brown v. Maryland*[24]. In all of these cases except that of *Cohens*, jurisdiction was assumed without any discussion of Section 25 itself. In the *Cohens* case the question was whether an act of Congress by which the city of Washington was authorized to establish a lottery was a "law" of the United States in the sense used in Section 25. The court ruled that it was.[25]

During these same years, in other cases less well-known, several points regarding the meaning of Section 25 were raised. In *Buel v. Van Ness* it was contended that the amount of the judgment was not sufficient to allow a writ of error to be issued. Justice Johnson, speaking for the court, explained that any reference in Section 25 to the preceding Section 22 of the Judiciary Act (where the amount of judgment was a factor in permitting appeals within the federal court system) was to the means of examining the disposing of cases, not to the description of cases which were eligible.

"This construction," wrote Johnson, "is fully supported by reference to the political object of the two sections. . .Questions of *meum and tuum* are those to which the twenty-second section relates; but those intended to be provided for by the twenty-fifth section are noticed only for their national importance and are deemed proper for an appellate tribunal, from the principles, not the sums, that they involve."[26]

In *Williams v. Norris*, the court held that the written opinion of a state court, filed among the papers, was not a part of the record and could not be examined under Section 25 to ascertain the question decided. It was the record alone which must show that one of the questions described by Section 25 necessarily arose.[27]

In *Montgomery v. Hernandez*, Justice Trimble pointed out: "Under [the provisions of the 25th Section], we have no authority to reexamine the whole case. We can reexamine so much and such parts of it only as come within some one or other of the classes of questions enumerated in the act of Congress, and so much of the case as must necessarily be decided to arrive at such question. . .It is not every misconstruction of an act of Congress by a state court that will give this court appellate jurisdiction. It is where the party claims some title, right, privilege, or exemption under an act of Congress, and the decision is against such right, title, privilege, or exemption."[28]

During the 1829 term the court took jurisdiction of two cases originating in state courts involving constitutional clauses. In both cases the question of jurisdiction was discussed, jurisdiction upheld and the judgments of the state courts affirmed. In *Wilson v. Blackbird Creek Marsh Co.*, the defendants in error contended that the Supreme Court did not possess jurisdiction because the record of the High Court of Errors and Appeals of Delaware did not show that the constitutionality of the act of the state legislature was drawn in question. Chief Justice Marshall answered that, "It is not necessary to state in terms on the record, that the Constitution or a law of the United States was drawn in question. It is sufficient to bring the case within the provisions of the twenty-fifth section of the Judicial Act, if the record shows that the Constitution or a law or a treaty of the United States must have been misconstrued, or the decision could not be made."[29]

The same objection was made to jurisdiction in the case of *Satterlee v. Matthewson.* Here Justice Washington, referring to the principles of construction applicable to Section 25, spoke for the court: "One of these principles is that if it sufficiently appears from the record itself, that the repugnancy of a statute of a state to the Constitution of the United States was drawn into question, or that that question was applicable to the case, this court has jurisdiction of the cause under the section of the act referred to; although the record should not, in terms, state a misconstruction of the Constitution of the United States, or that the repugnancy of the statute of the state to any part of that Constitution was drawn into question."[30]

The meaning of the terms "final judgment" and "any suit" came up to the Supreme Court for interpretation in *Weston v. Charleston*, the first case under Section 25 in which the opinion of the court was divided. The Court of Common Pleas of South Carolina granted a writ of prohibition restraining the City Council of Charleston from taxing stock of the United States. The Constitutional Court of the State reversed the writ, whereupon an appeal was taken to the Supreme Court of the United States, on the ground that the tax was inconsistent with the Constitution. The first question was—is a writ of prohibition a suit? Chief Justice Marshall, speaking for the majority, answered in the affirmative. "The term [suit] is certainly a very comprehensive one," he said, "and is understood to apply to any proceeding in a court of justice which the law affords him. The modes of proceeding may be various, but if a right is litigated between parties in a court of justice, the proceeding by which the decision of the court is sought is a suit."

The next question was—is a writ of prohibition a final judgment? "We think also that it was a final judgment in the sense in which that term is used in the twenty-fifth section of the Judicial Act," Marshall continued. "If it were applicable to those judgments and decrees only in which the right was finally decided, and could never again be litigated between the parties, the provisions of the section would be confined within much narrower limits than the words import, or than Congress could have intended. Judgments in actions of ejectment, and decrees in chancery dismissing a bill without prejudice, however deeply they might affect rights protected by the Constitution, laws, or treaties of the United States, would not be subject to the revision of this court. A prohibition might issue restraining a collector from collecting duties, and this court would not revise and correct the judgment. The word 'final' must be understood in the section under consideration, as applying to all judgments and decrees which determine the particular cause."[31]

Justice Johnson, acknowledging that the motion to obtain a writ of prohibition is a suit, opposed jurisdiction in the case because the writ of prohibition was not a final judgment or decree. "A prohibition," he contended, "especially where it is refused, as in this case, is not final and concludes nobody." An additional objection of Johnson's was that the suit to which Section 25 referred must be one in which the Supreme Court possessed or could exercise the power to enter judgment and award execution; but the Supreme Court did not possess the power to issue a prohibition to a state court or state officer. "Congress," he said, "has not pretended to vest in it such authority. And I am well satisfied that this power has been withheld from the courts of the United States *ex industria.* For every provision of the Constitution and the uniform policy of the government has been to prevent the immediate action of the one government upon the constituted authorities of the other, a collision which it was a leading object in the Constitution to avoid, because its effects were unavoidably and fully anticipated."[32]

Once again, in *Craig v. Missouri*, the court held that under the 25th section of the Judiciary Act it was not necessary that the record should state, in so many words, that the validity of a state law was questioned on the ground of its repugnancy to the Constitution of the United States, but that it was sufficient, if the record showed that it must have been so, and that the decision was in favor of the validity of the state law.[33] However, two justices, Thompson and McLean, though deferring to the precedents, doubted the wisdom of that interpretation. For McLean, the questioning of the validity of the statute "should not be left to inference, but be clearly stated in the proceeding."[34]

Menard v. Aspasia presented an entirely novel, though easily solvable problem to the court. The Supreme Court of Missouri had held the defendant in error, Aspasia, entitled to her freedom under the ordinance of 1787. The plaintiff in error, Menard, contended that the Missouri court had erred. The Supreme Court dismissed the writ for want of jurisdiction.

"If the decision of the Supreme Court of Missouri had been against Aspasia," declared McLean, "it might have been contended that the revising power of this court, under the twenty-fifth section of the Judiciary Act, could be exercised. In such a case the decision would have been against the express provision of the ordinance in favor of her liberty; and on that ground, if that instrument could be considered, under the circumstances, as an act of Congress within the twenty-fifth section, the jurisdiction of this court would be unquestionable. But the decision was not against but in favor of the express provision of the ordinance. . .[The title of the plaintiff] does not arise under an act of Congress. This is essential to give jurisdiction under this head."[35]

Thus it was quite clear that when a state court upheld a right given by a law of Congress, there was no ground on which the Supreme Court could revise the judgment.

Another aspect of the Supreme Court's revisory powers over judgments of state courts was considered in *Worcester v. Georgia.* The majority of the court assumed jurisdiction under Section 25 without discussion, in this politically delicate case in which they reversed the judgment of the Superior Court of Gwinett County, Georgia, on the ground that the law of Georgia under which the plaintiff, Worcester, was convicted, was repugnant to the Constitution, treaties and laws of the United States.[36] Justice McLean, in a concurring opinion, added a commentary on the question of jurisdiction.

"Doubts have been expressed whether a writ of error to a state court is not limited to civil cases," began McLean. "These doubts could not have arisen from reading the above section. Is not a criminal case as much a suit as a civil case?

What is a suit but a prosecution? And can anyone suppose that it was the intention of Congress, in using the word 'suit,' to make a distinction between a civil prosecution and a criminal one?

"It is more important that jurisdiction should be given to this court in criminal than in civil causes, under the twenty-fifth section of the Judiciary Act. Would it not be inconsistent, both with the spirit and letter of this law, to revise the judgment of a state court in a matter of controversy respecting damages, where the decision is against a right asserted under the Constitution or a law of the United States; but to deny the jurisdiction, in a case where the property, the character, the liberty and life of a citizen may be destroyed, though protected by the solemn guarantees of the Constitution?"[37]

This observation, implicitly concurred in by the majority in this case as well as in such earlier ones as *Cohens v. Virginia*, presents the anomalous situation of upholding the Supreme Court's power to re-examine convictions in certain cases in state tribunals, at the same time that no such appellate power in criminal cases existed in prosecutions originating in the lower federal courts.[38]

Marshall's final contribution to the interpretation of Section twenty-five was to give a liberal reading of the rights which might be claimed by the party seeking redress in the Supreme Court. The third ground for jurisdiction under Section twenty-five refers to decisions "against the title, right, privilege or exemption specially set up or claimed by either party, under such clause of the said Constitution, treaty, statute or commission." Counsel for the defendant in error, Armas, interpreted this clause to mean that a case can arise under the Constitution, law or treaty, only when the right *is created by* the Constitution, law or treaty.

The Chief Justice replied: "In support of his motion, the counsel has, we think, in his argument, prescribed too narrow a principle for the action of this court. . .This construction would defeat the obvious purpose of the Constitution as well as of the act of Congress. The language of both instruments extends the jurisdiction of this court to rights *protected by* the Constitution, treaties, or laws of the United States, from whatever source those rights may spring."[39]

During Taney's first term on the bench, the Supreme Court, speaking through Justice Story, took the opportunity to review and summarize the interpretation given to Section 25 over the preceding years. "To bring a case within the twenty-fifth section of the Judiciary Act," wrote Story, "it must appear upon the face of the record: 1. That some one of the questions stated in that section did arise in the state court. 2. That the question was decided by the state court, as required in the same section. 3. That it is not necessary that the question should appear on the record to have been raised, and the decision made in direct and positive terms, *ipsissimis verbis*, but that it is sufficient if it appears, by clear and necessary intendment, that the question must have been raised and must have been decided in order to have induced the judgment. 4. That it is not sufficient to show that a question might have arisen or been applicable to the case, unless it is further shown on the record that it did arise, and was applied by the state court to the case."[40]

This interpretation represented a sharp modification of the earlier rule laid down in *Miller v. Nicholls*,[41] that it was sufficient to give jurisdiction that an act of Congress was applicable to the case even if it was not drawn in question. Henceforth it would be necessary to show that the question did arise in the state court and was applied to the case.

In the *Charles River Bridge* case, a writ of error to the Supreme Judicial Court of Massachusetts, the majority of the court assumed jurisdiction of the case and proceeded to affirm the judgment of the state court.[42] McLean, however, took an entirely different approach to the case: concluding that the state act establishing the Warren Bridge was not repugnant to the Constitution, he held that the court did not possess jurisdiction to re-examine the judgment of the state court.[43] But McLean seems to have missed the point of Section 25, whose second class of cases refers to those "where is drawn in question the validity of a statute of, or an authority exercised under any state, on the ground of their being repugnant to the Constitution, treaties or laws of the United States, and the decision is in favor of such their validity." In order to have reached the conclusion that the case involved the divesting of vested rights rather than the unconstitutional impairment of a contract, it was necessary to examine the merits of the case first, and to do so involved taking jurisdiction. Thus Taney's position was the correct one, first to take jurisdiction to determine whether or not a constitutional right had been violated as a result of the state judgment, and then to affirm the state judgment on determination that no such right was involved. Yet McLean had a point: if in each instance that vested rights were divested by the exercise of the eminent domain, the Supreme Court was called upon to "act as a court of supervision for the correction of errors, its powers may be invoked in numberless instances."[44]

A few years later the court was asked to take jurisdiction of a case in which the Supreme Court of Missouri had decided against the validity of a state law, as repugnant to the Constitution of the United States. The Chief Justice dismissed the case for want of jurisdiction, pointing out that Section 25 authorized the court to re-examine a judgment of the state court in such a case only when the decision was in favor of the validity of the state law.

"The policy of this distinction is obvious enough," wrote Taney. "The power given to the Supreme Court by this act of Congress was intended to protect the general government in the free and uninterrupted exercise of the powers conferred on it by the Constitution, and to prevent any serious impediment from being thrown in its way while acting within the sphere of its legitimate authority. The right was therefore given to this court to re-examine the judgments of the state courts, where the relative powers of the general and state government had been in controversy, and the decision had been in favor of the latter. It may have been apprehended that the judicial tribunals of the states would incline to the support of state authority against that of the general government, and might, moreoever, in different States, give different judgments upon the relative powers of the two governments, so as to produce irregularity and disorder in the administration of the general government. But when, as in the case before us, the state authority or state statute is decided to be unconstitutional and void in the state tribunal, it cannot, under that decision, come in collision with the authority of the general government; and the right to re-examine it here is not necessary to protect this government in the exercise of its rightful powers. In such a case, therefore, the writ of error is not given, and the one now before us must be dismissed for want of jurisdiction."[45]

The statute of Kentucky which was held invalid by the state court of Missouri is the same one which was upheld by the state court of Kentucky and subsequently affirmed to be valid by the Supreme Court of the United States in *Briscoe v. Bank of Kentucky*.[46] Although the court's interpretation of its jurisdiction under Section 25 was a correct one, in the *Griffith* case the incapacity of the Supreme Court to take jurisdiction revealed a flaw in Section 25, insofar as that section was designed to achieve uniformity of decisions on the same point throughout the nation. Taney's explanation of the policy of Section 25 gives an entirely different emphasis to the law than that previously given by those concerned with uniformity. The result of this limitation in Section 25 was to permit the same law to be both valid and invalid (under the Constitution of the United States), depending on the state in which the controversy arose. There was nothing the Supreme Court could do to impose uniformity.

Perhaps one of the most difficult cases arising under Section 25 to confront the Supreme Court was that of *Holmes v. Jennison*, a writ of error to the Supreme Court of Vermont, to revise the judgment of the state court on *habeas corpus* proceedings.[47] Both the treaty-making power of the United States government as well as its exclusive authority to carry on relations with foreign countries were involved in the case, but before those substantial questions could be met it was necessary to overcome the objections to jurisdiction.

The first question was whether the state court's refusal to discharge the prisoner Holmes was a final judgment in the sense in which that term was employed in Section 25. Chief Justice Taney held that since the judgment given by the

Supreme Court of Vermont determined the particular case before them (the *habeas corpus* proceedings), it was a final judgment within the meaning of the act of Congress. Three other justices agreed with him in this opinion and one more, Catron, concurred on this point in a separate opinion. Only Justice Baldwin dissented, the other two judges remaining silent.[48]

The second question was whether the proceeding before the state court was a "suit." Citing Marshall's opinion in *Weston v. Charleston*, with approval, Taney held: "We entirely concur in the definition of the word 'suit,' as used in the act of 1789. It makes the act of Congress consistent with the principles of justice, and interprets it according to the natural meaning of its words; and it is too plain for argument that according to this definition the proceedings upon the *habeas corpus* was a suit in the Supreme Court of Vermont."[49]

The division of the court was the same on this point as on the preceding one. Baldwin's dissent was based on a distinction between "the cause itself," the arrest of Holmes, and the inquiry into the arrest, the *habeas corpus* proceedings. "There can. . .be no final decision of 'any suit,' the 'original suit,' or 'the cause,' on a writ of *habeas corpus*," he declared. A case such as this could be brought within the law," he continued, "only by a successive train of implication upon implication, till ingenious reasoning may fasten it to some expression which may be thought to justify the assumption of the power." [50]

The third question was whether the proceedings involved a federal question. Here Catron dissented from the conclusion of Taney (and the three judges who accompanied him) that the arrest of Holmes was repugnant to the prohibition on the states to enter into any agreement, without the consent of Congress, with any foreign state. Catron contended that since there was no explicit *agreement* on the part of the State of Vermont, there was no conflict with the Constitution and therefore no federal question to give jurisdiction.[51] Since Thompson, Barbour and Baldwin also failed to discover a federal question, the resulting 4-4 division compelled the court to dismiss the writ of error for want of jurisdiction.

Thus a very narrow interpretation of what constituted a federal question undid the results of a generous reading of the terms "final judgment" and "suit" and kept the Supreme Court from passing on the state's right to extradite criminals to foreign countries.

The case of *Gordon v. Longest* presented for the first time the delicate problem of a removal of cause from the state court to the federal court being denied by the highest court of the state. The Supreme Court reversed the judgment of the state court and directed the cause to be removed to the circuit court of the United States. In reaching this conclusion, Justice McLean, the author of the court's opinion, suggested that, "A more summary remedy might have been pursued by the defendant than the one which this court can now give him." The "more summary remedy" referred to by McLean is not specified, but the implication is that the reference is to a *mandamus* which might have been issued by the circuit court of the United States to the state court.[52]

During the 1830's and 1840's, at virtually every term the Supreme Court was called upon to re-examine the judgment of state courts. In addition to the cases already mentioned, writs of error were issued under Section 25 in *Dobbins v. Erie County*[53], *Prigg v. Pennsylvania*[54], *The License Cases*[55], and the *Passenger Cases*[56], among others. Furthermore, in several other cases the court continued its interpretation of Section 25. In *Armstrong v. Treasurer of Athens County*[57], Justice Catron reviewed the prerequisites for bringing a case before the Supreme Court. In *Pepper v. Dunlap*[58], it was held that no writ of error lies in a case in which the highest court of a state remands the cause to a lower state court for further proceedings. And in *Scott v. Jones*[59], the majority ruled that the court could not re-examine under Section 25 the judgment of a state court concerning the validity of a statute passed by the territorial government of Michigan before Michigan became a state.

In this last case, Justice Woodbury declared: "The principle under which the Judiciary Act of 1789 allows this interference of ours in relations between the two governments, always of so sensitive and responsible a character, is that no government can be efficient or just without the means of self-protection; and hence that those who act under it, or claim rights beneath the shield of its laws, should, within its own territory, be able to appeal to its own tribunals for relief, whenever their claims under it are decided against in the courts of the states. But prejudices here are to be guarded against as well as there; and hence the paramount rule of construction in all cases of this kind ought to be not to interfere at all, unless the decision is shown to come clearly within the letter and spirit of the act of Congress permitting an appeal; and, when interfering, not to overrule the judgment of the state court unless clearly erroneous."

The obvious design of this section of the Judiciary Act, continues Woodbury in a later portion of his opinion, "was to prevent partiality in [the state tribunals] against the authority and agents of the general government; to hold the protecting supervision in respect to its own Constitution, treaties and acts of Congress, for purposes of self-preservation and self-defense, and finally, to insure uniformity in the construction and operation of them over the whole Union."[60]

In 1851, in *Strader v. Graham*, the court ruled that the question whether slaves held in Kentucky are made free by going into Ohio, with the permission of their master, is purely a question of local law, over which the court could not take jurisdiction under a writ of error to the Court of Appeals of the State of Kentucky. The writ of error was thus dismissed for want of jurisdiction.[61]

In *Butler v. Pennsylvania*[62], as in the Charles River Bridge case many years earlier, Justice McLean dissented from the majority's affirmation of the state court's judgment that a state law repealing an appointment to a state office was not an impairment of the obligation of a contract because the original appointment did not amount to a contract. McLean agreed that there was no contract and held that therefore the case should have been dismissed for want of jurisdiction rather than affirmed.[63]

Further clarification of the rules laid down in *Crowell v.*

Randall[64] appeared in cases decided during the 1850's. In *Grand Gulf Railroad v. Marshall*, Chief Justice Taney stated: "The party is authorized to bring his case before the court because a state court has refused to him a right to which he is entitled under the Constitution or laws of the United States. But if he omits to claim it in the state court, there is no reason for permitting him to harass the adverse party by a writ of error to this court, when, for any thing that appears in the record, the judgment of the state court might have been in his favor if its attention had been drawn to the question."[65]

This same position was taken by the Chief Justice in *Maxwell v. Newbold* where *Miller v. Nicholls* was made to yield to *Crowell v. Randall:* "Experience showed that [the rule in *Miller v. Nicholls*] was not a safe one; and that it might sometimes happen, that although in one view of the subject an act of Congress or a clause of the Constitution might be applicable to a case, yet the state court, upon a different view of the case, might have decided upon principles of state law altogether independent of any provision in the Constitution or laws of the United States, and in nowise in conflict with either. And if this court reversed the judgment, upon the assumption that a right claimed under the Constitution or laws of the United States, and to which the party was entitled, had been denied to him, the reversal would sometimes be for a supposed error which the state court had not committed, and upon a point which the state court had not decided."[66]

This interpretation, more than a question of deference to the state tribunals, was a warning to the litigants to raise the federal question in the state court in the first instance and not to wait to bring it up before the justices of the Supreme Court.

In *Bridge Proprietors v. Hoboken Co.*, however, a case in which the validity of a state statute was drawn in question as contrary to the Constitution of the United States, the Supreme Court held that it was not necessary to state in the pleadings in so many words the specific clause in the Constitution supposed to render the act invalid.

"It would be a new rule of pleading, and one altogether

superfluous," held Justice Miller, "to require a party to set out specially the provision of the Constitution of the United States on which he relies for the action of the court in the protection of his rights. If the courts of this country, and especially this court, can be supposed to take judicial notice of anything without pleading it specially, it is the Constitution of the United States. And if the plaintiff and defendant in their pleadings, make a case which necessarily comes within some of the provisions of that instrument, this court surely can recognize the fact without requiring the pleader to say in words: 'This paragraph of the Constitution is the one involved in this case'. . .The true and rational rule is that the court must be able to see clearly, from the whole record, that a certain provision of the Constitution, or act of Congress, was relied on by the party who brings the writ of error, and that the right thus claimed by him was denied."[67]

During the 1850's many other important cases reached the Supreme Court under Section 25, often without discussion of the question of jurisdiction. Among these were: *Cooley v. Board of Wardens*[68], *Piqua Branch v. Knoop*[69], *Ohio Life Insurance v. Debolt*[70], *Taylor v. Carryl*[71] and *Ableman v. Booth*[72]. Reviewing these cases as well as those listed previously, it is clear that without Section 25 of the Judiciary Act it would have been impossible for the Supreme Court to have exercised its constitutional function; that had it not existed from the beginning it would have had to be created. In *Martin v. Hunter's Lessee*, *Cohens v. Virginia* and the *Booth* case the court clearly demonstrated that Section 25 was the vehicle through which the supremacy clause of the Constitution was to be exercised. But once this supremacy had been asserted, the court was careful to stay within the letter and spirit of Section 25 and avoid usurpation of the prerogatives of the state courts. Although the reversals of judgments were more dramatic and contributed more to the development of substantive constitutional law, the frequent dismissals of writs of error for want of jurisdiction as well as the large number of cases in which the judgments of the state courts were affirmed, attest to the prudence and deference by which the Supreme Court steered its course.

2. *General Conflicts of Jurisdiction*

The first case to come before the Supreme Court involving the interference of a federal court with proceedings in a state tribunal was that of *Diggs v. Wolcott*, decided in 1807. Here the appellee had filed a bill in chancery in the Superior Court of the State of Connecticut, praying for an injunction prohibiting the appellants from proceeding with a suit at law in an inferior state court. On petition of the appellants, the suit in chancery was removed to the Circuit Court of the United States for the District of Connecticut, which issued an injunction against further proceedings at law in the state court. Against this decision, the plaintiff in the original suit appealed to the Supreme Court, which, "being of the opinion that a circuit court of the United States had not jurisdiction to enjoin proceedings in a state court, reversed the decree."[73]

The theory underlying this decision was clearly stated by the Chief Justice in another case decided at the same term: "The state courts are not, in any sense of the word, inferior courts, except in the particular cases in which an appeal lies from their judgment to this court. . .They are not inferior courts, because they emanate from a different authority and are the creatures of a distinct government."[74]

On the other hand, in *United States v. Peters*, the Supreme Court clearly announced that the legislatures of the states have no power to annul judgments of the federal courts nor to deprive the nation of the means of enforcing its own laws in its own tribunals.[75] Also Justice Story, in the Circuit Court of Rhode Island, held that, "It is not competent for the legislature of Rhode Island to suspend process in the courts of the United States."[76] And when a state court of Kentucky issued an injunction against the execution of a judgment obtained in a circuit court of the United States, the Supreme Court held that the state court had no jurisdiction to enjoin a judgment of a court of the United States.[77]

Excepting the cases of *Martin v. Hunter's Lessee* and

Cohens v. Virginia, which have previously been discussed in Chapter Two, it was not until 1835 that the Supreme Court had occasion to refer to the relationship of the federal courts to the states. In *Beers v. Haughton*, Justice Story declared that "state laws cannot control the exercise of the powers of the national government, or in any manner limit or affect the operation of the process or proceedings in the national courts."[78]

In the first year of Taney's accession to the court, an important case involving conflict of jurisdictions came up for decision. The question was whether a levy on property (in this case, slaves) carried out by the officer of one court—in this case, the sheriff acting under orders of the state court—withdraws the property from the reach of process issued subsequently by another court—the levy of a U.S. marshal under orders of a federal court. It is noteworthy that the Supreme Court, so nationalistic in other matters, and so jealous of its own appellate power, where that power was appropriate, did not decide the issue on a federal vs. state basis but on the rule of "first come-first served."

"The first levy," wrote McLean, "whether it were under the federal or state authority, withdraws the property from the reach of the process of the other." This because "a most injurious conflict of jurisdiction would be likely, often, to arise between the federal and the state courts, if the final process of the one could be levied on property which had been taken by the process of the other."[79]

Two additional decisions affirmed the earlier prohibitions against state interferences with proceedings before the federal courts. The court held in *Wallace v. McConnell* that once jurisdiction had been vested in the circuit court of the United States, it cannot be divested by any subsequent proceeding in a state court;[80] and in *Duncan v. Darst*, that a state officer, acting under a state insolvent law, cannot discharge from imprisonment a debtor arrested under an order of a circuit court of the United States.[81]

On the other hand, in *Ex parte Dorr*, it was held that no court of the United States can issue a writ of *habeas corpus* to bring up a prisoner confined by state process.[82] Also, the District Court of Pennsylvania declared, in a charge to the jury, that in order to avoid a conflict of jurisdiction between the courts, Congress had provided that no writ of injunction could be granted by any of the courts of the United States to stay proceedings in any of the state courts, and if any fraud or irregularity had been committed in the state court proceedings it was for that court to make the necessary correction free of federal interference.[83] Still another circuit court decision, *Tobey v. County of Bristol*, emphasized the incompetence of the federal courts to interfere with state proceedings. "This court, as a court of equity, possesses no revisory power over the acts of the state tribunals in the exercise of their jurisdiction. It has no authority to compel them to do their duty, or to abstain from the exercise of their functions."[84]

In *Ex parte Christy*, a case dealing with the Bankrupt Law of 1841, Justice Story suggested (in a dictum) that under the provisions of Section 6, the district courts of the United States possessed full jurisdiction to suspend or control all proceedings in the state courts "either then pending or thereafter to be brought, by any creditor or person having any adverse interest to enforce his rights or obtain remedial redress against the bankrupt or his assets after the bankruptcy." This control was to be exercised, according to Story, "not by acting on the courts, over which it possesses no authority, but by acting on the parties through the instrumentality of an injunction or other remedial proceedings in equity."[85]

However, this doctrine was explicitly rejected by the court five years later, when Story was no longer a member, in *Peck v. Jenness*, which denied that the Bankrupt Act conferred any such jurisdiction. The state court, declared Justice Grier, "was an independent tribunal, not deriving its authority from the same sovereign, and, as regards the district court, a foreign forum, in every way its equal. The district court has no supervisory power over it." Story had admitted as much by carefully pointing out that the district court had authority only to act on the parties, not on the state court. However the Grier decision went further in denying the district court the authority to enjoin the plaintiff, directly or indirectly. "An attempt to enforce the decree," concluded Grier, "would probably have been met with resistance and resulted in a collision of jurisdictions much to be deprecated."[86]

During the 1850's the federal courts continued to emphasize the separation of jurisdictions: *In re Veremaitre*, a conflict involving *habeas corpus:* "It is a principle acknowledged by all well-informed citizens, that the line of jurisdiction between national and state jurisdiction, should be so strongly marked, that every court shall abide by that line. To prevent all conflict of jurisdiction there should be no encroachment on either side."[87] Also *Rogers v. Cincinnati:* "The circuit court of the United States has no power to enjoin a procedure in a state court."[88] Also *Catherwood v. Gapete*[89] and *Sadlier v. Fallen*[90], where Justice Curtis rejected the interference of state laws and state courts with process of the circuit courts of the United States.

In 1855, in *Pulliam v. Osborne*, the Supreme Court affirmed its decision in *Hagan v. Lucas*, when it ruled that where officers of state and federal courts are both invested with authority to seize property under judgments of their respective courts, "the tribunal which first acquires possession of the property, by the seizure of its officer, may dispose of it so as to vest a title in the purchaser."[91]

A more delicate problem of a similar nature arose a few years later in the Circuit Court of Ohio involving the priority of jurisdiction. A suit was commenced in the state court on the fourteenth of October. Summons was issued but had not yet been served two days later when a bill of equity was filed in the circuit court of the United States by different plaintiffs against the same defendant. The latter court issued a subpoena which was served the same day, at the same time that a receiver was named and assignees were enjoined not to dispose of the assets they held. At a later hour of the same day, the state court appointed the sheriff as receiver under the state court proceedings and ordered the assignees to deliver the assets to him. The injunction of the circuit court notwithstanding, the sheriff obtained possession of the assets, whereupon the plaintiffs in the federal action sought the support of the circuit court.

Justice McLean's ruling in the case was that the priority of jurisdiction is determined by the time at which process is served rather than by the date of the commencement of the suit. Therefore, the fact that the suit in the state court was commenced two days earlier was of no avail to the state court plaintiffs since the state court process was served subsequently to that of the federal court. After the federal court had served process and issued its injunction, held McLean, the state court had no authority to take action or make orders in regard to the subject matter over which jurisdiction had been exercised by the circuit court. McLean's final words were: "We do not doubt that. . .the superior court. . .will direct the receiver [the sheriff] to restore the assets to the possession of the receiver of this court."[92]

A much more serious conflict of jurisdictions was presented to the Supreme Court the following year in *Ableman v. Booth* and *United States v. Booth.* Booth had been charged by the United States commissioner with having aided and abetted the escape of a fugitive slave and was committed to the custody of the United States Marshal, Ableman. Booth thereupon applied to one of the justices of the Supreme Court of the State of Wisconsin for a writ of *habeas corpus*, alleging illegal imprisonment. The writ was issued and the state judge ordered the marshal to discharge Booth and set him at liberty, which was accordingly done. Booth was then tried before the District Court of the United States, found guilty and sentenced to fine and imprisonment. Once more he applied for a writ of *habeas corpus* to the State Supreme Court which again decided that his imprisonment was illegal and discharged him.

Chief Justice Taney, speaking for a unanimous court, held that state courts have no power to review or reverse the judgment of the courts of the United States, and that an attempt to do this by virtue of a writ of *habeas corpus*, does violence to the jurisdiction of the federal courts and is a violation of the law and Constitution of the United States.

In reversing the judgment of the Supreme Court of Wisconsin, Taney wrote: "We do not question the authority of the state court, or judge, who is authorized by the laws of the state to issue the writ of *habeas corpus*, to issue it in any case where the party is imprisoned within its territorial limits, provided it does not appear, when the application is made, that the person imprisoned is in custody under the authority of the United States. And it is the duty of the marshal, or other person having the custody of the prisoner, to make known to the judge or court, by a proper return, the authority by which he holds him in custody. . .But after the return is made, and the state judge or court is judicially apprized that the party is in custody under the authority of the United States, they can proceed no further. . .And although, as we have said, it is the duty of the marshal, or other person holding him, to make known by a proper return the authority under which he detains him, it is at the same time imperatively his duty to obey the process of the United States, to hold the prisoner in custody under it, and refuse obedience to the mandate or process of any other government. And consequently, it is his duty not to take the prisoner, nor suffer him to be taken, before a state judge or court upon a *habeas corpus* issued under state authority."

If the state judge, notwithstanding his lack of authority, were to attempt to interfere with the marshal's custody of the prisoner, Taney continued, it would be the marshal's duty to resist the attempt, "and to call to his aid any force that might be necessary to maintain the authority of law against illegal interference."[93] [94]

The final note of warning reflects in greater degree the tensions of the pre-Civil War years than the general relationships existing between the federal and state courts for, as we have seen, the number of cases to come before the federal courts involving a conflict of jurisdictions were few,[95] considering the years which had passed and the opportunities for mutual interference. If the federal courts were powerless to prevent the outbreak of open hostilities between the opposing forces of the North and the South, at least they were successful in keeping the federal and state judges—with their marshals and sheriffs—from one another's throats, through the wise policy of sharply delineated jurisdictions. In those few cases where the conflict was over the possession of property or the custody of prisoners, the courts laid down rules which, no matter how grating to the losing side, were easy to apply and conducive to peace. It may further be noted that the federal courts showed no overbearing bias toward their own jurisdiction, since a review of the cases decided reveals that the state courts were as often the beneficiary of their judgments as those of the federal government. Only when the constitutional supremacy of the national government (and its courts) was at stake did the federal courts adopt a nationalistic tone in coming to a decision.

3. Conflicts with State Courts in Admiralty Cases

A more specialized area in which conflicts arose between the federal and state courts, especially during the decade immediately preceding the Civil War, was that of cases involving admiralty jurisdiction. We shall see in Chapter Seven how the geographical and topical limits to admiralty jurisdiction evolved, principally at the expense of state jurisdiction. Here we shall examine the *modus operandi* worked out to resolve actual disputes involving the courts' possession of ships and other vessels.[96]

The first case to come before the federal courts—and it is interesting to note that only one of the twenty cases worth mentioning came before the Supreme Court—was that of *The Robert Fulton*, decided by the Circuit Court of New York in 1826. Prior to the filing of a libel in the district court of the United States and the subsequent issuance of a decree by that court, the sheriff had attached the vessel under the process of the state court. The claimant in the state proceedings thereupon appealed to the circuit court for a reversal of the decree on the basis of his own superior prior claim. This thesis was accepted by Justice Thompson of the Circuit Court, on the ground that in cases of concurrent jurisdiction *in rem*, the right to maintain the jurisdiction attaches to that tribunal which first exercises it and takes possession of the thing. The court advised the United States marshal that on finding that the ship was held by the sheriff, he should have so reported to the district court, "and all further proceedings of the district court would have been arrested, and no conflict of jurisdiction could have arisen."[97]

Two years later a similar but not identical conflict came before the court in the case of *The Florenzo*. Here the sheriff had taken possession of the ship in order to satisfy the execution of a state judgment in favor of a simple creditor; the marshal subsequently attempted to attach the ship under a proceeding for forfeiture under a law of the United States. District Judge Betts, acknowledging the earlier ruling in *The Robert Fulton*, carefully distinguished the two cases: the first was a case of parallel proceedings under the same state law, the present was a case involving two laws, one of which, that of the United States, gave an anterior (and superior) title to the vessel. In ruling that jurisdiction belonged to the United States court, the judge presented a practical argument in defense of his policy: if possession of property by a state sheriff was to exclude the marshal from taking possession in order to execute the laws of the United States, state process could effectively prevent the operation of the revenue laws, in particular the laws against smuggling.[98]

In a case decided by the District Court of Maine in the same year, Judge Ware held that the rule that possession belongs to the jurisdiction which first lays hand on the property applies only when both claimants or creditors stand in the same relation to the property. "But the reason no longer holds," the judge declared, "when the claim of one of the parties is in its nature a privileged claim." Here the claim in the federal court was that of seamen for wages due; the claim in the state court was that of various general creditors. As the claim for wages was universally considered to be a privileged claim, the jurisdiction then must attach to the admiralty court, regardless of precedence of possession.[99]

This exception to the "priority of possession" rule was extended several years later by Justice Story in a case in which process of the state court had been served prior to the United States marshal's attachment of cargo under a libel for freight. Here Story held that the right of a court of admiralty to proceed by a suit *in rem* could not be superseded by a suit in the state court. "The admiralty suit," he declared, "asserts a paramount right against all persons whatever, whether claiming above or under that process."[100]

These four cases constituted a prelude to the case of *The Royal Saxon*, a controversy which commenced in 1847 and was not finally decided until a divided Supreme Court submitted judgment eleven years later, by which time the ship had undoubtedly rotted away.

On November 17, 1847, the *Royal Saxon* was attached by the sheriff under order of the state court in a proceeding for debt. Two months later, in January of the following year, Wall, a seaman, filed a libel *in rem* in the District Court of Pennsylvania for wages due while in the service of the ship. On January 29th, the state court ordered the sale of the vessel.

Six days later the district court ordered the marshal to sell the vessel. Citing the precedents of the two previous cases, District Judge Kane held that a vessel may be libelled and sold in a court of admiralty under a paramount lien, such as seaman's wages,[101] notwithstanding that she had been previously attached by process of the state court and was still in the custody of the sheriff.[102]

On February 9th, five days after Judge Kane handed down his decision, the *Royal Saxon* was sold by the sheriff under the order of the state court to Ward; six days later the vessel was sold and delivered by the marshal to Taylor. On February 24th the sheriff replevied the vessel from possession of Taylor and delivered it to Ward. Subsequently, Taylor filed a libel in the circuit court for repossession of the vessel, at the same time that the right of property in the ship was pending before the Supreme Court of the State of Pennsylvania.

The circuit court, in effect, evaded the issue by holding, simultaneously, that the sale of the *Royal Saxon* by order of the court of Pennsylvania could not divest the lien in the admiralty for seaman's wages; but that the conflict of ownership resulting from the two sales was an issue which must be decided by the court which first took cognizance of the question of possession and property, namely the state court. This conclusion was founded on the necessity of avoiding the "unpleasant collision of jurisdiction which would otherwise ensue," and an eternal march and countermarch of sheriff and marshal and of replevin and libel. "It would exhibit a humiliating spectacle," wrote Justice Grier, "to have a ship delivered by the state officer to Ward yesterday, restored to Taylor by the court of admiralty today—to be retaken by the process of the state court tomorrow, and so on alternately."[103]

In deferring to the State Supreme Court, Grier presumed that said court would give as much consideration to the legitimacy of Taylor's title and the principles of maritime law as the federal court itself. The replevin suit was, however, decided favorably to Ward. Taylor, who did not give up easily, brought the case before the Supreme Court of the United States on a writ of error under Section 25 of the Judiciary Act.

Before this complicated and well-litigated controversy reached the Supreme Court—where it was not decided until 1858[104]—a number of other cases of conflicting jurisdiction came before the lower courts. In *The Celestine*, the District Court of Wisconsin held that it had no jurisdiction in admiralty of a suit of a domestic creditor against a domestic vessel, but that if it had jurisdiction, the vessel, having been previously attached by the sheriff of Racine County and in the custody of the law, could not be subsequently attached by the marshal.[105] Similarly, in *Auther v. The Atlantic*, Justice Campbell held that the sale of a vessel under a decree of a state court extinguished prior maritime liens under the general maritime law, thus excluding the federal court from proceeding further in admiralty.[106] The same position was taken two years later by Justice Curtis in the Circuit Court of Maine.[107]

In the federal courts in Michigan, however, an entirely different tack was taken. District Judge Wilkins, in deciding in favor of the purchaser under a sale by the district court against the purchaser under a prior sale by the state court, in a case in which the facts were similar to those in *The Royal Saxon*, held that proceedings *in rem* were peculiar to the admiralty courts and that whenever municipal law makes use of the remedy *in rem* against vessels, it comes in direct conflict with the constitutional admiralty and maritime jurisdiction of the United States. The state legislature, he stated, had no power to divest a lien existing in admiralty, and the possession of the vessel by the sheriff could not so divest the admiralty lien.[108] The decree was upheld by Justice McLean when the decision was brought before the circuit court on appeal. McLean's position was that the deciding factor was not the priority in time of one attachment against another but the priority in nature of the maritime lien over the domestic lien, which gave the paramount jurisdiction and disposition of the vessel to the admiralty court.[109]

Again, in *Ashbrook v. The Golden Gate*, the District Court of Missouri held that the state law governing liens could not interfere with the operation of the general maritime law and the jurisdiction of the admiralty courts. Here District Judge Wells, in a lengthy opinion, echoed the earlier conclusion of Judge Kane in *Wall v. The Royal Saxon*, to the effect that state court proceedings were *in personam* and that only admiralty and maritime proceedings in the courts of the United States could be *in rem.* Denying that there could exist a concurrent jurisdiction *in rem*, Wells insisted that the maritime lien could not be divested by the state law or the proceedings under it.[110] [111] And in *The N.W. Thomas*, Justice McLean, disapproving the decision in *Auther v. The Atlantic*,[112] held that a lien for seaman's wages was prior to a claim for supplies under the state law and upheld the decree of the district court ordering the sale of the vessel despite a prior sale under state law.[113]

The delicacy and complication arising from the conflict of jurisdictions is well-illustrated by the case of *The Gazelle.* This ship had been arrested by the sheriff under state process. Two weeks later the district court ordered the marshal to arrest the ship in a suit for seaman's wages. The sheriff refused to permit the marshal to take possession of the vessel, whereupon the marshal desisted. The district judge decided, therefore, that he could take no jurisdiction over the vessel, refusing to pass on the question of whether the marshal could have proceeded to execute the order of the court by force. Subsequently the ship was sold by the sheriff. The district judge then granted the motion of the libellant to issue another warrant to arrest the vessel which was now in the hands of the purchaser. The marshal thereupon arrested the ship which was sold by order of the district court. In reviewing the proceedings, Judge Sprague said: "Although the sheriff was permitted to hold possession of the vessel, until he had sold her on execution, and had terminated his custody by delivery to the purchaser, such sale and delivery did not divest or impair the lien of the libellants. The purchaser took the vessel *cum onere.*" Thus a direct clash between marshal and sheriff and federal court and state court was avoided at the same time that the court upheld the superiority of the paramount admiralty lien. Only the purchaser *cum onere* had to pay.[114]

Shortly afterward a similar case arose in the same court. Here Judge Sprague took the time to expand on his previous opinion and comment on the relationship between the two conflicting jurisdictions and laws. "The whole people of a state," he declared, "with all the sovereignty they possess, have no right to impair or impede such law, and can confer no power to do so upon any of its officers. Now the law which gives to a seaman a paramount right to wages, and the jurisdiction of the courts of the United States, authorized, as it is, by the express words of the Constitution, are universally admitted. How, then, can a subordinate state officer have a right to defeat or obstruct the enforcement of such law, under the authority of such courts? This would be going even beyond the doctrine of nullification."[115]

With the exception of *The Robert Fulton* and *The Oliver Jordan* and a handful of cases of a similar nature, none of which involved libels for seamen's wages, the tendency of the lower court decisions was to uphold the paramount claim of the admiralty court in conflicts of jurisdiction. But until 1858, no case had come before the Supreme Court for decision. In May of that year the case of *The Royal Saxon* finally reached the higher court under the title of *Taylor v. Carryl.* The result must have taken the legal profession by surprise, because one of the justices composing the five-man majority, Justice McLean, inexplicably sided with the position of Justice Campbell, which he had rejected only the year before on circuit.

Campbell, speaking for the majority, drew directly on the decisions of *The Robert Fulton* and *The Oliver Jordan* and *Hagan v. Lucas*[116] as well as the leading English case, *Paine v. Drew*, to conclude that the Supreme Court of Pennsylvania was correct in finding for the purchaser under the state sale and against Taylor. For the majority it was once more a simple matter of "first come-first served"; the question of the paramountcy of the admiralty lien was completely ignored. Put simply, the court decided that when a vessel had been seized under a process of attachment in a state court and was in the actual custody of the sheriff, no valid seizure could be made of her so as to give jurisdiction in proceedings *in rem* in the district court of the United States sitting in admiralty. Nor was any encouragement given to the procedure followed and approved by the district court in *The Gazelle*.[117] [118]

In a strong dissent by Chief Justice Taney, joined by three colleagues, the minority declared that the rule of *Hagan v. Lucas* was not applicable in a case where the two jurisdictions in conflict were not equal in standing. Carefully explaining that the conflict was not one between the federal courts as such and the state courts as such, Taney insisted that it was a question of the relative powers of an admiralty court and a common-law court. Where the admiralty lien—as in this case—was prior and paramount in nature, the state jurisdiction must yield even if the state had first attached the vessel. Taney repeated the thesis presented in several of the earlier lower court decisions, that only the admiralty proceeding could be *in rem*. To the argument that the serving of the process of the district court was an infringement on the rights of a different sovereignty, Taney replied that, "The Constitution of the United States is as much a part of the law of Pennsylvania as its own Constitution, and the laws passed by the general government pursuant to the Constitution are as obligatory upon the courts of the states as upon those of the United States; and they are equally bound to respect and uphold the acts and process of the courts of the United States, when acting within the scope of its legitimate authority."[119]

Notwithstanding the decision in this case, two years later

the District Court of Ohio held void a state judgment in a "quasi-admiralty proceeding *in rem*" on the ground that no state had the power to proceed *in rem* against a vessel. Although the facts in the case were different from those in *Taylor v. Carryl*, it is worthwhile noting that the decision in the latter case was not used as a license to further debilitate the powers of the federal admiralty courts.[120]

Finally, the case of *The Reindeer* partially vindicated Taney's position in the case of *The Royal Saxon.* The facts were simple: on January 26, 1861, an allegation was made that the ship was fitted out for the slave trade, in violation of an act of Congress of 1794. On July 20th the sheriff of Newport County, Rhode Island, attached the ship under the order of the state court. The United States Government then applied to the District Court of Rhode Island for an attachment, in a proceeding for forfeiture, notwithstanding the sheriff's prior seizure of the vessel. The marshal was ordered to seize the vessel, which action was upheld by the circuit court on the ground that forfeiture attaches at the time the wrongful act is committed and from that moment the owner is divested of his title, which becomes vested in the United States. Therefore, notwithstanding *Taylor v. Carryl*, the state attachment could not defeat the operation of the federal court proceedings.[121] [122]

In *Taylor v. Carryl*, Taney had attempted to draw a parallel between the privileged status of libels for mariners' wages and forfeiture proceedings, contending that if the latter would oust the jurisdiction of a state court proceeding, so would the former. Although Taney did not live to see a reversal of *Taylor v. Carryl*, the courts did nothing to extend the decision in that case. Thus, at Taney's death, there was still a considerable degree of confusion in this delicate area of conflict.

4. The State as Defendant: The Eleventh Amendment

The second section of Article III of the Constitution declared, among other things, that, "The judicial power shall extend to controversies between a State and citizens of another State." Section 13 of the Judiciary Act added: "The Supreme Court shall have exclusive jurisdiction of all controversies of a civil nature, where a state is a party, except between a state and its citizens; and except also between a state and citizens of other states, or aliens, in which latter case it shall have original but not exclusive jurisdiction."

The question involved in *Chisholm v. Georgia*[123], the first case to be decided by the Supreme Court, was whether it possessed jurisdiction over a suit initiated by a citizen of South Carolina against the State of Georgia. The answer, given in the form of individual opinions of the justices, though not unanimous, was affirmative. Justice Blair saw the issue as a simple matter of reading the Constitution. For him, the clause extending judicial power to controversies between a state and citizens of another state was equally intended to include controversies in which the state was the defendant. "If this Court should refuse to hold jurisdiction of a case where a state is a defendant," stated Blair, "it would renounce part of the authority conferred, and consequently part of the duty imposed on it by the Constitution."[124]

Justice Iredell, on the other hand, took another approach to the question of jurisdiction, and in so doing concluded that the State of Georgia could not be sued by a citizen of another state. In the earliest assertion on record of the doctrine of judicial restraint on the part of the Supreme Court, Iredell argued that the court had to receive its authority as to the manner of its proceeding, not from the Constitution alone but from Congress acting in accordance with the Constitution. The court was not free to interpret the extension of the word "controversy" as used in the Constitution but was bound by the directions of the legislature. Since Congress had not directed the court to issue writs in a case involving a private action for recovery of money against a State, the court was bound by "the principles and usages of law," namely, the common law. The part of the common law which applied here was that part which prescribed remedies against the crown.

This brought Iredell to the question of sovereignty. The crown could not be sued because it was sovereign. Were the states sovereign? Yes, contended Justice Iredell. "Every state in the Union, in every instance where its sovereignty has not been delegated to the United States, I consider to be as completely sovereign as the United States are, in respect to the powers surrendered. The United States are sovereign as to all the powers of government actually surrendered; each state in the Union is sovereign as to all the powers reserved. It must necessarily be so, because the United States have no claim to any authority but such as the states have surrendered to them."

Furthermore, argued Iredell, "A state does not owe its origin to the government of the United States, in the highest or in any of its branches. It was in existence before it. . .A state is altogether exempt from the jurisdiction of the courts of the United States, or from any other exterior authority, unless in the special instances where the general government has power derived from the Constitution itself."[125]

Employing Iredell's argument based on the sovereignty of the state, Justice Wilson reached a contrary conclusion. "Do the people of the United States form a nation?" asked Wilson. Yes, he replied. Is a state sovereign? No. "The citizens of Georgia, when they acted upon the large scale of the Union, as a part of the 'people of the United States,' did not surrender the supreme or sovereign power to that state; but, as to the purposes of the Union, retained it to themselves. As to the purposes of the Union, therefore, Georgia is not a sovereign state.

"Could the Constitution of the United States vest a jurisdiction over the State of Georgia?" Yes, he replied. The states were the work of the people and the people "could alter, as they pleased, their former work; to any given degree, they could diminish as well as enlarge it. Any or all of the former state powers they could extinguish or transfer." In short, "The Constitution ordained and established by those people, and. . .in particular by the people of Georgia, could vest jurisdiction or judicial power over those states and over the State of Georgia in particular."

And, continued Justice Wilson, the Constitution had done so. The people of the United States intended to bind the several states not only by the legislative power of the national government but by the executive power and the judicial power as well. It was incongruous "that any man or body of men, any person, natural or artificial, should be permitted to claim successfully an entire exemption from the jurisdiction of the national government."

Having countered Iredell's assertion of state sovereignty with the doctrine that sovereignty lies in the people, Wilson concluded: "But, in my opinion, this doctrine rests not upon the legitimate result of fair and conclusive deduction from the Constitution; it is confirmed, beyond all doubt, by the direct and explicit declaration of the Constitution itself. . .'The judicial power of the United States shall extend to controversies between a state and citizens of another state.'. . .Could this strict and appropriated language describe with more precise accuracy the cause now depending before this tribunal? Causes and not parties are weighed by justice in her equal scales; on the former, solely, her attention is fixed; to the latter she is, as she is painted, blind."[126]

Continuing Wilson's discussion of sovereignty, Chief Justice Jay outlined the historical genesis of that doctrine in the United States. "From the crown of Great Britain," he writes, "the sovereignty of their country passed to the people of it. . .The people, in their collective and national capacity, established the present Constitution. It is remarkable that in establishing it the people exercised their own rights and their own proper sovereignty, and, conscious of the plenitude of it, they declared with becoming dignity, 'We, the people of the United States, do ordain and establish this Constitution.' Here we see the people acting as sovereigns of the whole country, and, in the language of sovereignty, establishing a constitution by which it was their will that the state governments should be bound, and to which the state constitutions should be made to conform."

As to the suability of the State of Georgia, there is no doubt that one state may be sued by another state. Why, then, argues Jay, does it make any difference if one private citizen or one hundred thousand citizens acting through their state government initiate a suit against another state?

Furthermore, says Jay, since the Constitution is designed, among other things, to establish justice and insure domestic tranquility, the extension of the judicial power "to controversies between a state and citizens of another state" should not be understood in a limited sense but should be "construed liberally."

"It is politic, wise and good, that not only controversies in which a state is plaintiff, but also those in which a state is defendant, should be settled." Had the Constitution intended to exempt states from being sued by private citizens, the wording would have expressly exempted them. But the wording is unambiguous; there is no such exemption. Further, such an exemption would have violated the spirit of the Constitution which insures justice "to the few against the many, as well as to the many against the few."[127]

The direct and immediate consequence of the decision in *Chisholm v. Georgia* was the proposal, in 1794, and the ratification, in 1798, of the Eleventh Amendment[128] which reads:

"The judicial power of the United States shall not be construed to extend to any suit in law or equity, commenced or prosecuted against one of the United States by citizens of another state, or by citizens or subjects of any foreign state."

In dismissing the case of *Hollingsworth v. Virginia*, the Supreme Court held that the amendment being constitutionally adopted, they could not exercise any jurisdiction, in any case, past or future, in which a state was sued by the citizens of another state, or by citizens or subjects of any foreign state.[129]

The first case to come before the Supreme Court involving the interpretation and application of the Eleventh Amendment was one arising from a conflict of authority between the federal courts and the State of Pennsylvania. Ever since 1778, Gideon Olmstead had been trying to recover the prize money awarded to him for the capture of the sloop *Active* by the Court of Appeals in prize cases established by Congress during the war. This court had overruled an earlier verdict by the admiralty court of the State of Pennsylvania, which had awarded three-fourths of the prize to the officers of two other ships, one of which belonged to the State of Pennsylvania. The state, however, refused to abide by the decision of the Congressional Court and had placed the proceeds in the hands of the state treasurer, David Rittenhouse. It was not until 1803 that Judge Peters of the United States District Court of Pennsylvania decreed that the funds be paid over to Olmstead. The state refused to order the funds to be turned over and Judge Peters refrained from making any order to carry his decree into effect.

Six years later the case came before the Supreme Court on an application by Olmstead for a *mandamus* against Judge Peters. Before issuing the *mandamus*, the court examined the question of jurisdiction and the contention that the federal courts were deprived of jurisdiction by the Eleventh Amendment of the Constitution. Chief Justice Marshall, speaking for the court, held that the fact that a state has an interest in the subject matter of a suit between individuals, which it may choose to assert, does not oust the courts of the United States of jurisdiction.

"The right of a state to assert, as plaintiff, any interest it may have in a subject which forms the matter of controversy between individuals, in one of the courts of the United States, is not affected by this amendment," wrote Marshall, "nor can it be so construed as to oust the court of its jurisdiction, should such claim be suggested. The amendment simply provides that no suit shall be commenced or prosecuted against a state. The state cannot be made a defendant to a suit brought by an individual; but it remains the duty of the courts of the United States to decide all cases brought before them by citizens of one state against citizens of a different state, where a state is not necessarily a defendant."

The decision of the Court of Appeals of Congress had annulled the sentence of the state admiralty court and had thereby extinguished the interest of the State of Pennsylvania in the *Active*. The property was now in the possession of the executrixes of David Rittenhouse, as an individual, and not of the State of Pennsylvania.

"Since then," concluded Marshall, "the State of Pennsylvania had neither possession of nor right to the property on which the sentence of the district court was pronounced, and since the suit was neither commenced nor prosecuted against that state, there remains no pretext for the allegation that the case is within that amendment of the Constitution which has been cited; and, consequently, the State of Pennsylvania can possess no constitutional right to resist the legal process which may be directed in this cause."[130]

When the attempt of the United States Marshal to serve process issued by Judge Peters in accordance with the Supreme Court's mandate met with armed resistance on the part of state troops led by General Bright, the latter was brought before the United States Circuit Court for Pennsylvania, charged with resisting the laws of the United States. Once more, in that court, the questions of jurisdiction and the Eleventh Amendment were argued and decided.

Here Justice Washington said: "It is certain that the suit in the district court was not commenced or prosecuted against the State of Pennsylvania. She was in no respect a party to that suit. . .

"The state cannot be forced into court, but she may come there, if she pleases, in pursuit of her rights, and will no doubt do so upon all proper and necessary occasions. But if, on the other hand, the mere claim of interest by a state in the subject in dispute between two citizens can have the magic effect of suspending all the functions of a court of justice over that subject, and of annihilating its decrees when pronounced, this effective and necessary branch of our government, and of all free governments, may be rendered useless at any moment at the pleasure of a state. If the suit be prosecuted against a state, the court perceives at once its want of jurisdiction, and can dismiss the party at the threshold. But if a latent claim in the state, not known, perhaps, by any of the litigant parties, is sufficient to oust the jurisdiction, to annul the judgment when rendered, and to affect all the parties concerned, with the consequences of carrying a void judgment into execution, the federal courts may become more than useless; they will be traps in which unwary suitors may be insnared to their ruin.

"To illustrate this position the district attorney mentioned many very strong and very supposable cases. I will add one other. A sues B for a debt, or for property, either real or personal, in his possession. Conscious that he must pay the money or lose his possession in consequence of the unquestionable title of his adversary, B pays over the money, or conveys the property, even pending the suit, to a third person for the use of the state, and by this operation arrests the further progress of the suit, or avoids the judgment, whenever it shall pass. A doctrine so unjust, and big with consequences so alarming, and so fatal to the general government, should have strong and unequivocal words to support it. The court would be very mischievously employed in supplying them. We should convert this amendment, this sacrifice made to state pride, into an engine to demolish altogether one of the essential branches of the general government."[131] [132]

It was not until twelve years later that the Supreme Court was again called upon to give an interpretation of the Eleventh Amendment. In *Cohens v. Virginia*, after establishing the comprehensive principle that the Supreme Court has appellate jurisdiction over cases arising under laws of the United States even when one of the parties is a state, Chief Justice Marshall went on to examine the applicability of the Eleventh Amendment to the case. Noting that the original suit had been commenced by the state against an individual, Marshall held that the amendment was not a bar to the examination of a judgment against an individual who later had recourse to the appellate jurisdiction of the Supreme Court:

"If a suit, brought in one court, and carried by legal process to a supervising court, be a continuation of the same suit, then this suit is not commenced nor prosecuted against a state. It is clearly, in its commencement, the suit of a state against an individual, which suit is transferred to this court, not for the purpose of asserting any claim against the state, but for the purpose of asserting a constitutional defence against a claim made by a state."

To fortify his argument as well as to allay the fears of the states that their sovereignty was in danger, Marshall explained that the same procedure applied in suits initiated by the government of the United States, where writs of error had been issued for the removal to the Supreme Court of judgments in favor of the United States, on the motion of individual defendants: "It has never been suggested that such a writ of error was a suit against the United States and therefore not within the jurisdiction of the appellate court."[133]

The decision in *Cohens v. Virginia* was logical and in no way could be said to do violence to the spirit of the Eleventh Amendment. The decision in *Osborn v. United States Bank*, however, went far to circumvent the amendment and return things to the way they were at the time of the *Chisholm* case. This was a suit commenced by the United States Bank against officers[134] of the State of Ohio who had seized assets of the bank in accordance with the law of the state. The appellants contended that the real controversy was between the bank and the State of Ohio ("The interest of the state is direct and immediate, not consequential. The process of the court, though not directed against the state by name acts directly upon it, by restraining its officers. The process, therefore, is substantially, though not in form, against the state,") and that therefore the Eleventh Amendment was a bar to the suit.

The bank, however, contended that in all cases in which jurisdiction depended on the character of the party, reference is made to *the party on the record*, "not to one who may be interested, but is not shown by the record to be a party." Marshall readily adopted this argument and made it the basis of the court's opinion: "It may, we think, be laid down as a rule which admits of no exception, that in all cases where jurisdiction depends on the party, it is the party named in the record. Consequently the Eleventh Amendment, which restrains the jurisdiction granted by the Constitution over suits against states is, of necessity, limited to those suits in which a state is a party on the record."[135] [136]

In *Cohens v. Virginia*, the court had taken the wide ground that a case depending on the character of the cause was cognizable in the federal courts, whoever may be the parties, provided, of course, that jurisdiction had been given by Congress. Jurisdiction in the Osborn case rested on the Congressional act authorizing the Bank of the United States to sue in the federal courts. Under the rule of *Cohens*, then, it would seem that the federal court could have taken jurisdiction of the present case, even if the state had been a party to the case.[137] Was it necessary, then, for Marshall to demonstrate that the state was not a party on the record? Either way the *Osborn* opinion would seem to constitute a gratuitous invitation to litigants to circumvent the Eleventh Amendment: if a federal question was involved it was permissible to prosecute a suit directly against the state; if there was no federal question, the suit should be commenced against an officer of the state rather than the state itself.

It is no wonder then that Justice Johnson dissented on the question of jurisdiction. He argued that it was not averred that the case was one "arising under" a law of the United States and in fact was not such a case, and that the principle adopted by the majority would extend the jurisdiction of the court indefinitely.[138]

At the same term, the court also ruled that the fact that a state is one of the stockholders in a banking corporation does not prevent the corporation from being sued in the courts of the United States. "The state does not, by becoming a corporator, identify itself with the corporation," wrote Marshall. "The Planters' Bank of Georgia is not the State of Georgia, although the state holds an interest in it. It is, we think, a sound principle, that when a government becomes a partner in any trading company, it divests itself, so far as concerns the transactions of that company, of its sovereign character, and takes that of a private citizen."[139]

In *Governor of Georgia v. Madrazo*, the roles of the judges were reversed. Marshall held that where the governor of a state is sued, not by his name but in his official character, and the claim is made upon him solely by reason of his holding the office of governor, the suit is, in effect, against the state, which must be considered as the real party on the record, and therefore, under the Eleventh Amendment, cannot be sustained.[140]

If *Chisholm v. Georgia* was reversed by the Eleventh Amendment, still the amendment did not accomplish its intended purpose. Its apparently clear and broad coverage was restricted and diluted by the Marshall Court in the cases cited, especially in the *Osborn* case, and nothing was done during the Taney period to alter the earlier interpretation.

Furthermore, the amendment did nothing to settle the controversy over state sovereignty. That conflict was to burst forth time after time both within and without the court until a final decision was reached by arms.

One other case involving the state as defendant, but unrelated to the Eleventh Amendment, is worthy of mention. The Constitution extended the judicial power to controversies between two or more states and gave to the Supreme Court original jurisdiction over such cases. When Rhode Island sued Massachusetts over a disputed boundary, the question was whether the Supreme Court possessed jurisdiction over such a controversy.

The majority of the court, in an opinion written by Justice Baldwin, upheld the jurisdiction. "Though the Constitution does not, in terms, extend the judicial power to all controversies between two or more states," he wrote, "yet it in terms excludes none, whatever may be their nature or subject. . .'Controversies between two or more states,' 'all controversies of a civil nature, where a state is a party,' are broad comprehensive terms, by no obvious meaning or necessary implication excluding those which relate to the title, boundary, jurisdiction or sovereignty of a state."

Baldwin, examining the state of things at the time the Constitution was adopted, concluded that controversies between states other than those referring to boundaries were not contemplated—"and it would be a most forced construction to hold that these were excluded from judicial cognizance, and that it was to be confined to controversies to arise prospectively on other subjects." Further, if the judicial power could not settle such disputes, controversies over boundaries would be interminable and would necessarily lead to the submission of the weaker states to the stronger.

To the objection that the controversy was of a political rather than a civil nature, Baldwin replied that it was nothing more than the judicial determination of a geographic point, based on the interpretation of an agreement—a matter of an ordinary judicial nature.

The opinion concluded with a distinction between political and judicial powers and questions: "The former is that which a sovereign or state exerts by his or its own authority, as reprisal and confiscation; the latter is that which is granted to a court or judicial tribunal. So of controversies between states; they are in their nature political, when the sovereign or state reserves to itself the right of deciding on it; makes it the 'subject of a treaty, to be settled as between states independent,' or 'the foundation of representations from state to state.' This is political equity, to be adjudged by the parties themselves, as contra-distinguished from judicial equity administered by a court of justice, decreeing the *equum et bonum* of the case, let who or what be the parties before them."[141]

Nonetheless Taney dissented, insisting that the judicial power did not extend to suits merely involving "sovereignty and jurisdiction," rather than the title to land or rights of property in the soil. "Contests for rights of sovereignty and jurisdiction between states over any particular territory," wrote the Chief Justice, "are not, in my judgment, the subjects of judicial cognizance and control, to be recovered and enforced in an ordinary suit, and are, therefore, not within the grant of judicial power contained in the Constitution."[142] Taney's dissent is consistent with his position in *Pennsylvania v. The Wheeling Bridge Co.*,[143] even if at odds with his general philosophy of comprehensive jurisdiction.

5. *Following State Court Decisions*

The 34th section of the Judiciary Act provided, "That the laws of the several states, except where the Constitution, treaties or statutes of the United States shall otherwise require or provide, shall be regarded as rules of decision in trials at common law in the courts of the United States where they apply."

The logic of this provision was clear: to prevent the development of conflicting constructions of the same law. But before the federal courts could apply the construction given by the state, it was necessary to establish the criteria for determining what that construction was.

The first time that such a problem arose, Chief Justice

Marshall, without referring explicitly to Section 34, admitted that were the act of the State of Pennsylvania in question to be construed for the first time, the Supreme Court would place a different interpretation on it than that given by the courts of the state; but that the court would yield to the construction of the state courts because, "in construing the statutes of a state, on which land titles depend, infinite mischief would ensue, should this court observe a different rule from that which has been long established in the state."[144]

In a case before the Circuit Court of Pennsylvania, Justice Washington, in an *obiter dictum*, interpreted Section 34 to refer both to state laws in force prior to the Judiciary Act as well as to laws passed subsequently.[145]

In *Polk's Lessee v. Wendall*, the Supreme Court held: "In cases depending on the statutes of a state, and more especially in those respecting titles to land, this court adopts the construction of the state *where that construction is settled* and can be ascertained."[146] Again, in *Mutual Assurance Society v. Watt's Executors*, the court held: "This court uniformly acts under the influence of a desire to conform its decisions to those of the state courts on their local laws."[147]

But in *Campbell v. Claudius*, a case before the Circuit Court of Pennsylvania, Justice Washington declared that the state laws have no binding effect in the federal courts as to remedies.[148]

It was not until 1823 that the members of the Supreme Court disagreed among themselves as to the application of Section 34. In *Daly's Lessee v. James*, the majority decided to defer to the decision of the Supreme Court of Pennsylvania on the basis of that court's disposition of a single case.[149] Justice Johnson, however, dissented, with the following statement: "As precedents entitled to high respect, the decisions of the state courts will always be considered; and in all cases of local law, we acknowledge an established and uniform course of decisions of the state courts, in the respective states, as the law of this court; that is to say, that such decisions will be as obligatory upon this court as they would be acknowledged to be in their own courts. But a single decision on the construction of a will cannot be acknowledged as of binding efficacy, however it may be respected as a precedent."[150]

On the other hand Johnson, speaking for the court in the case of *Shelby v. Guy*, recognized that the federal courts must defer to the "fixed and received construction" of statute laws in each state, even if the Supreme Court doubted the propriety of that construction and even if this rule would lead the Supreme Court into accepting different constructions where the same statute had been adopted by several states, whose courts might differ in construing the statute.[151]

In the following year, the court held that the reference to "the laws of the several states," in Section 34, was not limited to statute law but included the common law as well, and that the Supreme Court must defer to the state's construction of its own common law.[152]

A more difficult problem was presented in *Neal v. Green.* In 1816, in *Patton's Lessee v. Easton*, the Supreme Court had adopted the construction of a state law based on decisions which had been made in the state court. Subsequently, the state court revised its opinion and gave a different construction to the same statute. The Circuit Court of Tennessee held that in the present case it should employ the construction given by the Supreme Court of the United States, at least until the question could be reviewed by the latter court.[153]

On appeal to the Supreme Court, the question was raised whether it should adhere to its own previous decision or yield to the more recent opinion of the tribunals of Tennessee. One argument was that once the Supreme Court had accepted a construction given by the state court and had conformed its own decisions to those of the state, the construction must be considered final, lest there be recognized a power in the state courts to revise the decisions of the Supreme Court. The contrary position was that the judicial exposition given by the state must be the deciding factor and should not be disregarded even if it involved a change in interpretation.

Reversing the judgment of the circuit court, McLean held

that the Supreme Court must conform its decisions to the settled law of the State at the time the decision is made. "The same reason which influences this court to adopt the construction given to the local law, in the first instance," wrote McLean, "is not less strong in favor of following it in the second, if the state tribunals should change the construction. . .The inquiry is, what is the settled law of the state at the time the decision is made. . .As the federal tribunals profess to be governed by this rule, they can never act inconsistently by enforcing it. If they change their decision, it is because the rule on which that decision was founded has been changed."[154] [155]

Following the decision in *Green v. Neal's Lessee* and *United States v. Morrison*[156]—where the Supreme Court ordered the circuit court to reverse its judgment and conform to an interpretation of a state law given by the state tribunal after the circuit court judgment had been made—the federal courts were (temporarily) wary of anticipating the decisions of the state courts. Thus in *Springer v. Foster*, Justice Story held that the Circuit Court of Massachusetts would reserve judgment on the construction of a state law until it had been decided by the state court where the very point in question was then pending.[157]

At the same time, the Supreme Court began to examine the constructions of the state tribunals with greater care. In *Groves v. Slaughter*, Justice Thompson pointed out that it was necessary to look into the state court decisions, "to see whether there has been such a fixed and settled construction given to the constitution [of the state] as to preclude this court from considering it an open question." In this case, the court held that the construction of the state constitution was still an open question because the only case relied on was one in which the two judges of the state court were divided in opinion.[158]

Perhaps the most difficult and controversial decision made by the court under Section 34 was that of *Swift v. Tyson:* difficult because it is hard to determine just how far Justice Story's opinion was meant to reach; controversial because the decision is still being debated.[159] The only thing which is quite clear is that Story held that the 34th section of the

Judiciary Act did not apply to the construction of contracts or to questions of general commercial law. These questions were ones for the federal courts to determine in accordance with "the general principles and doctrines of commercial jurisprudence," which went beyond "the laws of the several states" and were, therefore, not dependent on the decisions of state tribunals.

In order to reach this decision, however, Story was forced to state the dubious conclusion that the words—"laws of the several States"—did not include the decisions of the local tribunals. "In the ordinary use of language," said Story, "it will hardly be contended that the decisions of courts constitute laws. They are, at most, only evidence of what the laws are, and are not themselves laws. . .The laws of a state are more usually understood to mean the rules and enactments promulgated by the legislative authority thereof, or long-established local customs having the force of laws."

"In all the various cases which have hitherto come before us for decision," Story continued, "this court has uniformly supposed that the true interpretation of the thirty-fourth section limited its application to state laws strictly local, that is to say, to the positive statutes of the state, and the construction thereof adopted by the local tribunals, and to the rights and titles to things having a permanent locality, such as the rights and titles to real estate, and other matters immovable and intraterritorial in their nature and character."[160]

Now, in a certain sense it is true that the Supreme Court had always been fastidious about extending the operation of state law beyond the territory of the state,[161] and it was perhaps justifiable to strive for a federal judge-made commercial law in preference to a series of conflicting decisions made by the state tribunals; but the question remained whether Story's reading of Section 34 was correct. In *Jackson v. Chew*, the court upheld the decisions of state tribunals in cases growing out of the common law, while in *Shelby v. Guy* the court was willing to suffer the charge of inconsistency in its desire to give the benefit of the doubt to the states in the application of Section 34. Further, and perhaps of greater importance, Story's distinction between state court decisions on local law (which he accepted) and state court decisions on commercial law (which he rejected) is nowhere to be found in Section 34 itself.[162]

However Section 34 emerged from *Swift v. Tyson*, the practical effects of the decision were unambiguous. Thus in *Carpenter v. Providence Washington Insurance Co.*, the court held that questions of general commercial law concerning the construction and legal effect of a contract of insurance, were not local in their character and that therefore the Supreme Court was not bound by the decisions of the state courts thereon. [163]

From now on the going began to get heavier for the state tribunals. During the 1845 term the Supreme Court declared both that a rule of property could be settled by a single case[164] and could not be settled by a single case.[165] A strong dissent was filed in the latter case by Justice McKinley, who held that the federal courts must defer to the construction of the state tribunals, regardless of whether the rule had been settled by frequent decisions or a single one.[166]

A further whittling away of positions taken earlier occurred in *Rowan v. Runnels*, a case revolving around the same article of the constitution of Mississippi which applied in *Groves v. Slaughter.* Here, ignoring the court's decision in *Green v. Neal's Lessee*, the majority held that its ruling in the *Groves* case was still law even if the state tribunals had meanwhile given a different interpretation to the state constitution. "We can hardly be required," said Taney, "by any comity or respect for the state courts, to surrender our judgment to decisions since made in the state, and declare contracts to be void which upon full consideration we have pronounced to be valid."[167] Taney's preoccupation was to protect the validity of contracts entered into on the strength of the Supreme Court's previous decision against being annulled retroactively by the subsequent decisions of the state courts. It is not clear, however, what the court would have decided had the contract been made after the state court ruling had been handed down, nor is the decision in this case reconciled with that of *Green v. Neal's Lessee.* The confusion of the lower federal courts might well be imagined when in the *Green* case they were overruled for adhering to the Supreme Court's judgment, while in the Rowan case they were reversed for not adhering to it.

Justice Daniel dissented from the opinion of the court. Holding that the decisions of the Supreme Court of Mississippi were "familiar, unequivocal, uniform, numerous," he contended: "That any or all of these expositions may have been made posterior to the decision of the cause of *Groves v. Slaughter*, I hold to be perfectly immaterial, insofar as this circumstance can affect their force and validity. If these expositions establish the meaning of the constitution of Mississippi, such meaning must have relation to the period of the consummation of that instrument. The Constitution has always been the same thing from the time of its adoption."[168] True as this statement may be, Daniel ignored the majority's unwillingness to accept a doctrine of "the contractor beware," when the contract had been made on the strength of the Supreme Court's interpretation of the validity of the constitutional provision rather than on the provision itself, pure and simple. To have deferred to the state tribunal here would have been to mislead the contracting parties.

That the sanctity of contract underlay the decision in *Rowan v. Runnels* is further affirmed by the court's unanimous opinion in *Nesmith v. Sheldon*, upholding the state court interpretation of a state statute against a prior circuit court interpretation, where the question of contract was not involved. Here, the rule of *Green v. Neal's Lessee* was once more followed.[169]

In *Williamson v. Berry*, the Supreme Court again chose to follow its own judgment rather than that of the Supreme Court of the State of New York, in a question of the jurisdiction of the state court of chancery under a private act of the state legislature. On the narrow ground that the decision of the state court concerned only the party for whose benefit such a law was passed and therefore could not become a rule for other cases, the majority of the court held that Section 34 did not apply.[170]

Nelson, joined by Catron and Taney, dissented. For them

the question of jurisdiction was, like other matters of local law, one which belonged to the courts of the state to expound and settle; and when so settled, "it becomes a rule of decision for the federal courts sitting in the state, and administering her laws."[171]

Piqua Branch v. Knoop[172] presented the court with a problem somewhat similar to that which arose in *Rowan v. Runnels.* Under a law of 1845 a charter had been given by the State of Ohio to the State Bank, limiting the rate at which the latter was to be taxed in the future. In accordance with earlier decisions of the state court of Ohio such a stipulation was considered to be consonant with the constitution of the state. Subsequently, a new statute established a different and more costly method of taxation. The Supreme Court of Ohio upheld the validity of the latter statute, on the ground that the constitution of the State prohibited the state legislature from tying up the hands of subsequent legislatures in the exercise of its taxing powers. The bank appealed to the Supreme Court of the United States on the ground that the obligation of its contract had been impaired.

A majority of the court held that, in effect, a contract had been entered into between the state and the bank and that the second statute was an unconstitutional impairment of the contract. To the argument that the Supreme Court must defer to the state court in the interpretation of the constitution of the state, the majority presented two answers: first, the Supreme Court adopts the *settled* construction of the state constitution, existing when a contract is made and acquiesed in by all branches of the government and rejects a more recent decision made by the highest court of the State subsequent to the contract; and, secondly, the Supreme Court reserves to itself "the final authority to determine whether a contract existed, the nature of its obligations, and whether a state law has impaired these obligations."[173] Thus, in questions involving the Constitution of the United States—certainly in cases involving contracts—the Supreme Court, not the state court, was to determine the meaning as well as the validity of both state laws and state constitutions.

The opinion of the court was by no means unanimous. Justices Catron and Campbell filed separate dissents, Daniel concurring with the latter. Catron ignored completely the rule in *Rowan v. Runnels* (to which Daniel had earlier dissented) and the ultimate right of the Supreme Court to decide questions involving the obligation of contracts. For Catron, the latest state court interpretation of the state constitution was all that was necessary to know.[174]

In *Ohio Life Insurance Co. v. Debolt*, decided at the same term, six different opinions were filed. By a 5-4 majority the court affirmed the judgment of the state court that there was no impairment of the obligation of contract in the case before it. Chief Justice Taney's opinion (concurred in by Grier) was composed of six points, only the last of which—whether there was a contract or not—received the support of the other justices making up the majority. On his first five points, which did not decide the case but discussed general questions, Taney received the support of Grier and three of the justices who formed the minority in the final disposition of the case.[175]

The third of these questions was how to resolve the conflicting decisions of state courts concerning the construction of their own constitution and laws. Here Taney wrote: "When the constitution of a state, for nearly half a century, has received one uniform and unquestioned construction by all the departments of the government, legislative, executive, and judicial, I think it must be regarded as the true one. It is true that this court always follows the decision of the state courts in the construction of their own constitution and laws. But where those decisions are in conflict, this court must determine between them."

The court, continued Taney, must adopt the construction of the state constitution which it received from the state authorities at the time the contract was made. "It was upon this ground that the court sustained contracts made in good faith in the State of Mississippi, under an existing construction of its own constitution, although a subsequent and contrary construction, given by the courts of the state, would have made such contracts illegal and void." *Rowan v.*

Runnels was confined to contracts made with citizens of other states, "but the principle applies with equal force to all contracts which come within its jurisdiction.

"The sound rule," concluded Taney, "is, that if the contract when made was valid by the laws of the state, as then expounded by all the departments of its government, and administered in its courts of justice, its validity cannot be impaired by any subsequent act of the legislature of the state, or decision of its courts, altering the construction of the law."[176]

Pease v. Peck demonstrates how far the court had wandered from *Green v. Neal's Lessee.* Justice Grier, speaking for the court, said: "In all cases where there is a settled construction of the laws of a state, by its highest judicature, established by admitted precedent, it is the practice of the courts of the United States to receive and adopt it without criticism or further inquiry. But when this court has first declared a question arising under state laws, we do not feel bound to surrender our convictions on a contrary subsequent decision of a state court. . .When the decisions of the state court are not consistent, we do not feel bound to follow the last, if it is contrary to our own convictions—and much more is this the case where, after a long course of consistent decisions, some new light suddenly springs up, or an excited public opinion has elicited new doctrines, subversive of former safe precedent. Cases may exist also, when a cause is got up in a state court for the very purpose of anticipating our decision of a question known to be pending in this court. Nor do we feel bound in any case in which a point is first raised in a circuit court, to reverse that decision contrary to our own convictions, in order to conform to a state decision made in the meantime. Such decisions have not the character of established precedent declarative of the settled law of a state."[177]

Perhaps the most important case in which a state law was regarded as a rule of decision in a federal court was the Dred Scott case. But here, despite an unsettled course, the majority of the court found no difficulty in adopting the most recent decisions of the Supreme Court of Missouri as the unquestioned exposition of the state law on the status of slaves. "We are satisfied," said the Chief Justice, "upon a careful examination of all the cases decided in the state courts of Missouri referred to, that it is now firmly settled by the decisions of the highest court in the state, that Scott and his family upon their return were not free but were, by the laws of Missouri, the property of the defendant."[178]

Justice Nelson, in a separate opinion, held that "the settled course of decision, at the time this case was tried" was to be considered the law of the state. "Certainly it must be," he continued, "unless the first decision of a principle of law by a state court is to be permanent and irrevocable. The idea seems to be that the courts of a State are not to change their opinions or, if they do, the first decision is to be regarded by this court as the law of the state." Nelson, however, contended that in only one case in the state courts had a slave who had been brought temporarily into a free territory been granted freedom by the court, and that decision had not been followed in subsequent decisions.[179]

It is interesting to compare Nelson's "settled course of decision, at the time the case was tried" with the rule in *Pease v. Peck* or Taney's opinion in the *Ohio Life Insurance* case, involving contract, where the decisive point was not what rule prevailed at the time the case came to trial but what rule prevailed at the time the contract was made. The crucial point here is that the Supreme Court did not yield to the state courts in cases involving contracts alleged to be impaired, because it retained a supervisory role under the contract clause, but yielded on questions of real and personal property (which comprehended slaves) where no constitutional prohibition on state action existed.

Justice McLean, dissenting, cited a series of Missouri court decisions dating from 1824 to 1836 where freedom had been granted to slaves under similar circumstances. He also referred to the strong dissent of Chief Justice Gamble of the Missouri Supreme Court in *Dred Scott v. Emerson.*[180] "These decisions," wrote McLean, "which come down to the year 1837, seemed to have so fully settled the question, that since that time there has been no case bringing it before the court for any reconsideration, until the present. . .When Dred

Scott, his wife and children, were removed from Fort Snelling to Missouri, in 1838, they were free, *as the law was then settled*, and continued for fourteen years afterwards, up to 1852, when the above decision was made. . .Such was the settled law of Missouri until the decision of Scott and Emerson.[181]

"And does such a case constitute a rule of decision for this court—a case to be followed by this court?" McLean continued. "The course of decision so long and so uniformly maintained established a comity or law between Missouri and the free states and territories where slavery was prohibited, which must be somewhat regarded in this case. Rights sanctioned for twenty-eight years ought not and cannot be repudiated with any semblance of justice, by one or two decisions, influenced, as declared, by a determination to counteract the excitement against slavery in the free states."[182]

McLean concludes: "I am strongly inclined to think that a rule of decision so well settled as not to be questioned, cannot be annulled by a single decision of the court. Such rights may be inoperative under the decision in the future; but I cannot well perceive how it can have the same effect in prior cases."[183]

Justice Curtis applied an entirely different criterion to the problem in his own separate dissent. For him, the question was not what had been determined by the state court of Missouri or whether any settled construction of state law existed, but what were the convictions of the justices of the Supreme Court of the United States. For Curtis, the question did not depend on any statute or local usage but on the rules of international law and the principles of universal jurisprudence and, therefore, the Supreme Court was not bound by the decisions of the state court on the subject. "Sitting here to administer the law between these parties," Curtis wrote, "I do not feel at liberty to surrender my own convictions of what the law requires, to the authority of the decision in 15 Missouri Reports."[184] This case, declared Curtis, in effect, went beyond the borders of the State of Missouri and should be governed by *Swift v. Tyson.*

As if in reply to McLean, Justice Grier, in a case decided

in the Circuit Court of Pennsylvania during the same year, stated that the court, on questions relating to real estate, would not examine the conflicts of construction or concern itself with a comparison of the respect due the majority and minority opinions of the state court, but would take the law "as it appears to be settled by the last decision, without entering upon the question whether on true principles it was rightly or wrongly decided."[185]

In *Morgan v. Curtenius*, however, the Supreme Court virtually overturned the decision in *Green v. Neal's Lessee* when it held that a change in the position of a state court in regard to a statute, pending a writ of error from the circuit court to the Supreme Court, could not work to make erroneous what had been rightly decided in the circuit court.[186]

Again, the Circuit Court of Ohio held that the obligation of the federal courts to follow the state laws as rules of decision was limited to cases at law, and did not apply to a circuit court of the United States when sitting as a court of chancery. "The circuit court of the United States, sitting in chancery," said District Judge Willson, "is governed by the principles and usages of equity as peculiar to themselves and as contra-distinguished from courts of common law."[187]

Lest there remain any doubt regarding the Supreme Court's independent power to examine for itself the construction of statutes when called upon to decide whether a legislative act created a contract, the court held, in *Jefferson Branch Bank v. Skelly*, that in every case where a subsequent statute is asserted to impair the obligation of a contract found in a former statute, it is necessary to decide independently of the state court on the existence of a contract in the first statute.[188]

Unfortunately, the last two cases to be decided by the Taney Court, involving *the authority* to be given to the decisions of the state courts, still left the problem unresolved. In *Leffingwell v. Warren*, after stating that, "The construction given to a statute of a state by the highest judicial tribunal of such state is regarded as a part of the statute, and is as binding upon the courts of the United States as the text." Justice Swayne, the spokesman for the court, held: "If the highest judicial tribunal of a state adopts new views as to the proper construction of such a statute and reverses its former decisions, this court will follow the latest settled adjudications."[189]

This return to the doctrines of *United States v. Morrison* and *Green v. Neal's Lessee* was short-lived and merely apparent, for in *Gelpcke v. City of Dubuque*, decided the following year, the majority of the court followed the line of decisions since *Rowan v. Runnels.*

The case involved the validity of bonds subscribed to by a municipality in accordance with the state constitution. From 1853 until 1859 the state courts of Iowa had held that the constitution permitted municipal corporations to subscribe to the bonds of railroads extending beyond the limits of the city or county. In the latter year, however, the Supreme Court of Iowa reversed its position, in *The State of Iowa v. The County of Wapello.* Upholding the validity of the bonds, the Supreme Court of the United States ruled that the fact that the state court had now decided that its earlier decisions were erroneous could have no effect upon transactions carried out prior to the Wapello decision, however it might affect future transactions.

Justice Swayne, again speaking for the court, pointed out that the key words in the *Leffingwell v. Warren* decision were "the latest *settled* adjudications." Without determining whether or not the present case fell within that rule, Swayne declared: "It cannot be expected that this court will follow every such oscillation, from whatever cause arising, that may possibly occur. . .We are not unmindful of the importance of uniformity in the decisions of this court, and those of the highest local courts, giving constructions to the laws and constitutions of their own states. It is the settled rule of this court in such cases to follow the decisions of the state courts. But there have been heretofore, in the judicial history of this court, as doubtless there will be hereafter, many exceptional cases."[190]

Justice Miller, dissenting, declared that the principle on which the court rested its decision was one which in the present case went "a step in advance of anything heretofore ruled by it on the subject," and that the court "has taken a position which must bring it into direct and unseemly conflict with the judiciary of the states."

The majority of the court, wrote Miller, "have said to the federal court sitting in Iowa, 'You shall disregard this decision of the highest court of the state on this question. Although you are sitting in the State of Iowa and administering her laws, and construing her constitution, you shall not follow the latest, though it be the soundest, exposition of its constitution by the supreme court of that State, but you shall decide directly to the contrary; and where that court has said that a statute is unconstitutional, you shall say that it is constitutional.'...

"Thus we are to have two courts, sitting within the same jurisdiction, deciding upon the same rights, arising out of the same statute, yet always arriving at opposite results, with no common arbiter of their differences.

"The Supreme Court of Iowa," continued Miller, "is not the first or the only court which has changed its ruling on questions as important as the one now presented. I understand the doctrine to be in such cases not that the law is changed, but that it was always the same as expounded by the later decision, and that the former decision was not and never had been the law, and is overruled for that very reason. The decision of this court contravenes this principle, and holds that the decision of the court makes the law, and in fact, that the same statute or constitution means one thing in 1853, and another thing in 1859."

Then Justice Miller, warming up to his argument, attempted to strike down the distinction made by the majority between rules of property and matters of contract: "If the deed by which a man supposes he has secured to himself and family a homestead, fails to comply in any essential particular with the statute or constitution of the state, as expounded by the most recent decision of the state court, it is held void by this court without hesitation, because it is a rule of property, and the last decision of the state court must govern, even to overturning the well-considered construction of this court. But if a gambling stockbroker of Wall Street buys at twenty-five per cent of their par value the bonds issued to a railroad company in Iowa, although the court of the state, in several of its most recent decisions, has decided that such bonds were issued in violation of the Constitution, this court will not follow that decision but resort to some former one, delivered by a divided court, because in the latter case it is not a rule of property, but a *case of contract.* I cannot rid myself of the conviction that the deed which conveys to a man his homestead, or other real estate, is as much a contract as the paper issued by a municipal corporation to a railroad for its worthless stock, and that a bond when good and valid is property. . .

"And when the construction of a constitution is brought to bear upon the questions of property or no property, contract or no contract, I can see no sound reason for any difference in the rule for determining the question.

"I think I have sustained, by this examination of the cases,"[191] wrote Miller in conclusion, "the assertion made in the commencement of this opinion that the court has, in this case, taken a step in advance of anything heretofore decided by it on this subject. That advance is in the direction of a usurpation of the right which belongs to the State courts, to decide as a finality upon the construction of state constitutions and state statutes. This invasion is made in a case where there is no pretense that the constitution, as thus construed, is any infraction of the laws or Constitution of the United States."[192]

But this was precisely the point which the majority insisted was the justification of the Supreme Court's intromission in the case. The municipal bonds were, in effect, in the nature of a contract, the obligation of which had been impaired not by the legislature but by the judiciary of the State. Five years later, Justice Swayne, in *Butz v. Muscatine*, stated: "This right can no more be taken away by *subsequent judicial decisions* than by subsequent legislation. It is as much within the sphere of our power and duties to protect the contract from the former as from the latter."[193]

Thus we have seen that Section 34 proved to be one of the most difficult and delicate provisions of the Judiciary Act to carry into effect. From a naive acceptance of state laws, as interpreted by state courts, the Supreme Court gradually developed a highly sophisticated rule which was as wont to ignore the state courts as to stretch exceptions to deferring to them. Swayne's "immolation" and Miller's "usurpation" may both have been exaggerations, but they underlay the vital differences in judicial philosophy regarding the appropriate spheres of the conflicting state and federal jurisdictions.

CHAPTER FOUR

Footnotes:

[1] See Chapter Two, pp. 49-51, above.

[2] See Chapter Two, pp. 94-96, above.

[3] Italics added.

[4] Strictly speaking, Section 25 cases came before the Supreme Court on a writ of error, which limited the higher court to the examination of errors of law on the record—and only those related to the questions enumerated in Section 25.

[5] *Olney v. Arnold,* 3 Dallas 308 (1796).

[6] *Clerke v. Harwood,* 3 Dallas 342 (1797). See Warren, I. p. 444, note.

[7] *Calder v. Bull,* 3 Dallas 386 (1798).

[8] *Hallet v. Jenks,* 3 Cranch 210 (1805).

[9] *Gordon v. Caldcleugh,* 3 Cranch 268 (1806).

[10] 7 Cranch 164 (1812).

[11] 7 Cranch 589 (1813).

[12] 7 Cranch 603 (1813).

[13] Chapter Two, pp. 49-51 ff. and Chapter Five, pp. 212-214, below.

[14] The final clause in Section 25 reads: "But no other error shall be assigned or regarded as a ground of reversal in any such case as aforesaid, than such as appears on the face of the record, and immediately respects the before-mentioned questions of validity or construction of the said constitution, treaties, statutes, commissions, or authorities in dispute."

[15] *Martin v. Hunter's Lessee*, 1 Wheaton 304 (1816).

[16] 2 Wheaton 363 (1817).

[17] 3 Wheaton 433 (1818).

[18] 4 Wheaton 311 (1819). See *Crowell v. Randall*, p. 144, below.

[19] 4 Wheaton 311 (1819).

[20] 4 Wheaton 518 (1819).

[21] 5 Wheaton 1 (1820).

[22] 6 Wheaton 264 (1821).

[23] 9 Wheaton 1 (1824).

[24] 12 Wheaton 419 (1827).

[25] See Chapter Two, p. 51, and Chapter Five, p. 214, for discussion in this case of appellate jurisdiction in general.

[26] *Buel v. Van Ness*, 8 Wheaton 312 (1823).

[27] 12 Wheaton 117 (1827).

[28] 12 Wheaton 129 (1827).

[29] 2 Peters 245 (1829).

[30] 2 Peters 380 (1829).

[31] *Weston v. Charleston*, 2 Peters 449 (1829). This interpretation was cited with approval by Taney in *Holmes v. Jennison*, 5 Peters 540; 561-568 (1840). See below, pp. 146-148.

[32] Dissent of Johnson, *op. cit.*, 2 Peters 47-472.

[33] 4 Peters 410 (1830).

[34] 4 Peters 451-452 (1830).

[35] 5 Peters 505 (1831).

[36] 6 Peters 515 (1832).

[37] Concurring opinion of McLean, *op. cit.*, 6 Peters 567.

[38] See Chapter Five, pp. 209-10, below.

[39] *New Orleans v. Armas,* 9 Peters 223 (1835). Italics added. In this particular case, however, the court dismissed the writ of error on finding that the title set up by the plaintiff was not protected by treaty.

[40] *Crowell v. Randall,* 10 Peters 368 (1836).

[41] See p. 138, above.

[42] *Charles River Bridge v. Warren Bridge,* 11 Peters 420 (1837).

[43] Dissent of McLean, 11 Peters 582-583. A similar position was taken by Justice Grier in his dissent to jurisdiction in *Bridge Proprietors v. Hoboken Co.,* 1 Wallace 116 (1864).

[44] McLean was preoccupied with the flood of cases which might be brought before the Supreme Court, as well as the need for mutual forbearance between the federal and the state tribunals. Cf. *Mills v. St. Clair County,* 8 Howard 569 (1850).

[45] *Commonwealth Bank of Kentucky v. Griffith,* 14 Peters 56 (1840). Affirmed in *Walker v. Taylor,* 5 Howard 64 (1847).

[46] 11 Peters 257 (1837).

[47] See Chapter Two, p. 61 and Chapter Six, pp. 281-283 ff.

[48] Only eight justices took part in this case.

[49] Opinion of Taney, *Holmes v. Jennison,* 14 Peters 540; 561-568 (1840).

[50] Opinion of Baldwin, *op cit.,* 14 Peters 620-633.

[51] Opinion of Catron, 14 Peters 597.

[52] 16 Peters 97 (1842). See Chapter Three, pp. 112 and 128, where this remedy was respectively approved and disapproved by circuit courts. In the latter case; *Hough v. Western Transporation Co.,* 12 FC 581 (1864), District Judge Drummond refers to the suggestion of McLean as a "mere *dictum.*"

[53] 16 Peters 435 (1842).

[54] 16 Peters 539 (1842).

[55] 5 Howard 504 (1847).

[56] 7 Howard 284 (1849).

[57] 16 Peters 281 (1842).

[58] 5 Howard 51 (1847).

[59] 5 Howard 343 (1847).

[60] *Op. cit.* pp. 374 ff. Justice McLean dissented. Inexplicably, four years later the court took jurisdiction of a case of a similar nature on a writ of error to the Supreme Court of Texas. It is not clear why the court did not deny jurisdiction when they themselves admitted that the 25th section conferred no power to annul the laws passed before Texas became a state. *League v. De Young,* 11 Howard 185 (1851). However, in a third case, *Miners' Bank v. State of Iowa,* 12 Howard 1 (1852), the writ of error was dismissed.

[61] 10 Howard 82 (1851). Justice Nelson based his argument in the Dred Scott case on the precedent of this case, a somewhat weak base, since by dismissing the case for want of jurisdiction the court did not consider the merits.

[62] 10 Howard 402 (1851).

[63] *Op. cit.,* 10 Howard 419.

[64] See p. 144, above.

[65] 12 Howard 165 (1852).

[66] *Maxwell v. Newbold,* 18 Howard 511 (1856).

[67] 1 Wallace 116 (1864).

[68] 12 Howard 299 (1852).

[69] 16 Howard 369 (1854).

[70] 16 Howard 416 (1854).

[71] 20 Howard 583 (1858).

[72] 21 Howard 506 (1859). See Chapter Two, pp. 94-96 and p. 156, below, for more on this case.

[73] 4 Cranch 179 (1807).

[74] *Ex parte Bollman,* 4 Cranch 97 (1807).

[75] 5 Cranch 115; 136 (1809). See Chapter Two, p. 44.

[76] *Babcock v. Weston,* Case 703, 2 FC 306 (1812).

[77] *McKim v. Voorhies,* 7 Cranch 279 (1812).

[78] 9 Peters 329; 359 (1835). Affirmed in *Keary v. Farmers Bank,* 16 Peters 89 (1842).

[79] *Hagan v. Lucas,* 10 Peters 400 (1836). See reference to this case in *Taylor v. Carryl,* below, p. 164.

[80] 13 Peters 136 (1839). See reference to this case in *Campbell v. Emerson,* Case 2,357, 4 FC 1162 (1839).

[81] 1 Howard 301 (1843).

[82] 3 Howard 103 (1845).

[83] *Atkinson v. Purdy,* Case 616, 2 FC 112 (1844).

[84] Case 14,065, 23 FC 1313 (1845), Story.

[85] 3 Howard 292; 318 (1845).

[86] 7 Howard 612; 624-626 (1850). See Warren II, pp. 182-185.

[87] Case 16,915, 28 FC 1147 (1850), District Court, S.D. New York.

[88] Case 12,008, 20 FC 1111 (1852), Circuit Court Ohio.

[89] Case 2,513, 5 FC 286 (1854), Circuit Court, Massachusetts.

[90] Case 12,209, 21 FC 136 (1854).

[91] 17 Howard 471 (1855).

[92] *Bell v. Ohio Life & Trust Co.,* Case 1,260, 3 FC 110 (1858).

[93] This *modus operandi* is reminiscent of the circumstances surrounding the Olmstead case in the City of Philadelphia earlier in the century. *United States v. Peters,* 5 Cranch 115 (1809).

[94] *Ableman v. Booth* and *United States v. Booth,* 21 Howard 506 (1859). See Warren, II, pp. 342 ff. for subsequent history of the case.

[95] See also Chapter Six, pp. 186 ff. below, for references to clashes involving the writ of *habeas corpus.*

[96] Admiralty cases were, with few exceptions, *in rem* proceedings; that is, the sentence of the court acted upon *the thing itself* (the ship), and could not be executed unless the court had possession of *the thing.*

[97] Case 11,890, 20 FC 869 (1826).

[98] Case 4,886, 9 FC 316 (1828), District Court, S.D. New York.

[99] *Poland v. The Spartan,* Case 11,246, 19 FC 912 (1828). Almost thirty years later, in a case entitled "Anonymous," the same judge held that the marshal had no right to disturb the possession of a vessel by the sheriff, when the right claimed by the libellant in the federal court was not paramount to that of the creditor in the state court. Here the libel was for materials furnished in building the ship, in its nature not a maritime lien. Case 452, 1 FC 1008 (1857).

[100] *Certain Logs of Mahogany,* Case 2,559 5 FC 374 (1837), Circuit Court Massachusetts.

[101] The rationale behind the privileged nature of seamen's wages was that justice could not be obtained except through an expeditious proceeding because, if the only remedy was a protracted common law suit, the seaman would be forced to stay on shore to litigate, thus losing future employment for an indefinite time, or be forced to forego recovery if he preferred to sail.

[102] *Wall v. The Royal Saxon,* Case 17,093, 29 FC 61 (1848). Kane makes an interesting distinction between the *in personam* nature of the state court proceedings and the *in rem* nature of the admiralty proceeding.

[103] *Taylor v. The Royal Saxon,* Case 13,803, 23 FC 797 (1849).

[104] See below, pp. 163-164.

[105] Case 2,541, 5 FC 338 (1851). The latter rule (*dictum* in this case) followed the decision in *The Robert Fulton.*

[106] Case 668, 2 FC 238 (1853), Circuit Court, E.D. Louisiana.

[107] *The Oliver Jordan,* Case 10,503, 18 FC 679 (1855). See also *Lewis v. The Orpheus,* Case 8,330, 15 FC 492 (1858), District Court Massachusetts, Ware.

[108] *Riggs v. The John Richards,* Case 11,827, 20 FC 784 (1856).

[109] *The John Richards,* Case 7,361, 13 FC 707 (1856), Circuit Court, Michigan.

[110] Case 574, 2 FC 10 (1856). This opinion is worth examining in detail for its treatment of *in rem* and *in personam* proceedings, common law remedies provided by the 9th section of the Judiciary Act, and the rationale behind the concentration of admiralty power in the federal courts: "If the state courts can have jurisdiction in admiralty cases conferred on them by state statutes, to proceed *in rem*, so they can proceed in equity, and this would constitute them, to all intents and purposes courts of admiralty. . .If there is an average of fifty counties to each state, and twenty justices of the peace to each county, we should then have in these United States, thirty-one thousand courts of admiralty and maritime jurisdiction. . .The effect of this must be, it appears to me, to embroil the United States with foreign nations, and the several states with each other, and to produce retaliatory laws and proceedings, and endless conflict, uncertainty and mischief."

[111] The judgment of Wells was affirmed by the Circuit Court of Missouri, though the latter court took pains not to disturb the state law insofar as it did not interfere with the operation of the admiralty and maritime jurisdiction of the United States. *Hill v. The Golden Gate*, Case 6,491, 12 FC 155 (1857).

[112] p. 161, above.

[113] Case 10,386, 18 FC 502 (1857), Circuit Court, S.D. Ohio.

[114] He received what was left of the proceeds of the second sale after payment of the seaman's wages. Case 5,289, 10 FC 127 (1858), District Court, Massachusetts.

[115] *The Julia Ann*, Case 7,577, 14 FC 35 (1858). Here the dispute was between the purchaser under the state sale and the purchaser under the admiralty sale. The court had no difficulty upholding the latter.

[116] See above, pp. 158, 161 and 153, respectively.

[117] *Taylor v. Carryl*, 20 Howard 583 (1858).

[118] The decision in this case was well summarized by Justice Nelson in *Freeman v. Howe*, decided three years later: "The majority of the court were of opinion that, according to the course of decisions in the case of conflicting authorities under a state and federal process, and in order to avoid unseemly collision between them, the question as to which authority should, for the time, prevail, did not depend upon the rights of the respective parties to the property seized, whether the one was paramount to the other, but upon the question, which jurisdiction had first attached by the seizure and custody of the property under its process."

[119] Dissent of Taney, *Taylor v. Carryl*, 20 Howard 600-617. As a

practical solution, Taney would have the creditor before the state court apply to the registry of the admiralty for the amount awarded him by the state court, "if there was surplus enough after paying the superior and preferred claims for maritime liens." For Taney's general remarks on admiralty jurisdiction in this case, see Chapter Seven, p. 357 below. Suffice it to say here that this decision was the greatest blow to the ever-encroaching admiralty power since Taney's accession to the court.

[120] *The Isabella,* Case 7,100, 13 FC 158 (1860).

[121] *United States v. The Reindeer,* Case 16,144, 27 FC 753 (1861).

[122] On appeal to the Supreme Court, the decision of the Circuit Court was affirmed. The court held that the ship was first in the custody of the collector; and that the state attachment suit was collusive, in order to defeat the federal jurisdiction. The Supreme Court did not rule on whether suits for forfeiture would oust state seizure or not, though this seems to be the point ruled by the circuit court. *The Slavers (Reindeer),* 2 Wallace 383 (1865).

[123] 2 Dallas 419 (1793).

[124] 2 Dallas 450-451.

[125] 2 Dallas 435; 448.

[126] 2 Dallas 457; 464; 465; 466.

[127] 2 Dallas 473-477.

[128] See Chapter Two, p. 32 above. See also Warren I, p. 100.

[129] 3 Dallas 378 (1798).

[130] *United States v. Peters,* 5 Cranch 115 (1809). See also Chapter Two, p. 44.

[131] *U.S. v. Bright,* Case 14,647, 24 FC 1232; 1235-36 (1809).

[132] Washington first presented the broader argument to show that the Eleventh Amendment did not apply to this case. He then added that the amendment was limited to suits "in law or equity" and did not apply to suits such as this, involving questions of admiralty and maritime jurisdiction. To the contention of the counsel for the defendant that the amendment should be so construed as to extend to admiralty cases, Washington interposed: "Would we be justified by any rule of law in admitting such an interpretation, even if a reason could not be assigned for the omission of those words in the amendment itself? I think not. In our various struggles to get at the spirit and

intention of the framers of the Constitution, I fear that this invariable charter of our rights would, in a very little time, be entirely construed away, and become at length so disfigured that its founders would recollect very few of its original features." *Op. cit.*, p. 1236.

[133] *Cohens v. Virginia,* 6 Wheaton 264; 378-412 (1821). See also Chapter Five, p. 214 below.

[134] The auditor and the treasurer of the state. The state asserted title to the funds in contest.

[135] *Osborn v. United States Bank,* 9 Wheaton 738; 846-857 (1824).

[136] Marshall argues that there is a significant difference between the reference in the Constitution to cases "affecting" foreign ministers and the reference to controversies "between a state and citizens of another state" where the term "affecting" is deliberately omitted. The term "affecting" was used in conjunction with the foreign ministers to give the widest possible coverage both to the person of the minister and his staff: "Therefore, jurisdiction does not depend on the party named in the record. But this language changes when the enumeration proceeds to states. Why this change? The answer is obvious. In the case of foreign ministers, it was intended for reasons which all comprehend, to give the national courts jurisdiction over all cases by which they were in any manner affected. In the case of states, whose immediate or remote interests were mixed up with a multitude of cases, and who might be affected in an almost infinite variety of ways, it was intended to give jurisdiction in those cases only to which they were actual parties." (p.855).

[137] "[The judicial department] is authorized to decide all cases, of every description, arising under the Constitution or laws of the United States. From this general grant of jurisdiction, no exception is made of those cases in which a state may be a party. . .We think a case arising under the Constitution or laws of the United States, is cognizable in the courts of the Union, whoever may be the parties to that case." (Marshall in *Cohens v. Virginia,* 6 Wheaton 382.)

[138] Dissent of Johnson, *Osborn v. United States Bank,* 9 Wheaton 881.

[139] *Bank of the United States v. Planters' Bank,* 9 Wheaton 904 (1824). Johnson, dissenting, contended that the defendant corporation was exempt from suit under the 11th Amendment. (9 Wheaton 911).

[140] 1 Peters 110; 122-124 (1828). Here Justice Johnson dissented, holding that, for a number of reasons, the 11th Amendment was not a bar to this suit: first, he contends, it is a suit in admiralty, properly before the district court; and, second, it is a suit prosecuted by the state. 1 Peters 125-135.

[141] *Rhode Island v. Massachusetts,* 12 Peters 657; 720-738 (1838).

[142] Dissent of Taney, *op. cit.,* pp. 752-753. See Chapter Five, pp. 220-221.

[143] 9 Howard 647 (1850).

[144] *McKeen v. Delancy's Lessee,* 5 Cranch 22 (1809).

[145] *Golden v. Prince,* Case 5,509, 10 FC 542; 543 (1814).

[146] 9 Cranch 87 (1815). (Italics added.)

[147] 1 Wheaton 279; 290 (1816).

[148] Case 2,356, 4 FC 1161 (1817). Rule affirmed in *Wayman v. Southard,* 10 Wheaton 1 (1825).

[149] 8 Wheaton 495 (1823).

[150] Dissent of Johnson, *op. cit.,* p. 542.

[151] 11 Wheaton 361 (1826).

[152] *Jackson v. Chew,* 12 Wheaton 153 (1827).

[153] *Neal v. Green,* Case 1263, 17 FC 1263 (1829).

[154] *Green v. Neal's Lessee,* 6 Peters 291; 295-299 (1832).

[155] Referring to the decision in this case, McLean held, in a concurring opinion in *Worcester v. Georgia,* that the rule underlying Section 34 was reciprocal, and that just as the decisions of the courts of a state form the rule for the decisions of the Supreme Court on questions arising under state laws, so the decisions of the Supreme Court must form the rule for the state courts in matters arising under the laws of the United States. 6 Peters 572-573 (1832).

[156] 4 Peters 124 (1830).

[157] Case 13,265, 22 FC 1007 (1841).

[158] 15 Peters 449; 497; 499 (1841).

[159] See Gerald T. Dunne, *Justice Joseph Story,* Simon & Schuster, 1970, pp. 403-414.

[160] *Swift v. Tyson,* 16 Peters 1 (1842).

[161] See, for example, *Ogden v. Saunders,* 12 Wheaton 368-369 (1827) where the final outcome of the case depended on the fact that a question of extra-territoriality was involved.

[162] In *Erie Railroad v. Tompkins,* 304 U.S. 64 (1938), the court held that Story had written an "unconstitutional opinion." Dunne (*op. cit.,* p. 403) states that Justice Reed, in a concurring opinion, "held in effect that Story did not write an unconstitutional opinion but merely misconstrued a statute."

[163] 16 Peters 495 (1842).

[164] *Carroll v. Safford,* 3 Howard 441 (1845).

[165] *Lane v. Vick,* 3 Howard 464 (1845).

[166] Dissent of McKinley, *op. cit.,* pp. 478-483.

[167] 5 Howard 134 (1847).

[168] Dissent of Daniel, *op. cit.,* p. 140.

[169] *Nesmith v. Sheldon,* 7 Howard 812 (1849).

[170] 8 Howard 495 (1850).

[171] *Op. cit.,* pp. 558-565.

[172] 16 Howard 369 (1854).

[173] Benjamin F. Wright, *The Contract Clause,* p. 80.

[174] *Piqua Branch v. Knoop,* 16 Howard 398-405. Campbell dissented on the ground that the Act of 1845 did not constitute a binding contract concerning the taxation of the bank.

[175] Curtis' concurrence with Taney (in which Nelson joined) is given at 16 Howard 450-451; McLean's at 16 Howard 389-391 (1854).

[176] Opinion of Taney, *Ohio Life Insurance Co. v. Debolt,* 16 Howard 416; 431-432 (1854).

[177] 18 Howard 595; 598-599 (1856).

[178] Opinion of Taney, *Dred Scott v. Sandford,* 19 Howard 393; 452-453 (1857).

[179] Opinion of Nelson, *op. cit.,* pp. 465-467.

[180] McLean quotes Gamble as regarding the question "as conclusively settled by repeated adjudications of this court. . .In this state it has been recognized from the beginning of the government as a correct position in law, that a master who takes his slave to reside in a state or territory where slavery is prohibited, thereby emancipates his slave." *Op. cit.*, p. 553 ff.

[181] Italics added.

[182] Compare Grier in *Pease v. Peck*, above—"where an excited public opinion has elicited new doctrines, subversive of former safe precedent." 18 Howard 598-599.

[183] Dissent of McLean, *Dred Scott v. Sandford*, 19 Howard 550-560. McLean's suggestion is indeed novel, that the decision should have a prospective effect on future parties but should have no effect on the parties before the court. This "concession," however, should not detract from the merits of McLean's argument.

[184] Dissent of Curtis, *op. cit.*, pp. 603-605. The reference is to *Dred Scott v. Emerson.*

[185] *Smith v. Shriver*, Case 13,108, 22 FC 659 (1857).

[186] 20 Howard 1 (1858).

[187] *Burt v. Keyes*, Case 2,212, 4 FC 858; 861 (1861).

[188] 1 Black 436 (1862).

[189] 2 Black 599 (1863).

[190] 1 Wallace 175; 205-207 (1864). Rather dramatically, Swayne added: "We shall never immolate truth, justice and the law, because a state tribunal has erected the altar and decreed the sacrifice."

[191] Miller distinguished the present case from *Rowan v. Runnels*, where the Supreme Court had previously established a rule of its own and which involved citizens of different states in a contract, rather than relations between a city and a railroad company of the same State. He excluded the opinion of Taney in *Ohio Life Insurance Co. v. Debolt* on the ground that it received the concurrence only of Grier. See p. 184, above. Thirdly, he insisted that the question in this case had never been closed until the decision of *State of Iowa v. Wapello County* in the state court.

[192] Dissent of Miller, *Gelpcke v. City of Dubuque*, 1 Wallace 207-220.

[193] 8 Wallace 575; 584 (1869). Italics added.

CHAPTER FIVE:

JURISDICTION

No clear line can be drawn between the terms *judicial power* and *jurisdiction;* nor, for the purpose of studying Article III of the Constitution, is it necessary to draw such a line. The word *power* is generally used in reference to the means employed in carrying jurisdiction into execution; the term *jurisdiction* refers to the capacity of the court to exercise its powers. Judicial power also comprehends a wider meaning in American constitutional history, one which has been discussed in Chapter Two, above: the judicial versus the executive and legislative power; judicial review; judicial supremacy.

Jurisdiction is also comprehended within the term judicial power; in the words of Justice Thompson, "power, as used in the Constitution, would seem to embrace both."[1] Section 2 of Article III refers specifically to the jurisdiction of the federal courts:

"The judicial power shall extend to all cases, in law and equity, arising under this constitution, the laws of the United States, and treaties made or which shall be made, under their authority; to all cases affecting ambassadors, other public ministers and consuls; to all cases of admiralty and maritime jurisdiction; to controversies to which the United States shall be a party; to controversies between two or more States; between a State and citizens of another State; between citizens of different States; between citizens of the same State claiming lands under grants of different States, and between a State, or the citizens thereof, and foreign states, citizens or subjects.

"In all cases affecting ambassadors, other public ministers and consuls, and those in which a State shall be party, the

Supreme Court shall have original jurisdiction. In all the other cases before mentioned, the Supreme Court shall have appellate jurisdiction, both as to law and fact, with such exceptions, and under such regulations as the Congress shall make."

We have already examined controversies involving the states themselves and in a subsequent chapter we will treat special problems of jurisdiction, such as diversity of citizenship and admiralty and maritime jurisdiction. Our immediate interest is in the nature of original and appellate jurisdiction; cases arising under the Constitution and laws of the United States; the exceptions and regulations which Congress is authorized to make; criminal jurisdiction; and the special jurisdiction of the Circuit Court of the District of Columbia.

The Judiciary Act of 1789 was a comprehensive law establishing the judicial courts of the United States, specifying the powers of those courts and delineating their jurisdiction. Of special interest are Section 9, giving the district courts "cognizance of all crimes and offenses that shall be cognizable under the authority of the United States;" and Section 11, giving the circuit courts "cognizance. . .of all suits of a civil nature at common law or in equity, where the matter in dispute exceeds, exclusive of costs, the sum or value of five hundred dollars, and the United States are plaintiffs, or petitioners; or an alien is a party, or the suit is between a citizen of the state where the suit is brought, and a citizen of another state."

The first case involving the interpretation of the Supreme Court's original jurisdiction was an indictment of a foreign consul for offenses committed within the United States. The case was brought before the Circuit Court of Pennsylvania, where counsel for the defendant argued that under the Constitution the Supreme Court possessed exclusive original jurisdiction over consuls as well as ambassadors. Both Justice Wilson and Judge Peters upheld Section 13 of the Judiciary Act granting "original, but not exclusive jurisdiction of all suits. . .in which a consul, or vice-consul, shall be a party." "I am of the opinion," said Wilson, "that although the Constitution vests in the Supreme Court an original jurisdiction, in cases like the present, it does not preclude the legislature from exercising the power of vesting a concurrent jurisdiction, in such inferior courts, as might by law be established."[2] Justice Iredell dissented: "I do not concur in this opinion, because it appears to me that for obvious reasons of public policy, the Constitution intended to vest an exclusive jurisdiction in the Supreme Court upon all questions relating to the public agents of foreign nations. Besides, the context of the judiciary article of the Constitution seems fairly to justify the interpretation, that the word 'original' means 'exclusive' jurisdiction."[3]

In 1796, for the first time, the Supreme Court commented on the nature of its appellate power. The immediate question was whether a writ of error or an appeal was the proper mode of bringing equity and admiralty cases before the Supreme Court.[4] A majority of four held that a writ of error was the mode prescribed by the Judiciary Act.

The more important question concerned the power of Congress to make exceptions and regulations governing the appellate power. Pointing out that the appellate jurisdiction was qualified by the Constitution itself, "inasmuch as it is given 'with such exceptions, and under such regulations, as the Congress shall make'," Chief Justice Ellsworth continued: "Here then is the ground, and the only ground on which we can sustain an appeal. If Congress has provided no rule to regulate our proceedings, we cannot exercise an appellate jurisdiction; and if the rule is provided, we cannot depart from it. The question, therefore, on the constitutional point of an appellate jurisdiction, is simply whether Congress has established any rule for regulating its exercise."

Asserting that in accordance with the 22nd section of the Judiciary Act, causes of admiralty and maritime jurisdiction are to be brought up from the lower courts on a writ of error, Ellsworth adds: "The law may, indeed, be improper and inconvenient; but it is of more importance, for a judicial determination, to ascertain what the law is than to speculate upon what it ought to be."[5]

Wilson, dissenting, argued that the remedy by writ of error does not comprehend admiralty causes and that "appeal is the natural and proper mode of removing an admiralty cause." He contended that such an appeal is expressly sanctioned by the Constitution and was nowhere restricted by the Judiciary Act. But even if a positive restriction existed by law, Wilson continued, "it would, in my judgment, be superseded by the superior authority of the constitutional provision."

Wilson's thesis was that removal of a case to the Supreme Court by *appeal* was implicit in the constitutional term "appellate jurisdiction," and that it was not necessary for Congress to stipulate such a remedy which had already been given. "The legislature might, indeed, have made exceptions, and introduced regulations upon the subject," Wilson acknowledged; "but as it has not done so, the case remains upon the strong ground of the Constitution, which in general terms, and on general principles, provides and authorizes an appeal."[6] [7]

Beyond the technical, though important, question in this case—whether admiralty causes were to be removed to the Supreme Court by appeal or by writ of error—was the more essential query of whether there were inherent in the appellate jurisdiction given by the Constitution certain modes and means of judicial procedure and capacity, or whether it was necessary in all cases that Congress first spell out the regulations governing the operation of the courts. Here the majority determined that since appeal was nowhere explicitly authorized by the Judiciary Act, the only remedy open was writ of error, given in Section 22; the minority, on the other hand, held that since appeal was not prohibited by any law of Congress, the removal by appeal, implicit in the constitutional grant, was appropriate for this kind of cause.

Three years later an even more important issue came before the court. The question was whether Congress could restrict or narrow a jurisdiction explicitly given by the Constitution. The constitutional grant extended jurisdiction to controversies between citizens of different states. Section 11 of the Judiciary Act included a proviso, barring jurisdiction of the federal courts in actions on assigned promissory notes where no action would have been possible had the note not been assigned.[8] The counsel for the plaintiff, arguing in favor of jurisdiction, contended that

Congress could no more limit than enlarge the constitutional grant; that if the controversy was between citizens of different states, the judicial power of the United States extended to it.

The Supreme Court, however, held otherwise. Chief Justice Ellsworth pointed out that the circuit court was of limited jurisdiction and depended for that jurisdiction on the grant of Congress. "The fair presumption is," he stated, "that a cause is without its jurisdiction till the contrary appears." The Chief Justice rejected the argument that in every case to which the judicial power of the United States extends, the federal courts may exercise jurisdiction, without intervention of Congress to distribute and regulate the power.[9]

In a separate opinion, Justice Chase expressed his agreement: "The notion has been frequently entertained that the federal courts derive their power immediately from the Constitution; but the political truth is that the judicial power (except in a few specified instances) belongs to Congress. If Congress has given the power to this court we possess it, not otherwise; and if Congress has not given the power to us, or to any other court, it still remains at the legislative disposal. Besides, Congress is not bound, and it would perhaps be inexpedient to enlarge the jurisdiction of the federal courts to every subject, in every form, which the Constitution might warrant."[10]

Although in a certain sense it was true that the judicial power belonged to Congress, it was not within the power of Congress to grant to the Supreme Court any original jurisdiction which went beyond the constitutional grant. This principle was clearly affirmed by the court in *Marbury v. Madison* where it was decided that Congress cannot confer on the Supreme Court any original jurisdiction. Those who argued to the contrary alleged that since "the clause, assigning original jurisdiction to the Supreme Court, contains no negative or restrictive words, the power remains to the legislature to assign original jurisdiction to that court in other cases than those specified in the article which has been recited; provided those cases belong to the judicial power of the United States."

Chief Justice Marshall, however, supported by a

unanimous court, held that Congress was not at liberty to give the court appellate jurisdiction where the Constitution has given original, or original jurisdiction where the Constitution has given appellate. "Affirmative words are often, in their operation, negative of other objects than those affirmed," he stated, "and in this case, a negative or exclusive sense must be given to them, or they have no operation at all."[11]

Two years later, in *United States v. More*, an even more important rule was announced by the Supreme Court. Section 22 of the Judiciary Act had authorized final judgments and decrees in *civil* actions and suits in equity to be brought before the Supreme Court on a writ of error, provided the *matter in dispute* exceeded the sum of two thousand dollars. A similar provision was included in the Act of 1803, establishing the Circuit Court for the District of Columbia. When a defendant was acquitted before the latter court on an indictment for taking fees to which he was not entitled, the government appealed to the Supreme Court. Before investigating the merits, the court stated that it was first necessary to determine whether it possessed jurisdiction. Here was a criminal indictment, not a civil action or suit in equity; it was incumbent on the government to point to the source of jurisdiction in such a case. The Attorney General argued that criminal jurisdiction was exercised by the courts of the United States, under the description of "all cases in law and equity arising under the laws of the United States"; that the appellate jurisdiction of the Supreme Court was extended to the enumerated cases, "with such exceptions, and under such regulations, as the Congress shall make"; and that "the Supreme Court possessed appellate jurisdiction in criminal as well as civil cases,. . .unless there should be some exception or regulation made by Congress, which should circumscribe the jurisdiction conferred by the Constitution." No exception in regard to criminal cases had been made; therefore, argued the Attorney-General, the Supreme Court possessed appellate jurisdiction.

The court, however, held that the jurisdiction of the Supreme Court had been regulated by act of Congress and, as in the previous case, "an affirmative description of its powers must be understood as a regulation, under the Constitution, prohibiting the exercise of other powers than those described." Determining that the appellate jurisdiction over cases arising from the Court of the District of Columbia was confined by positive words to civil cases ("matter in dispute"), the writ of error was dismissed for want of jurisdiction.[12]

Although this ruling concerned appellate jurisdiction over the Circuit Court of the District of Columbia, it applied equally to all the other circuit courts of the United States. Thus there was but one mode of obtaining review of a criminal case by the Supreme Court, and that was by a certificate of division from the circuit court when the two judges of that court were divided.[13] This interpretation of the jurisdiction of the Supreme Court meant, in practice, that in criminal cases the circuit court and not the Supreme Court was to be the court of last resort. Whether or not this ruling was just or wise, it was consistent with the Supreme Court's position that its jurisdiction depended not on the Constitution or any inherent prerogative powers but on the will of Congress. Similarly, the rule explains the otherwise anomalous fact that virtually no criminal cases were to come before the Supreme Court until a later era, when appeals were based on the privation of constitutional rights.

The doctrine of legislative regulation of jurisdiction was affirmed in other cases arising during the early period of the Marshall Court. In *Ex parte Bollman*, the Chief Justice Stated: "Courts which originate in the common law possess a jurisdiction which must be regulated by common law, until some statute shall change their established priciples; but courts which are created by written law cannot transcend that jurisdiction. . .This opinion is not to be considered as abridging the power of courts over their own officers, or to protect themselves and their members from being disturbed in the exercise of their functions. It extends only to the power of taking cognizance of any question between individuals, or between the government and individuals. To enable the court to decide on such questions, the power to determine it must be given by written law."[14]

In *Bank of the United States v. Deveaux*, the court held that the Bank of the United States did not have the right to sue in a circuit court on the principle that the case arose under a law of the United States, notwithstanding the constitutional provision that the judicial power shall extend to all cases, in law and equity, arising under the Constitution and laws of the United States. The Judiciary Act did not extend jurisdiction to the entire constitutional grant, insofar as the right to plead and be impleaded in the courts of the United States depended on the nature of the case. That the case arose under a law of the United States was not sufficient to give jurisdiction.[15]

Once more, in *Durousseau v. United States*, the court emphasized the role of Congress in establishing the jurisdiction of the courts. Denying that the appellate jurisdiction of the court extended to every case not excepted by Congress, Marshall continued: "They have not declared that the appellate power of the court shall not extend to certain cases but they have described affirmatively its jurisdiction, and this affirmative description has been understood to imply a negative on the exercise of such appellate power as is not comprehended within it."

The rule that affirmative words are negative of other objects than those affirmed, however, was not to be taken as an absolute; the rule is founded on the intent of the legislature, and "only where that manifest intent appears" can the rule be applied. Exceptions "are implied from the intent manifested by the affirmative description of [the court's] powers. It would be repugnant to every principle of sound construction to imply an exception against the intent." Thus the court held that upon this principle it possessed appellate jurisdiction, by writ of error, over the judgments of the District Court of the Territory of Orleans even if the act of March 26, 1804, did not expressly stipulate this jurisdiction.[16]

Returning once again to the extent to which the constitutional grant established by its own force the appellate jurisdiction of the Supreme Court, the court once more made it clear that the jurisdiction depended on legislative action within the constitutional grant. "Although the judicial power of the United States extends to cases arising under the laws of the United States," wrote Justice Johnson in *McIntire v. Wood*, "the legislature has not thought proper to delegate the exercise of that power to its circuit courts, except in certain specified cases."[17]

The most thorough analysis of appellate jurisdiction was presented by Justice Story in *Martin v. Hunter's Lessee*, decided in 1816. Although the immediate question involved the constitutionality of Section 25 of the Judiciary Act, giving the Supreme Court the power to revise judgments of the state tribunals, Story dedicated the first portion of his opinion to a general treatment of judicial power and jurisdiction. Up to this point, the court had acknowledged that the constitutional grant of appellate jurisdiction was not binding in itself without legislative enactment. Story, however, placed an entirely different interpretation on the clause: "In all the other cases before mentioned, the Supreme Court shall have appellate jurisdiction both as to law and fact, with such exceptions and under such regulations as the Congress shall make." For the judge from Massachusetts, the exceptions referred to were merely intended "as a limitation upon the preceding words to enable Congress to regulate and restrain the appellate power, as the public interests might, from time to time, require." Thus the provision in Section 22 of the Judiciary Act, requiring a minimum of two thousand dollars in the matter in dispute, might be cited as an exception to the appellate jurisdiction.

For Story, the wording of Article III—"the judicial power shall be vested. . .the judicial power shall extend"—was imperative.[18] Congress had the obligation—not the discretion—to vest and extend the judicial power; the term "shall" was obligatory. This conclusion, universally accepted, was then followed by a more controversial proposition: "If, then, it is a duty of Congress to vest the judicial power of the United States, it is a duty to vest the whole judicial power. The language, if imperative as to one part, is imperative as to all." Story's reasoning was that if Congress might refuse to vest the jurisdiction in any one class of cases enumerated in the Constitution, it might then be able to defeat the jurisdiction as to all cases, since the Constitution did not give preference to any one class.

Story then proceeds to point out an important distinction in Section 2 of Article III, between cases depending on the nature of the controversy and those depending on the parties. In the first class—cases in law and equity arising under the Constitution and the laws of the United States; cases affecting ambassadors; cases of admiralty and maritime jurisdiction—the judicial power extends to *all* cases; in the second class, the judicial power extends to controversies, but not all controversies.

"From this difference of phraseology," writes Story, "perhaps a difference of constitutional intention may, with propriety, be inferred. It is hardly to be presumed that the variation in the language could have been accidental. It must have been the result of some determinate reason, and it is not very difficult to find a reason sufficient to support the apparent change of intention. In respect to the first class, it may well have been the intention of the framers of the Constitution imperatively to extend the judicial power either in an original or appellate form to all cases; and in the latter class to leave it to Congress to qualify the jurisdiction, original or appellate, in such manner as public policy might dictate."[19] [20]

This portion of Story's opinion is, however, *dicta.* Not only is it much broader than the question before the court, but Story himself adds: "But even admitting that the language of the Constitution is not mandatory, and that Congress omits to vest the judicial power in courts of the United States, it cannot be denied that when it is vested, it may be exercised to the utmost constitutional extent." Thus his judgment in this case is not dependent on his prefatory remarks, no matter how appropriate they may be. The real test of Story's position would have been a case arising under a law of the United States in which jurisdiction was denied by the circuit court on the ground that there was no authorization for it in the Judiciary Act, and where the plaintiff argued that jurisdiction was given directly by the constitutional grant extending judicial power to *all* cases arising under the laws of the United States. Judging from the opinions of other cases of the period, Story would have upheld such a jurisdiction, in accordance with the views laid down in *Martin v. Hunter's Lessee*, while his colleagues, including Marshall, would have upheld the power of Congress to regulate and make exceptions to jurisdiction, even in the first class of cases enumerated by Story.[21]

In *Cohens v. Virginia* the court was faced with the problem of whether it possessed appellate jurisdiction over a case in which a state was a party, when the Constitution clearly stated that in all cases in which a state shall be a party, the Supreme Court shall have original jurisdiction. This case originated in a local court of Virginia and was brought before the Supreme Court under Section 25 of the Judiciary Act. Counsel for Virginia contended that the constitutional provision cited above excluded the exercise of appellate jurisdiction. Chief Justice Marshall, however, reiterating the distinction made by Story in the previous case of two classes of cases—one dependent on the nature of the controversy, the other dependent on the character of the parties—held that the grant of original jurisdiction in cases in which a state is a party was not exclusive; that when a state is a party to a case over which the Supreme Court possessed appellate jurisdiction by the nature of the controversy—as in this case where a law of the United States was alleged to be involved—the appellate jurisdiction of the court "was not arrested by the circumstance that a state was a party."

Distinguishing the rule of construction employed in this decision from that postulated in *Marbury v. Madison*, Marshall said: "The truth is that where the words confer only appellate jurisdiction, original jurisdiction is most clearly not given; but where the words admit of appellate jurisdiction, the power to take cognizance of the suit originally does not necessarily negate the power to decide upon it on an appeal, if it may originate in a different court. It is, we think, apparent that to give this distributive clause the interpretation contended for, to give its affirmative words a negative operation in every possible case, would, in some instances, defeat the obvious intention of the article. . .The court may imply a negative from affirmative words, where the implication promotes, not where it defeats the intention."[22]

This conclusion was sound and necessary for, as Marshall pointed out, a contrary rule would exclude the Supreme Court from the revision of the judgments of state courts in which the state was the plaintiff and the defendant claimed a right under the Constitution or a law of the United States. It is interesting to note, however, that it was no longer possible to rely on the *dicta* in *Marbury v. Madison* that "affirmative words are often negative of other objects than those affirmed," for the decision in this case necessitated a proviso reading, "except when they are not." As Marshall pointed out, it was necessary to ascertain the intention of the constitutional provision, and to do so it was necessary to go beyond the words. Thus generalizing *dicta* as to the meaning of terms employed might prove more harmful than helpful.

In the same year, Justice Washington of the Circuit Court of Pennsylvania commented further on the jurisdiction of the federal courts over cases enumerated in the Constitution but omitted from the Judiciary Act. "Cognizance of cases arising under the Constitution, laws of the United States, or treaties," he wrote, "is not assigned by the act to either of the courts which it establishes; and, consequently, neither of them could take jurisdiction in those cases, since the article of the Constitution, above recited, leaves to Congress the distribution of the judicial powers, not assigned to the Supreme Court, amongst the inferior courts which that body might ordain. The powers therefore not bestowed upon those courts by legislative provision remain dormant, until some law should call them into action, by designating the particular tribunal which should be authorized to exercise them."[23]

In a parallel case involving the Bank of the United States, the Circuit Court of Kentucky declared that "the circuit court can only exercise such portions of [the judicial] power as are expressly conferred upon it by Congress. . .The judicial power of the United States is, by the Constitution, declared to extend to eleven numerated classes. This may properly be said to be the potential judicial power; to be called into action, either by some subsequent provisions of the Constitution, or by law, or by both. . .The Constitution defines the portion of the judicial power vested in that

Supreme Court and leaves the residue to be distributed among the inferior courts which might be established by law; and to be vested, or not vested, in them respectively, from time to time, according to the sound discretion of Congress. It follows that a court, created by law, can only exercise the jurisdiction which the law confers upon it. It cannot assume jurisdiction under the Constitution alone, without legal power being superadded. It will be conceded further, that the circuit courts of the United States will not and cannot take cognizance by implication."

However, as was decided in the previous case, the court held that the Bank of the United States could sue or be sued in the circuit courts, not by virtue of the constitutional grant and even less under the Judiciary Act which made no provisions for such jurisdiction, but under the very act which incorporated the Bank.[24] The Constitution left the distribution of jurisdiction to the discretion of Congress; the Judiciary Act did not cover the entire field: "Congress might well, therefore, in any subsequent statute, as they have done in the charter of the bank, provide for a case not provided for in the judicial act, and give jurisdiction beyond the provisions of that act within the limits of the judicial power of the Union."[25]

In *Osborn v. Bank of the United States*, the Supreme Court upheld the constitutionality of the clause in the Act of 1816 incorporating the Bank of the United States, which authorized the bank to sue in the federal courts. In order to uphold this jurisdiction, it was necessary to show that, barring diversity of citizenship, a case arising under a law of the United States was involved. Counsel for the plaintiff in error as well as Justice Johnson, in dissent, contended that this case depended on general principles of law rather than on an act of Congress, and that the proper tribunal in the first instance was a state court. If, during the proceedings, it was shown that a federal case was involved, appeal could be made to the Supreme Court under Section 25 of the Judiciary Act.

The majority of the court, with Marshall as its spokesman, rejected this interpretation. "First," said the Chief Justice, "We think. . .that when a question to which the judicial power of the Union is extended by the Constitution forms an ingredient of the original cause, it is in the power of Congress to give the circuit court jurisdiction of that cause, although other questions of fact or of law may be involved in it." The ingredient of the original cause to which the judicial power extended in this case was the act of Congress establishing the bank. "Every act of the bank," said Marshall, "grows out of this law, and is tested by it. To use the language of the Constitution, every act of the bank arises out of this law." Thus it was not necessary, as Johnson contended, to look further for a federal case since, by definition, every act of the bank fitted that description.

To Johnson's argument that causes such as the present one were properly cognizable in the first instance in state courts, Marshall replied that, with the exception of cases in which original jurisdiction is given by the Constitution to the Supreme Court, "there is none to which the judicial power extends, from which the original jurisdiction of the inferior courts is excluded by the Constitution. Original jurisdiction, so far as the Constitution gives a rule, is coextensive with the judicial power."[26]

In *Ex parte Watkins*, an attempt was made to circumvent the earlier ruling of the Court that the Supreme Court has no appellate jurisdiction in criminal cases. Here the petitioner had applied to the Supreme Court for a writ of *habeas corpus* following judgment by the circuit court under which he had been committed to prison. The petitioner contended that he had been indicted for an offense not punishable criminally by federal law. The petition, however, was turned down, when the court held that it could not examine indirectly by a writ of *habeas corpus* what it could not revise directly on a writ of error. "We have no power to examine the proceedings on a writ of error," said Marshall, "and it would be strange if, under color of a writ to liberate an individual from unlawful imprisonment, we could substantially reverse a judgment which the law has placed beyond our control. An imprisonment under a judgment cannot be unlawful, unless that judgment be an absolute nullity," he continued, "and it is not a nullity if the court has general jurisdiction of the subject, *although it should be erroneous.*"[27]

Similarly, in a case involving capital punishment before

the Circuit Court of Massachusetts, Justice Story reiterated that, "The circuit courts have final jurisdiction of all cases of crimes; and no writ of error or appeal lies to the Supreme Court in any such cases. . .The only mode contemplated by the law of the United States to revise the opinions of the judges of the circuit courts in criminal cases is when the judges are divided in opinion at the trial; and then the point of division may be certified to the Supreme Court for a final decision under the judicial act of 1802."[28]

The case of *United States ex rel. Stokes v. Kendall* posed the important question of whether the Circuit Court of the District of Columbia possessed a special jurisdiction which went beyond that of the other circuit courts.[29] The latter courts were established by the Judiciary Act of 1789, or subsequent acts written in accordance with it. The Supreme Court had previously determined that the legislative grant of jurisdiction to those courts was not as wide as the constitutional grant, and that they did not possess, by virtue of that law, jurisdiction over all cases arising under the Constitution or laws of the United States.

The Circuit Court of the District of Columbia was established by the Act of February 27, 1801. Section 5 of that act provided, "That the said court shall have cognizance of all crimes and offenses committed within the said District, and of all cases in law and equity between parties, both or either of which shall be resident, or shall be found within the said District. . ." Section 3 read, "The Circuit Court of the District of Columbia, and the judges thereof, shall have all the powers vested in the circuit courts, and the judges of the circuit courts of the United States."

Stokes v. Kendall first came before the Circuit Court for the District of Columbia. There Judge Cranch held that the Circuit Court of the District had jurisdiction in all cases arising under the Constitution and laws of the United States and, as the present was a case arising under a law of the United States, the court possessed jurisdiction. This conclusion was reached by following two lines of reasoning. First, the 5th section of the act of February 27th was sufficient to give the Circuit Court of the District jurisdiction over all cases arising under the Constitution or laws of the United States, because such cases were obviously comprehended in the grant of cognizance of "*all* cases in law and equity."[30]

The second source of jurisdiction was Section 3 of the same act, giving the Circuit Court of the District "all the powers vested in the circuit courts." In order to determine what these powers were, said Cranch, it was necessary to refer to the act of February 13th of the same year, modifying the original Judiciary Act. Although this act of February 13th was later repealed and was no longer of any validity in determining the powers and jurisdiction of the circuit courts in general, it controlled, argued Cranch, the interpretation of Section 3, because it was in effect when the Circuit Court of the District was established.

"The only circuit courts. . .then existing," wrote Cranch, "were those ordained and established by the Act of Congress of the 13th of February, 1801;. . .and by the Eleventh section it was enacted, among other things, that the said courts respectively should have cognizance of. . .'all cases in law or equity arising under the Constitution and laws of the United States.' " Thus, by reading these two laws together, the conclusion was reached that the Circuit Court of the District of Columbia also was given jurisdiction of "all cases in law and equity arising under the Constitution and laws of the United States."[31] [32]

On appeal to the Supreme Court, the interpretation of Judge Cranch was upheld on both points. Justice Thompson, speaking for the majority, referred to the Act of February 27th as "the delegation, to the Circuit Court, of the whole judicial power in the District, and in the very language of the Constitution; which declares that the judicial power shall extend to all cases in law and equity arising under the laws of the United States."

Further on he reiterated: "We are then to construe the third section of the Act of 27th of February, 1801, as if the eleventh section of the Act of 13th of February, 1801, had been incorporated at full length; and by this section it is declared that the circuit courts shall have cognizance of all cases in law or equity, arising under the Constitution and laws of the United States, which are the very words of the Constitution, and which is, of course, a delegation of the whole judicial power, in cases arising under the Constitution and laws, etc."[33] [34]

Chief Justice Taney dissented from the conclusion reached by the majority of the court. He could see no reason for the legislature to have given the Circuit Court for the District a power not granted to the other circuit courts. His opinion, however, was confined to the point whether the circuit court had the power to issue a *mandamus*, and did not consider the question of whether the Circuit Court for the District possessed jurisdiction in general as wide as the constitutional grant. His argument was, on the one hand, that a *mandamus* was not a case in law or equity and therefore was not included in the terms of Section 5 of the Act of February 27th; and, on the other hand, that Section 3 did not incorporate Section 11 of the Act of February 11th because, first, the Act of February 11th had been repealed and, secondly, because Section 3 referred to powers and Section 11 to cognizance.[35]

Justice Barbour filed a separate dissent in which he argued that there was no difference between the jurisdiction of the Circuit Court of the District under Section 5 of the Act of February 27th and that of the other circuit courts under the original Judiciary Act.[36]

The outcome of the case was the establishment—whether by intentional legislative act or by judicial interpretation—of a wider jurisdiction in the Circuit Court for the District of Columbia than in any of the other circuit courts, a unique exception to the limitations which the original Judiciary Act had placed on the constitutional grant of judicial power.

Of an entirely different nature was the controversy concerning the original jurisdiction of the Supreme Court over suits brought by one state against another to determine a question of disputed boundary. The opponents of such a jurisdiction did not doubt the power of the court to hear such a controversy where a property right was at issue, but claimed that the mere determination of a boundary line was a political issue and was not of a judicial character. The majority of the court, however, held that it was precisely such disagreements which the framers of the Constitution had in mind when they extended the judicial power to "controversies between two or more states," and that there was no basis for a settlement of such disputes other than in a court of justice.

Political power, said Justice Baldwin in the majority opinion, "is that which a sovereign or state exerts by his or its own authority, as reprisal and confiscation; [judicial power] is that which is granted to a court or judicial tribunal." There was no doubt in the minds of the majority that the Constitution intended boundary disputes to be decided by judicial power.

In discussing the 3rd Article of the Constitution in general terms, Baldwin reiterated the conclusion reached by the court in earlier cases: "It was necessarily left to the legislative power to organize the Supreme Court, to define its powers consistently with the Constitution as to its original jurisdiction, and to distribute the residue of the judicial power between this and the inferior courts. . .No department could organize itself; the Constitution provided for the organization of the legislative power, and the mode of its exercise, but it delineated only the great outlines of the judicial power, leaving the details to Congress. . .The distribution and appropriate exercise of the judicial power must therefore be made by laws passed by Congress, and cannot be assumed by any other department; else, the power being concurrent in the legislative and judicial departments, a conflict between them would be probable, if not unavoidable."[37]

In *Gittings v. Crawford*, the Circuit Court of Maryland echoed the early decision of *United States v. Ravara*, that the 2nd Section of the 3rd Article of the Constitution, declaring that "in all cases affecting ambassadors, other public ministers, and consuls. . .the Supreme Court shall have original jurisdiction," does not conflict with and render unconstitutional the ninth section of the Judiciary Act, giving jurisdiction to the district courts of the United States, in civil cases, against consuls and vice-consuls. "There are no express words of exclusion in the clause which confers original jurisdiction, in the cases mentioned, upon the

Supreme Court," wrote Taney. "The original jurisdiction conferred on the Supreme Court is not inconsistent with the exercise of original jurisdiction on the same subjects by the inferior courts of the United States, and there is no necessity, therefore, for implying an intention to exclude them. . .The true rule in this case is, I think, the rule which is constantly applied to ordinary acts of legislation, in which the grant of jurisdiction over a certain subject matter to one court, does not, of itself, imply that jurisdiction is to be exclusive. In the clause in question, there is nothing but mere affirmative words of grant, and none that import a design to exclude the subordinate jurisdiction of other courts of the United States on the same subject matter."[38]

Although Taney does not pursue the question further, the implication of this decision is that Congress could give to the district or circuit courts original jurisdiction of any of the cases in which original jurisdiction is granted to the Supreme Court by the Constitution (for instance, cases affecting ambassadors or controversies between one state and another), thus converting the reference to original and appellate jurisdiction into a mere prohibition on the scope of the Supreme Court's original jurisdiction: the Supreme Court *may* take original jurisdiction in four enumerated cases and in no others, but even then the Congress may grant original jurisdiction in those same four cases to inferior courts and, in effect, leave the Supreme Court without any original jurisdiction in practice.

Another old question which was revived in a case before the circuit court was the constitutionality of the proviso in Section 11 of the Judiciary Act excluding jurisdiction over promissory notes assigned to citizens of another state. In a *dictum*, the Circuit Court of Ohio cast doubts on the constitutionality of that restrictive clause. "Insofar as this law is restrictive of the constitutional right of a non-resident," said the court, "it is, in my judgment, unconstitutional. If Congress can impose this restriction, they may go farther and impose other restrictions, as their disrection may dictate. In this way a constitutional right may be modified or taken away in whole or in part, as Congress may determine. This is a new and most dangerous principle, and cannot be maintained."[39]

An even stronger position was taken on this subject by the Circuit Court of Michigan. Recognizing that the law had been sustained by the Supreme Court, the circuit court declared: "A clearer and more palpable infraction of this constitutional provision could not be well-imagined. . .The only answer to this argument that has been attempted is that the jurisdiction is given to the courts of the United States by Congress, and that they can not exercise jurisdiction, except in certain cases, under the Constitution. It is often said that a bad reason is better than none; but this can scarcely come under that denomination. If Congress, in attempting to carry out the provisions of the Constitution, shall repudiate a part of its provisions, it is the duty of the Supreme Court to declare such legislation void."[40]

Another problem to come before the Supreme Court was the validity of the Bankrupt Act of 1841, which permitted no appeal from the judgment of the District Court. In upholding this feature of the law, Justice Story said: "Congress possesses the sole right to say what shall be the form of proceedings, either in equity or at law, in the courts of the United States, and in what cases appeal shall be allowed or not. It is a matter of sound discretion, and to be exercised by Congress in such a manner as shall in their judgment best promote the public convenience and the true interests of the citizens. Because the proceedings are to be in the nature of summary proceedings in equity, it by no means follows that they are not entirely consistent with the principles of justice, and adapted to promote the interest as well as the convenience of all suitors. Because there is no appeal given, it by no means follows that the jurisdiction is either oppressive or dangerous. No appeal lies from the judgments either of the district court or circuit court in criminal cases; and yet, within the cognizance of one or both of these courts are all crimes and offenses against the United States, from those which are capital down to the lowest misdemeanors, affecting the liberty and the property of the citizens. And yet there can be no doubt that this denial of appellate jurisdiction is founded in a wise protective public policy."[41]

In *Cary v. Curtis*, the court upheld the Act of March 3, 1839, which provided for no recourse to the courts to recover money paid to a Customs collector under protest. Justice Daniel, speaking for the majority, upheld the thesis that "the judicial power of the United States, although it has its origin in the Constitution, is (except in enumerated instances applicable exclusively to this court) dependent for its distribution and organization, and for the modes of its exercise, entirely upon the action of Congress, who possesses the sole power of creating the tribunals (inferior to the Supreme Court) for the exercise of the judicial power, and of investing them with jurisdiction either limited, concurrent, or exclusive, and of withholding jurisdiction from them in the exact degrees and character which to Congress may seem proper for the public good. To deny this position," concluded Daniel, "would be to elevate the judicial over the legislative branch of the government, and to give to the former powers limited by its own discretion merely."[42]

In order to avoid elevating the judicial over the legislative branch of government, however, the Court was willing to entrust to the discretion of Congress the right to a judicial revision of an executive decision. Although the Constitution nowhere guaranteed such a right, a minority of the Court assumed that the right existed by the nature of government. Justice Story, who thirty years earlier in *Martin v. Hunter's Lessee* had insisted that the entire judicial power, especially cases arising under the Constitution or laws of the United States, be vested in one of the courts of the United States, dissented from the majority opinion, which denied to the courts jurisdiction to revise the decisions of executive officers if no such revision was explicitly provided for by law. If Congress has the right to deny to citizens right to recover money in any court and leaves to the Secretary of the Treasury the final authority to withhold or restore that money, argued Story, "then I must say that it seems to me to be not what I had hitherto supposed it to be; a government where the three great departments, legislative, executive, and judicial, had independent duties to perform, each in its own sphere; but the judicial power, designed by the Constitution to be the final and appellate jurisdiction to interpret our laws, is superseded in its most vital and important functions. . .If Congress possesses a constitutional authority to vest such summary and final power of interpretation in an executive functionary, I know of no other subject within the reach of legislation which may not be exclusively confided in the same way to an executive functionary. . .I deny the constitutional authority of Congress to delegate such functions to an executive officer, or to take away all right of action for an admitted wrong and illegal exercise of power in the levy of money from the injured citizens."[43]

Justice McLean filed a separate dissent: "The right to construe the laws in all matters of controversy is of the very essence of judicial power. Executive officers who are required to act under the laws, of necessity, must give a construction to them. But their construction is not final. When it operates injuriously to the citizen, he may, by any and every possible means through which it may be brought before the courts, have the construction of the law submitted to them, and their decision is final. . .If the Act of 1839 be what it is now construed to be, then I say the act is unconstitutional and void. It not only strikes down the rights of the citizen, but it inflicts a blow on the judicial power of the country. It unites, in the same department, the executive and judicial power."[44]

Despite these protests of Story and McLean, the Supreme Court had no intention of questioning the authority of Congress to restrict the jurisdiction of the courts of the United States nor to enlarge its own appellate jurisdiction by liberal interpretation. This conservative approach to jurisdiction appeared once more in *Barry v. Mercein*, a controversy involving the custody of a minor child. Chief Justice Taney pointed out that under Section 22 of the Judiciary Act the *matter in dispute* must exceed the sum of $2,000, "and in order, therefore, to give us appellate power under this section, the matter in dispute must be money, or some right, the value of which, in money, can be calculated and ascertained.

"In the case before us, the controversy is between the father and mother of an infant daughter. They are living separate from each other, and each claiming the right to the custody, care, and society of their child. This is the matter in dispute. And it is evidently utterly incapable of being reduced to any pecuniary standard of value, as it rises superior to money considerations.

"The question for this court to decide is, whether a controversy of this character can, by a fair and reasonable construction, be regarded as within the provisions of the 22nd section of the Act of 1789. Is it one of those cases in which we are authorized to reexamine the decision of a circuit court of the United States, and affirm or reverse its judgment? We think not. The words of the act of Congress are plain and unambiguous. They give the right of revision in those cases only where the rights of property are concerned, and where the matter in dispute has a known and certain value, which can be proved and calculated, in the ordinary mode of a business transaction. There are no words in the law which, by any just interpretation, can be held to extend the appellate jurisdiction beyond those limits, and authorize us to take cognizance of cases to which no test of money can be applied. Nor, indeed, is the limitation upon the appellate power of this court confined to cases like the one before us. It is the same in judgments in criminal cases, although the liberty or life of the party may depend on the decision of the circuit court."[45]

Again, in *United States v. New Bedford Bridge*, Justice Woodbury pointed out: "To enable this court to act, a case must not only fall within the judicial power of the United States, as conferred by the Constitution, but jurisdiction over it must have been conferred on the circuit court by some act of Congress. Such cases alone are those described in the judiciary act, as 'cognizable under the authority of the United States.' "[46]

Another equally important principle, later cited in the *Dred Scott* case, was that the consent of parties cannot give jurisdiction where jurisdiction has not been conferred by the Constitution or the law. This rule was clearly stated in the case of *Cutler v. Rae.*[47]

As if in answer to doubts expressed by the Circuit Courts of Ohio and Michigan, the Supreme Court, in *Sheldon v. Sill*, once more upheld the constitutionality of the proviso in the

11th Section of the Judiciary Act concerning assigned notes. Speaking for the court, Justice Grier said: "It must be admitted that if the Constitution had ordained and established the inferior courts, and distributed to them their respective powers, they could not be restricted or divested by Congress. But as it has made no such distribution, one or two consequences must result: either that each inferior court created by Congress must exercise all the judicial powers not given to the Supreme Court, or that Congress, having the power to establish the courts, must define their respective jurisdictions. The first of these inferences has never been asserted, and could not be defended with any show of reason, and if not, the latter would seem to follow as a necessary consequence. And it would seem to follow, also, that having a right to prescribe, Congress may withhold from any court of its creation jurisdiction of any of the enumerated controversies. Courts created by statute can have no jurisdiction but such as the statute confers."[48]

Jecker v. Montgomery presented the court with the interesting question, arising out of the Mexican War, of whether the President or any other executive office could establish prize courts which were competent to take jurisdiction of a case of capture. Carefully distinguishing between the military courts established in Mexico on a temporary basis from courts empowered to determine questions of prize, the Supreme Court held that the latter could be established only by an act of Congress. "Every court of the United States," said Chief Justice Taney, "must derive its jurisdiction and judicial authority from the Constitution or the laws of the United States. And neither the President nor any military officer can establish a court in a conquered country, and authorize it to decide upon the rights of the United States, or of individuals in prize cases, nor to administer the laws of nations." A sentence of such a court was therefore held to be without any validity.[49]

The case of *Pennsylvania v. Wheeling Bridge Co.* once more presented the court with the interpretation of its original jurisdiction in controversies involving states. When the case first came before the court, the majority took jurisdiction without discussion of the question. Justice

Daniel, however, dissented, on the ground that the State of Pennsylvania had no direct interest which would justify the assumption of original jurisdiction.[50]

Two years later, when the case came before the court a second time, the majority held that the state had a direct interest in the controversy involving its own property.[51] Daniel once more took issue with the majority, contending that Pennsylvania's appearance before the court was merely on behalf of certain of its citizens, rather than in defense of direct interests and rights, and that the proper forum was either in the state court or one of the lower federal courts. The medula of Daniel's objection was that, "If in all instances in which the citizens of one state have cause of action against a citizen or a corporation of a different state, the action can be prosecuted in the name of the state in which the claimant resides, although no peculiar or legal right or cause of action can be shown in such state sustaining the character of a private suitor, then the restriction as to cases of original jurisdiction is entirely abolished; the defending party, too, must be entitled to the same right of substitution, and all suits between citizens of different states, might, by this process, be transformed into suits between states, or suits to which states are parties: cases of original jurisdiction in this court." Daniel contended that original jurisdiction should be confined to cases in which a certain and direct interest, or an injury, or a right of property, on the part of the state, was proven.[52]

In another case of original jurisdiction, a boundary dispute between Florida and Georgia, the question arose as to whether the United States could intervene. Four justices denied this right, arguing that the constitutional grant of original jurisdiction did not comprehend cases in which the United States was a party. The majority, however, insisting on the right of the United States to be heard prior to any decision by the court, lest the interests of the nation as a whole be inadequately represented, skirted the constitutional restrictions by permitting the federal government to give testimony without actually becoming a party to the suit.[53]

Justice Curtis, joined by McLean, refused to accept this subterfuge and insisted that the ruling of the court was in violation of the constitutional distinction between original and appellate jurisdiction. Further, he insisted that the United States could not be a party to a judicial controversy with a state in any court. "There is," he declared, "nothing in the general plan of the Constitution, or in the nature and objects of the powers it confers, or in the relations between the general and state governments, to lead us to expect to find a grant of power over judicial controversies between the government of the Union and the several states."

Curtis then pointed out that a state could be sued only by its own consent; that nowhere had the states consented to be sued by the federal government. The State of Georgia, through the Constitution, had consented to be sued by the State of Florida, but had not consented to the intervention of a third party, no matter what the argument of necessity or natural justice. Nor was it within the power of Congress to confer such a right on the United States or any other party not enumerated in the constitutional provision.[54]

In *Dynes v. Hoover*, the court ruled that the sentence of a court-martial was not reviewable by any civil tribunal, provided that the military court had jurisdiction over the subject matter.[55]

In the following year, the Circuit Court of Massachusetts once more held that a writ of error does not lie from the Supreme Court to the Circuit Court in a criminal case, even when the prisoner was sentenced to be executed. Here George Searle, the lawyer for the defendant, presented a lengthy argument in which he attempted to prove the prisoner's right to be heard by the Supreme Court. His first proposition was that the Supreme Court was constitutionally bound to take appellate jurisdiction in all cases, whether civil or criminal, arising under the Constitution and laws of the United States, and that the decision in *United States v. More* was erroneous.

Searle contended that the entire jurisdiction of the Supreme Court, both original and appellate, was conferred directly by the Constitution and not by act of Congress. "Until 'exceptions' are made by Congress to the appellate jurisdiction conferred by the Constitution," he stated, "that jurisdiction includes all cases whatsoever, civil and criminal, arising under the Constitution and laws of the United States, except such as are included in the original jurisdiction. The point we contend for is that Congress has no power whatever affirmatively to confer appellate jurisdiction on the Supreme Court. It only has a discretionary power 'to make exceptions' to the general appellate jurisdiction conferred by the Constitution, and also to 'make regulations' by which this general appellate jurisdiction shall be exercised."

Searle maintained that exceptions were "against equality and right, and adverse to the ascertainment of truth and the accomplishment of justice, and also adverse to uniformity and certainty in the law;" that consequently all such exceptions should be expressly and affirmatively made; "they cannot be implied by any acts of Congress whatever; much less can they be implied negatively or unnecessarily from any acts of Congress."

The lawyer for the defendant then proceeded to point out that Congress had never made any express exceptions to the general appellate jurisdiction, that it had conferred jurisdiction in certain cases, but that such grants were gratuitous since the Supreme Court already possessed that jurisdiction directly from the Constitution.

Turning to the case of *United States v. More,*[56] Searle claims that the Supreme Court erred in confusing the terms "exceptions" and "regulations"; that the "regulation" of the appellate jurisdiction in the Judiciary Act did not and could not imply that what was not explicitly granted was therefore excepted from the jurisdiction of the Supreme Court, because a regulation of one thing was not the same as an exception of another. The regulations enumerated in Section 22 of the Judiciary Act, he said, could not be "construed into 'exceptions' prohibiting appeals in criminal cases, which are not mentioned, and where not money, but life, liberty and character are in issue. Such a construction would not only be legally absurd, it would be morally atrocious. To hold that a regulation prescribing the mode of appeal in a civil suit where $2,000 are at stake, shall, by implication, be deemed a prohibition upon any appeal in a criminal case where one's life is at stake, would be an interpretation of the law as ludicrous and grotesque as it would be brutal and inhuman. It is a maxim of universal application that all interpretations are to lean to life and liberty."

Searle's second argument was that the defendant was entitled to Fifth Amendment due process of law, which not only comprehended trial by jury but the right to appeal. If the Third Article of the Constitution did give to Congress any discretionary power to withhold the right of appeal in a criminal case, continued Searle, the subsequent amendment superseded and annulled such a power.[57]

Justice Clifford rejected the argument of Searle. Conceding that authority might be vested in the Supreme Court to grant writs of error to the circuit courts to revise criminal cases in order to re-examine matters of law, Clifford declared that Congress had never conferred such a jurisdiction. Acknowledging that the counsel's proposition was "ingeniously put and well-argued," Clifford denied the basic assumption that "jurisdiction exists unless it be shown that it is excluded by some express exception in an act of Congress."

"It is as clear," said Clifford, "that the appellate jurisdiction of the Supreme Court, if Congress legislates upon the subject, must be exercised under such regulations as Congress shall prescribe, as it is that the appellate jurisdiction is conferred with such exceptions as Congress shall make. . .Congress, it is true, has not declared in express terms that the appellate jurisdiction of the Supreme Court shall not extend to criminal cases, nor to civil actions or suits in equity where the matter in dispute, exclusive of costs, does not exceed the sum or value of $2,000; but Congress has described affirmatively the appellate jurisdiction of that court, and that affirmative description has always been held 'to imply a negative on the exercise of such appellate power as is not comprehended within it.' " Thus Clifford's rebuttal relied on the very cases which Searle contended were erroneous.

It is difficult to determine from his opinion how Clifford would have ruled if there were no precedents dating from the early days of the court. On the one hand he argued that the detailed regulations concerning appeals in civil actions, suits in equity, causes of admiralty and maritime jurisdiction, and the omission of any regulations concerning review of criminal cases, pointed to the clear intention of Congress not to extend the appellate jurisdiction to the latter category of cases. On the other hand, he seems to yield to the repeated decisions of the Supreme Court because they "have been too long acquiesced in as sound expositions of the judiciary act to be changed without an act of Congress."

In a final observation, which goes beyond the case at hand but which throws some light on the prevailing attitudes, Clifford says: "Efforts have been made in Congress at different periods to extend the appellate jurisdiction of the Supreme Court so as to include criminal cases, but the measure has never received much support, as it was foreseen that it would increase the business of that court beyond what the judges could accomplish, and would necessarily lead to such delays as would tend to defeat the great purpose intended to be accomplished in the administration of criminal justice."[58]

The thesis underlying Clifford's denial of the petition was affirmed by the Supreme Court once again in *Ex parte Gordon* in 1862. Where a prisoner who had been convicted for the crime of piracy and sentenced to death applied for a writ of prohibition to be directed to the circuit court, the Supreme Court ruled: "In criminal cases, the proceedings and judgment of the circuit court cannot be revised or controlled here, *in any form of proceeding*, either by writ of error or prohibition. . .The only case in which this court is authorized even to express an opinion on the proceedings in a circuit court in a criminal case is where the judges of the cricuit court are opposed in opinion upon a question arising at the trail."[59]

Summing up the controversy between Searle's position and the rulings of the courts, we can make certain observations:

1. If Searle's argument were correct, then there would be no end to the cases in which the Supreme Court would have to take appellate jurisdiction under the Constitution. . .unless, of course, Congress made explicit exceptions to said jurisdiction.

2. Under the rule laid down by the Supreme Court in *United States v. More* and confirmed in these decisions, Congress exercised a veto power over the business of the Supreme Court which could be exercised without excepting cases from the appellate jurisdiction but merely by granting jurisdiction affirmatively in some few cases.

3. More importantly, under either interpretation of the clause in question, it was Congress which determined the appellate jurisdiction of the Supreme Court (though it can only limit, not create new jurisdiction not given by the Constitution), not the court itself which so determines. Likewise, Congress determined the jurisdiction of the inferior courts. Therefore, by virtue of its control over original jurisdiction in the inferior courts and appellate jurisdiction in the Supreme Court, *it exercised an indirect* (and not so indirect) *control over the exercise of the judicial power itself.* [60]

Clifford himself says: "The better opinion is that Congress cannot defeat the appellate jurisdiction of the Supreme Court by omitting to enact regulations for its exercise, as authorized by the Constitution."[61] But if the granting of jurisdiction is a matter of Congressional discretion, even if what Clifford says is true, the jurisdiction may be narrowed down, in an extreme case, to only one class of cases—and who is there to decide that such a restriction is unconstitutional? Yet if such a restriction were unconstitutional, where is the line to be drawn? If such a restriction were unconstitutional, how can appellate jurisdiction in criminal cases be excluded?

4. In the last resort, the choice is between Story's position in *Martin v. Hunter's Lessee* ("it is the duty of Congress to vest the whole judicial power;. . .if it were otherwise, this anomaly would exist: that Congress might successively refuse to vest the jurisdiction in any one class of cases. . .and thereby defeat the jurisdiction as to all") and a reliance on Congressional discretion. Although a potential danger lies in the latter alternative (for reasons stated by Story as well as arguments given by Searle), the granting of complete and unrestricted appellate jurisdiction to the Supreme Court in all cases would, as Clifford pointed out and as experience

proved, flood the Supreme Court with an excess of business. Thus, reliance on Congressional discretion, despite the potential dangers, seemed and seems to be the better course, out of prudence if not out of abstract theory or a literal interpretation of the clause in question.

CHAPTER FIVE

Footnotes:

[1] *Kendall v. United States ex rel. Stokes,* 12 Peters 524 (1838).

[2] *United States v. Ravara,* Case 16,122, 27 FC 713 (1793). See also Chapter Six, p. 240.

[3] *Idem.*

[4] An appeal brought both the law and the facts; a writ of error, only the law.

[5] *Wiscart v. Dauchy,* 3 Dallas 321 (1796).

[6] *Idem,* dissent of Wilson (joined by Paterson), 3 Dallas 324-327.

[7] Congress, by the act of February 13, 1801, gave an appeal in equity and admiralty cases. This act was repealed in 1802. Again Congress gave an appeal in the act of March 3, 1803.

[8] The purpose of this proviso was to exclude suits between citizens of the same state by assigning notes to a citizen of a second state.

[9] *Turner v. Bank of North America,* 4 Dallas 8 (1799).

[10] *Idem,* concurring opinion of Chase, 4 Dallas 10.

[11] *Marbury v. Madison,* 1 Cranch 137; 173-176 (1803). See Chapter Two, p. 39 and Chapter Three, pp. 107-109 for more on this case.

[12] 3 Cranch 159 (1805), Marshall. See also Story's opinion in *Ex parte Kearney,* 7 Wheaton 38; 42 (1822): "It is to be considered that this court has no appellate jurisdiction confided to it in criminal cases, by the laws of the United States. It cannot entertain a writ of error, to revise the judgment of the circuit court, in any case where a party has been convicted of a public offense. And undoubtedly the denial of this authority proceeded upon great principles of public policy and

convenience. If every party had a right to bring before this court every case in which judgment had passed against him for a crime or misdemeanor or felony, the course of justice might be materially delayed and obstructed and, in some cases, totally frustrated."

[13] Act of April 29, 1802.

[14] *Ex parte Bollman,* 4 Cranch 75; 93-94 (1807).

[15] 5 Cranch 61 (1809). The court, however, upheld jurisdiction under the "diversity of citizenship" clause.

[16] 6 Cranch 307 (1810). The court held that the *intent* of Congress was to give the Supreme Court the same appellate jurisdiction here as was given over the District Court of Kentucky by Section 10 of the Judiciary Act.

[17] 7 Cranch 504 (1813).

[18] Taking issue with Story's interpretation, Justice Johnson, in a concurring opinion, held that the words "shall extend to" were used in a future sense and implied no imperative. 1 Wheaton 374-375.

[19] Story's explanation for the distinction is "the vital importance of all the cases enumerated in the first class to the national sovereignty."

[20] *Martin v. Hunter's Lessee,* 1 Wheaton 304; 327-340 (1816). See also Chapter Two, p. 49.

[21] We have seen previously how Marshall accepted legislative limitations on the constitutional grant of jurisdiction. This difference alone is enough to contradict the allegation that the real author of this opinion was Marshall, whose name did not appear because of a personal interest in the outcome of the case.

[22] 6 Wheaton 264; 392-405 (1821).

[23] *Bank of the United States v. Northumberland Bank,* Case 931, 2 FC 726 (1821).

[24] The case was considered to be one arising under a law of the United States, the law in question having given the right to sue.

[25] *Bank of the United States v. Roberts,* Case 934, 2 FC 728 (1822), Per Curiam.

[26] *Osborn v. Bank of the United States,* 9 Wheaton 738; 818-827 (1816). Dissent of Johnson, 9 Wheaton 874; 885-889.

[27] 3 Peters 193 (1830). (Italics added.)

[28] *United States v. Gilchrist,* Case 15,204, 25 FC 1287; 1317-1318 (1834).

[29] For the significance of such a ruling, see Chapter Three, pp. 117 and 121-122 above, under "*Mandamus*".

[30] This conclusion is consistent with an earlier ruling of the Supreme Court that, "By the fifth section of the same act, the courts of the District are vested generally with jurisdiction of all causes in law and equity." *Bank of Columbia v. Okely,* 4 Wheaton 235 (1819), Johnson.

[31] Case 15,517, 26 FC 702 (1837).

[32] This latter line of reasoning, especially coming from Judge Cranch, leaves much to be desired, for only four years earlier the same judge had made a point of distinguishing between the words "power" or "powers" and "jurisdiction." In *United States v. Williams,* Case 16,712, 28 FC 647 (1833), Cranch had stated: "We are, therefore, referred to the act of February 13th, 1801, for our powers; but not for our jurisdiction. . .No two ideas can be more distinct than 'power' and 'jurisdiction'. . .By thus using both terms, it is evident that Congress did not consider either of them alone as sufficient to convey the ideas included in both; and that the word 'power,' as applied to a court, did not necessarily include the idea of jurisdiction; nor the word jurisdiction that of power. Still less does the word 'powers' (in the plural) which is the term used in the grant of the powers of this court, imply jurisdiction, particularly, if the jurisdiction of the court, as in the present case, be expressly given in a separate and distinct section."

[33] *Kendall v. United States ex rel. Stokes,* 12 Peters 524 (1838).

[34] Thompson's treatment of the terms "power" and "jurisdiction" or "cognizance" was more consistent with his reasoning than that of Cranch. Part way through his opinion, Thompson remarked: "Some criticisms have been made at the bar, between the use of the terms 'power' and 'cognizance' as employed in those sections. It is not perceived how such distinction, if any exists, can affect the construction of this law. That there is a distinction, in some respects, cannot be doubted; and, generally speaking, the word 'power' is used in reference to the means employed in carrying jurisdiction into execution. But it may well be doubted whether any marked distinction is observed and kept up in our laws, so as in any measure to affect the construction of those laws. *Power must include jurisdiction,* which is generally used in reference to the exercise of that power in courts of justice. *But power, as used in the Constitution, would seem to embrace both.*" (Italics added.)

[35] *Idem,* dissent of Taney, 12 Peters 626-641.

[36] *Idem,* dissent of Barbour, 12 Peters 641-653. Justice Catron also dissented.

[37] *Rhode Island v. Massachusetts,* 12 Peters 657 (1838). Taney dissented, contending that "contests for rights of sovereignty and jurisdiction between states over any particular territory, are not, in my judgment, the subjects of judicial cognizance and control, to be recovered and enforced in an ordinary suit." 12 Peters 752-753. He did not, however, offer an alternative solution. See Chapter Four, pp. 175-6.

[38] Case 5,465, 10 FC 447 (1838).

[39] *Dundas v. Bowler,* Case 4,410, 8 FC 28 (1843). In view of the fact that the proviso had hitherto been held valid by the courts and because it was possible to uphold jurisdiction in this case on other grounds, the court stopped short of declaring the proviso void.

[40] *Brainard v. Williams,* Case 1,804, 4 FC 7 (1846). There is no indication, however, that this opinion had any practical consequence.

[41] *Ex parte Christy,* 3 Howard 292 (1845). See also *Nelson v. Carland,* 1 Howard 265 (1843) and Catron's dissent.

[42] 3 Howard 236; 244-245 (1845).

[43] *Idem,* dissent of Story, 3 Howard 253 ff. The majority claimed that the citizen was not without judicial remedy: "[The claimant] might have asserted his right to the possession of the goods or his exemption from the duties commanded, either by replevin, or in an action of detinue, or perhaps by an action of trover." 3 Howard 250.

[44] *Idem,* dissent of McLean, 3 Howard 263 ff.

[45] 5 Howard 103 (1847). This decision is curious and inexplicable when compared with the earlier decision of *Lee v. Lee,* 8 Peters 44 (1834), where the Supreme Court took jurisdiction of a petition for freedom and held: "On the part of the defendant in error a preliminary objection has been made to the jurisdiction of this court, growing out of the Act of Congress of the 2nd of April, 1816, which declares that no cause shall be removed from the Circuit Court for the District of Columbia to the Supreme Court, by appeal or writ of error, unless the *matter in dispute* shall be of the value of $1,000, or upwards.

"The *matter in dispute* in this case is the freedom of the petitioners. The judgment of the court below is against their claims to freedom; the matter in dispute is, therefore, to the plaintiff in error, the value of their freedom; and this is not susceptible of pecuniary valuation. Had the judgment been in favor of the petitioners, and the writ of error brought by the party claiming to be the owner, the value of the slaves as property would have been the *matter in dispute*, and affidavits might be admitted to ascertain such value. But affidavits estimating the value of freedom are entirely inadmissible, and we entertain no doubt of the jurisdiction of the court." 8 Peters 47-48, Thompson. (Italics added.)

[46] Case 15,867. 27 FC 91; 103 (1847), Circuit Court, Massachusetts.

[47] 7 Howard 729; 731 (1849).

[48] 8 Howard 411 (1850).

[49] 13 Howard 498; 515 (1852).

[50] 9 Howard 647 (1850). Dissent of Daniel, 9 Howard 659. Joined in by Taney.

[51] 13 Howard 518 (1852). The state had invested considerable sums in means of transportation connecting with the Port of Pittsburgh, which was the destination of steamboats plying the Ohio River and passing beneath the defendant's bridge at Wheeling.

[52] *Idem*, dissent of Daniel, 13 Howard 594 ff. Both Daniel and Taney further held that the case was incorrectly brought in equity when the remedy was at law.

[53] *Florida v. Georgia*, 17 Howard 478; 493-495 (1855).

[54] *Idem*, dissent of Curtis, 17 Howard 496-512. Dissents were also filed by Daniel and Campbell. The latter stated that the United States had "no title to appear as a party to the record, nor in any undefined and uncertain relation to it." 17 Howard 514-522.

[55] 20 Howard 65 (1858).

[56] It is interesting to note that in the earlier case it was the government which argued in favor of appellate jurisdiction over criminal cases.

[57] Argument of George W. Searle, *United States v. Plumer*, Case 16,055, 27 FC 551; 552-556 (1859).

[58] *Idem*, Opinion of the Court (Clifford), 27 FC 558-561. Clifford makes no reply to Searle's argument concerning due process.

[59] 1 Black 503 (1862), Taney. (Italics added.)

[60] See the post-Civil War case of *Ex parte McCardle*, where Congress literally removed the case from the jurisdiction of the United States courts while still pending and prior to a final decision. 7 Wallace 506 (1869).

[61] *United States v. Plumer*, above.

CHAPTER SIX:

SPECIAL PROBLEMS OF JURISDICTION

The federal courts faced many special problems of jurisdiction, arising out of the Constitution and legislative acts. The principal jurisdictional conflicts to which the courts devoted their attention during the pre-Civil War period involved authority over common-law crimes, the standing of corporations, the status of Negroes, the writ of *habeas corpus* and admiralty and maritime jurisdiction.

1. Jurisdiction over Common-Law Crimes

Perhaps the easiest problem to resolve and the one which gave rise to a minimum of polemics was that of the common-law jurisdiction of the federal courts. However, the final conclusion which was reached was not the starting point, and it was several decades before the question was put to rest.

It is to be remembered that both in the English legal system and that of the states which, with the exception of Louisiana, was based on the former, the courts had jurisdiction over common-law as well as statutory crime—and at that time the bulk of criminal cases involved violations of the common law. When the new government was formed and courts were established to deal with criminal as well as civil cases, the question arose as to whether or not there was such a category as a federal common-law crime, which could be tried and punished before its own courts.

The first time the question came up in a court of the United States was in the case of *United States v. Smith*, in 1792. Here it was held, by the Circuit Court of

Massachusetts, that the federal courts have common-law jurisdiction of criminal cases and may punish a crime though there be no express statute for that purpose. The defendant was charged and found guilty of the crime of passing counterfeit bank bills of the Bank of the United States. Before sentencing, his attorney moved in arrest of judgment on the ground that there was no federal statute on the subject; that the offense was only a common-law one; and that the state courts exclusively had jurisdiction of such offenses. The court, however, held that, "the federal courts had jurisdiction of all causes or cases in law of equity arising under the said Constitution and the laws of the United States; that this was a case arising under those laws, for those bills were made in virtue thereof, though there was no statute describing or punishing the offense of counterfeiting them; and therefore to counterfeit them was a contempt of and a misdemeanor against the United States, and punishable by them as such."[1]

The following year the Circuit Court of Pennsylvania handed down a ruling of the same tenor in the *Case of Henfield.* Here an American citizen was indicted for aiding and assisting a French privateer in taking British vessels, in contravention of treaty and the law of nations. The court held that the federal judiciary had jurisdiction over such offenses and could punish the offender according to the forms of the common law. In a note attached to the case, reference was made to "the much controverted position that the federal courts have common-law cognizance of offences against the sovereignty of the United States."[2]

Again, in Pennsylvania, the Circuit Court held that the defendant was indictable and triable in the federal courts for the common-law offense of sending anonymous and threatening letters with intent to extort money.[3]

It was not until 1798 that judicial doubts were raised over the question of jurisdiction over common-law offenses. The defendant, Worrall, was indicted in the federal courts for attempting to bribe the Commissioner of Revenue of the United States, in the absence of any act of Congress defining such an offense. The court was divided: Chase, the Circuit Justice, being of opinion that there was no common law of the United States, and that no offenses against the United States were punishable except as provided by statute; while Judge Peters thought that the United States possessed the common-law power to punish misdemeanors.[4]

The attorney for the defense argued that, "It is incumbent upon the prosecution to show that an offer to bribe the commissioner of the revenue is a violation of some constitution or legislative prohibition. . .Can the offence, then, be said to arise under the Constitution or the laws of the United States? And if not, what is there to render it cognizable under the authority of the United States?" He went on to attack the idea that if a federal officer is concerned, federal jurisdiction automatically extended to other persons in any case in which the officer might be involved.

As for the claim that the common law is the law of the United States, counsel contended that, "The nature of our federal compact will not, however, tolerate this doctrine. . .Congress may make all laws which shall be necessary and proper for carrying into execution the powers of the general government. But here is no reference to a common-law authority: Every power is a matter of definite and positive grant; and the very powers that are granted cannot take effect until they are exercised through the medium of law. Congress has undoubtedly a power to make a law, which should render it criminal to offer a bribe to the commissioner of the revenue; but not having made the law the crime is not recognized by the federal code, constitutional or legislative; and, consequently, it is not a subject on which the judicial authority of the Union can operate."

The prosecution replied that in both the cases of Henfield and Ravara, a common law of the United States was recognized under which both indictments were upheld; and that unless the offense was punishable in the federal courts it would not be punishable at all, since it was certainly not cognizable before any state tribunal.

Thereupon Justice Chase interrupted: "Do you mean, Mr. Attorney, to support this indictment solely at common-law? If you do, I have no difficulty upon the subject. The indictment cannot be maintained in this court."

Agreeing with defendant's counsel, Chase continued: "The question, however, does not arise about the power, but about the exercise of the power: whether the courts of the United States can punish a man for any act, before it is declared by a law of the United States to be criminal? Now, it appears to my mind to be as essential that Congress should define the offenses to be tried, and apportion the punishment to be inflicted, as that they should erect courts to try the criminal, or to pronounce a sentence on conviction.

"It is attempted, however, to supply the silence of the Constitution and statutes of the Union by resorting to the common law for a definition and punishment of the offence which has been committed; but in my opinion, the United States, as a federal government, have no common law; and consequently no indictment can be maintained in their courts, for offenses merely at the common law. . .

"The question recurs: when and how have the courts of the United States acquired a common-law jurisdiction in criminal cases? The United States must possess the common law themselves, before they can communicate it to their judicial agents. Now, the United States did not bring it with them from England; the Constitution does not create it; and no act of Congress has assumed it. Besides, what is the common law to which we are referred? Is it the common law entire, as it exists in England; or modified, as it exists in some of the states; and of the various modifications, which are we to select, the system of Georgia or New Hampshire, of Pennsylvania or Connecticut?"

In conclusion, Chase followed the road of judicial restraint: "Upon the whole it may be a defect in our political institutions; it may be an inconvenience in the administration of justice that the common law authority, relating to crimes and punishments, has not been conferred upon the government of the United States, which is a government in other respects of a limited jurisdiction; but judges cannot remedy political imperfections, nor supply any legislative omission."[5]

Judge Peters upheld the precedent of the earlier cases and the argument of the prosecution: "The power to punish misdemeanours is originally and strictly a common-law power, of which I think the United States are constitutionally possessed. It might have been exercised by Congress in the form of a legislative act; but it may also, in my opinion, be enforced in a course of judicial proceeding. Whenever an offence aims at the subversion of any federal institution, or at the corruption of its public officers, it is an offence against the well-being of the United States; from its very nature, it is cognizable under their authority; and, consequently, it is within the jurisdiction of this court, by virtue of the eleventh section of the judicial act."[6]

In the following year, in the Circuit Court of Connecticut, the defendant was indicted for accepting a commission from the French Republic and cruising against and capturing British property. No question of jurisdiction was raised, and he was convicted.[7]

The case of *United States v. Meyer*, before the Circuit Court of Pennsylvania, was, according to the editors of *Federal Cases*, "an indictment for libel, and is cited in Wharton's *Precedents of Indictments* as an instance of the exercise by the federal courts of jurisdiction over offenses of a purely common-law origin. The case is nowhere reported, opinion not now accessible."[8]

And in the year 1806, Justice Washington summed up the matter in *United States v. McGill* when he said: "I have often decided that the federal courts have a common-law jurisdiction in common-law cases."[9]

Then, in 1812, the course of two decades was turned around, on the first occasion that the question was brought before the Supreme Court. Ignoring the circuit court decisions previously cited, Justice Johnson, speaking for the court, held that the jurisdiction of the courts of the United States did not extend to common-law criminal cases.

"The course of reasoning which leads to this conclusion," he wrote, "is simple, obvious, and admits of but little illustration. The powers of the general government are made up of concessions from the several states—whatever is not expressly given to the former, the latter expressly reserve. The judicial power of the United States is a constitutent part of those concessions—that power is to be exercised by courts organized for the purpose, and brought into existence by an effort of the legislative power of the Union. Of all the courts which the United States may, under their general powers, constitute, one only, the Supreme Court, possesses jurisdiction derived immediately from the Constitution, and of which the legislative power cannot deprive it. All other courts created by the general government possess no jurisdiction but what is given them by the power that creates them, and can be vested with none but what the power ceded to the general government will authorize them to confer.

"The legislative authority of the Union," Johnson continued, "must first make an act a crime, affix a punishment to it, and declare the court that shall have jurisdiction of the offence. Certain implied powers must necessarily result to our courts of justice from the nature of their institution. But jurisdiction of crimes against the state is not among those powers; all exercise of criminal jurisdiction in common-law cases we are of the opinion is not within their implied powers."[10]

But Justice Story was unsatisfied with this ruling and, notwithstanding this decision, the following year in the Circuit Court of Massachusetts, attempted to ground the common-law jurisdiction of the federal courts on a sound legal argument.

"There can be no doubt," he wrote, "that Congress may, under the Constitution, confide to the circuit court jurisdiction of all offences against the United States. Has it so done? The Judicial Act of 24th of September, 1789, Section 11, provides that the circuit court 'shall have exclusive cognizance of all crimes and offences cognizable under the authority of the United States...' No subsequent act has narrowed the jurisdiction; it remains therefore in full operation. *The jurisdiction is not, as has sometimes been supposed in argument, over all crimes and offences specially created and defined by statute. It is of all crimes and offences 'cognizable under the authority of the United States,'* that is, of all crimes and offences to which by the Constitution of the United States, the judicial power extends. The jurisdiction could not, therefore, have been given in more broad and comprehensive terms."

For Story, "all offences against the sovereignty, the public rights, the public justice, the public peace, the public trade and the public police of the United States, are crimes and offences against the United States." Among the examples of offenses of which the federal courts had cognizance, independent of any statute, Story cited: treason, embezzlement of the public records, bribery and resistance of the judicial process, riots and misdemeanors on the high seas, frauds and obstructions of the public laws of trade, and robbery and embezzlement of the mail.

As for the problem of punishment, "The common law affords the proper answer. It is a settled principle that where an offence exists to which no specific punishment is affixed by statute, it is punishable by fine and imprisonment."[11]

Had this sweeping jurisdiction of Story's prevailed, the potential power of the federal courts would have been virtually unlimited, at least until checked by Congress. The courts would have been called on to play an active role not only in defining, interpreting and even creating categories of public offenses; their discretion in handing out punishments would have been unbounded, and they would have found themselves faced with the problem posed by Justice Chase: which version of the common law was to be followed?[12]

Judge Davis did not concur with this opinion. Even Story himself expressed his desire to have the matter reviewed by the higher court. The case was then certified to the Supreme Court which, in an unsatisfactory opinion, overruled Story and upheld the earlier decision of *United States v. Hudson.* Justice Johnson, giving the opinion of the court, stated: "Upon the question now before the court, a difference of opinion has existed, and still exists, among the members of the court. We should, therefore, have been willing to have heard the question discussed upon solemn argument. But the Attorney General has declined to argue the cause and no counsel appears for the defendant. Under these circumstances, the court would not choose to review their former decision in the case of the *United States v. Hudson*, or draw it into doubt. They will, therefore, certify an opinion to the circuit court in conformity with that decision."[13]

It is no wonder that Story added: "I do not take the

question to be settled by that case."[14] But despite his dissent, the question was settled. In 1818 the Circuit Court of Maryland pointed out that the courts of the United States have no common-law jurisdiction in criminal cases and will not punish an offense at common law unless punishable by statute.[15] In 1840, the Circuit Court of Arkansas refused to take jurisdiction of a case involving robbery within Indian territory because there was no law of Congress punishing the crime of robbery committed on land. As District Judge Benjamin Johnson pointed out: "The United States have no unwritten criminal code, to which resort can be had as a source of jurisdiction."[16]

Seven years later the same judge quashed an indictment against an accessory before the fact, no law of Congress existing to provide for punishment: "This court is only authorized to try and punish such crimes as Congress expressly or by necessary implication has visited with known and certain penalties, and the court has no common-law jurisdiction in that respect. The defects in the Criminal Code of the United States have been severely felt, but it is for Congress, not this court, to interpose and apply the corrective."[17]

In the same year, the Circuit Court of Massachusetts rejected an indictment against a bridge corporation for obstructing navigation for want of jurisdiction, Congress not having declared the act charged to be an offense against the United States. In a lengthy opinion, Justice Woodbury demonstrated that neither the power of Congress to regulate commerce nor the admiralty and maritime jurisdiction enabled the courts to punish any act as a crime, unless the Constitution, a treaty or a law made it a crime and conferred authority on the court to punish it. The court did not deny the power of Congress to act on the subject but insisted that legislation must declare what obstructions shall be illegal and in what court the offense shall be tried.

"To enable this court to act," said Woodbury, "a case must not only fall within the judicial power of the United States, as conferred by the Constitution, but jurisdiction over it must have been conferred on the circuit court by some act of Congress. Such cases alone"—and here we have the belated reply to Story—"are those described in the judiciary act, as 'cognizable under the authority of the United States.' "

Reiterating the fact that the United States had no unwritten code to give it jurisdiction, Woodbury proceeded to speculate on "the unqualified adoption of some whole code of laws in a Constitution. Had there been a provision in it like that of our ancestors at Plymouth Rock, respecting the Mosaic Code, directing the laws of any country or sovereign to be in force till Congress could make better ones, and offences under them to be prosecuted in any courts created by Congress, the difficulty in this case would have been cured, if the conduct of the respondents should amount to an offence under those laws. Or had there been a provision of a like tenor, adopting the common law, or the civil law, or the admiralty law, as a whole, and placing the execution of them in charge of this court, then our jurisdiction would be clear. . .But no such clause exists, and none is likely to exist. . .It is also very inconvenient to adopt in any Constitution any code as a part of the law of the land, without at the same time proceeding to make it alterable by legislation alone, as the interests and wants and experience of society might require. . .Hence the common-law of England has been considered as not put in force, directly or indirectly, by means of any clause in the Constitution of the United States, so as to create, make, or help to make any thing an offence which has not been made so by the Constitution itself, or acts of Congress passed under it. . .And however courts may properly resort to the common law to aid in giving construction to words used in that Constitution and those laws, the body of the common law, as such, does not alone give jurisdiction in any case, and enable the court to declare any acts to be offences under the United States and to try them, where the Constitution and the acts of Congress have been silent concerning them."[18]

The upshot of this narrow interpretation of the federal courts' jurisdiction over criminal offenses was a victory for the civil rights doctrine, that no man shall be punished unless legally tried by virtue of a law passed prior to the commitment of the offense. The rule laid down in *United States v. Hudson* and followed ever since was, in its way, the first step toward establishing a meaningful due process of law.

2. *Diversity of Citizenship. The Corporation as Citizen.*

Section 2 of Article III of the Constitution describes the cases and controversies to which the judicial power of the United States was to extend. The framers contemplated various situations in which the federal courts should exercise jurisdiction along with or in place of the state courts. The Judiciary Act of 1789—and later modifications—implemented the constitutional grant.

Perhaps the one state of circumstances which most clearly justified recourse to the federal tribunals in the minds of the framers was the case involving a controversy between citizens of different states. The First Congress promptly granted to the circuit courts original cognizance[19] of civil suits between a citizen of the state where the suit is brought and a citizen of another state.[20] The controversies which were to come before the courts under this heading proved to constitute the bulk of their business.

But from the beginning the application of this jurisdictional grant posed problems. In the first place, the court ruled that it was necessary for the parties to aver their citizenship on the record before the courts could take jurisdiction under this section of the Judiciary Act.[21] A few years later, in *Strawbridge v. Curtis*, the Supreme Court held that where there are more than one plaintiff or defendant, each one must be capable of suing or being sued in the federal courts; that is, there must exist a diversity of citizenship as to all plaintiffs and all defendants.[22]

In 1808 a case came before the Circuit Court of Georgia in which a corporation, the Bank of the United States, was the plaintiff. The court ruled to dismiss the case for want of jurisdiction on the ground that the Constitution takes no notice of corporate bodies in enumerating the cases in which the circuit courts have jurisdiction over persons. Said the court: "A corporation cannot with propriety be denominated a citizen of any state, so that the right to sue in this court under the Constitution can only be extended to corporate bodies by a liberality of construction, which we do not feel ourselves at liberty to exercise."[23]

The following year, in a landmark decision, the Supreme Court reversed the lower court. The court held that the capacity of a corporation to sue in the courts of the United States depends upon the citizenship of its members; that if all the members of the corporation are citizens of a state other than that of the other party, the court may take jurisdiction.

Chief Justice Marshall begins his examination of the question by admitting, "That invisible, intangible, and artificial being, that mere legal entity, a corporation aggregate, is certainly not a citizen. Consequently," he concludes. "[it] cannot sue or be sued in the courts of the United States unless the rights of the members, in this respect, can be exercised in their corporate name.

"If the corporation be considered as a mere faculty," Marshall continues, "and not as a company of individuals who, in transacting their joint concerns, may use a legal name, they must be excluded from the courts of the Union."

But Marshall sees no reason to exclude these groupings of persons from the federal courts. Consequently, he holds that, "the controversy is, in fact and in law, between those persons suing in their corporate character, by their corporate name for a corporate right, and the individual against whom the suit may be instituted. Substantially and essentially, the parties in such a case, where the members of the corporation are aliens, or citizens of a different state from the opposite party, come within the spirit and terms of the jurisdiction conferred by the Constitution on the national tribunals.

"The term 'citizen,' " he adds, "ought to be understood as it is used in the Constitution, and as it is used in other laws. That is, to describe the real persons who come into court, in this case, under their corporate names. . .The court feels itself authorized. . .to look to the character of the individuals who compose the corporation."[24]

Combining this interpretation with the rule laid down in *Strawbridge v. Curtis*, as the matter then stood a corporation could sue in the corporate name if *all* the members of the corporation were citizens of a state other than that of the other party. This compromise satisfied virtually no one—with the exception of small, locally owned insurance companies—and yet it was to remain the law of the land for thirty-five years. Had the court adopted the legal fiction that a corporation was a citizen, the problem posed by *Strawbridge v. Curtis* would have been avoided; had the court upheld the Circuit Court of Georgia by refusing "the liberal construction" which was necessary to permit the Bank of the United States to sue,[25] it is highly probable that with the passing of time a constitutional amendment could have been obtained granting the federal courts a clear and explicit jurisdiction over corporate bodies.

Meanwhile, the courts were otherwise restricting the applicability of the diversity of citizenship clause. In *Hepburn v. Ellzey*,[26] the Supreme Court held that the citizens of the District of Columbia, not being citizens of any state, cannot sue in the courts of the United States as citizens of any state. Some years later, following the same line of reasoning, the court refused to take jurisdiction in a case where the plaintiff was a citizen of the Mississippi Territory and the defendant a citizen of a state.[27]

Other cases involving this clause were concerned with the locus of citizenship. In *Cooper v. Galbraith*, the Circuit Court of Pennsylvania held that if a citizen of one state thinks proper to change his domicile and to remove to another state, with a *bona fide* intention to reside there, he becomes instantly a citizen of that state and may sue in the courts of the United States as such.[28] In another case, before the Circuit Court of Virginia, Marshall stated that "a citizen of the United States must be a citizen of that state in which his domicile is placed," domicile being (according to Vattel), "the habitation fixed in any place, with an intention of always staying there."[29] In *Butler v. Farnsworth*, Justice Washington stated that the intention of the party in changing the place of his residence was material, "But this intention is to be collected from the acts, and not from the declarations of the party."[30] In *Picquet v. Swan*, the Circuit Court of Massachusetts refused to take jurisdiction in a case where the defendant, a citizen of the United States, a resident in a foreign country, was not a citizen of any state of the

Union.[31] In another case the court held that the presumption was that an American citizen was a citizen of some state unless there was "very strong evidence of his being a mere wanderer, without a home."[32]

In 1826, the Circuit Court of New York dismissed a suit against the Pacific Insurance Company when it was proved that three of the stockholders were not citizens of New York. (Ironically, the plaintiff had moved from the District of Columbia to the State of Virginia for the sole purpose of bringing the suit in the courts of the United States. The court held that whether the change of residence was *bona fide* was a question for the jury, but the question was never decided since the case was dismissed on the other grounds.)[33]

Also, the Circuit Court of Pennsylvania dismissed a suit where four members of a corporation were citizens of the State of New Jersey. The court turned down the plaintiff's request to limit the suit to those defendants who were citizens of Pennsylvania, in accordance with the long-standing rule that where there was a joint interest all the defendants must be under the jurisdiction of the court. When the plaintiff insisted that the parties to the suit were the officers of the corporation, all citizens of Pennsylvania, the court referred to the rule in the *Deveaux* case in which it was decided that all the members of the corporation and not just the officers were party to the suit.

But Justice Washington, who gave the opinion in this case, took the opportunity to express his dissatisfaction with the rules which he applied: "We very truly regret that the authorities and the course of reasoning which has been stated, lead us inevitably to the conclusion that the jurisdiction cannot be sustained in this case. . .; and we freely acknowledge that we have struggled, as far as duty would sanction, to discover such reasons as we could safely and conscientiously abide by, to authorize us in coming to a different conclusion. Our duty is to follow where the rules of law or equity and right reason lead, without looking to the consequences, although from a view of these consequences, we may be permitted, as we have done, to express our regret that the law is as we have stated it, or as we apprehend it to be. For it is very certain that if we are correct in our view of it, very few corporations can enjoy the privilege of suing, or being sued, in the courts of the United States, where a plea similar to the present is interposed; since it can seldom happen, we presume, but that some of their members reside in other states than that in which the business of the corporate body is transacted, and in which the suit is brought. Whether Congress can, or will, by legislative provisions, secure to corporations the privilege of suing, and to others that of suing them in the courts of the nation, in cases where some of the corporators are citizens of a state or states other than that in which the suit is brought, rests with that body in its wisdom to decide."[34]

Congress, however, took no action on the subject, and some years later, in a case where one member of the plaintiff-corporation was a citizen of the same state as the defendant, Justice Story reiterated the *Deveaux-Strawbridge* rule: "It has been repeatedly decided in the courts of the United States that to entitle a corporation to sue in the circuit courts of the United States, all members of that corporation must be citizens of some state of the United States, other than that state of which the defendant is a citizen."[35]

These three circuit court interpretations were confirmed by the Supreme Court as late as 1840, in a case in which two stockholders of a corporation were citizens of the same state as that of the original plaintiffs in the suit. Here Justice Barbour held for a unanimous court that the doctrines of *The Bank of the United States v. Deveaux* and *Strawbridge v. Curtis* continued to be the law of the court.[36]

Then in 1844, in a decision which was to expand the jurisdiction and business of the federal courts beyond measure, the Supreme Court reversed itself. In *Louisville Railroad Company v. Letson*, the court held unanimously[37] that a corporation is, "substantially, within the meaning of the law, a citizen of the state which created it, and where its business is done, for all the purposes of suing and being sued."

Holding that the doctrines laid down in the *Strawbridge* and *Deveaux* cases could not be sustained by a sound and comprehensive course of professional reasoning, and rejecting the consequences and inferences which had been drawn from the latter case, Justice Wayne re-examined the question with the object of finding a way to extend jurisdiction to corporations. Looking to the consequences, which Justice Washington had refrained from doing twenty years earlier, Wayne denied that the word "citizen" was used in the Constitution and the laws of the United States in a sense which necessarily excluded corporations.

"A corporation, created by a state, to perform its functions under the authority of that state," wrote Wayne, "seems to us to be a person, although an artificial one, inhabiting and belonging to that state, and therefore entitled, for the purpose of suing and being sued, to be deemed a citizen of that state."

In treating the corporation as a citizen for legal purposes, the court simultaneously solved the problem of the locus of citizenship: "A suit, then, brought by a citizen of one state against a corporation by its corporate name in the state of its locality, by which it was created, and where its business is done by any of the corporators who are chosen to manage its affairs, is a suit, so far as jurisdiction is concerned, between citizens of the state where the suit is brought and a citizen of another state."[38] [39]

Subsequent to the Letson case, the federal courts assumed jurisdiction over corporations without further objection. However, in the case of *Rundle v. Delaware and Raritan Canal Co.*, in which the court took jurisdiction without discussion, Justice Catron, in a concurring opinion, stated his own interpretation of the earlier case; namely, that the true parties that sue and are sued are the president and directors of the corporation as trustees and representatives of the stockholders. "If the president and directors are citizens of the state where the corporation was created," contended Catron, "and the other party to the suit is a citizen of a different state. . ., then the courts of the United States can exercise jurisdiction under the Third Article of the Constitution." Thus, for Catron, it was the narrow ground presented by Justice Wayne which was to furnish the rule for the courts.

In upholding the jurisdiction of the federal courts over

corporations within these limits, Catron presented a practical reason for his position, pointing out that if the United States courts were ousted of this jurisdiction, private citizens would be compelled to submit their rights to judges and juries of the state courts and "to contend with powerful corporations, in local courts, where the chances of impartial justice would be greatly against them; and where no prudent man would engage with such an antagonist if he could help it."[40]

Justice Daniel, in the first of a series of strong dissents, rejected totally the idea that the Constitution authorized the federal courts to exercise jurisdiction over corporations. For this strict constructionist, not only *Louisville Railroad Co. v. Letson* but *Bank of the United States v. Deveaux* was wrong. For Daniel, the correct doctrine was that laid down by the Circuit Court of Georgia in 1808.

Daniel begins his analysis by insisting that "the term 'citizen' is designed to apply to man in his individual character, and to his natural capacities; to a being, or agent, possessing social and political rights, and sustaining social, political, and moral obligations." In distributing judicial power, the Third Article extends it to "the natural physical beings composing these separate communities and can, by no violence of interpretation, be made to signify artificial, incorporeal, theoretical, and invisible creatures. A corporation, therefore, being not a natural person but a mere creature of the mind, invisible and intangible, cannot be a citizen of a state or of the United States, and cannot fall within the terms of the power of the above-mentioned Article, and can therefore neither plead nor be impleaded in the courts of the United States."

Turning to the *Deveaux* case, Daniel criticizes the ruling of Marshall, which permitted the courts to look beyond the party of record, the corporation aggregate, to the members who composed the corporation. This, for Daniel, was the initial error of the court. The second error was the decision in the Letson case to create a category of "quasi-citizen, to be called into existence for particular purposes; a being without any of the attributes of citizenship, but the one for which he may be temporarily and arbitrarily created, and to be dismissed from existence the moment the particular purposes of his creation shall have been answered." Contending that the term "citizen" retains the same meaning wherever used in the Constitution, he asserts that the court's "corporation-citizen" could "aspire to the office of President of the United States, (or to the command of armies, or fleets, in which last example, so far as the character of the commander would form a part of it, we should have the poetical romance of the spectre ship realized in our republic.)"

In conclusion, Daniel holds that by no sound or reasonable interpretation can a corporation be transformed into a citizen, or treated as a citizen; that Article Three cannot be made to embrace controversies to which corporations are parties, where diversity of citizenship is necessary to jurisdiction; and that the case before the court should be dismissed for want of jurisdiction.[41]

The following year, in concurring with the court's dismissal of a bill in equity, but dissenting from the reasons given for the dismissal, Daniel could not resist the temptation to add, that to the extent that citizenship and corporate existence were identical, "a corporation can be a citizen, and a citizen can become a corporation. The process by which the latter transformation may be accomplished has not yet been pointed out. We are told. . .that a corporation is an invisible, intangible, artificial creature. In one sense, at least, the citizen may render himself invisible and intangible—he may abscond."[42] This remark did little to advance the cause of judicial interpretation except to demonstrate the bitterness which Daniel felt toward what he considered a judicial usurpation.

These attacks of Daniel on the Letson decision prompted the court, by a 6-3 division, to reiterate the position outlined ten years earlier by Justice Wayne. In defense of the extension of jurisdiction to corporations, Justice Grier argues that the right of a citizen to sue other citizens in the federal courts cannot be taken away by the fact that a state has permitted these citizens to group together and operate in a corporate form. "A citizen who has made a contract, and has a 'controversy' with a corporation, may also say, with equal truth, that he did not deal with a mere metaphysical abstraction, but with natural persons; that his writ has not been served on an imaginary entity, but on men and citizens; and that his contract was made with them as the legal representatives of numerous unknown associates, or secret and dormant partners." The faculties of contracting, suing and being sued in a collective name, "conferred on them by state legislation for their own convenience, cannot be wielded to deprive others of acknowledged rights. It is not reasonable that those who deal with such persons should be deprived of a valuable privilege by a syllogism, or rather sophism, which deals subtly with words and names, without regard to the things or persons they are used to represent."

The case for jurisdiction, then, arises from the injustice and impropriety which would result if jurisdiction were denied. The spirit rather than the literal terms used in the Constitution must prevail. The argument from consequences is clear in Grier's conclusion: "The right of choosing an impartial tribunal is a privilege of no small practical importance, and more especially in cases where a distant plaintiff has to contend with the power and influence of great numbers, and the combined wealth wielded by corporations in almost every state. It is of importance also to corporations themselves that they should enjoy the same privileges in other states, where local prejudices or jealousy might injuriously affect them."[43]

In summary, Grier's position is that the corporation cannot be a citizen; that the real parties to the suit are the directors or legal representatives of the corporation and not the stockholders; that the law *presumes* that the residence of the legal representatives is in the state which incorporated the corporation, regardless of the actual residence of said representatives; in short, a presumption of law replaces the usual necessity to aver the citizenship of the party and to support the averment with proof. In the court's desire to make corporations amenable to the jurisdiction of the United States courts, the majority establishes a rule which discriminates between corporate parties and natural parties, in that neither legal presumptions nor fictions can be resorted to in the averment of citizenship made by natural persons.

This opinion gave rise to three dissents. Catron, insisting on the doctrine he presented in the *Rundle* case, that the court must look to the citizenship of the president and directors of the company, which must be averred and not presumed, remarked that under the court's ruling, if a corporation were to receive a charter in more than one state, it might sue or avoid suit at will, claiming citizenship in accordance with its convenience.[44]

Daniel's dissent is of greater interest for his style of expression and the vehemence of his remarks than for its content, his point having previously been made more than once: "There cannot be a more striking example than is instanced by the case before us, of the mischiefs that must follow from disregarding the language, the plain words, or what may be termed the body, the *corpus*, of the Constitution, to ramble in pursuit of some *ignis fatuus* of construction or implication, called its spirit or its intention—a spirit not unfrequently about as veracious and as clearly connected with the Constitution as are the spirits of the dead with the revolving tables and chairs, which, by a fashionable metempsychosis of the day, they are said to animate."

Ignis fatuus No. 1, the *Deveaux* case, "was succeeded by the case of *Letson v. The Cincinnati and Louisville Railroad Company*, in which, by a species of judicial resurrection, this party, the corporation, was *deterre*, (raised up again), but was not restored to the full possession of life and vigor, or to the use of all his members and faculties, nor even allowed the privilege of his original name; but semi-animate, and in virtue of some rite of judicial baptism, though 'curtailed of his natural dimensions,' he is rendered equal to a release from the thralldom of constitutional restriction, and made competent at any rate to the power of commanding the action of the federal courts. This is *ignis fatuus* No. 2. Next in order is the case of *Marshall v. The Baltimore and Ohio Railroad Company.* This is indeed the *chef d'oeuvre* amongst the experiments to command the action of the spirit in defiance of the body of the Constitution. It is compelled, from the negation of that instrument, by some necromantic influence, potent as that by which, as we read, the resisting Pythia was constrained to yield her vaticinations and an occult futurity.

"Thus does it appear to me," continues Daniel, "that this

court has been led on from dark to darker, until at present it is environed and is beaconed onward by varying and deceptive gleams, calculated to end in a deeper and more dense obscurity. In dread of the precipices to which they would conduct me, I am unwilling to trust myself to these rambling lights; and if I cannot have reflected upon my steps the bright and cheering day-spring of the Constitution, I feel bound nevertheless to remit no effort to halt in what, to my apprehension, is the path that terminates in ruin."

Again, warning against the attempted usurpation by the federal government on the pretext of protecting the people of the states, Daniel writes: "The effect of this practice is to reduce the people of the states and their governments under an habitual subserviency to federal power, and gives to the latter what ever has been and ever must be the result of intervention by a foreign, a powerful and interested mediator, the lion's share in every division. For myself, I would never hunt with the lion. I would anxiously avoid his path and as far as possible keep him from my own, always bearing in mind the pregnant reply told in the Apologue as having been made to his gracious invitation to visit him in his lair; that although in the path that conducted to its entrance innumerable footprints were to be seen, yet in the same path there could be discerned *nulla vestigia retrorsum.*"

In a bitter finale—which was by no means Daniel's last word on the subject—the conservative judge from Virginia wrote:

"By the disciples of this new morality, it seems to be thought that the mandates or axioms of the Constitution, when found obstructing the way to power, and when they cannot be overstepped by truth or logic, may be conveniently turned and shunned under the denomination of abstractions or refinements; and the loyal supporters of those mandates may be borne down under the reproach of a narrow prejudice of fanaticism incapable of perceiving through the letter, and in contradiction of the language of the charter, its true spirit and intent; and as being wholly behind the sagacity and requirements of the age."[45]

The third dissent was submitted by Justice Campbell. His opinion is principally a broadside against corporations and only secondarily a discussion of jurisdiction. While his colleagues seemed to fear the consequences of ousting the jurisdiction of the federal courts over corporations, Campbell was wary of the additional power which these corporations might acquire through access to the courts: "The litigation before this court, during this term, suffices to disclose the complication, difficulty, and danger of the controversies that must arise before these anomalous institutions shall have attained their legitimate place in the body politic. Their revenues and establishments mock at the frugal and stinted conditions of state administration; their pretensions and demands are sovereign, admitting impatiently interference by state legislative authority. And from the present case, we learn that, disdainful of 'the careless arbiters' of State interests, they are ready 'to hover about them' in 'efficient and vigilant activity,' to make of them a prey; and, to accomplish this, to employ corrupting and polluting appliances. [46] I am not willing to strengthen or to enlarge the connections between the courts of the United States and these litigants."[47]

Two years later a case came before the Supreme Court which put its doctrine to a severe test. In *Dodge v. Woolsey*, a stockholder in a corporation, citizen of a state other than that in which the company was incorporated, brought a suit in equity in the federal courts against the tax collector of the State of Ohio, the directors of the corporation and the corporation itself. In accordance with the rule of *Deveaux*, the bill would have been dismissed on the face of it without further examination; but in accordance with the new doctrine, the majority (6-3) found no difficulty in assuming jurisdiction. At the same time that they upheld the rule that the citizenship of the corporation was that of the state in which it was incorporated and not that of the stockholders, they established the precedent that a stockholder could sue in the federal courts a corporation of which he was a member, provided that he was not from the incorporating state.[48]

This decision was objected to by the same dissenters of the previous case. Here it was Campbell rather than Daniel who wrote the dissent. It was no longer possible, he argued, to presume that the corporators were citizens of the State of Ohio when one of them had just averred that he was a citizen of another state. Whatever value that presumption might have under another set of circumstances, it could not hold up when facts proven before the court contradicted the presumption. Further, the jurisdiction could be upheld only in the event that a corporation could be a citizen in the sense used in the Constitution, and it was the understanding of the majority that the court had held otherwise in *Marshall v. Baltimore and Ohio Railroad.*

"The question then is," Champbell continued, "can a corporation belonging to a state, and whose officers are citizens, upon some hope or assurance that the opinions of the courts of the United States are more favorable to their pretentions, by any combination, contrivance, or agreement with a non-resident shareholder, devolve upon him the right to seek for the redress of corporate grievances, which are the subjects of equitable cognizance in the courts of the United States, by a suit in his own name?"

Looking to the future, the minority predicted that "if a foreign shareholder, upon the real or affected indifference of a board of directors, or on some imaginary or actual obstacle to relief, arising in the state of opinion in the courts of the state, can draw questions of equitable cognizance into the courts of the United States, in which corporate rights are involved, or evils threatened or inflicted on corporate property, making the corporation and its managers parties, then a very compendious method of bringing into the courts of the United States all questions in which these artificial beings are concerned has been invented, and the most morbid appetite for jurisdiction among all their various members will be gratified, and upon a class of cases where grave doubts exist whether those who made the Constitution ever intended to confer any jurisdiction whatever."[49]

It was not surprising that by now individuals who sought to sue corporations in the federal courts were somewhat confused as to the proper manner in which to present them. When the plaintiff gave as the jurisdictional credentials of the Lafayette Insurance Company the bare fact that it was "a citizen of the State of Indiana," the court admonished: "The averment that the company is a citizen of the State of Indiana can have no sensible meaning attached to it. This court does not hold that either a voluntary association of persons, or an association into a body politic, created by law, is a citizen of a state within the meaning of the Constitution. And therefore, if the defective averment in the declaration had not been otherwise supplied, the suit must have been dismissed."[50] Fortunately for the plaintiff, he had the foresight to reply that the company had been incorporated under the laws of the State of Indiana and had its principal place of business in that state.

But two years later, when the *Covington Drawbridge Company* was referred to in the same meager style, "citizens of the State of Indiana," the court decided the averment to be sufficient on the ground that the statute incorporating the company was a public law, "of which the circuit courts and this court are bound to take judicial notice, without it being pleaded or offered in evidence."

Chief Justice Taney, who intervened publicly in the dispute for the first time, explained that the court had held in the *Letson* case "that the members of the corporate body must be presumed to be citizens of the state in which the corporation was domiciled, and that both parties were estopped from denying it. And that, inasmuch as the corporators were not parties to the suit in their individual characters, but merely as members and component parts of the body or legal entity which the charter created, the members who composed it ought to be presumed, so far as its contracts and liabilities are concerned, to reside where the domicile of the body was fixed by law, and where alone they could act as one person; and to the same extent, and for the same purposes, be also regarded as citizens of the state from which this legal being derived its existence and its faculties and powers."

The Chief Justice continued: "Now no one, we presume, ever supposed that the artificial being created by an act of incorporation could be a citizen of a state in the sense in which the word is used in the Constitution of the United States,[51] and the averment was rejected because the matter averred was simply impossible."[52]

Thus to circumvent the objections raised by Justice Daniel in his poetic dissent to the idea that a corporation was a citizen, and a citizen a corporation, the court now created the legal fiction that the citizenship of the shareholders was *presumed* to be that of the state in which their company was incorporated. (The idea that a shareholder might be a member of various companies incorporated in different states and, by association, a citizen of as many states, was not contemplated by the court.)

Justice Campbell, apparently worn out by the discussion, was convinced by this approach and concurred with the opinion of the court. Justice Daniel, unyielding, dissented.

The following year a case came before the court involving the Philadelphia, Wilmington and Baltimore Railroad Company and a citizen of Delaware. The railroad was averred to be a body corporate in the State of Maryland, even though one of the three companies of which the corporation was formed was originally incorporated in the State of Delaware. But Daniel was still there: "Some cursory recapitulation will, however, be attempted of previous decisions made here, as evincing the progress of relaxation and inconsistency from the first departure from what, by me at least, are deemed sound, legal, and constitutional principles, down to the remarkable instance exemplified in the case before us."

After reviewing the cases of the preceding half-century, Daniel contends that the court has now gone to the extreme of accepting an averment that a corporation is "in" a state, "but whether in its organized constitution, or by the citizenship of its president and directors, or by its individual members or whether in either character it is or is not *of* Maryland, is left to the court to supply." This was in defiance of the rule that citizenship must be averred expressly and cannot be inferred from residence or locality.

Daniel's principal objection here is that three corporations created by three distinct states have "by some professional magic" been converted into one. "These three *quasi*-citizens of different states are transformed into one and, although threefold in form, less than one; and by this transformation are brought into tribunals where real citizens are not permitted to litigate without averring, and if denied, not without proving the truth and reality of their character in obedience to the command of the Constitution. In the present instance, this may subserve the convenience of the individual, but in another the mischiefs incident to such a relaxation would be apparent and serious. It would be putting in the power of separate corporations, deriving their origin from distinct sources by claiming a joint name or title, to select at will, for its purposes, a forum within that jurisdiction, within which either corporate body was created. The averments of citizenship and residence being dispensed with by this court, no check is left to such a combination and irregularity; and by this practice there is extended to artificial bodies, which are not and cannot, from the nature of things, be citizens, privileges which belong by the Constitution to citizens only, and upon proof, if required, of the reality of their character as such."[53]

By 1862 the Chief Justice was finally able to say that it was the settled doctrine of the court that a suit by or against a corporation, in its corporate capacity, is a suit by or against citizens of the state which created it, and no averment to the contrary will be heard to defeat the jurisdiction. The decision was unanimous. Justice Daniel was dead.

However, it would have given Daniel some consolation to know that in the case before the court, where the plaintiff was a corporation created by the laws of the States of Ohio and Indiana, and the defendant was a citizen of Indiana, the court refused to take jurisdiction because there was not the necessary diversity of citizenship.

"It follows," said Taney, "that this suit in the corporate name is, in contemplation of law, the suit of the individual persons who compose it, and must therefore be regarded and treated as a suit in which citizens of Ohio and Indiana are joined as plaintiffs in an action against a citizen of the last-mentioned state. Such an action cannot be maintained in a court of the United States, where jurisdiction of the case depends altogether on the citizenship of the parties. And, in such a suit, it can make no difference whether the plaintiffs sue in their own proper names, or by the corporate name and style by which they are described."[54]

Thus the right of the corporation to sue and its liability to being sued in the federal courts under the diversity of citizenship clause was firmly established after more than fifty years of vagaries. The corporation had almost become a citizen[55] and perhaps *would* have become one had the court not retreated[56] under the attacks of Justice Daniel. It is ironic that after the Chief Justice's effort to deny the status of citizenship to the corporation, company officials themselves, in the second half of the twentieth century, should be the first to speak of corporate citizens. Perhaps we will yet live to see realized the spectre ship which Justice Daniel so feared.

In the cases involving diversity of citizenship, especially those dealing with the status of corporations in terms of the federal courts' jurisdiction over them, there is a clear conflict between two distinct schools of constitutional interpretation: on the one hand we find that of Wayne and Taney whose aim, or at least result, is subordination of words and terms to desired ends, in this case the extension of jurisdiction to cases in which corporations are parties to a controversy; on the other hand, we find the strict, logical and consistent efforts of Daniel to interpret the words and terms of the Constitution without regard to consequences, convenience or external criteria. Consciously or unconsciously, the Taney-Wayne school takes the position that the Constitution must be "adapted" to the circumstances prevailing, to changing conditions and needs, and that it is not necessary to resort to constitutional amendments to carry out these adaptions. Daniel, on the other hand, consistent with his insistence on judicial restraint and in accordance with his underlying idea that the ultimate sovereignty lies with the framers of the Constitution and the succeeding generations of American citizens, ignores all Procrustean attempts to adapt the Constitution to the necessities or politics of the time, insisting that such changes, if desired and desirable, are matters for the ultimate sovereign—the people—to carry out.

3. The Negro as Citizen

If the judicial standing of the corporation was

satisfactorily resolved by the courts, the same cannot be said for those persons who were living in the United States and were members of the Negro race. The same court which discovered a formula by which to extend jurisdiction over corporate litigants was unable, or rather, unwilling, to permit Negroes to appear before it.

It is not true, however, to say that the Supreme Court did not entertain jurisdiction in any case involving Negroes. They did; but not where it was necessary to prove a diversity of citizenship. With few exceptions, the cases they heard were up on appeal from the District Court of the District of Columbia, which had jurisdiction over local matters where the citizenship of the parties was not an issue. In the other federal courts, where diversity of citizenship was a prerequisite, it was not possible to take jurisdiction in cases involving petititions for freedom where both parties were resident of the same state or where the presumption was that one of the parties, the Negro, was not a citizen.

Notwithstanding this unproved presumption, in 1806 the Circuit Court of Pennsylvania took jurisdiction over a suit by a former Congressman from South Carolina against his former Negro slave, then residing in Pennsylvania, in which the plaintiff claimed that the defendant was not entitled to his freedom by virtue of the law of Pennsylvania. The court upheld the freedom of the defendant. Its value as a precedent, however, was limited: the question of jurisdiction was not argued—the plaintiff could not present his suit unless the former slave was held to be a citizen of Pennsylvania, and the defendant could not plead to the jurisdiction without denying his own citizenship; and, unfortunately for legal history, this decision of Justice Washington was not appealed to the Supreme Court. Nonetheless, it is interesting to note, in light of the later decision in the *Dred Scott* case, that jurisdiction was taken in a case in which one of the parties was a former Negro slave.[57]

Other cases of questionable relevance came before the circuit courts; it is worthwhile, nonetheless, to mention them for the light they throw on prevailing attitudes. In 1823, a Negro British seaman was arrested by the authorities of the State of South Carolina under a state law authorizing the seizure and imprisonment of free Negroes brought into the state on board of out-of-state vessels. The seaman petitioned the circuit court for his freedom. The court took jurisdiction to the extent of declaring the state law unconstitutional but did not order the prisoner released because he was held by the state, a case to which the court's power to issue the writ of *habeas corpus* did not extend. The fact that the prisoner was a Negro was not, however, any obstacle to the decision; but since jurisdiction over his petition was denied and diversity of citizenship was not at issue, the case furnishes us with no positive precedent.[58]

In 1827, in *Curranee v. McQueen*, the Circuit Court for the Second Circuit entertained jurisdiction of a suit by a Negro plaintiff, born in Jamaica, and brought into Georgia during his minority. Again, there was no argument concerning jurisdiction and no appeal to the Supreme Court. Nor is the citizenship of the parties stated.[59] Ten years later the District Court of Maine upheld the right of a Negro slave from Guadaloupe to maintain a suit in admiralty for tort in the courts of the United States. Here the court said: "The court certainly is not bound to enforce against him, a personal incapacity derived from the law of his domicile, because that law can have no force in this country any further than our law on the principles of comity chooses to adopt it; and every nation will judge for itself how far it is consistent with its own interest and policy to extend its comity in this respect. If the legislative power has prescribed no rule, the courts must of necessity decide in each individual case as it is presented." But here jurisdiction was not taken under Section 11 of the Judiciary Act.[60]

Some years earlier, however, a case came before the Supreme Court which was more to the point—so much so that Chief Justice Taney took pains to explain it away in his opinion in the *Dred Scott* case. Darnall, the defendant, was the son of a white father and a Negro slave mother. The father had left property to the son and the question arose whether the bequest was valid. In order to determine the point, the plaintiff, Le Grand, brought suit in the Circuit Court of Maryland. The question of jurisdiction was raised neither there nor on appeal to the Supreme Court.[61]

Though it was clear, then, that the court took jurisdiction of a case where one party was a descendant of a slave, Taney later argued that this by no means meant that the Supreme Court had held that a descendant of a slave may sue or be sued in the courts of the United States, because "Le Grand raised no objection to the jurisdiction of the court [and] there was nothing in the record before the court to show that Darnall was of African descent. The character or citizenship of the parties," added Taney, "had no connection with the question of jurisdiction, and the matter in dispute had no relation to the citizenship of Darnall."[62]

These few inconclusive cases were the prelude to one of the most important and controversial cases of the pre-Civil War era, *Dred Scott v. Sandford.*[63] On his return to Missouri after a long absence in the free State of Illinois and the Minnesota Territory with his master, Dr. Emerson, an Army doctor, Dred Scott sued for his freedom in the state courts. A divided bench denied his petition, holding that the law of Missouri where he was then domiciled still considered him a slave, despite his long residence in free territory. On the death of Dr. Emerson, Dred Scott became the property of a citizen of New York, Sandford. Assuming the existence of the diversity of citizenship necessary to bring a suit in the federal courts, Scott's lawyers determined to obtain a ruling in the courts of the United States and brought suit against Sandford in the Circuit Court of Missouri. Jurisdiction over the case was assumed by the court but this petition was also turned down. Thereupon Scott appealed to the Supreme Court.

At the threshold, the court was faced with the problem of jurisdiction—was there or was there not the necessary diversity of citizenship? That parties from two different states were involved, there could be no doubt; but was Dred Scott a citizen?

In order to speak of the opinion of the court it is necessary to speak of the opinions of nine justices, for seldom had so many points of view been presented in one case.[64]

The first query was: could the Supreme Court revise and reverse the circuit court's assumption of jurisdiction when averment of citizenship was not properly shown? To Justices Catron and McLean the question was no longer open to examination; the circuit court having assumed jurisdiction, the Supreme Court must do likewise. Justices Nelson and Grier did not pass judgment on the issue. But the Chief Justice and Justices Wayne, Daniel, Campbell and Curtis insisted that the Supreme Court retained the power to revise and reverse rulings with respect to jurisdiction. It is noteworthy that Curtis formed a part of this *ad hoc* majority in light of the fact that the result of his revision was to uphold the jurisdiction.

The second and most important question was: can persons whose ancestors were Negroes of the African race sustain a suit in the circuit courts of the United States as citizens of a state different from that of the adverse party? Here Justice Curtis replied with a vehement "Yes." McLean, who had previously assumed that the question of jurisdiction was not an issue, did not speak further on the subject, nor did Nelson or Catron pass on the question. But the five other judges were in agreement that descendants of the African race were not citizens in the constitutional sense of the term and could not sue in the courts of the United States under the diversity of citizenship clause.[65]

Taney begins his exposition on the status of Negroes by asserting that they did not and do not compose a portion of the sovereign people of the United States who alone are the citizens referred to in the Constitution: "They are not included, and were not intended to be included, under the word 'citizens' in the Constitution, and can therefore claim none of the rights and privileges which that instrument provides for and secures to citizens of the United States.

"It is true," the Chief Justice continues, "every person, and every class and description of persons, who were at the time of the adoption of the Constitution recognized as citizens in the several states, became also citizens of this new political body; but none other; it was formed by them, and for them and their posterity, but for no one else."

Thus, if neither Negro slaves nor their descendants, whether they had become free or not, were citizens of the several states at the time of the adoption of the Constitution, this class of persons could not become citizens in the future; that they were not then acknowledged as a part of the people or intended to be included was an obvious fact.[66]

At the time that the Constitution was adopted, "The number that had been emancipated. . .were but few in comparison with those held in slavery; and they were identified in the public mind with the race to which they belonged, and regarded as a part of the slave population rather than the free. It is obvious that they were not even in the minds of the framers of the Constitution when they were conferring special rights and privileges upon the citizens of a state in every other part of the Union."

Further, argues Taney, no state in freeing a former Negro slave can transmit to him the rights of citizenship of the United States. The state may give the right to vote to free Negroes and mulattoes, "but that does not make them citizens of the state, and still less of the United States."[67]

Daniel's argument went even further, if that was possible. In a simple syllogism he asserted: a slave is property; property cannot be a citizen; therefore, a slave cannot be a citizen. As to emancipated Negroes: "It is difficult to conceive by what magic the mere *surcease* or renunciation of an interest in a subject of *property*, by an individual possessing that interest, can alter the essential character of that property with respect to persons or communities unconnected with such renunciation. Can it be pretended that an individual in any state, by his single act, though voluntarily or designedly performed, yet without the cooperation or warrant of the government, perhaps in opposition to its policy or its guarantees, can create a citizen of that state?" Emancipation is merely the abdication or abandonment of the master's interest or ownership in his property; it is the state alone which can grant citizenship. But not even the states could bestow citizenship of the United States; they "could not add to or change in any respect the class of persons to whom alone the character of citizen of the United States appertained at the time of the adoption of the federal Constitution. They could not create citizens of the United States by any direct or indirect proceeding."[68]

Justice McLean attempted to refute the argument of the

Chief Justice: "[The plaintiff] is averred to have had a Negro ancestry, but this does not show that he is not a citizen of Missouri, within the meaning of the act of Congress authorizing him to sue in the circuit court. . .Being born under our Constitution and laws no naturalization is required, as one of foreign birth, to make him a citizen."

On the status of the Negroes at the time of American independence and the framing of the Constitution, McLean said: "While I admit the government was not made especially for the colored race, yet many of them were citizens of the New England States, and exercised the right of suffrage when the Constitution was adopted."[69]

Justice Curtis pursued McLean's thesis in greater detail: "To determine whether any free persons, descended from Africans held in slavery, were citizens of the United States under the confederation, and consequently at the time of the adoption of the Constitution of the United States, it is only necessary to know whether any such persons were citizens of either of the states under the confederation, at the time of the adoption of the Constitution.

"Of this there can be no doubt. At the time of the ratification of the articles of confederation, all free native-born inhabitants of the States of New Hampshire, Massachusetts, New York, New Jersey, and North Carolina, though descended from African slaves, were not only citizens of those states, but such of them as had the other necessary qualifications possessed the franchise of electors, on equal terms with other citizens.

"I can find nothing in the Constitution which, *proprio vigore*, deprives of their citizenship any class of persons who were citizens of the United States at the time of its adoption, or who should be native-born citizens of any state after its adoption; nor any power enabling Congress to disenfranchise persons born on the soil of any state, and entitled to citizenship of such state by its constitution and laws. And my opinion is," continued the judge from Massachusetts, "that, under the Constitution of the United States, every free person born on the soil of a state, who is a citizen of that state by force of its constitution or laws, is also a citizen of the United States."

To the assertion that the Constitution was made exclusively by and for the white race, Curtis replied: "It has already been shown that in five of the thirteen original states colored persons then possessed the elective franchise, and were among those by whom the Constitution was ordained and established. If so, it is not true, in point of fact, that the Constitution was made exclusively by the white race. And that it was made exclusively for the white race is, in my opinion, not only an assumption not warranted by anything in the Constitution, but contradicted by its opening declaration, that it was ordained and established by the people of the United States, for themselves and their posterity. And as free colored persons were then citizens of at least five states, and so in every sense part of the people of the United States, they were among those for whom and whose posterity the Constitution was ordained and established."

In conclusion, Curtis wrote: "That as the plea to the jurisdiction in this case shows no facts, except that the plaintiff was of African descent, and his ancestors were sold as slaves, and as these facts are not inconsistent with his citizenship of the United States, and his residence in the State of Missouri, the plea to the jurisdiction was bad, and the judgment of the circuit court overruling it was correct."[70]

Thus the court was divided over a matter of fact, or better, the interpretation of a fact—whether or not Negroes were citizens at the time the Constitution was adopted. It is difficult to reconcile the ease with which the same court refused jurisdiction to one class of persons—Negroes—while extending it to another—corporations—whose claim was even more tenuous. At least it could be said that Justice Daniel was consistent.

For the second time, a decision of the Supreme Court was overruled by a constitutional amendment. But the Fourteenth Amendment was not so much a direct reply to the Dred Scott decision as the result of changed attitudes emerging from changed circumstances following the Civil War.

4. The Writ of Habeas Corpus.

The writ of *habeas corpus* was one of the many writs inherited from the English common law and incorporated into the American judicial system. Its purpose was to inquire into the cause of commitment and protect prisoners against illegal imprisonment. It was only natural for Congress to grant the courts of the United States the power to issue this writ; but Section 14 of the Judiciary Act of 1789 surrounded this power with subtle limitations.

Section 14 provided that the courts of the United States "shall have power to issue writs of *scire facias, habeas corpus,* and all other writs not specially provided for by statute, which may be necessary for the exercise of their respective jurisdictions, and agreeable to the principles and usages of law. And that either of the justices of the Supreme Court, as well as judges of the District Courts, shall have power to grant writs of *habeas corpus* for the purpose of an inquiry into the cause of commitment. Provided, that writs of *habeas corpus* shall in no case extend to prisoners in jail, unless where they are in custody, under or by color of the authority of the United States, or are committed for trial before some court of the same, or are necessary to be brought into court to testify."

Three principal problems arose in the application of this grant of power to the federal courts: the power of the Supreme Court to issue the writ of *habeas corpus;* the power of the lower courts to issue the writ, and the power of the federal courts to issue the writ in the case of prisoners not held in jail under the authority of the United States government.

The first case involving *habeas corpus* which came before the Supreme Court was that of *United States v. Hamilton,* in which the court granted the writ where the prisoner had been committed to jail by the judge of the district court on the charge of treason. The court ordered the prisoner to be admitted to bail.[71]

It was not until ten years later that the first recorded case involving *habeas corpus* came before one of the circuit courts. In *Ex parte Cabrera,* a secretary of the Spanish legation was arrested and jailed by the state authorities of Pennsylvania. The prisoner turned to the Circuit Court of Pennsylvania, claiming that by the law of nations he was immune from civil or criminal prosecution. The court, however, ruled that it was not authorized by law to issue a writ of *habeas corpus* and discharge a prisoner held by the state nor interfere in any way with the jurisdiction of the courts of the state. Pointing to the fourteenth section of the Judiciary Act, Judge Washington necessarily concluded that Cabrera did not fall under any of the requisites to jurisdiction by the federal courts: he was not a prisoner in jail, nor in custody by authority, nor committed for trial before any court of the United States; nor was he wanted to testify in the court. "The consequence is, that, by express injunctions of the law, this writ of *habeas corpus* cannot extend to the present case.

"The question is not," asked Washington, "whether Congress might, within the terms of the Constitution, have conferred the power on the courts of the United States [to relieve a public minister from criminal process under state authority]; but, have they done it?. . .The question then is, has this court jurisdiction of the present cause, by virtue of any law of Congress, so as to discharge from confinement any person, no matter what may be his character or privilege, committed by a warrant from the governor, or any judicial magistrate of this state?"

Having determined that the answer was "No," Washington continued to give his own ideas on the topic: "Whether it would have been wise in Congress to have vested in the national courts the power of deciding, in some way or other, every national question authorized by the Constitution, is another point. I am one of those, I confess, who have always thought it would have been better if the legislature of the Union, in alloting to the several courts the jurisdiction they were to exercise, had occupied the whole ground marked out by the Constitution; but I am not one of those who think it a commendable quality in a judge to enlarge, by construction, the sphere of his jurisdiction: that of the federal courts is of a limited nature, and cannot be extended beyond the grant. Whether the petitioner may or ought to be relieved in the courts of this state, it would be improper in me to say. It is clear that upon this motion, we cannot relieve him."[72]

In *Ex parte Burford*, the prisoner had been first committed by justices of the peace of the District of Columbia. On *habeas corpus* proceedings before the circuit court, the latter recommitted the prisoner, issuing an order which was considered to be a new cause of commitment, superseding the earlier one. On the authority of *U.S. v. Hamilton*, the Supreme Court granted the writ of *habeas corpus* to revise the proceedings of the circuit court. The judges of the Supreme Court were unanimously of the opinion that the commitment by the circuit court was illegal, "for want of stating some good cause certain, supported by oath." The prisoner was discharged.[73]

The following year a decision of greater importance was made by the court.[74] Bollman had been charged with treason and committed by the circuit court. The prisoner, who was being held for trial, petitioned the Supreme Court to issue a writ of *habeas corpus* to inquire into the cause of his commitment. The question was whether under Section 14, the Supreme Court possessed such an authority. Justice Johnson replied in the negative. For him, the provision authorizing "either of the justices" of the Supreme Court to grant writs of *habeas corpus* for the purpose of inquiring into the cause of commitment was limited to the action of an individual judge in his chambers, but did not extend to the Supreme Court as a body. As to the first clause of the section, in order that the courts of the United States might issue writs of *habeas corpus*, the writ must be "necessary for the exercise of their respective jurisdictions." But, argued Johnson, the Supreme Court possessed neither original nor appellate jurisdiction over criminal cases and therefore the issuance of the writ of *habeas corpus* in a case of treason could by no means be necessary to their jurisdiction, since the jurisdiction itself did not exist. Further, Johnson contended that the judicial proceeding was original rather than appellate, and that in accordance with the decision of *Marbury v. Madison* it was unwarranted.[75]

The majority of the court, however, disagreed with Johnson's interpretation. In the first place, the court held that the Congress would hardly have given a power to issue the writ of *habeas corpus* to one of the judges of the court and denied it to the court as an assembled body; the reason for inserting the second sentence of Section 14 was to make provision for times when the courts were not in session. Second, the issuance of the writ in order to examine into the cause of commitment by the circuit court was not an original proceeding but a part of the Supreme Court's appellate jurisdiction. And, finally, the clause, "which may be necessary for the exercise of their respective jurisdictions," referred only to the antecedent, "and all other writs not specially provided for by statute," and not to the writs of *scire facias* and *habeas corpus.* [76] Going beyond a grammatical foundation for his position, Chief Justice Marshall asserted:

"It may be worthy of remark that this act was passed by the First Congress of the United States, sitting under a Constitution which had declared 'that the privilege of the writ of *habeas corpus* should not be suspended, unless when, in cases of rebellion or invasion, the public safety might require it.'

"Acting under the immediate influence of this injunction, they must have felt, with peculiar force, the obligation of providing efficient means by which this great constitutional privilege should receive life and activity; for if the means be not in existence, the privilege itself would be lost, although no law for its suspension should be enacted. Under the impression of this obligation, they give to all the courts the power of awarding writs of *habeas corpus.*"

As to the nature of the present proceeding, Marshall explained that the jurisdiction which the court was now asked to exercise was clearly appellate: "It is the revision of a decision of an inferior court, by which a citizen has been committed to jail. It has been demonstrated at the bar that the question brought forward on a *habeas corpus* is always distinct from that which is involved in the case itself. The question whether the individual shall be imprisoned is always distinct from the question whether he shall be convicted or acquitted of the charge on which he is to be tried, and, therefore, these questions are separated, and may be decided in different courts.

"The decision that the individual shall be imprisoned must always precede the application for a writ of habeas corpus, and this writ must always be for the purpose of revising that decision, and therefore appellate in its nature." The court thereupon granted the motion for *habeas corpus* to bring up the body of Bollman to examine into the cause of his commitment.[77]

Thus, as Circuit Court Judge McAllister was to explain fifty years later, the "masterly decision of Chief Justice Marshall, in *Ex parte Bollman*,. . .settled that the words, 'which may be necessary for the exercise of their respective jurisdictions,' apply only to the writs referred to in the last antecedent clause, thus leaving the writs enumerated, *scire facias* and *habeas corpus*, unrestricted, save as limited by the proviso to this section."[78] The same judge who was unable to interpret the Bill of Rights as a limitation on the acts of the state legislatures,[79] here, in the face of opposition, gave the widest possible interpretation to the privilege of the writ of *habeas corpus*, thus belying the charge that he did not give a high place to civil liberties.

In 1812, the Circuit Court of Tennessee decided the first of a long series of cases which were to come before the circuit courts, concerning the right of members of the Armed Forces to obtain discharge under *habeas corpus* proceedings. "The judges, by law," stated District Judge McNairy, "are vested with the power to issue writs of *habeas corpus* in all cases where citizens are illegally confined. Men constrained to enlist by force, or enlisted under the age of twenty-one, without the consent of their parents. . .are legally confined. . .and are therefore entitled to their discharge upon a writ of *habeas corpus*."[80]

In *Ex parte Kearney*, the Supreme Court laid down the important rule that it had no authority to issue the writ of *habeas corpus* to review a commitment to jail by a circuit court for contempt of that court. Commitment for contempt was equivalent to a judgment, said Justice Story, and the Supreme Court cannot revise circuit court judgments of this nature; it cannot do indirectly what it is not permitted to do directly; provided that the circuit court possessed jurisdiction, the Supreme Court could not act.[81]

In *Elkinson v. Deliesseline*, a circuit court for the second time examined the proviso of Section 14. A Negro British seaman was arrested by the state authorities of South Carolina under a state law authorizing the seizure and imprisonment of free Negroes brought into the state on board of out-of-state vessels. The prisoner turned to the Circuit Court for a writ of *habeas corpus*. After striking down the state law as unconstitutional, Justice Johnson searched for a remedy—but could find none within the power of the federal courts. Under Section 14 of the Judiciary Act, these courts could not issue the writ unless the prisoner was in custody under the authority of the United States. The prisoner's counsel, however, contended that this case should be excepted from the proviso, insofar as his constitutional right to *habeas corpus* had been abridged and because the prisoner could not be said to be in confinement under state authority if the state law under which he was arrested was void.

To this argument, Johnson replied: "But what are the courts of the United States to do? We cannot undertake to judge when that crisis has arrived which the Constitution contemplates; nor are we to undertake to define and limit that meaning of those words, 'the privilege of the writ of *habeas corpus*.' Every state in the Union may have had different provisions limiting and defining the extent of this privilege; some, perhaps, confining themselves to the privilege as it stood at common law, others adopting some or all of those statute provisions which have wrought such a change in its practical utility. It can, then, only be left to Congress to give an uniform and national operation to this provision of the Constitution. In legislating on this subject they have confined us to those cases in which the party is confined under United States authority, or is necessary to be introduced into its courts as a witness.

"On the second point, it is to be observed that the proviso to the fourteenth section of the Judiciary Act imposes on the petitioner the necessity of maintaining the affirmative of his being confined under United States authority; so that it is not enough to negate his being in custody under State authority, for the consequence is only that he is confined arbitrarily and without authority by a state officer, a case to which our power to issue this writ does not extend."[82]

That the interpretation of this proviso was not uniform was demonstrated by a case which came before the Circuit Court of Rhode Island the following year. Here the court issued a writ of *habeas corpus* to the grandfather of a minor child to bring the child before the court, on petition of the child's father who claimed that the child was wrongfully detained. There was no discussion of the court's authority to issue the writ in such a case and the case was settled by the parties prior to the judgment of the court, but what is significant is that the writ was issued where there was no detention by the authorities of the United States. The presiding judge of the court was the latitudinarian Justice Story; perhaps he concluded that the proviso applied only in cases where the person detained was in jail.[83]

Returning to the ruling in *Ex parte Kearney* some years later, the Supreme Court, in the first of two cases involving Watkins, held that it had no authority to issue *habeas corpus* when the prisoner was in prison by virtue of a judgment of the circuit court, rendered in a criminal prosecution: the judgment of the circuit court is sufficient cause in itself for commitment and cannot be looked into by the Supreme Court.

Turning to the historic use of the writ of *habeas corpus*, Marshall wrote: "No law of the United States prescribes the cases in which this great writ shall be issued, nor the power of the court over the party brought up by it. The term is used in the Constitution as one which was well understood; and the Judicial Act authorizes this court, and all the courts of the United States and the judges thereof, to issue the writ 'for the purpose of inquiring into the cause of commitment.' This general reference to a power which we are required to exercise, without any precise definition of that power, imposes on us the necessity of making some inquiries into its use, according to that law which is in a considerable degree incorporated into our own. The writ of *habeas corpus* is a high prerogative writ known to the common law, the great object of which is the liberation of those who may be imprisoned without sufficient cause. It is in the nature of a writ of error, to examine the legality of the commitment. . .The *habeas corpus* act of 31st of Charles II excepts from those who are entitled to its benefits persons committed for felony or treason, plainly expressed in the warrant, as well as persons convicted or in execution.

"The exception of persons convicted applies particularly to the application now under consideration. The petitioner is detained in prison by virtue of the judgment of a court, which court possesses general and final jurisdiction in criminal cases. Can this judgment be reexamined upon a writ of *habeas corpus?*

"The writ is, as has been said, in the nature of a writ of error, which brings up the body of the prisoner with the cause of commitment. The court can undoubtedly inquire into the sufficiency of that cause; but if it be the judgment of a court of competent jurisdiction, especially a judgment withdrawn by law from the revision of this court, is not that judgment in itself sufficient cause? Can this court, upon this writ, look beyond the judgment, and reexamine the charges on which it was rendered? A judgment, in its nature, concludes the subject on which it was rendered, and pronounces the law of the case. The judgment of a court of record, whose jurisdiction is final, is as conclusive on all the world as the judgment of this court would be. It is as conclusive on this court as it is on other courts. It puts an end to inquiry concerning the fact, by deciding it."

Again: "The judgment of the circuit court in a criminal case is of itself evidence of its own legality, and requires for its support no inspection of the indictments on which it was founded. The law trusts that court with the whole subject, and has not confided to this court the power of revising its decisions. We cannot usurp that power by the instrumentality of the writ of *habeas corpus.* The judgment informs us that the commitment is legal, and with that information it is our duty to be satisfied."

The Chief Justice distinguished this case from the preceding ones of Hamilton, Burford and Bollman by pointing out that in no one of the earlier cases was the prisoner confined under the judgment of a court.[84] What is strange, however, is that the same *habeas corpus* act which Marshall cited as his authority for not issuing the writ of *habeas corpus* in the case of convicted persons, also excepts persons committed for treason from its benefits, yet Marshall found no difficulty in issuing the writ in the case of Bollman years earlier.

Three years later the same prisoner applied to the Supreme Court for a writ of *habeas corpus* on the ground that he had been illegally confined in jail beyond the nine-month term set by the circuit court. Here the Supreme Court issued the writ because the prisoner was being held by order of the marshal rather than under the judgment of the circuit court, and ordered him to be discharged.[85] Justice Johnson dissented, maintaining that the Supreme Court had no jurisdiction in the case because it was not one of appellate jurisdiction. The prisoner, he said, should have applied to the circuit court and not to the Supreme Court, a point well-taken, but ignored by the majority. Johnson then proceeded to deny the authority and correctness of all the cases from Hamilton through to Kearney.[86]

In *Ex parte Randolph*, a case heard by the Circuit Court of Virginia, it was held that the writ of *habeas corpus* extended to commitments under civil process as well as criminal. The petitioner had been arrested and held in custody by a distress warrant issued from the Treasury Department for alleged debt to the United States.[87]

Until 1833 the federal courts were prohibited from granting writs of *habeas corpus* in cases of prisoners in jail under state authority. But on March 2nd of that year, Congress passed the Force Bill to provide for the enforcement of laws of Congress and for the protection of federal enforcing officers against state imprisonment. By that law, the authority to grant writs of *habeas corpus* was extended to cases of prisoners in state jails, committed or confined by authority or law, for any act done or omitted to be done in pursuance of a law of the United States, or any order, process, or decree of any judge or court thereof. The authority was given to any of the justices of the Supreme Court or a judge of any District Court of the United States.[88] Although the law was passed in reply to the doctrine of nullification, it was not resorted to until many years later, when in the 1850's federal officers attempting to enforce the Fugitive Slave Act were imprisoned by authorities of the Northern states determined to oppose the law.

The first case involving *habeas corpus* to reach the Taney Court, *Holmes v. Jennison*,[89] did not involve Secton 14 but the interpretation of Section 25 of the Judiciary Act. The case is considered inconclusive because the court divided 4-4 on the question of jurisdiction. However, a careful examination of the Chief Justice's opinion (joined in by Story, McLean and Wayne), and concurred in separately by Catron, reveals that certain important points were decided.

Holmes, a Canadian,[90] was a fugitive from justice in his country; he escaped into Vermont where he was arrested by authority of the state. The Governor of Vermont, Jennison, prepared to turn Holmes over to the Canadian authorities. Thereupon Holmes applied to the state court for a writ of *habeas corpus.* The Supreme Court of Vermont refused to discharge him and gave judgment, remanding him to the state authorities. The prisoner then applied to the Supreme Court of the United States on a writ of error to revise the state court's decision, under Section 25 of the Judiciary Act. The first question was whether the court could take jurisdiction of the writ of error. Over the strong dissent of Justice Baldwin, a majority of five held that the Supreme Court did possess jurisdiction over a writ of error to a state court, to revise its decision on *habeas corpus* proceedings, where the decision of the state court otherwise meets with the requisites laid down in Section 25.[91] A proceeding by *habeas corpus* is a suit within the meaning of Section 25, they held, and a refusal to discharge a defendant is a final judgment in such a suit. Where the first four justices named failed to convince their colleague Catron was whether the suit involved a federal question; Catron dissented on this point.

Justice Baldwin, who had just filed a dissent to the jurisdiction of the court in the *mandamus* case of *Decatur v. Paulding*,[92] also held that it was improper to issue a writ of error in this case. He expressed his opposition to any interference with the proceedings of the Supreme Court of

Vermont on the ground that, "it is not within the appellate jurisdiction of this court, under the twenty-fifth section of the Judiciary Act, because the order of that court on a *habeas corpus* is not a judgment on which a writ of error can be brought." His three principal objections were that it was not a civil action; that the order to recommit, to bail, or to discharge was not a final judgment; and that the action of the court was discretionary, and no writ of error lies in a case depending on the discretion of the court.

If the Judiciary Act had been intended to embrace a writ of error on *habeas corpus* proceedings, Baldwin argued, "some provision appropriate to the case would have been made; its entire omission affords the most conclusive evidence to the contrary; or if anything is wanting to remove all doubt, it will be found in the nature and object of the great writ, this constitutional privilege. It was designed to afford a speedy remedy to a party unjustly accused of a crime without obstructing or delaying public justice, both of which objects would be defeated by the delays consequent upon a writ of error, as it may be taken out by either party; if it can be by one, the court can make no distinction between them, as it is a writ of right. For these reasons I am fully convinced that no writ of error can be issued by this or a circuit court, under the authority of the Judiciary Act, to revise a proceeding on a writ of *habeas corpus* by any judge or court of the United States." Baldwin concluded that no writ of error could issue either to a circuit court or to a state court on *habeas corpus* proceedings.

His final comment was that if the Supreme Court were to assume jurisdiction where all the provisions of the Judiciary Act were not complied with, "it must usurp power to carry into effect a judgment which the law does not recognize, and consequently makes no provision for its execution. It is dangerous, at least, if not unwise or rash, to exercise a power which may be given by the Constitution, but which Congress has given no authority to execute, or given in terms so obscure, that to so construe them is in substance the exercise of legislative power, by the judicial department."[93]

In short, for Baldwin the judgment of the state court on *habeas corpus* proceedings could not be reviewed by the

Supreme Court of the United States *even if* the constitutional rights of the prisoner were involved. It is interesting to compare this limited interpretation of the court's jurisdiction not only with that of the majority but with the opinions given in two other cases. In *Elkinson v. Deliesseline*, Justice Johnson, who otherwise was over-cautious when it came to the Supreme Court's jurisdiction over *habeas corpus* proceedings, clearly implied that the jurisdiction existed under Section 25 when he pointed out that the state law, by placing the prisoner in the hands of the sheriff without the intervention of a state court of justice, deprived the prisoner of the benefit of Section 25.[94] And in *Ex parte Milligan*, the court cited favorably Taney's conclusion that "the proceeding by *habeas corpus* was a suit."[95]

This case is more of academic than practical interest, because no further cases of this kind were brought to the attention of the Supreme Court, despite the Court's willingness to review state court *habeas corpus* proceedings under Section 25.

Seven years later, in *Barry v. Mercein*, the Court was called upon to decide a similar case, which differed from *Holmes v. Jennison* principally in that the writ of error was to a circuit court rather than to a state court. The lower court had denied the writ in a case where a father had petitioned to have brought before the court his minor child, whom he alleged was imprisoned and detained by his wife and mother-in-law. Here the Supreme Court held that the writ of error did not lie to re-examine the judgment of the circuit court. The Chief Justice pointed out that in accordance with Section 22 of the Judiciary Act, the Supreme Court could not reexamine the lower court judgment unless the matter in dispute exceeded the sum of $2,000. Distinguishing this decision from the earlier one, Taney wrote: "Before we speak more particularly of the construction of this section, it may be proper to notice the difference between the provisions contained in it, and those of the twenty-fifth section, in the same act of Congress, which gives the appellate power over the judgments of the State courts. In the latter case, the right to reexamine is not made to depend on the money value of the thing in controversy, but upon the character of the right in dispute, and the judgment which the state court has pronounced upon it; and it is altogether immaterial whether the right in controversy can or cannot be measured by a money standard."[96] It should also be pointed out that this decision differs from that in the *Burford* and *Bollman* cases in that the former were direct *habeas corpus* proceedings to inquire into the cause of commitment, whereas the *Barry* case involved a review of a lower court's judgment to grant or not to grant the *habeas corpus.*

In The Matter of Metzger, decided at the same term, the court further limited its jurisdiction over *habeas corpus* proceedings by deciding that it had no authority to issue the writ to inquire into the cause of commitment when a fugitive was imprisoned on a warrant issued by the District Judge in chambers, because the Supreme Court had no appellate jurisdiction over decisions made by justices or judges at chambers.[97]

Meanwhile, the courts decided that they were not empowered to issue a writ of *habeas corpus* to bring up a prisoner confined by state process, for any other purpose save to examine him as a witness;[98] nor could they discharge on *habeas corpus* a prisoner who had been committed by either House of Congress for contempt.[99]

One of the most complicated cases arising before the federal courts was that of Kaine, a fugitive from justice, held under the order of a United States commissioner for extradition to Great Britain. The prisoner applied for discharge on a writ of *habeas corpus* to the Circuit Court of New York. The court was willing to take jurisdiction of the case but refused to release Kaine, after determining that the commissioner had jurisdiction and had committed the prisoner on the basis of legal evidence.[100] Kaine thereupon applied at chambers for a writ of *habeas corpus* to Circuit Court Justice Nelson, who expressed the opinion that the commissioner did not possess jurisdiction, allowed the writ, and ordered the case adjourned to the Supreme Court for final decision.

When the twofold case came before the Supreme Court, it was unanimously decided that a single justice, at chambers, while the court was in recess, could not on *habeas corpus* proceedings remit a case to the Supreme Court for decision; thus the adjourned case was summarily dismissed for want of jurisdiction. As to the case coming up from the circuit court, the members of the higher court divided: seven justices held that the Supreme Court had authority to issue the writ of *habeas corpus* to review the judgment of the circuit court, but four of them decided not to exercise the jurisdiction because the judgment of the circuit court was correct.[101] The other three justices (Nelson, Taney and Daniel) who upheld the jurisdiction, also held that the prisoner should be discharged on the merits. Justice Curtis denied that the court could take jurisdiction at all.

The majority made no reference to the underlying question of jurisdiction. Nelson, in his opinion, contended that the prisoner was committed by the circuit court whose proceedings on *habeas corpus* had superseded the order of detention made by the commissioner; that in any event, if *habeas corpus* can issue to review commitments made by order of a marshal, as in *Ex parte Watkins*, so too could they issue when detention was ordered by a commissioner; and that, as a general rule, the Supreme Court has appellate jurisdiction to issue the writ in all cases where a prisoner is in custody under or by color of the authority of the United States.

"It has been argued," wrote Nelson, "that great inconvenience would arise, if the writ of *habeas corpus* could issue from this court into any part of the Union to bring up a prisoner on a petition that he was illegally restrained of his liberty under the authority of the United States, as the proceeding must be attended with delay and expense, by reason of the great extent of our territory. But it must be remembered that in the case of a right of property involved, dependent upon the laws of the Union, and a decision against it, the party against whom the decision has been made in a state court, however small the amount in controversy, is entitled to a writ of error to this court, to bring up the case for review, by the twenty-fifth section of the same act in which the fourteenth section is found. And I am yet to learn that the right of the liberty of the citizen is not as dear to him, and entitled to be guarded with equal care by the

Constitution and laws, as the right of property, notwithstanding the supposed inconvenience."[102]

Justice Curtis rejected the conclusion of Nelson that the Supreme Court had appellate power over the proceedings of the commissioner since, according to him, there was no law to authorize such a revision; he also denied that the prisoner had been committed by the circuit court, holding that the cause of commitment was the warrant of the commissioner and that the order of the circuit court dismissing the writ of *habeas corpus* and remanding the prisoner did not supersede the action of the commissioner.[103]

The final outcome was to deny the writ of *habeas corpus* (on the merits) and order the petition dismissed. Thereupon Nelson, once more at chambers, took up the adjourned case which the Supreme Court had not decided for want of jurisdiction. After holding that a decision under one writ of *habeas corpus*, refusing the discharge of a prisoner, was no bar to the issuance of successive writs, Nelson ordered the prisoner discharged on the grounds that the commissioner did not possess jurisdiction and that the nature of the proof submitted was insufficient.[104] Thus by the peculiar rules concerning the appellate jurisdiction of the Supreme Court, an individual justice had the last word in the face of the opposition of a majority of his colleagues.

The release of Kaine, however, was an exception to the course followed in other similar cases. In the following year District Judge Betts, in the same Circuit Court of New York, held that although the circuit court was authorized to determine whether a commissioner had jurisdiction of a case, it could not, on *habeas corpus* proceedings, inquire into the merits of the committing magistrate's decision; the guilt or innocence of the accused could not be tried under *habeas corpus.*[105]

Meanwhile the circuit courts were beginning to make use of the powers conferred on them by the Act of March 2, 1833. In *Ex Parte Jenkins*, the Circuit Court of Pennsylvania held that it may issue a *habeas corpus* to bring before it one of its deputy marshals, arrested and put in jail under state process, for his conduct in executing a writ issued under the Fugitive Slave Law.[106] And in *United States ex rel*

Garland v. Morris, the District Court of Wisconsin held that the owner of an escaped slave, who apprehends the slave in accordance with the act of Congress authorizing such action, is a person within the Act of March 3, 1833, and is entitled to be discharged by a federal court on a writ of *habeas corpus* when arrested under state process for assault and battery committed in the apprehension of the slave.[107]

In *United States ex rel. Wheeler v. Williamson*, the question came before the District of Pennsylvania whether it had jurisdiction to issue the writ of *habeas corpus* in a case where the persons detained were not being held under the authority of the United States. Here the owner of slaves petitioned for the writ to be issued to a private citizen who had removed the slaves from the rightful owner to bring said slaves before the court. The court upheld the use of *habeas corpus* in this case on the ground that at common law the writ issued "whenever a citizen was denied the exercise of his personal liberty, or was deprived of his rightful control over any member of his household, his wife, his child, his ward, or his servant." In a sweeping extension of the use of *habeas corpus* to virtually any case, District Judge Kane went on to say that "the Congress was denied the power of limiting or restricting or qualifying the right, which it was thus forbidden to suspend. I do not, indeed, see that there can be a restriction or limitation of a privilege which may not be essentially a suspension of it. . .And it has appeared to me, that if Congress had undertaken to deny altogether the exercise of this writ by the federal courts, or to limit its exercise to the few and rare cases that might peradventure find their way to some one particular court, or to declare that the writ should only issue in this or that class of cases, to the exclusion of others in which it might have issued at the common law, it would be difficult to escape the conclusion that the ancient and venerated privilege of the writ of *habeas corpus* had not been in some degree suspended, if not annulled."[108]

Ex parte Wells[109] presented another delicate problem to the Supreme Court. Wells had been convicted of murder by the Circuit Court of the District of Columbia and sentenced to be executed. The President of the United States had granted the prisoner a conditional pardon, offering to change the punishment meted out by the court to imprisonment for life. The question on the merits was whether the condition was legal, but the preliminary question was whether the Supreme Court could issue a writ of *habeas corpus* to examine the circuit court's refusal to discharge the prisoner on a prior *habeas corpus.* As had occurred in the case of Kaine, the majority assumed jurisdiction without argument.

Justice McLean, dissenting from the majority's decision on the merits,[110] concurred with them in taking jurisdiction. "This court has no power to revise, in this form, the judgment of the circuit court under the law in a criminal case," said McLean, "but, as in the case of Watkins, we may decide whether the individual is held by legal custody." The court was free to examine the detention, argued McLean, because the prisoner was held not under the original conviction of the circuit court but under the order of commutation by the President, which was a superseding commitment.[111]

As in the case of Kaine, Justice Curtis, this time joined by Campbell, dissented on the point of jurisdiction, holding again that a writ of *habeas corpus* cannot issue from the Supreme Court to examine a criminal sentence of the circuit court. He objected to the revision of a sentence on *habeas corpus* which could not be revised by law on a writ of error. "It seems to me," said Curtis, "that the refusal of a writ of error in criminal cases is not only idle but mischievous, if a writ of *habeas corpus,* which is certainly a very clumsy proceeding for the purpose, may be resorted to, to bring the record of every criminal case, of whatever kind, before the court." Curtis feared that in the future, convicted prisoners would follow the roundabout route of applying to the circuit court for a writ of *habeas corpus* and, if unsuccessful, "bring into action the appellate power of this court, and by a writ of *habeas corpus* out of this court stop the execution of a sentence, which we have no power to reverse."[112]

Once more a case came before the courts involving the interpretation of the proviso of Section 14. A state judge, whose presence on the state court was necessary for the pursuit of the petitioner's suit, was illegally detained by private persons. The petitioner applied to the Circuit Court of California to issue a writ of *habeas corpus* to have the judge released from confinement and brought before the court. The judge, in issuing the writ, held that the evident object of the proviso, "and a most salutary one, was to prevent any possible conflict between the federal and state tribunals, which would result from leaving in the former the power to relieve persons confined in jail by state courts and state magistrates." The purpose of the proviso was to prevent the writ from being issued to any person in jail, unless confined under or by color of the authority of the United States; but where the individual was not in jail but illegally deprived of his liberty, the federal courts were free to make use of the writ.[113]

Whatever validity this ruling had in the Circuit Courts of California or Pennsylvania (where *Wheeler v. Williamson* had been similarly decided), it was rejected two years later by the Circuit Court of Ohio, demonstrating the danger of generalizing from one circuit court to all the other federal courts. Rejecting Marshall's ruling in *Ex parte Bollman* that the clause, "which may be necessary to the exercise of their respective jurisdictions," was not a limitation on the writ of *habeas corpus*, the court ruled that the first clause of Section 14 did not authorize the courts to issue a *habeas corpus*, unless it was necessary in aid of jurisdiction in a case or proceeding there pending; and therefore the case of a father claiming the custody of an infant child, not being ancillary to the exercise of jurisdiction, was not one in which the court could issue a *habeas corpus*. Thus the opinions in the *Bollman* case were inverted and Justice Johnson's dissent was treated as authority.

The judge completely rejected the thesis of Judge Kane in *Wheeler v. Williamson*, that the framers of the Constitution contemplated restraints resulting from the relations of master and servant, guardian and ward, parent and child, or husband and wife. "It was doubtless intended to protect against those invasions of personal liberty which are perpetuated under color of legal or official authority," said the court. "The framers of the Constitution had in view those outrages and usurpations which characterized the worst periods in the history of the British nation, by which the personal liberty of the citizen was invaded, from political considerations, but with the forms of legal authority. As a remedy for such abuses of power, and disregard of legal and constitutional rights, the judges of the courts of the United States are invested with the authority to issue the writ of *habeas corpus* and inquire into the cause of commitment."[114] It is difficult to explain this opinion of the court[115] except to say that it was an error—certainly the portion overruling the doctrine of Marshall.

Once again the courts were called upon to make use of the writ under the Act of March 2, 1833. In one case a marshal of the United States was arrested and confined in a state jail on the order of the state judge for not complying with a writ of *habeas corpus* issued by the state judge to the marshal to bring up the body of a fugitive slave detained by the marshal in compliance with the warrant of a United States commissioner.[116] A similar case involving the same marshal came before the same court the following year after the marshal had been sentenced by the state judge for contempt of court for not making a sufficient return to the writ of *habeas corpus;*[117] and in *Ex parte Sifford,*[118] a similar case involving several deputy marshals came before the same court. In all three cases brought before the court on writs of *habeas corpus*, the prisoners were discharged.

In the second of these cases, the court gave the following interpretation to the Act of 1833: "It is insisted by the counsel who oppose the discharge of the marshal that this provision of the act of Congress applies only to the case of a federal officer who is confined or imprisoned by state authority under an unconstitutional state law; and reference is made to the historical fact that the Act of 1833 was passed to meet the then existing exigency growing out of the threatened opposition of one of the states of the Union to the national legislation for the imposition and collection of duties on imports. To this it may be replied that whatever may have been the peculiar circumstances under which the act passed, the section above quoted is still in full force, and obligatory as a law of the United States. And it may be fairly inferred that while the purpose was, at the date of its passage, to provide against a great danger then pending, it has been deemed expedient that it should be continued as a remedy against nullification in any form in which it might be presented."[119]

During the Civil War the courts were called upon on several occasions to give rulings on their *habeas corpus* powers; however, these cases will be treated in a future study with others arising out of the Civil War, and which continued to come before the court even into the 1870's.

Unconnected with the war, the Supreme Court handed down one more ruling involving *habeas corpus.* In *Pratt v. Fitzhugh*, the court held that a judgment or order of the circuit court discharging prisoners on a writ of *habeas corpus* was not a judgment which the higher court could revise, inasmuch as the only appellate jurisdiction it could exercise was under Section 22 of the Judiciary Act, and that section limited writs of error to cases where the matter in dispute exceeded the sum of two thousand dollars.[120]

When Taney's term came to an end, the courts had by no means completed their interpretation of their *habeas corpus* jurisdiction. The Supreme Court had yet to rule on the right of the lower courts to issue *habeas corpus* in the case of private restraints and detentions; thus the circuit courts were divided as to the use of the writ in such cases.[121] The court had still to pass on its power to revise judgments of military courts, directly or indirectly, on *habeas corpus* proceedings. The ruling in *The Matter of Metzger* was to come up for reexamination and criticism. And other matters of importance were still to be decided.

Perhaps the only significant conclusion that could be made concerning the writ of *habeas corpus* is that the Marshall Court attempted to give it as wide a use as was consonant with the law, and yet the jurisdiction of both the lower and higher courts was being continually restricted so as not to give it an unlimited vitality or permit it to become a substitute for the writ of error in criminal cases. The courts, in short, left unanswered as many questions as they had solved.

CHAPTER SIX

Footnotes

[1] Case 16,323, 27 FC 1147 (1792), Circuit Court, Massachusetts.

[2] Case 6,360, 11 FC 1099; 1120 (1793), Wilson, joined by Iredell and Peters. (Henfield was acquitted.)

[3] *United States v. Ravara,* Case 16,122a, 27 FC 714 (1794), Jay (with Peters).

[4] *United States v. Worrall,* Case 16,766, 28 FC 774 (1798), Circuit Court, Pennsylvania.

[5] See Chapter Two, p. 99 (fn. 16).

[6] Notwithstanding the division of the court, the prisoner was sentenced to three months' imprisonment and a fine of two hundred dollars. In a note appended to the case it is stated: "The oddest part of the case is that though Judge Chase expressly denied that there was jurisdiction, and though there must have been at best a divided bench, the court, 'after a short consultation,' imposed a sentence of unequivocally common-law stamp. The most rational interpretation is that Judge Chase had used this 'short consultation' to acquaint himself with the views of his brethren on the Supreme bench, about which, after Henfield's case, there could then have been no doubt."

[7] *Williams' Case,* Case 17,708, 29 FC 1330 (1799), Ellsworth.

[8] Case 15,761, 26 FC 1242 (1799).

[9] Case 15, 676, 26 FC 1088 (1806), Circuit Court, Pennsylvania.

[10] *United States v. Hudson,* 7 Cranch 32; 32-33; 34 (1812). The case was one of libel.

[11] *United States v. Coolidge,* Case 14,857, 25 FC 619 (1813). Italics added.

[12] We will come across this same problem when we examine the application of admiralty law.

[13] *United States v. Coolidge,* 1 Wheaton 415 (1816).

[14] *Idem.*

[15] *United States v. Hare,* Case 15,304, 26 FC 148 (1818).

[16] *United States v. Terrel*, Case 16, 452, 28 FC 40 (1840).

[17] *United States v. Ramsay*, Case 16,115, 27 FC 694 (1847).

[18] *United States v. New Bedford Bridge*, Case 15,867, 27 FC 91 (1847).

[19] "Concurrent with the courts of the several states."

[20] Judiciary Act of 1789, Section 11. Conditions concerning the amount in dispute were attached but these were frequently changed and in no way affected the conflict over the meaning of "citizen".

[21] *Shedden v. Curtis*, Case 12,736, 21 FC 1218 (1793), Circuit Court, Virginia; *Bingham v. Cabot*, 3 Dallas 382 (1798).

[22] 3 Cranch 267 (1806).

[23] *Bank of the United States v. Deveaux*, Case 916, 2 FC 692 (1808).

[24] *Bank of the United States v. Deveaux*, 5 Cranch 61 (1809).

[25] At a later date, referring to this case, Justice Washington said: "If then the court could view the bank of the United States only in its corporate character, the legal consequence would have been to exclude all corporations, foreign and domestic; from the privilege. . .of suing and being sued in the courts of the United States." *Kirkpatrick v. White*, Case 7,850, 14 FC 685 (1826), Circuit Court, Penna.

[26] 2 Cranch 445 (1804).

[27] *New Orleans v. Winter*, 1 Wheaton 91 (1816).

[28] Case 3,193, 6 FC 472 (1819).

[29] *Prentiss v. Barton*, Case 11,384, 19 FC 1276 (1819).

[30] Case 2,240, 4 FC 902 (1821), Circuit Court, Eastern District, Pennsylvania.

[31] Case 11,134, 19 FC 609 (1828).

[32] *Rabaud v. D'Wolf*, Case 11,519, 20 FC 148 (1826), Circuit Court, New York.

[33] *Catlett v. Pacific Insurance Co.*, Case 2,517, 5 FC 291 (1826).

[34] *Kirkpatrick v. White*, Case 7,850, 14 FC 685 (1826).

[35] *Bank of Cumberland v. Willis,* Case 885, 2 FC 648 (1839), Circuit Court, Maine.

[36] *The Commercial and Railroad Bank of Vicksburg v. Slocomb,* 14 Peters 60 (1840).

[37] The decision was criticized later by Justice Daniel in *Rundle v. Delaware and Raritan Canal Co.*

[38] 2 Howard 497 (1844). On a narrower ground the court held that it was no longer of importance that many of the members of the corporation were citizens of a state other than that in which the corporation was created or did business; it was sufficient that some of the members were citizens of the state where the suit was brought. But this narrower ground was subordinated by the court itself to the broader argument stated above.

[39] For more on this decision, see discussion of *stare decisis* in Chapter Two.

[40] Concurring opinion of Catron, 14 Howard 80; 95 (1853).

[41] Dissent of Daniel, *Rundle v. Delaware and Raritan Canal Co.,* 14 Howard 95-102.

[42] Concurring opinion of Daniel, *Northern Indiana Railroad Co. v. Michigan Central Railroad Co.,* 15 Howard 249-251 (1854).

[43] *Marshall v. Baltimore and Ohio Railroad,* 16 Howard 314 (1854).

[44] *Idem,* dissent of Catron, 16 Howard 338.

[45] *Idem,* dissent of Daniel, 16 Howard 338-347.

[46] In this case, plaintiff had demanded the sum of $50,000 for obtaining or attempting to obtain favorable legislation for the railroad company.

[47] *Idem,* dissent of Campbell, 16 Howard 347-354.

[48] 18 Howard 331 (1856), Wayne.

[49] *Idem,* dissent of Campbell, 18 Howard 362-369.

[50] *The Lafayette Insurance Co. v. French,* 18 Howard 404 (1856). (French was the original plaintiff.)

[51] We have already seen that Justice Wayne said: "A corporation, created by a state. . .seems to us to be a person. . .entitled, for the

purpose of suing and being sued, to be deemed a citizen of that state." (See *Letson* case, above.) (See Warren II, p. 120 ff.) Warren states: "The Court decided, in *Louisville Railroad Co. v. Letson,* that for the purposes of a suit in a federal court brought on the ground of diverse citizenship, a corporation was presumed to be a citizen of the state in which it was chartered." In *Paul v. Virginia,* 8 Wallace 65; 175 (1869), Justice Field wrote: "In no case which has come under our observation, either in the state or federal courts, has a corporation been considered a citizen within the meaning of that provision of the Constitution, which declares that the citizens of each state shall be entitled to all the privileges and immunities of citizens of the several states."

[52] *Covington Drawbridge Co. v. Shepherd,* 20 Howard 227 (1858).

[53] *Philadelphia, Wilmington and Baltimore Railroad Co. v. Quigley,* dissent of Daniel, 21 Howard 202; 215-218 (1859).

[54] *The Ohio and Mississippi Railroad Co. v. Wheeler,* 1 Black 286 (1862).

[55] Wayne's opinion in the Letson case.

[56] Taney's opinion in *Covington Drawbridge Co. v. Shepherd.*

[57] *Butler v. Hopper,* Case 2,241, 4 FC 904 (1806). No reference was made to this case by either of the dissenting justices in the *Dred Scott* case. The only apparent difference in the cases is that in the earlier one the former slave was the defendant; in the latter, the plaintiff.

[58] *Elkinson v. Deliesseline,* Case 4,366, 8 FC 493 (1823), Circuit Court, South Carolina, Johnson.

[59] Case 3,488, 6 FC 984 (about 1827, exact date not given).

[60] *Polydore v. Prince,* Case 11,257, 19 FC 950 (1837), Ware.

[61] *Le Grand v. Darnall,* 2 Peters 664 (1829).

[62] Opinion of Taney, *Dred Scott* case, 19 Howard 423-424 (1857).

[63] 19 Howard 393 (1857).

[64] See *Holmes v. Jennison,* 14 Peters 540 (1840); The *License Cases,* 5 Howard 504 (1847), and *The Passenger Cases,* 7 Howard 283 (1849), for other cases in which there were a multiplicity of opinions.

[65] Ordinarily, the case would have come to an end at this point. But notwithstanding the ruling on jurisdiction, the court determined to examine the merits of the suit. The Chief Justice, joined by Wayne,

contended that the Supreme Court had the duty to determine whether the circuit court erred in giving judgment for the defendant, and in order to so determine it must examine whether or not the facts relied on by the plaintiff entitled him to his freedom. Thus for Taney and Wayne, the examination of the merits was an integral part of the higher court's duty to revise errors—to dismiss the case for want of jurisdiction without such an examination was to allow possible errors to stand. This controversial ruling was not concurred in by the other members of the court: Daniel considered it proper but not necessary to examine the merits; Nelson, Grier, Campbell and Catron did not pass on the question; while McLean and Curtis held that nothing said by the Court which did not have a direct bearing on the jurisdiction of the Court could be considered as authority. For a summary of the opinion on the merits and further remarks on whether this part of the case was *obiter dicta* or not, see Chapter Two, pp. 87-89, above.

It is easy to lose one's way in this case, even in attempting to follow the final disposition. Three judges (Taney, Wayne and Daniel) ruled that judgment for the defendant Sandford must be reversed and a mandate issued, directing the suit to be dismissed for want of jurisdiction; Nelson and Catron (by implication) held that the judgment of the circuit court should be affirmed; Grier and Campbell concurred with *both* of these two points of view, contending that judgment should be affirmed *or* the suit should be dismissed for want of jurisdiction; McLean and Curtis held that the judgment of the circuit court should be reversed, while the latter added that the cause should be remanded for a new trial.

Only the fact that this case has been the subject of so much controversy and interpretation justifies such exact placing of the point over the "i."

[66] To the proposition in the Declaration of Independence that "all men are created equal," Taney contended that the clause "would not in any part of the civilized world be supposed to embrace the Negro race." 19 Howard 410.

[67] Opinion of Taney, *Dred Scott* case, 19 Howard 404-405; 406-407; 411-412; 421.

[68] *Idem*, opinion of Daniel, 19 Howard 475-476; 477; 482.

[69] *Idem*, dissent of McLean, 19 Howard 531; 537.

[70] *Idem*, dissent of Curtis, 19 Howard 571-573; 576; 582; 588.

[71] 3 Dallas 17 (1795). No opinion or argument was given.

[72] *Ex parte Cabrera*, Case 2,278, 4 FC 964 (1805). The prisoner was remanded to the custody of the state authorities.

[73] *Ex parte Burford*, 3 Cranch 448 (1806). In his dissent to *Ex parte Bollman*, Johnson stated that he had objected to this assumption of jurisdiction but had submitted "in silent deference to the decision of my brethren."

[74] *Ex parte Bollman,* 4 Cranch 75 (1807).

[75] *Idem,* dissent of Johnson, 4 Cranch 101-107.

[76] See the opinion of District Judge Kane in *United States ex rel. Wheeler v. Williamson,* Case 16,725, 28 FC 682 (1855) for an expanded version of Marshall's thesis.

[77] *Idem,* 4 Cranch 93-101. Washington and Livingston joined Marshall in the decision; Cushing and Chase were not present; Johnson dissented.

[78] *Ex parte Des Rochers,* Case 3,824, 7 FC 537 (1856), Circuit Court, California.

[79] *Barron v. Baltimore,* 7 Peters 243 (1833).

[80] *United States v. Anderson,* Case 14,449, 24 FC 813 (1812).

[81] *Ex parte Kearney,* 7 Wheaton 38 (1822).

[82] Case 4,366, 8 FC 493 (1823), Circuit Court, South Carolina.

[83] *United States v. Green,* Case 15,256, 26 FC 30 (1824).

[84] *Ex parte Watkins,* 3 Peters 193 (1830).

[85] *Ex parte Watkins,* 7 Peters 568 (1833).

[86] *Idem,* dissent of Johnson, 7 Peters, 579-583.

[87] Case 11,558, 20 FC 242 (1833).

[88] Section 7 Act of March 2, 1833.

[89] 14 Peters 540 (1840).

[90] Canada was still part of Great Britain.

[91] See Chapter Four, pp. 146-148.

[92] 14 Peters 497 (1840).

[93] Dissent of Baldwin, *Holmes v. Jennison,* 14 Peters 614-633.

[94] *Op. cit.,* above, pp. 277-278.

[95] 4 Wallace 2; 113 (1867).

[96] 5 Howard 103 (1847).

[97] 5 Howard 176 (1847).

[98] *Ex parte Dorr,* 3 Howard 103 (1845).

[99] *Ex parte Nugent,* Case 10,375, 18 FC 471 (1848), Circuit Court, District of Columbia.

[100] *In re Kaine,* Case 7,598, 14 FC 84 (1852), Circuit Court, S.D. New York, Betts (District Judge).

[101] *In re Kaine,* 14 Howard 103 (1853), Catron (joined by McLean, Wayne and Grier).

[102] *Idem,* dissent of Nelson, 14 Howard 129-135.

[103] *Idem,* dissent of Curtis, 14 Howard 117-129.

[104] *Ex parte Kaine,* Case 7,597, 14 FC 78 (1853), Circuit Court, Southern District, New York.

[105] *Ex parte Van Aernam,* Case 16,824, 28 FC 931 (1854).

[106] Case 7,259, 13 FC 445 (1853).

[107] Case 15,811, 26 FC 1318 (1854).

[108] Case 16,725, 28 FC 682 (1855).

[109] 18 Howard 307 (1856).

[110] The majority upheld the power of the President to grant conditional pardons.

[111] *Idem,* opinion of McLean, 18 Howard 316-318.

[112] *Idem,* dissent of Curtis, 18 Howard 328-331.

[113] *Ex parte Des Rochers,* Case 3,824, 7 FC 537 (1856), McAllister.

[114] *Ex parte Everts,* Case 4,581, 8 FC 909 (1858).

[115] The majority of opinions handed down by the Circuit Court of Ohio were "Opinions of the Court." The name of the judge was not given, so it is impossible at times to know whether the opinion was that of McLean or the District Judge.

[116] *Ex parte Robinson,* Case 11,935, 20 FC 969 (1855), Circuit Court, S.D. Ohio, McLean.

[117] *Ex parte Robinson,* Case 11,934, 20 FC 965 (1856), Leavitt.

[118] Case 12,848, 22 FC 105 (1857), Leavitt. Vallandingham was the counsel for the marshals.

[119] *Op. cit.,* 20 FC 965.

[120] 1 Black 271 (1862).

[121] See *Bennett v. Bennett,* Case 1,318, 3 FC 212 (1867), for a strong argument by District Judge Deady of the District Court of Oregon in favor of exercising the writ in private controversies.

CHAPTER SEVEN:

ADMIRALTY JURISDICTION

1. 1789-1847

In the period prior to the Civil War the federal courts were faced with only a limited number of cases arising under the commerce clause of Article I, calling on them to draw a line between the jurisdiction of the national government and that of the states; in part because regulation over commerce was only in its infancy, in part because non-maritime commerce was still principally of a local nature. Two of the principal commerce cases, in fact, dealt with problems of navigation on tidal waters.[1]

While controversies involving land commerce were few, the dockets of the courts were full with cases of admiralty and maritime jurisdiction, arising under Article III of the Constitution. Had these controversies been confined to technical questions such as rules of navigation, collisions, maritime insurance or the treatment of seamen, their interest would have been limited; however their scope was much wider, for it was precisely under this heading that the pre-Civil War courts were faced with the problem of drawing the line between their own jurisdiction and that of the state courts. This question in itself would justify an examination of the manner in which admiralty and maritime jurisdiction evolved; what makes the subject of even greater importance is the fact that the very right of trial by jury was involved.

The only direction which the Constitution itself has to give is that, "The judicial power shall extend to all cases of admiralty and maritime jurisdiction."[2] The Seventh Amendment adds: "In suits at *common law*. . .the right of trial by jury shall be preserved."

Section 9 of the Judiciary Act of 1789 enacts, "That the district courts shall have, exclusively of the several states, cognizance of all crimes and offences that shall be cognizable under the authority of the United States, committed within their respective districts, or upon the high seas;. . .*and shall also have exclusive original cognizance of all civil causes of admiralty and maritime jurisdiction*, including all seizures under laws of impost, navigation or trade of the United States, where the seizures are made, on waters which are navigable from the sea by vessels of ten or more tons burthen, within their respective districts as well as upon the high seas; saving to suitors, in all cases, the right of a common law remedy, where the common law is competent to give it;. . .And the trial of issues in fact, in the district courts, in all causes *except civil causes of admiralty and maritime jurisdiction*, shall be by jury."[3]

From the beginning we are faced—as was the court—with the questions: What is admiralty jurisdiction? What was it in England? What was it in the colonies and the states at the time of the adoption of the Constitution? For if the federal courts were to have exclusive jurisdiction of admiralty and maritime cases, it was of the utmost importance to know how far this jurisdiction extended. At the same time that the courts were exploring these general questions, they were called on to determine their jurisdiction in specific areas, such as prize, contracts, torts, seamen's wages and criminal offenses.

A case-by-case interpretation of the Constitution does not require the court to lay down an overall philosophy or rule. The admiralty and maritime jurisdiction of the United States, at the beginning, was no exception; the early cases were principally succinct decisions concerning the jurisdiction in the matter at hand or, at times, simple judgments on the merits. But before long the judges of the lower courts found it necessary to go back into history to establish their opinions on solid grounds; as a result, we have a great body of material concerning the scope of admiralty law. But the replies to the questions posed above were many and varied, for this was perhaps the most controversial jurisdictional problem to come before the pre-war courts.

The law of the seas is as old as navigation. Each seafaring community had its own code or built on that of its predecessors. The principal maritime codes which formed the base of the maritime law which existed at the time the Constitution was adopted were: the laws of the Rhodians, the *Consolate del Mare*, the Amalfitan Code, the laws of Oleron, the Black Book of the Admiralty, the laws of the Hanse Towns, the laws of Wistbury and the sea laws of Spain. By 1787 these codes could be divided into two principal groups: the admiralty laws of the Continent and the admiralty law of England, which, in turn, had an offshoot—the law of the vice-admiralty courts of the colonies. The first problem which the courts of the United States had to answer in order to determine the extent of their admiralty jurisdiction was—to which of these codes were they to refer?

The first reply, that of Judge Peters of the District Court of Pennsylvania, was very general: "This court must be governed in its decisions by the maritime code we possessed at the period. . .of our becoming an independent nation. . .as well as by the particular laws since established by our government, or which may hereafter be enacted." The court must be bound by the general law of nations, the judge went on to say, rather than "the varying and crooked line of discretion." He made mention of the known maritime codes but did not confine himself to any one in particular.[4]

Ten years later, in *United States v. McGill*, Justice Washington was more specific: "The words of the Constitution must be taken to refer to the admiralty and maritime jurisdiction of England (from whose code and practice we derive our system of jurisprudence, and, generally speaking, obtain the best glossary)."[5] This opinion was shared by Justice Johnson, who rejected the civil law of the Roman government as the basis for admiralty law and held that, "The admiralty law of Great Britain is the admiralty law here."[6] This entirely logical conclusion[7] was, however, only the first step toward the solution of the problem; as we shall see, the admiralty and maritime jurisdiction of England meant different things at different times.

While the lower courts were attempting to resolve this controversial problem, the Supreme Court was settling others. In *Glass v. The Sloop Betsey*, the court held that every district court of the United States possesses all the powers of a court of admiralty, both instance and prize.[8] And in *United States v. La Vengeance*, it was decided that in civil causes of admiralty and maritime jurisdiction, trial by jury was not necessary.[9]

Specific problems of jurisdiction in cases of contracts, torts and prize soon came before the lower courts. In 1806 Judge Peters of the District Court of Pennsylvania appended a note to the case of *Howland v. The Lavinia*, in which he wrote: "However applicable some general principles may be to its being within the jurisdiction of the admiralty, as a contract made on land 'to be performed on the sea,' I have always leaned against taking jurisdiction in disputed cases, such as freight, though ancient authorities would justify me in so doing. . .In transactions, where the commencement and consummation of the contract were exclusively on land, I have held it in general very disputable, at least, whether the jurisdiction attached, though the intermediate and indispensable portion of performance was on the sea."[10]

In the case of *The Emulous*, a vessel captured at New Bedford, within the ebb and flow of the tide, Justice Story ruled that the courts of the United States have jurisdiction over all prizes made in ports, as well as on the high seas, by virtue of the delegation of admiralty and maritime jurisdiction: "[Prize] jurisdiction is not confined to mere captures at sea. The prize jurisdiction does not depend upon locality, but upon the subject matter. . .The admiralty, therefore, not only takes cognizance of all captures made at sea, in creeks, havens and rivers, but also of all captures made on land, where the same have been made by a naval force, or by cooperation with a naval force."[11]

If the prize jurisdiction depended on subject matter and extended even to land captures, the admiralty jurisdiction as to torts depended upon locality and was limited to torts committed on the high seas or on waters within the ebb and flow of the tide, ruled Justice Story in the case of *Thomas v. Lane*. In an opinion which was surprisingly tentative for the foremost American admiralty advocate of his time, Story decided that torts committed on tide waters within foreign ports were within the admiralty jurisdiction, even if the common law courts refused jurisdiction to the admiralty over such cases occurring within English ports. In this case, however, the court dismissed the libel for want of jurisdiction, because it was not positively stated that the tide ebbs and flows in the harbor of Havana where the cause originated. Nor did Story state how the law would be if the case had arisen in an American port, though he implied that the admiralty jurisdiction would have been upheld.[12]

In a third case decided in the same First Circuit, Story held that the jurisdiction of the admiralty in cases involving contracts did not depend on the character of the parties but on the character of the contract, whether it was maritime or not.[13]

It was not until 1815, however, that the history of admiralty jurisdiction in England, the colonies and the United States was thoroughly investigated, in the case of *De Lovio v. Boit*. The immediate question was whether a policy of insurance was a maritime contract and therefore subject to the admiralty jurisdiction. Justice Story, before whom the case was brought in the Circuit Court of Massachusetts, held that the admiralty had jurisdiction over all maritime contracts, including ones of insurance,[14] wheresoever they be made or executed, and whatever may be the form of the stipulations. But in deciding this question, Story went beyond the immediate issue to examine the admiralty jurisdiction in general.

The history of admiralty jurisdiction in England may be divided into two eras: before and after the reign of Richard II

(1377-1400). In the earlier period the admiralty had cognizance of all questions of prize, torts and offenses upon the high seas, and in ports within the ebb and flow of the tide, as well as of maritime contracts and navigation. The forms of admiralty proceedings were borrowed from the civil law and were distinct from those of the common law; trials were held before judges of the admiralty rather than before juries. The admiralty courts can be traced back to the times of Richard I and the Laws of Oleron, through the ordinances of John, Henry III and Edward I, and up to the Black Book of the Admiralty of Edward III.

During the reign of Richard II, two statutes came into force which were to become the basis of future controversy between the advocates of the admiralty and the defenders of the common law. The first, 13 Richard II (1389) enacted that, "the admirals and their deputies shall not meddle henceforth of any thing done within the realm, but only of a thing done upon the sea;" the second, 15 Richard II (1391) stated in greater detail that, "of all manner of contracts, pleas and quereles and of all things done or arising within the bodies of counties, as well by land as water, and also of wreck of the sea, the admiral's court shall have no manner of cognizance, power nor jurisdiction; but all such manner of contracts, pleas and quereles and all other things rising within the bodies of counties, as well by land as by water, as afore, and also wreck of the sea, shall be tried, determined, discussed and remedied by the laws of the land, and not before or by the admiral, nor his lieutenant, in any wise."

The advocates of the admiralty claimed that these statutes were not intended to abridge or restrain the rightful jurisdiction of that court, but only to take away any pretense of entertaining suits upon contracts arising wholly upon land, not referring to maritime affairs, or upon torts and injuries which, though arising in ports, were not done within the ebb and flow of the tide. "Consistently with those statutes," concluded Story, "the admiralty may still exercise jurisdiction: 1) Over torts and injuries upon the high seas and in ports within the ebb and flow of the tide, and in great streams below the first bridges; 2) Over all maritime contracts arising at home or abroad; 3) Over matters of prize and its incidents."

The courts of the common law, on the other hand, held that the jurisdiction of the admiralty was confined by these statutes to "contracts and things exclusively made and done upon the high seas, and to be executed upon the high seas; that it has no jurisdiction over torts, offences or injuries done in ports within the ebb and flow of the tide; nor over maritime contracts made within the bodies of counties or beyond sea although they are, in some measure, to be executed upon the high seas."

"The courts of common law," declared Story, "by a silent and steady march, have gradually extended the limits of their own authority, until they have usurped or acquired concurrent jurisdiction over all causes, except of prize, within the cognizance of the admiralty." The particular villain for Story was Lord Coke (1552-1634), about whom he wrote: "It is well-known with what zeal, ability, and diligence he endeavored to break down the court of chancery, as well as the admiralty. It would have been fortunate for the maritime world if his labors in the latter had been as unsuccessful as in the former."

The purpose of Story was to demonstrate the error of the common lawyers who attempted to circumscribe the jurisdiction of the admiralty to the "high seas" and oust them from any matters occurring within the body of any county *(infra corpus comitatus)*. The common lawyers insisted that all ports and havens were within the bodies of counties where they possessed jurisdiction regardless of the ebb and flow of the tide, and that where the common law had jurisdiction the admiralty was excluded. The admiralty replied that the bodies of counties extended only to the high or low water mark and did not include waters between two necks of land; that they retained jurisdiction over all bodies of water affected by the ebb and flow of the tide, including ports and havens; and that the jurisdiction of the common law did not exclude that of the admiralty.

Story's own conclusion is: "The doctrine that the

admiralty is ousted by a concurrent jurisdiction of the common law would, if true, completely destroy its authority in all cases, except of prize; for in all others, the common law has now acquired or claimed a concurrent jurisdiction. It cannot, therefore, be maintained. There would be a much stronger reason for contending, upon sound principles, that where the admiralty possessed jurisdiction, the common law ought to be excluded."[15]

As for contracts, Story upheld the admiralty jurisdiction over all maritime affairs in general and all cases of maritime service and labor, contending that it was immaterial whether the contract be made on land or at sea, since the service itself is actually performed upon the sea. Story quotes with approval the judgment of Lord Mansfield: "The service at sea is the principal matter in consideration. The gist and foundation of the action (in the admiralty) is the marine service."

Summing up the admiralty jurisdiction in England, Story lays down the following rule, adopted from the English admiralty champion, Dr. Brown: "The jurisdiction of the admiralty depends, or ought to depend, as to contracts, upon the subject matter, i.e., whether maritime or not; and as to torts, upon locality, i.e., done upon the high seas, or in ports within the ebb and flow of the tide, or not."

For Story, this rule would have been sufficient to construe the constitutional grant of the admiralty courts of the United States. However, fearing that American followers of Lord Coke might insist on a contrary reading of English history, the judge from Massachusetts went beyond the above analysis to state: "In the United States, we are at liberty to reexamine the doctrines, and to construe the jurisdiction of the admiralty upon enlarged and liberal principles."

Story denies that the constitutional grant should be interpreted in terms of the admiralty jurisdiction acknowledged by the common law courts at the time of the American Revolution, or at the emigration of the earliest colonists. The correct interpretation is that acknowledged and exercised in the United States itself at the time of independence, or, in its place, the ancient and original jurisdiction of the admiralty prior to the statues of Richard

II. Story's argument is that the common law restrictions on admiralty jurisdiction are limited to the High Court of Admiralty in England but do not apply to the vice-admiralty colonial courts; and that in no case would the statutes of Richard II extend to the colonies. The Crown commissions, on the other hand, gave the courts which were established under the colonial government, "a most ample jurisdiction over all maritime contracts, and over torts and injuries, as well in ports as upon the high seas." This conclusion of Story's is a confirmation of an earlier ruling by District Judge Winchester of the District Court of Maryland, who in 1801 wrote: "The statutes of 13 and 15 Richard II have received in England a construction which must at all times prohibit their extension to this country."[16]

"At all events," Story reiterates, "there is no solid reason for construing the terms of the Constitution in a narrow and limited sense, or for ingrafting upon them the restrictions of English statutes, or decisions at common law founded on those statutes, which were sometimes dictated by jealousy and sometimes by misapprehension, which are often contradictory, and rarely supported by any consistent principle. The advantages resulting to the commerce and navigation of the United States from a uniformity of rules and decisions in all maritime questions, authorize us to believe that national policy, as well as judicial logic, require the clause of the Constitution to be so construed as to embrace all maritime contracts, torts and injuries or, in other words, to embrace all those causes which inherently belonged to the admiralty before any statutable restriction. . .The doctrine that would extend the statutes of Richard to the present judicial power of the United States seems little short of an absurdity. It is incorporating into the text of the Constitution an exception, not only unauthorized by its terms, but wholly inappropriate in phraseology to any other realm than England."

To support his argument, Story reasons that since the Supreme Court had on several occasions upheld the admiralty jurisdiction over seizures on waters navigable from the sea by vessels of ten or more tons, as well as within ports, the admiralty jurisdiction over such waters must be constitutional; and if constitutional in the case of seizures, so too in the case of torts. And to strengthen his conclusion that admiralty courts have jurisdiction over all maritime contracts, he points out that the word "maritime" was deliberately used in the phrase "admiralty and maritime jurisdiction" to include all maritime matters, and to dissipate any doubts which might have arisen if the word "admiralty" alone had been employed.[17]

At the same term that *De Lovio v. Boit* was decided, Justice Story made these additional remarks on the rivalry between the common law and the admiralty courts: "In the struggle between the courts of common law and the admiralty, which originated in the same spirit that attempted to break down the whole system of equity, it cannot be denied that the former have manifested a great degree of jealousy and hostility, fostered by strong prejudice and a very imperfect knowledge of the subject. It is not, therefore, to be wondered at that in such an unequal contest, where the power was all on one side, the admiralty should have lost many of its inherent rights. In more modern times when the jurisdiction of the admiralty has been better understood, a more liberal policy has been pursued and, where they have not been fettered by authority, judges have been more indulgent in allowing its exercise. The true doctrine was always asserted by the learned judges of the admiralty, and has been recently recognized by Mr. Justice Buller; that the jurisdiction as to contracts depends not upon the locality, but upon the subject matter of the contract. And I have not the slightest hesitation in holding that the admiralty has perfect jurisdiction over all maritime contracts. The decisions at common law on the subject of its jurisdiction have nothing to recommend them, and certainly are not binding on us. The Constitution and laws of the United States have confided to the courts of the United States cognizance of 'all civil causes of admiralty and maritime jurisdiction,' and what is the true limit of this jurisdiction must be judged of, not by hasty decisions upon prohibitions,[18] but by the history, practice and law, of the admiralty, as it is found expounded, with admirable learning and sagacity, by the judges who have presided in that court. . .Until I am taught a different rule by the highest tribunal, I shall continue to assert the original inherent powers of the admiralty in the full extent in which they were recognized in England until the unhappy controversies with the courts of common law."[19]

The following year the case of *United States v. Bevans* came before the Circuit Court of Massachusetts. Although this case arose under the Crimes Act of April 30, 1790, rather than Section 9 of the Judiciary Act, it affected the question of admiralty jurisdiction tangentially. Justice Story held that murder committed on a United States naval vessel, while lying in the channel of the harbor of Boston, at a considerable distance from shore, and outside the low-water mark, was an offense committed upon the "high seas," and consequently within the jurisdiction of the federal courts. The "high seas," said Story, "are that portion of the waters and arms of the sea beyond the low-water mark."[20]

Here Story's constant effort to extend the jurisdiction of the federal courts was overruled when the case came before the Supreme Court. Marshall held that the section of the law giving the federal courts cognizance of offenses committed on the high seas, or in any river, haven, basin or bay, was restricted to offenses committed "out of the jurisdiction of any particular state." The locus of the crime was within the jurisdiction of the State of Massachusetts, Marshall determined, and therefore beyond the reach of the federal jurisdiction.[21]

During the 1820's, two other members of the Supreme Court, within their respective circuits, confirmed Justice Story's interpretation of admiralty jurisdiction. In the case of *The Mary*, Justice Thompson declared, "We must look to our own Constitution and laws to ascertain the extent of [the admiralty] jurisdiction. . .Without undertaking to define the precise extent of this clause, 'all cases of admiralty and maritime jurisdiction,' I think I may safely say the terms are broad enough to embrace all maritime contracts, and if so, by the judiciary act, cognizance is given to the district courts."[22]

In *Zane v. The President*, Justice Washington held that if the subject matter of a contract concern the navigation of the sea, it is a case of admiralty and maritime jurisdiction, although the contract was made on land. "That this is a case of maritime contract, of which the admiralty has jurisdiction, is not disputed by the counsel for the appellee," he stated. "Although it was made at land, *infra corpus comitatus*, yet the subject matter of it concerned the navigation of the sea, and it is consequently maritime in its nature."[23]

In 1825 the Supreme Court itself for the first time attempted to draw a line as to the locality of admiralty jurisdiction, in a case involving seamen's wages, *The Thomas Jefferson*. The district court did not have admiralty jurisdiction of a suit for wages earned upon the Missouri River, above the ebb and flow of the tide, ruled the court. This decision was the logical corollary of Story's extension of admiralty jurisdiction to waters within the ebb and flow of the tide, and it was only just that Story himself wrote the opinion of the court: "In the great struggles between the courts of common law and the admiralty, the latter never attempted to assert any jurisdiction except over maritime contracts. In respect to contracts for the hire of seamen, the admiralty never pretended to claim, nor could it rightfully exercise any jurisdiction, except in cases where the service was substantially performed, or to be performed upon the sea, or upon waters within the ebb and flow of the tide. This is the prescribed limit which it was not at liberty to transcend. We say the service was to be substantially performed on the sea, or on tide water, because there is no doubt that the jurisdiction exists, although the commencement or termination of the voyage may happen to be at some place beyond the reach of the tide. The material consideration is whether the service is essentially a maritime service. In the present case the voyage, not only in its commencement and termination but in all its intermediate progress, was several hundreds of miles above the ebb and flow of the tide; and in no just sense can the wages be considered as earned in a maritime employment."[24]

In light of the doctrine which the court was to expound a generation later, it is important to emphasize the standards which Story applied: the sea or waters within the ebb and flow of the tide were the prescribed limits beyond which the admiralty jurisdiction could not extend; to be considered a maritime service it must be *substantially* performed on the sea or on tide water; a voyage which is confined to waters several hundreds of miles above the ebb and flow of the tide cannot be considered maritime.

The first outspoken opposition to Justice Story's reading of the history of admiralty jurisdiction came from Justice William Johnson in the case of *Ramsay v. Allegre*, a libel *in personam*[25] on a contract for repairs. The real object of his attack was an *obiter dictum* in a previous case, *The General Smith*,[26] in which it was held that the admiralty possessed jurisdiction over a suit *in personam* in cases of contracts for materials or repairs. Prefacing his opinion with the remark, "I think it high time to check this silent and stealing progress of the admiralty in acquiring jurisdiction to which it has no pretensions," Johnson proceeded to point out that the admiralty had been ousted of jurisdiction *in personam* over contracts for hundreds of years, with the sole exception of seamen's wages.

Whereas Story considered that the common law courts had encroached on the inherent prerogatives of the admiralty, Johnson's view was exactly the opposite: "The admiralty, before the time of Richard II, had arrogated to itself a scope of judicial, legislative, and ministerial power, which withdrew from the trial by jury, and placed under the surveillance of the crown, of which the admiralty was only the representative, more than half the jurisprudence, and particularly the commercial jurisprudence, of the kingdom."

The statutes of 13 and 15 Richard II, according to Johnson, were passed to set limits to this power. It was not, however, until the act of 2 Henry IV c. 11 that the admiralty could be effectually restrained. This latter statute provided double damages to anyone who was proceeded against in admiralty in contravention of the statutes of Richard II. Thereafter, the common law courts succeeded in ousting admiralty jurisdiction over all forms of contracts which were proper matters to be submitted to trial by jury, leaving the admiralty jurisdiction over matters which were proper for a court of equity, since there was no motive to transfer causes from one civil court—the admiralty—to another—chancery. If the admiralty retained jurisdiction over cases of seamen's wages it was because "their thoughtless character and ignorance renders them emphatically the wards of the admiralty."

To the contention that the decisions of the common-law courts are not conclusive against the admiralty jurisdiction, that the admiralty judges themselves should be heard, Johnson replies that the common-law prohibitions receive their authority from the King's Bench and are therefore conclusive.

Turning to the decision in *Stevens v. The Sandwich*, cited by Story in *De Lovio v. Boit*, Johnson argues that Judge Winchester erred in rejecting the statutes of Richard II and adopting the civil law as the guide to admiralty law: "The laws of the continent of Europe furnish no authority on this question." Nor could the justice from South Carolina conceive where the idea had originated that the admiralty and maritime jurisdiction vested by the Constitution of the United States was that which the admiralty possessed before the time of Richard II. Neither Judge Hopkinson, Bee, or Peters, the foremost American admiralty judges, had held the doctrine expressed by Winchester.

Turning to the immediate issue of contracts for materials or repairs, technically known as contracts of materialmen, Johnson traces the common-law prohibitions on admiralty jurisdiction up through the seventeenth century. To strengthen his argument he cites two rulings by State Admiralty Courts, in 1781 and 1786, respectively, which denied jurisdiction over contracts and service to be done on land within the body of a county.[27] "I should think here I have a right to demand," he continues, "if from the whole library of law books, and God knows we have enough of them already, 'camel loads,' a single attempt to proceed *in personam* upon a contract in the admiralty, except for seamen's wages can be extracted." As for the precedent of *De Lovio v. Boit*, a suit *in personam* on a policy of insurance, Johnson disposes of the case by pointing out that it was only a decision of a lower court and was not binding authority.

Justice Johnson concluded his opinion with this peroration: "I am fortifying a weak point in the wall of the Constitution. Every advance of the admiralty is a victory over the common law, a conquest gained upon the trial by jury.

The principles upon which alone this could have been maintained, are equally applicable to one-half the commercial contracts between citizen and citizen. Once establish the rights here claimed, and it may bring back with it all the admiralty usurpations of the fifteenth century. In England there exists a controlling power, but here there is none. Congress has, indeed, given a power to issue prohibitions to a district court, when transcending the limits of the admiralty jurisdiction. But who is to issue a prohibition to us, if we should ever be affected with a partiality for that jurisdiction? I, therefore, hold that we are under a peculiar obligation to restrain the admiralty jurisdiction within its proper limits."[28]

As if in reply to Johnson, Justice Story once more took up the cudgel in defense of the admiralty jurisdiction over maritime contracts. In an *obiter dictum* in the case of *Plummer v. Webb*,[29] Story objected to the practice of considering as infallible and irreversible authority, conclusive upon the conscience of American courts, every decision made by a court of common law on the subject of this jurisdiction. The courts of the United States should not be bound by hasty decisions made by jealous and hostile common-law courts whose restrictions were irregular and fluctuating; nor was it correct to accuse the admiralty courts of usurpation. The admiralty jurisdiction in America, reiterated Story, should be measured by the powers of the vice-admiralty courts and the doctrines of the admiralty judges, not by the prohibitions of the common-law courts.

The following year Judge Ware of the District Court of Maine expressed his wholehearted support of Story's doctrine. "I consider it as equally well-established," wrote Ware, "that the decisions of the common-law courts in England, as to the limits and extent of the admiralty jurisdiction, have not an authority in this country beyond the reasons on which they are founded. Every admiralty court in this country probably, most of them certainly, have in repeated instances taken cognizance of cases in which a prohibition would go in England."[30]

At the same time, the District Court of Pennsylvania was called upon to decide whether it possessed admiralty jurisdiction over disputes between part-owners of a vessel. The proctor for the complainants argued that the admiralty jurisdiction of the United States was not to be confined to that which survived in England, but included "all the jurisdiction of the English courts at an early period and all which the continental courts still exercise."

Judge Hopkinson, dismissing the petition, replied that whatever the jurisdiction of the admiralty in England, and whether or not the admiralty courts of the United States possessed an enlarged jurisdiction, the power asked for here had never been exercised before in an American court. "The courts of admiralty in England," he added, "may have been, at one period, too much constrained by the watchful and rigorous jealousy of the common law, but on the other hand the civilians have not been without ambition to extend their dominion; and, having the field very much to themselves on the continent, they may draw us over a wide range, if we follow them implicitly."[31]

When the case came before the circuit court on appeal, Justice Washington reversed the judgment of Hopkinson, holding that, (1) the jurisdiction of the district courts embraces all cases of a maritime nature, whether they be particularly of admiralty cognizance or not; and (2), "this jurisdiction, and the law regulating its exercise, are to be sought for in the general maritime law of nations, and are not confined to that of England or any other particular maritime nation." This decision is especially surprising in that twenty years earlier Justice Washington had reached the conclusion that, "The words of the Constitution must be taken to refer to the admiralty and maritime jurisdiction of England;"[32] and because Washington admitted that the law applicable to the case was not to be found in the admiralty court of England or the laws of Oleron and Wisbury but in the Marine Code of France, which hitherto had not been drawn on by the American courts as a source.

Going beyond anything that Justice Story had said, Washington argued that the French Marine Code was compiled from the prevailing maritime regulations of France and of other nations: "And why should not such parts of it as are purely of a general maritime character, which are adapted to the commercial state of this country, and are not inconsistent with the municipal regulations by which our courts are governed, be followed by the courts of the United States in questions of a maritime nature? I leave this question to be answered by those who would restrain the admiralty jurisdiction of the district court within the limits allowed by the common-law courts of England to be exercised by the high court of admiralty of that country."[33]

With this wide gamut of opinion, ranging from Justice Johnson's common-law court bias to Justice Washington's new-found eclecticism, it is no wonder that the lower court judges found it difficult to draw the line of jurisdiction. In *Sheckler v. The Geneva Boxer*, District Judge Walker took jurisdiction over a suit in admiralty by the crew of a vessel whose voyage was limited to the Ohio River between Cincinnati and Pittsburgh, well above the flow of the tide. This isolated case, however, is of dubious value because the *Federal Cases* editor states that it is "nowhere reported; opinion not now accessible," and adds that it is not known whether the question of jurisdiction was argued.[34]

In *Smith v. The Pekin*, the District Court of the Eastern District of Pennsylvania, without giving an opinion, upheld the admiralty jurisdiction over a contract for wages on a voyage on tide water between ports of adjoining states.[35] And in *Martin v. Acker*, the District Court of the Southern District of New York upheld the jurisdiction over a voyage on the Hudson River upon tide waters between two ports in the same state. Here Judge Betts holds that admiralty jurisdiction is completely independent of whether the voyage is interstate or intrastate, thus making it clear by implication that the admiralty jurisdiction is in no way dependent on the commerce clause of the Constitution. However, the judge errs in holding that "the remedies of the maritime law apply to all cases of admiralty and maritime jurisdiction on the rivers of the United States which are navigable to the sea for boats of ten tons burthen and upwards." The reference to such jurisdiction is limited, in Section 9 of the Judiciary Act, to *seizures*, and is nowhere extended to *all* cases of admiralty and maritime jurisdiction. This confusion or error or deliberate attempt to widen the admiralty jurisdiction, led

Judge Betts to anticipate the decision of the Supreme Court in *The Genesee Chief*[36] by some twenty years. "In the case of *The Thomas Jefferson*," wrote Betts in an *obiter dictum*, "the doctrines before recognized as having relation to all navigable waters were restrained to waters within the ebb and flow of the tide. It is difficult to discern any principle upon which that limitation can be applied to one description of navigable waters in the United States more than to another."[37]

At the same term, in *The Wave*, Judge Betts held that the district courts had admiralty jurisdiction over suits for pilotage even when the service was performed within the waters of the same state and the pilots were commissioned under a state law.[38] On appeal to the circuit court, Justice Thompson agreed that pilotage was a maritime service and that the admiralty courts in this country were not bound by the common-law court prohibitions against jurisdiction over pilotage service within the body of a county. Nonetheless, Thompson reversed the decree of the lower court on the ground that the State of New York, rather than the district courts of the United States, possessed jurisdiction over pilotage service: by the pilotage act of 1789, the subject matter was temporarily withdrawn from the cognizance of the general government and could not, therefore, be considered as "impliedly embraced" in the general delegation of admiralty and maritime jurisdiction. Thompson rejected the suggestion of Betts that the admiralty jurisdiction of the district court was exclusive of the jurisdiction of state tribunals, citing the clause in Section 9 of the Judiciary Act saving to all suitors the right of a common-law remedy, when the common-law is competent to give it. The suit, concludes Thompson, should be governed by the laws of the State of New York which were adopted by the pilotage act of 1789.[39]

By now it had become virtually an obligation for each judge in turn to submit an essay on the admiralty jurisdiction along with the judgment of the case at hand. Justice Baldwin was no exception. The immediate case involved a libel for seamen's wages and an off-set claimed by the respondents. In dismissing the claim for the off-set as being beyond the jurisdiction of the admiralty courts, Baldwin indulged in a history of the admiralty almost as lengthy as that of Justice Story in *De Lovio v. Boit*. "The jurisdiction of the admiralty was deemed a jewel of great lustre and value in the diadem or crown of the king," he began, "and was carried to great extent by the lord high admiral and his officers; but however it might be cherished and enlarged by them, in order to extend the King's and their power, and promote their interest, it was odious to the commons of England, who became alarmed at the encroachments upon the jurisdiction of the courts of common law, and called loudly for the redress of their grievance." Compelled to submit to the statute of 2 Henry IV c. 11, the admiralty "yielded with a bad grace. In the 8 James I, more than two hundred years after the statute of 2 Henry IV, the lord high admiral made a formal complaint on the subject to the King against the judges, concerning prohibitions granted to the court of admiralty. . .Such was the audacity of the pretensions of the admiralty, that it claimed to exercise jurisdiction in virtue of the King's patent, in defiance of the acts of Parliament."

Tipping his hat to the opinion of Justice Johnson in *Ramsay v. Allegre*, Baldwin proceeds to deny that the jurisdiction of the admiralty was more expansive in the colonies than in the mother country: "As appeals lay from the colonial courts of admiralty, the line of their jurisdiction was necessarily that which was the rule for the appellate court."

Turning to the Declaration of Rights of the colonies in October, 1774, Baldwin points out that one of the grievances was that Parliament had "extended jurisdiction of courts of admiralty not only for collecting said duties, but for the trial of causes merely arising within the body of a county." Among the acts of Parliament infringing their rights, the colonists complained against extending "the power of the admiralty courts beyond their ancient limits." And in the Declaration of Independence, the signers attacked the King "for depriving us in many cases of the benefit of trial by jury." All these documents, concluded Baldwin, expressed the colonists' resolution to combat the pretensions of the admiralty.

The true interpreters of the admiralty jurisdiction, continued Baldwin, were Judges Peters, Hopkinson and Bee, none of whom advocated an expanded jurisdiction. The true rule inherited by the colonists was: "All causes arising in the body of a county, or arising on the sea, unless of a maritime nature, were cognizable by the courts of common law, and the principles on which they granted prohibitions to the courts of admiralty were as much a part of the common law as the rules of descent. It was a part of that great system of English jurisprudence which the colonists adopted."

"It remains to inquire," wrote Baldwin, "whether [the American people] have, by the [Constitution], enlarged the civil jurisdiction of the admiralty, so as to extend it to causes arising within the body of a county, which were cognizable exclusively by the courts of common law in England. . .As the extension of admiralty jurisdiction beyond the line prescribed in England is necessarily a deprivation of the right of trial by jury, and a substitution of the civil for the common law in cases cognizable only by the latter in 1774, any construction which will give to the term admiralty and maritime jurisdiction a more expanded meaning than the term had in England, must be rejected. . .The jurisprudence of England is the test and standard to which these terms are to be referred, and by which they are clearly defined."

To further this argument, Baldwin refers to the provision of the Seventh Amendment, that in suits at common-law the right of trial by jury shall be preserved. If the admiralty were to take jurisdiction over suits which by the English system were suits at common-law, then the parties would be deprived of their constitutional right to a trial by jury; therefore, the only correct conclusion is that the admiralty courts cannot take jurisdiction over cases cognizable by the common law. "The decisions of the Supreme Court have conclusively established the principle that the terms cases in law and equity in the Constitution, and suits at common-law, in the Seventh Amendment, are therein used as they are defined by the common law; some powerful reasons ought therefore to be given why the term 'cases of admiralty and maritime jurisdiction' have not been used according to their common-law definition. . .By attempting to introduce the admiralty jurisdiction of the civil law, or those principles which were asserted in early times in its favor, a foundation is laid for interminable conflicts of jurisdiction between the courts of the state and the Union."

In conclusion, Baldwin said: "Judicial power must first annul the Seventh Amendment, or judicial subtlety transform 'a suit at common-law into a case of admiralty and maritime jurisdiction,' before I take cognizance of such a case as this without a jury. Both parties are citizens of Pennsylvania, the cause of action arose in the body of a county, the contract is governed by the common law, its subject matter is not of a maritime nature or regulated by public or maritime law; but in all its aspects, a suit upon it from its commencement to its close is cognizable only in a state court."[40]

Here we find summed up the medula of Baldwin's opposition to an expanded admiralty jurisdiction: the admiralty jurisdiction deprives the parties of a trial by jury; actions arising within the body of a county are proper matters for the common law courts; the proper forum is the state court rather than the federal one. This thesis is the antithesis of Story's point of view, though it is not certain that Story would have disagreed on this particular question of an off-set to wages.

Two years later, in *The Volunteer*, Justice Story once more reaffirmed the doctrine of *De Lovio v. Boit.* Again he criticized the courts of common law, whose decisions were "more the offspring of narrow prejudice, illiberal jealousy, and imperfect knowledge of the subject, than of any clear and well-considered principles." The admiralty jurisdiction, wrote Story, "is a rightful jurisdiction, highly promotive of the best interests of commerce and navigation." Again he insists that the prohibitions of the statutes of Richard II were never applicable to the vice-admiralty courts in the colonies. He does not, however, attempt to reply to Baldwin's objection that the colonists protested this vice-admiralty jurisdiction which deprived them of the trial by jury.[41]

While the lower courts were debating the extent of the admiralty jurisdiction, the Supreme Court, in *Peyroux v. Howard*, for the first time took jurisdiction of a case where a maritime service was performed on a navigable river, within the ebb and flow of the tide, within the body of a county, some hundred miles from the sea. A vessel had been repaired in the Port of New Orleans, and the only question before the court, as far as jurisdiction was concerned, was whether the tide in the Mississippi reached that point. "So far as. . .admiralty jurisdiction depends upon locality," said the court, "it is bounded by the ebb and flow of the tide, and if the influence of the tide is at all felt, it must determine the question."[42]

Here there was no problem of law but merely one of fact. For if the standard was to be the ebb and flow of the tide, it was necessary to determine in each case arising on a navigable river whether in fact the tide ebbed and flowed. In the last resort this decision would have to be made by the Supreme Court, whose appellate power in admiralty cases extended to both law and fact.[43]

But for Judge Hopkinson of the District Court of Pennsylvania, it was not enough that a vessel was in operation on tidewaters for the admiralty court to obtain jurisdiction over contracts relative to the service of the vessel. While willing to take jurisdiction over a contract for wages on board of a steamboat carrying passengers and cargo, plying between Philadelphia and ports in the State of Delaware,[44] Hopkinson refused where the wages were earned on a vessel employed in carrying fuel to the City of Philadelphia from the opposite shore of the Delaware River. A contract must be for maritime services, he ruled, in order for the admiralty to take jurisdiction; the activity of ferryboats and ordinary traffic along the river was not essentially maritime. "It was not enough," said Hopkinson, "that the thing floated on the water, and that the water was within the ebb and flow of the tide.

"The contract I am required to enforce must be maritime, or I have no right to touch it," Hopkinson continued. "Locality is not, of itself, enough to give jurisdiction to the admiralty in cases of contract. We must also look to the subject matter of the contract; to the nature of the service and employment. . .The court did not say or intimate [in *The Thomas Jefferson*], that every service performed on tidewater is, therefore and necessarily, a maritime service."

Hopkinson acknowledged the difficulty in establishing a rule or line which could be clearly drawn and would be universal in its application. Each case would have to be decided in accordance with circumstances. However, it was clear to Hopkinson that the admiralty jurisdiction did not extend to ferry boats used on tidewaters or to small boats used in bringing fruit or vegetables to the market.

Another point raised by Hopkinson was whether the persons employed aboard vessels were mariners engaged in marine services: "If the master should take with him a servant whose sole business should be to shave him or comb his hair, or another to amuse him with a violin, the service would be performed on the high sea, but would it be a maritime contract or service, for which a ship could be libelled and attached in the admiralty?"[45] [46]

At Marshall's death in 1835, the only thing which was clearly established by the court was that the admiralty had jurisdiction wherever the tidewater ebbed and flowed, and even this proposition was not unanimously held. It is interesting to note that Marshall himself took no part in the discussions of admiralty jurisdiction, and lent his name to no important ruling or doctrine. On circuit, apparently, no case of admiralty came before him, or was reported—neither one upholding or refusing the jurisdiction. It is not surprising, then, to read the conclusion reached by Beveridge: "Of admiralty law in particular he knew little."[47]

It would have been interesting to know where Marshall stood on the important issues raised by Story, Johnson, Baldwin, and their contemporaries, especially such issues as trial by jury, states' rights, and common-law vs. equity. Perhaps the explanation is that Richmond did not offer the opportunities of Boston, New York or Philadelphia. However, as we will see, another Virginia judge, Peter Daniel, possessed a dedication to the subject which would compensate for his predecessor's silence.

The first case involving the geographical limits of admiralty jurisdiction to be decided by the Taney Court furnished no clue to the revolutionary doctrine which Taney himself was to propose within the next twenty years. The steamboat *Orleans* was a vessel engaged in navigation from New Orleans upstream to interior towns on the Mississippi and tributary waters. The master of the boat sued *in rem* in the admiralty for wages which were due to him. Speaking for the court, Justice Story held that the case was not one of a steamboat engaged in maritime trade or navigation: "Though in her voyages she may have touched at one terminus of them, in tidewaters, her employment has been, substantially, on other waters. . .The true test of [admiralty] jurisdiction in all cases of the sort is whether the vessel be engaged, substantially, in maritime navigation; or in interior navigation and trade, not on tidewaters. In the latter case there is no jurisdiction. So that, in this view, the district court had no jurisdiction over the steamboat involved in the present controversy, as she was wholly engaged in voyages of such interior waters."

Story distinguished this case from that of *Peyroux v. Howard*, in that repairs in the earlier case had been made on tidewaters; it was the locality of the repairs rather than the waters over which the repaired vessel would travel which was decisive in the earlier case, a tenuous distinction which was not always applied. What is clear is that Story was unwilling to stretch the jurisdiction beyond tidewater even when presented with an opportunity to do so. By going so far up the river *within the body of a county* he had already done sufficient stretching for one generation.[48]

Even the rule of *Peyroux v. Howard* failed to command universal respect. Where a canal boat, built and used for service in the interior canals of Pennsylvania, and not on tidewater, was repaired at a place on the Schuykill River where the tide ebbed and flowed, the District Court of Pennsylvania refused to take jurisdiction over a suit involving the contract for repairs. Wrote Judge Hopkinson, ignoring the earlier cases decided in the Supreme Court: "The work was done at a place where the tide flowed. Can this give jurisdiction? I think not. It is the place where the vessel is to be engaged that is material to decide whether the contract for that service was maritime or not."[49]

However, where a vessel was employed to navigate both

on canals above tidewater and on tidewater rivers, the anti-admiralty Justice Baldwin "reluctantly" extended jurisdiction over the repair of a vessel, since the tidewater portion of the voyage was substantial.[50] But at the same time the District Court of New York ruled that the admiralty did not possess jurisdiction over a contract for the navigation of a boat on the Erie Canal from Albany to Rochester and back and thence to New York, because "the contract was not substantially one for navigating the vessel on tidewaters."[51] But where the voyage of a boat was confined to the tidewaters of the Hudson River between New York and Kingston, the same court held that the admiralty did possess jurisdiction over a seaman's suit to recover wages.[52] Similarly, Judge Betts ruled that a mariner, rendering services on board a vessel carrying coal between Philadelphia and New York, by way of the Delaware River and the Raritan Canal and River, may proceed in admiralty *in rem* against such vessel for his wages, even if the vessel be stripped of sails and masts and be towed by steamboats, since the service was performed substantially on waters within the ebb and flow of the tide. Not the least of the reasons for this liberal extension of jurisdiction is the assurance given to mariners that they will be able to obtain prompt and full payment for their labor, and that "this important and growing branch of trade" will have at its command sufficient numbers to insure "its active and profitable prosecution."[53]

It was obvious that the geographical limit of admiralty jurisdiction could not be determined by exact science; it was no longer a simple matter of hearing what the experts had to say concerning the "flux of the sea water, or the pressure backwards of the fresh water of a river."[54] Judge Betts had already expressed his skepticism over a principle which attempted to distinguish "one kind of water, adapted to general navigation, from another."[55] Now Justice Wayne, in determining that the admiralty jurisdiction extended over the Savannah River, between Savannah and Augusta, went on to say: "I do not mean, however, to assert that the grant of admiralty power, in the Constitution, is limited to the ebb and flow of the tide—that admiralty jurisdiction may not be maintained under the judicial act, as it is, above the flow of the tide and upon our great inland seas. It may be done without making any encroachment upon the trial by jury, in the legitimate use of that institution. I do not say it must be done. I am aware of the case of *The Thomas Jefferson.* It is authority, and I am bound by it; but I am not committed upon any of the points just suggested, nor to any interpretation which has been made of the grant of admiralty power in the Constitution, which gives a standard by which its jurisdiction is to be measured."[56]

This strong hint at the direction which the Supreme Court was soon to follow was accompanied the following year by an Act of Congress, extending the jurisdiction of the district courts to certain cases upon the Great Lakes and the navigable waters connecting them. This act of February 26, 1845, read:

"The district courts of the United States shall have, possess and exercise, the same jurisdiction in matters of contract and tort, arising in, upon, or concerning steamboats and other vessels of twenty tons burden and upwards, enrolled and licensed for the coasting trade, and at the time employed in business of commerce and navigation, between ports and places in different states and territories, upon the lakes and navigable waters connecting the said lakes, as is now possessed and exercised by the said courts, in cases of the like steamboats and other vessels employed in navigation and commerce, upon the high seas, or tidewaters, within the admiralty and maritime jurisdiction of the United States."

A clause was added, saving to the parties, "the right of trial by jury of all facts put in issue in such suits, where either party shall require it."

It is necessary to underline several features of this act: first, it was limited geographically to the Great Lakes and connecting waters—it was not an invitation to extend admiralty jurisdiction to navigable waters in general; second, it was limited to interstate commerce and navigation; finally, the reference to the high seas and tidewaters reflected the limits to which admiralty jurisdiction had hitherto been extended but could not be considered a definitive interpretation of the constitutional grant.

Before the Supreme Court was called upon to draw any

more lines, a number of geographical cases were decided in the lower courts. Judge Wells of the District Court of Missouri held that the admiralty had no jurisdiction over a ferryboat on the Missouri River, since the locality was thousands of miles above tidewater.[57] Judge Conkling of the Northern District of New York confirmed the ruling of Judge Betts that the admiralty did have jurisdiction over a contract for the transportation of flour from Albany to New York City on the Hudson River, even though the carrier was a towed canal boat, designed for use on the Erie Canal. "If the voyage in which the service had been rendered, or stipulated to be rendered," stated Judge Conkling, "was performed substantially on the sea or on tidewaters, it is immaterial that its commencement or termination happened to have been at some place beyond the reach of the tide. And, on the other hand, if the voyage was substantially on inland waters above the ebb and flow of the tide, the fact that the vessel entered tidewaters at one terminus of her voyage is insufficient to confer jurisdiction."[58]

Even when an entire voyage was within the ebb and flow of the tide, there was no certainty whether the courts would extend admiralty jurisdiction. In *Packard v. The Louisa*, Justice Woodbury, Story's successor, ruled that the employment of a vessel carrying and laying stone in Quincy River and Massachusetts Bay was not of a maritime character which would permit the exercise of admiralty jurisdiction. "The claim of a seaman on the vessel for his wages is, at any time, rather an equitable privilege than a technical hypothecation of the vessel. . .It is given in certain cases by admiralty law, and of course it cannot be sustained there, as that law is founded on the civil law, except where equitable. . .It must be an employment from one port to another, and not merely along shore or in the shore fisheries. It must also be at sea, not lying merely at a wharf; not as ferry boats, or merely carrying wood across a river. And it must be from one port to another, where the tide ebbs and flows, and not on fresh water. The person libelling must also be engaged in maritime duties on board."

"It is doubtful, therefore," continued Woodbury, "whether Packard's employment on board of the *Louisa*, partly in loading and laying stone, or the business of the sloop itself, could be regarded as strictly maritime and commercial. It seemed to be not wholly that of the sailor, whose services in and for the ship, and *whose reckless character in ocean dangers*, have made the law indulge him with this additional security."[59] [60]

Finally, in *Lowry v. The E. Benjamin*,[61] the uncertainty of the law was demonstrated when the District Court of Pennsylvania upheld the jurisdiction over a contract to be executed in part on the tidewaters of two rivers, the Raritan and the Delaware, and in part on the connecting fresh-water canals; whereupon, on appeal to the circuit court, the case was dismissed for want of jurisdiction.[62]

2. 1847-1851

Despite the objections of Johnson, Baldwin and some of the earlier lower court judges, the federal courts had fairly well established the rule that the admiralty jurisdiction extended to all waters within the ebb and flow of the tide. But it was not until 1847 that the Supreme Court, in *Waring v. Clarke*, positively asserted the doctrine that a case of collision on a navigable river, within the ebb and flow of the tide, was within the admiralty and maritime jurisdiction, even though the site of the accident was within the body of a county (*infra corpus comitatus*). This decision is not so important for the majority's explicit confirmation of a position long since accepted by the lower courts, as for the strong dissent of a minority which rejected the entire thesis of Justice Story and would have once more confined the admiralty to the high seas if it had had its way. By stretching the admiralty jurisdiction to its absolute limit—203 miles above the sea where the presence of tidewater was highly debatable—the majority pressed their point to an extreme that brought on a reaction; the reaction, in turn, pointed the way to a revolutionary doctrine which not even Justice Story had contemplated.

The site of the collision was at Bayou Goula on the Mississippi River, one hundred miles upstream from New

Orleans, where the effects of the tide were already considered tenuous at best. The vessels were engaged in local traffic and the parties were both residents of the State of Louisiana; indeed, of the same county. That the site was within the body of a county, there was no doubt; that it was within the ebb and flow of the tide, Justice Woodbury, dissenting, denied completely.

Because the opinion of the court was not unanimous, Justice Wayne found it necessary to retrace the history of admiralty jurisdiction in England and in the colonies. Wayne, as Story before him, insisted that whatever the admiralty jurisdiction was in England, it was different and more extensive in the American colonies.[63] In the case of New Hampshire, for instance, the jurisdiction extended to public streams, ports and fresh-water rivers. The vice-admiralty courts exercised jurisdiction over all maritime contracts, torts and injuries, in ports as well as on the high seas. The members of the convention who framed the Constitution, contended Wayne, had in mind the extended jurisdiction with which they were familiar.

"But, besides what we have already said," Wayne continued, "there is, in our opinion, an unanswerable constitutional objection to the limitation of 'all cases of admiralty and maritime jurisdiction,' as it is expressed in the Constitution, to the cases of admiralty and maritime jurisdiction in England when our Constitution was adopted. To do so would make the latter a part and parcel of the Constitution—as much so as if those cases were written upon its face. It would take away from the courts of the United States the interpretation of what were cases of admiralty and maritime jurisdiction. It would be a denial to Congress of all legislation upon the subject. It would make, for all time to come, without an amendment of the Constitution, that unalterable by any legislation of ours, which can at any time be changed by the Parliament of England, a limitation which never could have been meant, and cannot be inferred from the words, which extends the jurisdiction of the courts of the United States 'to all cases of admiralty and maritime jurisdiction.'

"The admiralty jurisdiction of the courts of the United

States," he concludes, "is not confined to the cases of admiralty jurisdiction in England when the Constitution was adopted."

Wayne next took up the proposition that the admiralty jurisdiction was ousted when the court of common law was competent to give a remedy in a trial by jury: neither the Seventh Amendment nor the saving clause of the 9th Section of the Judiciary Act took away the admiralty jurisdiction. The Seventh Amendment was limited to suits at common law, and the right to a trial by jury in such cases could in no way alter the procedures in admiralty cases or diminish the scope of the admiralty jurisdiction. As for the common law remedy reserved in the 9th Section of the Judiciary Act, it was an alternative offered to plaintiffs who preferred a trial by jury, but was not intended as a means by which the defendant "could at will force the plaintiff into a common law court, and in that way release himself and his property from all the responsibilities which a court of admiralty can impose upon both, as a security and indemnity for injuries of which a libellant may complain—securities which a court of common law cannot give."

Turning to the question of *infra corpus comitatus*, Wayne followed Story in rejecting the extension of the English common law court prohibitions to the admiralty jurisdiction of the United States. These restrictions on the admiralty were limited to England itself and then only for a given period; the true jurisdiction was the ancient one exercised before the statutes of Richard II, which prevailed in the colonies and was still followed on the continent.

"Our conclusion is," said the court, "that the admiralty jurisdiction of the courts of the United States extends to tidewaters, as far as the tide flows, though that may be *infra corpus comitatus;* that the case before us did happen where the tide ebbed and flowed *infra corpus comitatus*, and that the court has jurisdiction to decree upon the claim of the libellant for damages."[64]

Justice Catron presented a separate concurring opinion in which he argued that where the proceeding is against a vessel *in rem*, the common law courts are not competent to give a remedy; since "the remedy must be found somewhere. . .it seems to me to be a strange anomaly, that where no other court can afford the particular relief, in a case confessedly within the admiralty jurisdiction if occurring on the ocean, that the power did not exist because the trespass took place in the body of a state and county."[65] This rule would give to the admiralty jurisdiction over any and all torts, no matter where the locality, if the same tort were "within the admiralty jurisdiction if occurring on the ocean." Here the approach is one of available remedy rather than locality. The implications of this doctrine go far beyond anything hitherto proposed by the partisans of the admiralty.

Justice Woodbury, joined by Daniel and Grier, filed a lengthy dissent. For them the conflict was not an academic debate over the prerogatives of the admiralty court, but a question of the trial by the jury and the jurisdiction of state courts over local matters. "It is important to notice in the outset some unusual features in this case," wrote Woodbury. "The Supreme Court is called upon to try the facts as well as the law in it, and to decide them between parties in interest who belong to the same state, and as to a transaction which happened not on the high seas, as is usual in torts under admiralty jurisdiction, but two hundred miles above the mouth of the Mississippi River, within the limits of a county, and in the heart of the State of Louisiana. A question of jurisdiction, therefore, arises in this which is very important, and must be first disposed of. It involves the trial by jury as to trespasses of every kind happening between the ocean and the head of tidewaters in all the numerous rivers of the United States, as well as the rights of the citizens near them, in such disputes with their neighbors, to be tried by their own local tribunals and their own laws, rather than be subject to the great inconvenience and expense of coming hither, at such a distance, and under a different code to vindicate their just claims."

Woodbury, too, explored the admiralty jurisdiction as it had existed in England and concluded that, "No principle appears to be better settled there than that the court of admiralty has not jurisdiction over torts, whether to person or property, unless committed on the high seas, and out of the limits of a county." The admiralty was forbidden to try collisions within the body of a county, "because it was necessary to secure the highly prized trial by jury, rather than by a single judge, for everything happening where a jury could be had from the vicinage of the occurrence within a county, and because it secured a decision on their rights by the highly prized common law, inherited from their fathers, and with which they were familiar, rather than by the civil law or any other foreign code, attempted to be forced upon the commons and barons by Norman conquerors or their partisans.

"The controversy was not in England, and is not here," continued Woodbury, "a mere struggle between salt and fresh water—sea and lake—tide and ordinary current—within a county and without—as a technical matter only.

"But there are imbedded beneath the surface three great questions of principle in connection with these topics, which possess the gravest constitutional character. And they can hardly be regarded as of little consequence here, and assuredly not less than they possessed abroad, where they involve: 1) The abolition of the trial by jury over large tracts of country; 2) The substitution there of the civil law and its forms for the common law and statutes of the States; 3) And the encroachment widely on the jurisdiction of the tribunals of the states over disputes happening there between its own citizens."

When the admiralty is confined to matters connected with the ocean, with foreign intercourse, foreign laws, and foreign people; where it is desirable to have the law uniform; where matters are "extra-territorial, international and peculiar in some degree to the great highway of nations;" then "the admiralty law deserves the just tribute sometimes paid to it of expansive wisdom and elevated equity. And the vice-admiral is hence quaintly called 'the justice of the peace of the sea;' but who ever supposed him the justice of the peace two hundred miles inward from the sea?"

For Woodbury, the distinction between admiralty courts and common law courts in the United States was of greater, rather than less importance than in England, for here there was a contest between courts of the states and courts of the United States, while in England the courts were of one and the same government.

Woodbury insisted, as had Johnson and Baldwin previously, that the American courts were to look to the admiralty jurisdiction which prevailed in England when the Constitution was adopted. Contrary to the contention of Story, Woodbury claimed that the statutes of Richard II were in force in the colonies: "They were suited to the condition of those attached to the common law and jury trial in the colonies, no less than at home, and they were in favor of the rights and liberties of the subject, to be tried by his own and not foreign laws, and by a jury for all matters happening within the realm, and not on the high seas." The statutes came here with the colonies, as a part of the admiralty law. "They came here as much as Magna Charta or the Bill of Rights, and they should exist here now, in respect to all matters, with all the vigor that characterized them at home at the time of our Revolution. The principles, dear to freemen of the Saxon race—preferring the trial by jury and the common law, to a single judge in admiralty and the civil law—which were involved in these statutes, could be no less highly prized by our American fathers than their English ancestry, especially when we look to their numerous resolutions on this subject, both before and during the Revolution."

Woodbury attributed the concept of an expanded admiralty jurisdiction in the United States to a mistaken emphasis on tidewaters without the qualifying, "out of the body of the county." Thus the idea of tidewaters on the seacoast was altered, incorrectly, to tidewaters; and in the United States transformed into tidewaters, *infra corpus comitatus.* Further, it was error to confuse admiralty jurisdiction as to seizures on waters navigable by boats of ten tons' burden with jurisdiction over torts. Finally, for Woodbury, a case such as *Peyroux v. Howard* was no authority, since that was a case involving a contract rather than a tort.

To Wayne's argument that to equate the admiralty and maritime jurisdiction of the United States with the admiralty jurisdiction in England, was to make the latter a part and parcel of the Constitution and take away from the courts and

Congress the ultimate right to interpret and legislate on the subject, Woodbury replied that Congress was free to legislate under its power to regulate commerce and to give additional jurisdiction to the district courts, as it had done in the Act of 1845. But it was not for the courts to extend on their own initiative the admiralty jurisdiction with its denial of a trial by jury: "If desirable to have the United States courts try such cases rather than those of the states, they can be enabled to do it by express provisions, under the power to regulate foreign commerce and collect revenue, as is now done on the lakes; and reserving, as in that case, the right of trial by jury."

Then, in a rhetorical question which was soon to be taken up by the majority of the court as its face value, Woodbury asked: "And if such a change was required and intended, as some insist, by resorting to other than English law for a guide as to what were admiralty cases within the meaning of the Constitution, because something less narrow, geographically or otherwise, as it has been argued, something on a grander scale, and in some degree commensurate in length and breadth with our mighty rivers and lakes, was needed—as if a system which had answered for trade over all the oceans of the globe was not large enough for us—*then why not extend it at least over all our navigable waters, and not halt short at the doubtful, and fluctuating, and pent-up limits of tidewater?*"

The line drawn by the court was neither that of the civil law or the common law, Woodbury pointed out. "If this innovation had extended admiralty jurisdiction over all navigable waters, it would have been, at least, less vague, and found some vindication in its analogy to the civil code. But the rule of tidewater within a county and not on the sea conforms to no code nor precedent; neither marching boldly over all which is navigable, nor halting where the ocean meets the land; neither shunning to make wide inroads into the territories of juries, nor pushing as far as all which is nautical and commercial goes." In place of the flux and reflux of the tide on the high seas, without the body of a county or state, the court has substituted "the impulses from the tides at any and every distance from the ocean, sometimes encroaching from one to two hundred miles into the interior of counties and states, and prostrating those great pillars most valuable to the people of the states"—the jury trial and the common law.

Having virtually exhausted all avenues of opposition to an extended admiralty jurisdiction, Woodbury went on to say that there was no evidence of the influence of tides at Bayou Goula, the site of the collision; nor were the boats employed in maritime service. "This is a matter of local cognizance," he contended, "of mere state trade, of parties living in the same county, and doing business within the state alone; and should no more be tried without a jury, and decided by the laws of Oleron and Wistbury, or the *Consolate del Mare*, or the Black Book of Admiralty, than a collision between two wagoners in the same county."

Finally, as an afterthought, Woodbury expressed his doubts whether the justices of the Supreme Court possessed the qualifications for deciding the facts in admiralty cases: "The only good reason that the admiralty judge was ever intrusted with the decision of facts, rather than a jury, was that originally he was but a deputy of the admiral, and often a nautical man, acquainted with nautical matters and acting only on them; and now, in England, he calls to his aid, on facts, the experienced nautical officers of the Trinity House. . .He takes their opinions and advice on the facts as to collisions of vessels before he himself decides. The case is often fully argued before them first. But everything here is so different, and so much against the skill of judges of this court in settling facts, that in causes of doubt we are very likely, as has now happened, to disagree, and it is far better they should be examined by a jury in the vicinage of the collision."[66] This argument could be used against any admiralty jurisdiction, and it would seem that Woodbury favored concurrent jurisdiction with the common law courts even in the case of collisions which occurred on the high seas.

To comment on this exhaustive dissent would be almost superfluous. It is enough to underline the principal arguments: the preservation of the trial by jury should take precedent over any other considerations; the common law courts are most appropriate to matters arising within the body of a county, whether on land or water; any modifications in the extent of admiralty jurisdiction should be made by the Congress rather than by the courts; in all cases, the right to trial by jury should be saved; the members of the Supreme Court were not qualified to settle the facts. And left dangling for a future court to decide was the provocative query, which echoed the hint of Justice Wayne in *Bulloch v. The Lamar*—why draw the line at the point where the influence of the tide ceased?

If the decision in *Waring v. Clarke* was narrow, that of *New Jersey Steam Navigation Co. v. Merchants' Bank*, decided at the same term, was inconclusive. A contract had been made between an individual engaged in carrying specie and valuables of the Merchants' Bank of Boston, between New York and Providence, and the steamship company. On the night of January 13, 1840, the steamer *Lexington* caught fire and was consumed, resulting in the death of many passengers and the loss of $18,000 of the bank's property.

Four judges—Nelson, Taney, McLean and Wayne—held that the case was one of contract and that the courts of the United States possessed admiralty jurisdiction both *in personam* and *in rem* over contracts of affreightment entered into on land, to be executed on the sea. Two judges—Woodbury and Catron—were willing to take jurisdiction of the case only because it was one of a marine tort occurring on the high seas and not one of contract. Daniel and Grier dissented, denying that jurisdiction existed in either case.

Nelson, speaking for the advocates of admiralty jurisdiction, stated that the question had been settled by both legislative and judicial interpretation, "which ought not now to be distrubed." Nelson argued that the inclusion in Section 9 of the Judiciary Act of jurisdiction of causes arising under the revenue laws, and the reference to seizures on navigable waters without any mention of the common law test of *infra corpus comitatus*, demonstrated that from the beginning the American admiralty jurisdiction was wider than that which prevailed in England. Further evidence for the extended jurisdiction in the United States was the acceptance of suits of materialmen which were denied to the admiralty in England by the common law courts. Nelson's conclusion was that, "The authorities are decisive against expounding the constitutional grant according to the jurisdiction of the English admiralty, and in favor of a line of jurisdiction which fully embraces the contract in question." This conclusion leaves much to be desired since: (1) The legislative interpretation of the constitutional grant may or may not be constitutional; (2) Certain exceptions permitted in the scope of American admiralty jurisdiction do not mean that the English rule has been abandoned in general. This opinion, whether correct or not, lacks the forcefulness of those of Story and Wayne.

As a final observation, Nelson introduced a concept which could not help but confuse the entire question of admiralty jurisdiction. "The exclusive jurisdiction in admiralty cases was conferred on the national government as closely connected with the grant of the commercial power," he said. "It is a maritime court instituted for the purpose of administering the law of the seas. There seems to be ground, therefore, for restraining its jurisdiction, in some measure, within the limit of the grant of the commercial power, which would confine it, in cases of contracts, to those concerning the navigation and trade of the country upon the high seas and tidewaters, with foreign countries and among the several states. Contracts growing out of the purely internal commerce of the state, as well as commerce beyond tidewaters, are generally domestic in their origin and operation, and could scarcely have been intended to be drawn within the cognizance of the federal courts." [67] [68]

Woodbury, in upholding the admiralty jurisdiction in this case solely on the ground that the fire and damage was the result of gross neglect and therefore a tort committed on the sea, denied that the admiralty had jurisdiction over the contract under which the lost goods had been sent. He had little to add to his recent dissent in *Waring v. Clarke*, except the assertion that in some of the colonies, before the Revolution, the restraining statutes of Richard II had been expressly adopted; and that in accordance with those statutes, contracts made on land for the freight of goods by sea were not proper matters for the admiralty courts.

Justice Daniel completely rejected the suggestion of Woodbury that the case was one of tort, claiming that the jurisdiction of the admiralty in matters of tort is limited to "actions for assault, collision and spoil." For Daniel it was a simple proceeding *in personam* upon an express contract, entered into between the parties in the City of New York, properly cognizable before a common-law court, and not a case over which the admiralty court could exercise jurisdiction, either *in personam* or *in rem*, under the Constitution and laws of the United States.

This was Daniel's first commentary on the admiralty jurisdiction, and so it was only natural that he too would examine the question as if it had never before been explored. Daniel's premise was that the courts of the United States must look to the laws and policy of the mother country as guides. The underlying reason for this premise was the similarity of education and opinion between the colonies and England; a "national pride, and the partiality which naturally creates in the offspring admiration and imitation of the parent;" identity of civil and political rights and the uniformity and conformity always imposed by the mother country. For Daniel, the dominions of England might as easily adopt the ordinances of China or Tibet, as those of France, Genoa, Venice or any other portion of the continent.

Daniel cites as authority Sir Matthew Hale's *History of the Common Law*, which goes every bit as far as Coke to restrict the jurisdiction of the admiralty courts. "*Altum mare*," writes Daniel, "is given as the only legitimate province of the admiral's authority." In addition to Hale, Daniel cites Blackstone's, " 'All admiralty causes must, therefore, be causes arising wholly upon the sea.' Here, then," comments Daniel, "is the explicit declaration that it is the theatre, the place of their origin and performance exclusively, not their relation to maritime subjects which determines their forum." Daniel's conclusion is that as far as the jurisdiction of the English admiralty goes, in matters of contract it was limited to "maritime contracts made and to be executed upon the high sea, and to cases of hypothecation of the ship upon her voyage; and in matters of civil tort to cases also occurring upon the sea, without the body of the county."

Turning to the scope of admiralty jurisdiction in the colonies, Daniel rejects the argument that the term "maritime" employed in the constitutional and legal grant implies more than the word "admiralty" alone; he specifically opposes the "able, learned and ingenious effort" of Justice Story in *De Lovio v. Boit*, "to confer on the admiralty here powers not merely coextensive with the most ambitious pretensions of the English admiralty at any period of its existence, but powers that may be derived from the laws and institutions of almost every community of ancient or modern Europe, and covering not only seas and navigable waters, but men and their transactions having no necessary connection with waters of any description." Furthermore, adds Daniel, the decisions of the inferior courts are not binding on the judgment of the Supreme Court.

Daniel insists that the legitimate jurisdictions of the vice-admiralty courts in the colonies was no wider than that of the high court of admiralty—the former courts were subordinate and the jurisdiction was identical. He cites the opposition of the colonists to the pretensions of the admiralty and the resolutions and declarations described by Baldwin in *Bains v. The James and Catherine* and adds: "It would seem, then, reconcilable neither with reason nor probability that the men who made these solemn protests—that a community still warm from the contest induced by them—should, upon their emancipation from evils considered intolerable, immediately by a species of political suicide rivet those same evils indissolubly upon themselves." Daniel's conclusion is that the admiralty jurisdiction of the United States excludes both contracts made or torts committed within the body of a county.

"I am extremely diffident as to the wisdom and safety of enlarging a jurisdiction. . .which from the earliest traces of its existence. . .has always been exercised by rules and principles less congenial with our institutions then are the principles and proceedings of the common law," Daniel adds. "A jurisdiction substituting, too, for the invaluable safeguard to truth secured by confronting the witnesses with court and jury, a machinery by which the aspect and the force of testimony are graduated rather by the address and skill of the agents employed to fabricate it, than by its own intrinsic worth, and transferring the trial of facts resting upon credibility to a tribunal often remote and inconvenient, and constrained to decide on statements that may be merely colorable, often entirely untrue."[69]

In the same year that the two preceding cases were being decided by the Supreme Court, an indictment for building a bridge and obstructing a navigable river was brought before the Circuit Court of Massachusetts. In dismissing the indictment for want of jurisdiction, Justice Woodbury found occasion to comment further on the admiralty jurisdiction of the United States. "It is a matter of some regret," he wrote, "that Congress had not been a little more slow, cautious, and discriminating when they conferred jurisdiction in all civil cases, and had not either enumerated what is considered properly as civil cases in admiralty, specifying subjects and places, or referred to some era, or code, or country as to its civil admiralty jurisdiction as a guide." As things stood now, said Woodbury, some judges traced the power to the Saxon law, some to the Norman, some to the Saracen or Carthaginian, some to the Roman and some to the Turk or Crusader.

"It was of little consequence, comparitively, on the Continent, to preserve any settled lines between the admiralty and other courts," Woodbury continued, "as all of them followed the civil law and had no trials by jury. But when an attempt was made to transfer admiralty courts and powers to England, in which the common law and not the civil prevailed,. . .it soon became important, to protect themselves in the enjoyment of the common law and the trial by jury, to limit admiralty jurisdiction." It is even more important to discriminate here on account of state laws and state rights and to maintain the trial by jury, the "trial by neighbors in their own state tribunals and by their own laws, rather than at a distance and by a different code."

If the admiralty jurisdiction in civil causes was to be restricted to the rule prevailing in England at the time the Constitution was adopted, *a fortiori*, reasoned Woodbury, the admiralty jurisdiction over crimes should be limited and not created by judicial construction: "The whole leaning of the court, therefore, in case of any doubt, should be towards obtaining jurisdiction over commercial questions or crimes against navigation and trade by special legislation of Congress, rather than by broad constructions of any grants of mere admiralty power. Because there a jury can be used, under the power to regulate commerce."

Referring to the Act of 1845, Woodbury points out that the jurisdiction granted to the district courts over maritime matters on the Great Lakes was conferred under the power to regulate commerce and not under the grant of admiralty power, since the law would have been superfluous if the admiralty in itself possessed jurisdiction over the tideless lakes. Once more he concluded his opinion by extolling the inestimable right of the trial by jury.[70]

In the following year, Judge Ware of the District Court of Maine added a note on the question of jurisdiction to a case he had decided eight years earlier, a libel in admiralty for the loss of baggage shipped between the ports of Boston and Portland. Ware's position was diametrically opposed to the one of Woodbury and Daniel; he held that the jurisdiction of the admiralty courts in this country was more extensive than that of the high court of admiralty; that the terms "admiralty" and "maritime" are not synonymous; and that the constitutional grant refers to the law of nations rather than to the statute laws of England as they were enforced by the common-law courts.

Ware pointed out that the commissions of the vice-admiralty judges in the colonies extended to all that was ever claimed by the admiralty, and that the restraining statutes of Richard II were not in force in the colonies. Further, he rejected the idea that the framers of the Constitution would have "silently and without notice of any such intention, referred, for the sense and meaning of any of their words, to the signification which they had in laws and jurisprudence of a foreign nation." Thus Daniel's "mother country" had become Ware's "foreign nation." For Ware, "the common law was never in force in this country, any further than as it was adopted by common consent, or by the colonial legislatures. Beyond this, it was as much a foreign law as that of France and Holland."

By adding the word "maritime," argued Ware, the framers deliberately enlarged the jurisdiction of the admiralty; their intention was to include "a civil jurisdiction over causes civil and maritime, springing from a consideration purely maritime." The term was used to close the door against any doubt that the constitutional grant was limited to the narrow English admiralty jurisdiction.[71]

Ware then went on to answer the argument of Baldwin and Woodbury that the admiralty jurisdiction had been viewed with jealousy and distrust by the colonies: admitting this fact, it does not follow that the people would feel any hostility toward an admiralty jurisdiction exercised by their own government. Demonstrating a thoroughly nationalist philosophy which contrasted with the eighteenth century doctrine of states rights of the two justices mentioned above, Ware rationalized the enlargement of the admiralty jurisdiction under the Constitution by describing the changed circumstances: "While the colonial state remained, the people would naturally feel an objection to leave the decision of revenue causes to the court instead of the jury. The judges were strangers, and sent from abroad. They brought with them all the prejudices and partialities of Englishmen, in favor of their own country and people, and to this was added the bias, which the officers of the crown are always supposed to have, in favor of its prerogatives. Such officers were naturally viewed with jealousy and distrust. But under the Constitution a new order of things arose. The judges were our neighbors and kinsmen, and responsible to our own government. And the people might be willing to trust a larger measure of power to these than they would willingly see exercised by strangers and foreigners. There was no longer any foundation for the jealousy, and it no longer existed." This apology could hardly assuage Woodbury's fears concerning the loss of the trial by jury before persons drawn from the same vicinage.

In determining the meaning of the constitutional grant of admiralty jurisdiction, says Ware, we are to look to "the common and universal law that is acknowledged by all Christian and maritime nations"—the law of nations, rather than the jurisprudence of any one people in particular. And in this common law of the sea "we find these words, as understood by every people in the commonwealth of commercial and maritime nations, with the exception of England, to have a more comprehensive sense than that which confines them to the jurisdiction exercised by the high court of admiralty."

Following Nelson's lead, Ware goes on to equate the legislative power over commerce with the judicial power over admiralty jurisdiction: "The power of regulating commerce with foreign nations, and between the states, is granted by another article of the Constitution to the legislative department. This covers the whole maritime commerce of the country. The grant to the judicial department of the cognizance of all causes of maritime jurisdiction, makes the judicial coextensive with the legislative power. This is the only way in which we could be assured of having what is so important to a commercial nation, a uniform maritime law in all the states of the Union."

This argument of Ware and Nelson, though at first sight appealing, is fallacious. The implication is that the judicial power being coextensive with the legislative power, and Congress having the power to legislate over commerce, therefore the admiralty court has jurisdiction over maritime commerce. That federal courts have jurisdiction over maritime commerce may be so, but not necessarily in admiralty if, as Ware himself seems to say, the power stems from the commerce clause. There is no necessary relation between commerce and admiralty; otherwise land commerce would also come under the jurisdiction of the admiralty. It is possible that all admiralty jurisdiction is related to maritime matters but not necessary that all maritime matters come under the control of the admiralty.

Ware repeats the arguments of other partisans of the admiralty to drive home his point and, like Story, cannot resist the temptation to demolish Lord Coke. "The state of mind in which Lord Coke went into the controversy on the subject of the admiralty jurisdiction," he writes, "does not deserve the respectable name of prejudice. It was mere willfulness and passion. Brown says that he hated the civil law and everything connected with it. He was undoubtedly a man of an acute and vigorous mind, but it ran in a narrow groove. No man knew better the old law of England in all its ramifications of feudal technicalities and quibbling subtleties; but this was all, except the temporary politics of the days, that he did know. He talks about the gladsome light of jurisprudence, but no one at this day will look for this light in his ponderous volumes of insufferable tediousness, in which all things are jumbled together in a perfect chaos."

This injudicious judgment is followed by an equally passionate conclusion directed not at long-since-dead English judges, but at his own contemporary colleagues:

"We have a series of deliberate and well-considered decisions of the judiciary, and the quiet assent of the people to an unbroken and unvarying practice continued for more than half a century, all concurring in one point, that the admiralty and maritime jurisdiction, under the Constitution, is of larger extent than that of the English court of admiralty, and all repudiating the assumption that we are to look to the laws of England for the definition of those terms in the Constitution. If this cannot now be considered as a settled question of American jurisprudence under the great organic law of the government, we may, it seems to me, well say not only that no such question is settled, but that none ever will be or ever can be settled. And if every officer of the United States who is intrusted with a portion of the constitutional powers of the government, is at liberty to carry those powers into practice as he understands the Constitution, without any reference to the opinions of others, or to any settled and long-continued construction, this sacred instrument becomes a piece of wax, to be moulded into every variety of arbitrary and fantastic form that will harmonize with the varying idiosyncracies of these various officers.

"The only object of these observations is to vindicate the court in taking cognizance of causes of this description, and not to enumerate all the causes that are embraced by the terms of the Constitution; and if a contract for the transportation of goods on the high seas is not a case of maritime jurisdiction, then it seems to me that there is no such case."[72]

The next case to come before the Supreme Court, a suit

by the owners of a vessel against the consignee of cargo, was dismissed for want of jurisdiction on the ground that the dispute was one for a common-law court.[73] Justice Wayne, however, who was now the most outspoken advocate of the admiralty jurisdiction, dissented. His thesis was that the courts of the United States must look to the maritime courts on the continent as well as to the ancient practice and jurisdiction in England to determine whether a case was embraced by the constitutional grant, and if a case was within the jurisdiction of such courts—as was this one—it was properly brought before a court of the United States sitting in admiralty.[74]

In the following year, Judge Andrew Miller of the District Court of Wisconsin undertook to explain the Act of 1845 extending jurisdiction of the district courts to certain cases on the Great Lakes and connecting waters. For Miller, as for Woodbury, this statute was an exercise of the commerce power rather than a legislative extension of full admiralty powers; the act conferred what he termed "quasi-admiralty jurisdiction." In matters of contract and tort arising on the Lakes the court could take admiralty jurisdiction only if the conditions of the act were strictly complied with, and not by virtue of any general powers which an admiralty court possessed over cases arising on the seas and tidewaters.

Miller inferred that in passing the act Congress was pursuing the intimation of the Supreme Court in the case of *The Thomas Jefferson:* "Whether, under power to regulate commerce between the states, Congress may not extend the remedy by the summary process of the admiralty to cases of voyages on the western waters, it is unnecessary for us to consider. If the public inconvenience, from the want of a process of an analogous nature, shall be extensively felt, the attention of the legislature will doubtless be drawn to the subject."[75]

By now the Supreme Court was in the habit of taking jurisdiction over cases of tort or collision on navigable tidewater rivers without discussing the question of jurisdiction itself; opinions were limited to a judgment on the merits. But just as the majority was feeling sure of its position, Justice Daniel was warming up to a series of strong dissents which were to continue throughout the decade of the 1850's and up to the time of his death in 1860.

In *Newton v. Stebbins*, a case involving the collision of two vessels on the North River (New York), Daniel picked up where he had left off in the case of *The Lexington*, four years earlier: "My conclusions, thus stated, are fortified by the strong desire to preserve in fullest vigor that admirable institution of our Anglo-Saxon ancestors—whose elevating influence on the character even of the humblest man is perceived in his consciousness that he forms a part, an important, nay, an indispensable part in the administration of the laws—the venerable trial by jury; and, in the next place, by my conviction of the duty incumbent on all to maintain, with directness and in good faith, those distinctions and distributions with respect to the judicial power which the Constitution and laws of the United States have ordained, distributions which the power now claimed and exerted appears to confound and overthrow. . .Can it possibly be right thus summarily to abrogate the jurisdiction of the state courts over their own territory and their own citizens? If these things can be done it follows, of course, that the trial by jury, and the requisite as to citizenship of parties, ordained both by the Constitution and laws, may be abolished by the mere will of persons interested, or by the fiat of a tribunal by which neither citizenship nor trial by jury is held in regard. It would be difficult to adduce a more striking example of the irregularities here pointed out, than is furnished by one of the cases now before us—that of *Newton v. Stebbins.* This is a case which the evidence shows to have occurred between citizens of the same state, upon the narrow waters, and far within the interior of the state; and necessarily, therefore, within the body of a county of the state. It presents within that locality an instance of simple tort, the proper subject of trespass or case at common-law; yet this case, without regard to locality or citizenship, is wrested from the tribunals of the state and the common-law modes of trial, and transferred to a tribunal whose peculiar and appropriate jurisdiction, we are told by the English authorities, attaches only where there is no vicinage from which the *pais* can be summoned. I am compelled, therefore, to deny to the admiralty the constitutional authority to take cognizance of these cases."[76]

By the end of 1851 the courts had fairly well travelled as far as was possible along the lines which had been drawn by Justice Story in *De Lovio v. Boit.* But this process was by no means consistently in one direction, for as we have seen, the number of opinions on what Justice Daniel described as the "space and verge" of admiralty jurisdiction was almost as great as the number of cases decided by the courts. These opinions may be classified into several groups in accordance with the approaches which were taken. On the one hand, there was the question: Who should determine the scope of the admiralty jurisdiction? A second question was, Are the terms "admiralty" and "maritime" equivalent, or did the latter term add something to the former? A third query was, Was the admiralty jurisdiction coextensive with the power of Congress over foreign and interstate commerce?

The first group consisted of Justices Story and Wayne and their fellow partisans of the admiralty, who assumed that it was the prerogative of the judiciary to define the limits of jurisdiction. In the exercise of that prerogative, they attributed an additional significance to the term "maritime", denied completely the restraining statutes of England, and insisted that the admiralty jurisdiction in the United States went beyond that which prevailed in England at the time the Constitution was adopted. Although Story and Wayne differed as to the limits of the American jurisdiction—the former went back to the early admiralty powers before the statutes of Richard II while the latter looked to the continent for authoritative rules—they both agreed in extending the geographical jurisdiction up to the extreme limits of tidal influence on navigable waters.

Justice Woodbury, whose principal concern was for the maintenance of the trial by jury, resisted the encroachments of the admiralty into the interior of the country. Not so extreme as Justices Baldwin and Daniel, while denying to the judiciary the power to create an expanded admiralty jurisdiction, he trusted to Congress to draw the line in a growing country with a changing economy, provided that any extension of admiralty jurisdiction be accompanied by the trial by jury.

Justice Nelson's equation of the geographical reach of the admiralty with the scope of the national government over commercial activity, was tangential to the positions taken by the other groups but was to create its share of debate in the period to come.

The extreme conservative position was that of Justice Daniel, who insisted on a completely rigid and frozen jurisdiction, received in its entirety from the mother country, incorporating all the prohibitions of the common-law courts, and unchangeable except by constitutional amendment. Daniel's concern was not so much the trial by jury or the rights of the states as the utter rejection of judge-made law or judicially created jurisdiction.

3. 1852-1864

If *Waring v. Clarke* put to rest the debate over *infra corpus comitatus*, *The Genesee Chief v. Fitzhugh*[77] put an end to the ebb and flow of the tide. After more than fifteen years of virtual silence on the subject of admiralty jurisdiction, Chief Justice Taney, when he finally spoke, went beyond anything ever suggested by the English admiralty or Justice Story. Only Justice Wayne's hint in *Bulloch v. The Lamar*, Woodbury's rhetorical question in *Waring v. Clarke*, and the experience on the European continent could have prepared the legal profession for the revolutionary doctrine successfully propounded by the Chief Justice.

Strictly speaking, the greater part—or most significant innovation—of *The Genesee Chief* is *obiter dicta*, unless taken simultaneously as the opinion in the companion case of *Fretz v. Bull.*[78] The first of these cases was one involving a collision which took place on Lake Ontario; inasmuch as the court's discussion was limited to the Act of 1845 the opinion was authoritative. But the novel doctrine concerned neither the Act of 1845 nor the Great Lakes but navigable waters in general, above the ebb and flow of the tide, precisely the locus of the collision in *Fretz v. Bull.* The opinion of Taney, therefore, should be treated as if referring to both cases even if the court handed down separate opinions.[79]

Taney begins by asserting that the judicial limitation of admiralty powers to tidewaters "was narrower than the Constitution contemplated," a conviction which had been "growing stronger every day with the growing commerce on the lakes and navigable rivers of the western states." Taney pointed out that the lakes were indeed inland seas, bordered by different states and a foreign nation: "A great and growing commerce is carried on upon them between different states and a foreign nation, which is subject to all the incidents and hazards that attend commerce on the ocean. . .every reason which existed for the grant of admiralty jurisdiction to the general government on the Atlantic seas, applies with equal force to the lakes."

Upholding the Act of 1845 under the grant of admiralty jurisdiction, Taney explicitly rejects the argument that the Act can be supported under the commerce clause or the earlier suggestion of Justice Nelson that the power of Congress to regulate commerce is related to the admiralty jurisdiction. The jurisdiction of the courts of the United States and regulations of commerce, says the Chief Justice, "are entirely distinct things, having no necessary connection with one another, and are conferred in the Constitution by separate and distinct grants."

The commercial power is as extensive upon land as upon water, Taney points out: "And if the admiralty jurisdiction in matters of contract and tort which the courts of the United States may lawfully exercise on the high seas, can be extended to the lakes under the power to regulate commerce, it can with the same propriety and upon the same construction, be extended to contracts and torts on land when the commerce is between different states. If the power of regulating commerce can be made the foundation of jurisdiction in its courts, and a new and extended admiralty jurisdiction beyond its heretofore known and admitted limits may be created on water under that authority, the same reason would justify the same exercise of power on land"—and it would not be long before admiralty jurisdiction was exercised over land transport between the states or between the United States and neighboring countries.

Asserting then that the Act of 1845 was a regulation of admiralty jurisdiction on the Great Lakes and connecting waters, rather than the grant of a new jurisdiction—despite the title, "An act *extending* the jurisdiction of the district courts"—Taney concludes that the purpose of the act was to permit the right to a trial by jury in circumstances named in the act. Rather than an extension, the act is a limitation on the general exercise of admiralty powers.

Not content to include the lakes and connecting waters within the original constitutional grant of admiralty jurisdiction, the Chief Justice proceeds to extend the jurisdiction to *all* navigable waters rather than to "halt short at the doubtful, and fluctuating, and pent-up limits of tidewaters," as Justice Woodbury put it.[80] To fortify his thesis, he brings up a veritable battery of arguments:

First, it would be contrary to the first principles of government and contrary to the equal rights and privileges of the citizens of the states to confine the advantages of admiralty jurisdiction to the states bordering on the Atlantic and the tidewater rivers and to deny them to the citizens who border on the lakes and "the great navigable streams which flow through the western states."

Second, the ancient distinction between navigable tidewater rivers and other waters was an erroneous substitute for the real measure of admiralty jurisdiction which was "public navigable rivers." Since, in fact, all English navigable waters were within the ebb and flow of the tide, the description "tidewaters" came to replace the original term; but in the United States, where the rule of tidewater arbitrarily divided a public stream into two parts, one subject to the admiralty and one not, it was necessary to return to the original concept of public navigable waters. This problem did not exist in the original thirteen states nor before the discovery of steamboats which, of course, explains why the American courts continued to employ the rule of the tide.

This belated resort to the ancient rule was not the creation of a new jurisdiction for Taney but the necessary recognition of economic, geographical and technical changes. The decision in the case of *The Thomas Jefferson* in 1825 was made "when the commerce of the rivers of the West and on the lakes was in its infancy, and of little importance; there were no navigable waters in the United States upon which commerce, in the usual acceptation of the word, was carried on, except tidewater, until the valley of the Mississippi was settled and cultivated, and steamboats invented."

The case of *Waring v. Clarke*, continued Taney, "showed the unreasonableness of giving a construction which would measure the jurisdiction of the admiralty by the tide. For if such be the construction, then a line drawn across the River Mississippi would limit the jurisdiction, although there were ports of entry above it, and the water as deep and navigable, and the commerce as rich, and exposed to the same hazards and incidents, as the commerce below. The distinction would be purely artificial and arbitrary as well as unjust, and would make the Constitution of the United States subject one part of a public river to the jurisdiction of a court of the United States, and deny it to another part equally public and but a few yards distant.

"It is evident that a definition that would at this day limit public rivers in this country to tidewater rivers is utterly inadmissible. We have thousands of miles of public navigable water, including lakes and rivers in which there is no tide. And certainly there can be no reason for admiralty power over a public tidewater which does not apply with equal force to any other public water used for commercial purposes and foreign trade. The lakes and the waters connecting them are undoubtedly public waters; and we think are within the grant of admiralty and maritime jurisdiction in the Constitution of the United States."

Taney's only difficulty in establishing this new doctrine was the precedent of *The Thomas Jefferson*. This case, however, did not prove to be an unsurmountable obstacle since it had "no relation to rights of property. It was a question of jurisdiction only," a decision founded in error which must be corrected.[81]

Finally, Taney confronted the principle objection to the admiralty jurisdiction, which was the want of the trial by jury: "It is this feature in the admiralty practice which made it the object of so much jealousy in England in the time of

Lord Coke, and enabled him to succeed in his efforts to restrict it to very narrow limits." But for Taney, as for all partisans of the admiralty, "the interests of an extensive commerce and navigation" and the need for courts "acting more promptly than courts of common law" were overriding considerations to which a doctrinaire position such as Coke's must become subordinate. Further, under the Act of 1845, Taney pointed out, "the right to a trial by jury is undoubtedly secured to either party if he thinks proper to demand it."[82]

To comment on Taney's decision is virtually to dissent, for somehow it is difficult to swallow whole such a radical departure from the doctrine laid down by Justice Story, which, in itself, is controversial. The Chief Justice's distinction between the commerce power and the admiralty jurisdiction is well-taken, but it is his wider discussion of admiralty jurisdiction and his doctrine of navigable water which raise questions. Even his treatment of the Act of 1845 leaves unanswered the query: Why was the law entitled "an act *extending* jurisdiction," if the jurisdiction already existed? The only answer is that in 1845 Congress did not visualize such a broad constitutional grant as Taney did in 1852.

Second, Taney's thesis depended on a concession to a concession. The admiralty jurisdiction was designed to operate on the oceans; jurisdiction over tidewaters was a concession, and then originally only in ports and havens; inclusion of all navigable waters because it was unreasonable to draw a line at a given place across a river such as the Mississippi was stretching a point beyond its original purpose, and was a perfect example of the adage, "If you give him an inch, he'll take a mile." Nor was Taney's sleight of hand at equating the concept of tidal waters with navigable waters, and insisting that past references to the ebb and flow of the tide should now be understood as substitutes for public navigable streams entirely satisfactory. Nor did it answer the argument of those conservatives such as Woodbury, who were reluctant to see the maritime jurisdiction wander too far from the *mare*.

Finally, when Taney attempted to assuage his critics by

pointing out that the Act of 1845 provided for a trial by jury, he failed to face up to the fact that cases arising on navigable waters other than the Great Lakes and connecting waters did not provide that safeguard, since the Act of 1845 did not extend to them.

Justice Daniel predictably filed a dissent to this encroachment of the admiralty beyond anything hitherto proposed: "Without there having been ingrafted any new provision on the Constitution, without the alteration of one letter of that instrument, designed to be the charter of all federal power, the jurisdiction of the admiralty is to be measured by miles, and by the extent of territory which may have been subsequently acquired; a much less natural standard, surely, than the nature and character of the element to which it owes its origin. . .I cannot construe the Constitution by mere geographical considerations; cannot stretch nor contract it in order to adapt it to such limits, but must interpret it by my solemn convictions of the meaning of its terms, and by what is believed to have been the understanding of those by whom it has been formed."[83] But it was not until several years later, in the case of *Jackson v. James*, that he got around to replying to the doctrine of Taney in greater detail.[84]

Two years later the Supreme Court took jurisdiction over a libel in admiralty presented by a passenger on board a steamer, who was scalded by steam and hot water as the result of a boiler explosion on a voyage between Sacramento and San Francisco, within the ebb and flow of the tide. The question of jurisdiction was assumed without discussion.[85] But Justice Daniel, fighting a rear guard action, once more opposed the assumption of admiralty jurisdiction where the locality was *infra corpus comitatus* and neither marine nor nautical. Concerned lest no limit be placed on the admiralty jurisdiction, Daniel protested:

"It to my view seems manifest that an extension of admiralty jurisdiction over all waters affected by the ebb and flow of the tide, would not merely be a violation of settled and venerable authority, but would necessarily result in the most mischievous interference with the common law and internal and police powers of every community. Take one illustration, which may be drawn from subjects within our immediate view.

"In the small estuary which traverses the avenue leading to this courtroom, the tides of the Potomac regularly ebb and flow, although upon the receding of the tide this watercourse can be stepped over. Upon the return of the tide, there may be seen on this water numerous boys bathing or angling, or passing in canoes. Should a conflict arise amongst these urchins, originating either in collision of canoes or an entangling of fishing lines, or from any similar cause, this would present a case of admiralty jurisdiction fully as legitimate as that which is made by the libel in the case before us. Yet the corporate authorities of Washington would think strangely, no doubt, of finding themselves, by the exertion of a great national power designed for national purposes, ousted of their power to keep the peace, and to inflict upon rioters within their notorious limits the discipline of the workhouse."[86]

Daniel's fears were exaggerated, if the contemporary decisions in several lower court cases had any authority. In *Tome v. Four Cribs of Lumber*, decided by the Circuit Court of Maryland, Justice Taney ruled that the admiralty jurisdiction did not extend to the salvage of rafts anchored in a public navigable river as they were not vehicles intended for the navigation of the sea or arms of the sea. The controversy was one for the decision of a court of common law.[87] And in *The Ann Arbor*, an action *in rem* against a canal boat for a breach of contract of carriage from upstate Rome to New York City via the Erie Canal and Hudson River, the District Court of New York refused to take jurisdiction because the canal boat was not built to navigate tidewaters.[88]

Again, in *Wallis v. Chesney*, the District Court of Maryland applied the old rule of tidewaters in denying admiralty jurisdiction over contracts for freight carried on canal boats where the greater part of the voyage was on a canal. "Is the contract to carry this coal a maritime contract over which this court has jurisdiction? I think not. The contract is entire, and four-fifths of the distance this coal was carried was on a canal, clearly beyond the jurisdiction of this court." As authority, Judge Giles cited the rule in *The Lexington*, decided five years before *The Genesee Chief:* "But if the substantial part of the service under the contract is to be performed beyond tidewaters, or if the contract relates exclusively to the interior navigation and trade of a state, jurisdiction is disclaimed."[89]

Even after the decision in *The Genesee Chief*, a confusion existed as to whether the Act of 1845 operated as a limitation on the admiralty jurisdiction over navigable waters in the West. In *The Flora*, decided in 1853, the District Court of Illinois held that the jurisdiction of the district courts upon the Western lakes and rivers did not depend on that Act. For Judge Drummond, in a case of collision, if either craft was within the law and if the circumstances brought it within the admiralty jurisdiction "upon general principles of maritime law," the court could take cognizance of the case.[90]

However, to Justice Grier, the ruling in *The Genesee Chief* had an entirely different meaning. In *Jones v. Coal Barges*, he accepted the assumption of jurisdiction in admiralty over navigable rivers, which went beyond the Act of 1845, but limited the application of the jurisdiction to the facts and conditions stipulated in that Act. For him, a collision of coal barges on the Monongahela River was not a case for admiralty because the conditions of the Act of 1845 were not fulfilled.[91]

"The case of *The Genesee Chief v. Fitzhugh*," wrote Grier, "does not necessarily extend the sceptre of the admiralty over every stream whose occasional floods or factitious basins may suffice to float a steamboat. If it was unreasonable to refuse to ships and steamboats on our great lakes and rivers the benefit of the remedies afforded by courts of admiralty, it may be equally so to apply the principle and practice of the maritime law to everything that floats on a fresh-water stream. Every mode of remedy and doctrine of the maritime law affecting ships and mariners, may be justly applied to ships and steamboats, but could have no application whatever to rafts and flatboats. A court of admiralty is not needed to try common-law actions of trespass, nor to administer common-law remedies in any form."[92]

While Grier was unable to free himself from the

limitations of the Act of 1845, Judge Willson of the District Court of Ohio celebrated the decision of *The Genesee Chief:* "The Supreme Court has boldly, and we think wisely, overruled the case of *The Thomas Jefferson* and the *Orleans v. Phoebus;* and in so doing has shown the unreasonableness of giving a construction to the Constitution which would measure the jurisdiction of the admiralty by tide. The great and increasing magnitude of the commerce of the lakes, and the almost fabulous increase of the lake marine, has finally caused the courts to pause and inquire whether, in all its varied rights and business arrangements, there is anything to distinguish the great lake commerce from the other maritime commerce of the world. . .Independent of the Act of 1845, under the Constitution, the maritime law has the same application to cases upon the lakes as to those upon tidewaters. Congress doubtless has the power to prescribe the mode of proceeding in admiralty, as was done by the Act of 1845, in saving to the parties the right of trial by jury. The admiralty jurisdiction on the lakes, however, lies deeper and beyond the Act of 1845."[93]

However, lest it be thought that the inclusion of the lakes and navigable rivers in the original constitutional grant of admiralty jurisdiction implied a new doctrine concerning the geographical limit of criminal jurisdiction in admiralty, Judge Betts, in *United States v. Wilson*, made clear that the criminal jurisdiction, unlike the civil, was limited by Congressional statute; and that the particular offense before the court, the willful destruction of a vessel, was punishable by federal law only when committed on the high seas.[94] Thus the new broad doctrine of the Supreme Court was not interpreted to go so far as to obliterate the restrictions discussed at such great length by Justice Woodbury in *United States v. New Bedford Bridge.*[95]

Once more Justice Daniel was busy writing dissents on a variety of admiralty cases. In *Ship Howard v. Wissman*, he objected to entertaining jurisdiction over a contract between a shipper and the master of a vessel to transport a cargo of potatoes from Hamburg to the Port of New York. The proper forum for this suit, said Daniel, was a court of law.[96]

In *Durant v. Rea*, Daniel once more objected to taking

jurisdiction over a case of collision in the harbor of New York on the North River. Here he returned to his argument on behalf of state rights, holding that it is "an axiom or postulate that, by the admiralty jurisdiction vested by the Constitution of the United States, a power has not been, nor ever was intended to be delegated to these courts to supersede or control the internal police of the states in providing for the preservation of property, or the regulation of order, or the security of personal rights." For Daniel, every encroachment upon these prerogatives of the states was an "unwarrantable assumption in the federal government" and a "progressive decline in the health and vigor of the states." Objecting to the summary nature of admiralty proceedings which entailed the seizure of vessels and resulted in the suspension of business prior to an adjudication of rights, Daniel argued: "The guards which the wisdom and beneficience of the common law and equity jurisprudence of the country have thrown around the rights of property will tolerate no consequences like these; they require judgment before execution; and this single consideration, were there no other, should cause them to be cherished and maintained, rather than impugned or evaded."[97]

In a third case decided at the same term, Daniel opposed the court's assumption of jurisdiction over a petitory suit, in which the title to property in a vessel was litigated. The court affirmed an early ruling by Justice Story[98] extending the jurisdiction to such cases. Once more, Daniel insisted that the case was one for the local state courts and not a question justifying the interposition of the admiralty. First, it was never a legitimate portion of the English admiralty jurisdiction; second, it was not true as some would have it that the admiralty jurisdiction in this country was free and unfettered. To those who held the contrary opinion, Daniel asked: "Freed from the checks and restraints imposed upon such a jurisdiction in that country, from which the system was transferred to us, what are the checks imposed upon it here? Are there any such checks? Does it, either in theory or in practice, recognize any such—how or where are they defined or ascertained? Has it any system at all, or is it left to the judgment or fancy of those who assume to exercise power under its name?"

Thereupon Daniel turned on Mr. Arthur Brown, a professor of civil law in Ireland and author of a treatise on the admiralty which was high in the favor of the admiralty partisans. Daniel denied any authority to Brown's doctrines and stated that if the latter were adopted as law, "there is no excess of extravagance to be found. . .which will not find an apology, nay, a full justification, in the book of this civil-law doctor.[99]

"It seems singular, however, that Mr. Brown should be appealed to in support of the authority now claimed for the admiralty," Daniel continued, "when in truth his book again and again admits that such jurisdiction had been utterly repudiated in England as a sheer usurpation, and may appropriately be styled a jeremiad over the lost authority and splendor of a system which he would exalt to the control of every other branch of jurisprudence."[100]

Oblivious of Daniel's stand, the champions of the admiralty continued to drive nails into the coffin of the common-law restrictions. Although denying to the admiralty the power to administer relief as a court of equity where one party has equitable title to a vessel without possession, Judge Willson of the District Court of Ohio could not refrain from giving to the admiralty in general the widest possible jurisdiction. Turning to the question of whether the term "maritime" added anything to the word "admiralty," Willson insisted that the former word had a substantive meaning, which conferred upon the federal courts "a more enlarged and extended jurisdiction than was conceded by the common-law judges to the high court of admiralty in England;" the correct conclusion was that of Justice Washington in *Davis v. The Seneca*, where it was held that the jurisdiction was to be sought in the general maritime law of nations. "The district courts of the United States, sitting as courts of admiralty," Willson continued, "are not embarrassed by the restraining statutes of Richard II and Henry IV, but exercise a large jurisdiction, and are governed by the same principles of maritime law as are recognized by the courts of admiralty in the maritime nations of continental Europe."[101]

Under the enthusiasm of this doctrine, in a companion case decided before before the same court, Judge Willson extended the admiralty jurisdiction to a suit *in rem* over a contract for building a vessel which had not yet been launched or employed in navigation.[102] But this was too much even for the liberal Supreme Court, which overruled the principle two years later in *The People's Ferry Co. v. Beers.*[103]

In 1858 the Supreme Court decided the case of *The Royal Saxon*, which had been pending before the lower courts and the state courts of Pennsylvania for a period of ten years. The case involved a conflict of jurisdiction between the federal courts sitting in admiralty and the courts of the state, a subject treated elsewhere in this book.[104] What is of interest here are the general remarks of Chief Justice Taney on the subject of admiralty jurisdiction in his dissent in the case of *Taylor v. Carryl:*[105]

"I am sensible that among the highest and most enlightened minds, which have been nurtured and trained in the studies of the common law, there is a jealousy of the admiralty jurisdiction, and that the principles of the common law are regarded as favorable to personal liberty and personal rights, and those of the admiralty as tending in a contrary direction. And under the influence of this opinion, they are apt to consider any restriction upon the power of the latter as so much gained to the cause of free institutions. And as there is no admiralty jurisdiction reserved to the states, and the administration of justice in their courts is confined to questions of common law and chancery, the studies and pursuits of the jurists in the states do not generally lead them to examine into the history and character of the admiralty jurisdiction; nor to inquire into its usefulness, and indeed necessity, in every country extensively engaged in commerce."

Reviewing the struggle between the admiralty and the common-law courts in England, Taney stated: "The legislation of England, however, in the present age, when the principles of civil liberty and enlightened jurisprudence are better understood, shows that the restrictions upon the admiralty jurisdiction imposed by the King's Bench have been found unsuitable to the wants of a great commercial people, and that the enlargement of that jurisdiction is not regarded, at the present day, as adverse to the march of liberal and free institutions."

Taney argued that the long struggle between the two systems of law, culminating in the statutes of 3rd and 4th Victoria, passed in 1840, restoring to the admiralty most of its original jurisdiction, showed past doubt that the efforts of the King's Bench to take away the jurisdiction of the admiralty "did not arise from any anxiety to preserve free institutions, and that the charges made against the admiralty of favoring despotic principles and usurping powers which did not belong to it, are without foundation." The Chief Justice was convinced that the prejudice against the admiralty jurisdiction was the result of a convulsed period of English history which had long since been succeeded by an enlightened age.

Once more Taney attempted to answer his American critics by pointing out that, "There is nothing in the character and proceedings of the admiralty incompatible with the trial by jury. And, indeed, it has already been given to a certain extent by the Act of Congress of 1845, and may at the will of Congress be given in every case, if it is supposed the purposes of justice require it." Be that as it may, the Chief Justice failed to underline the fact that in practice admiralty cases were decided without a jury and that no constitutional provision existed to require Congress to provide a jury trial.

Overlooking these objections, Taney continued: "I can therefore see no ground for jealousy or enmity to the admiralty jurisdiction. It has in it no one quality inconsistent with or unfavorable to free institutions. The simplicity and celerity of its proceedings make a jurisdiction of that kind a necessity in every just and enlightened commercial nation. The delays unavoidably incident to a court of common-law, from its rules and modes of proceeding, are equivalent to a denial of justice where the rights of seamen or maritime contracts or torts are concerned, and seafaring men the witnesses to prove them."

In a concluding plea to transcend the jealousies and suspicions of Lord Coke, Taney wrote: "I can see no good reason for fostering in the common-law courts of this country, whether state or federal, opinions springing from prejudices which arose out of the conflicts of the times, and which tend to create jealousies and suspicions on their part, and produce discord instead of harmony and mutual good feeling in the tribunals of justice."[106]

It is difficult to find much harmony and mutual good feeling in the disposition of *Jackson v. James*, a case involving a collision on the waters of the Alabama River, above tidewater. Four opinions were filed, two in favor of jurisdiction, representing the majority, and two opposed.

What distinguished this case from those like *Fretz v. Bull*, which had arisen on the Mississippi River, was that the Alabama River, insofar as it was navigable, flowed only within that one state, whereas the Mississippi flowed through various states and formed the boundary between states in various portions of its course.

In presenting the opinion of the court Justice Grier boldly declared that the state courts of admiralty, before the adoption of the Constitution, had exercised jurisdiction over public navigable rivers connected with the sea, not only where these rivers were boundaries to or passed through other states, but also where they were wholly within one state. The interpretation of the constitutional grant, argued Grier, must be based on this early practice rather than on arbitrary distinctions introduced by the common-law courts.

After asserting that the constitutional grant included all navigable rivers, Grier then made the observation that it was not necessary for Congress to extend the jurisdiction by legislation to the Mississippi, Alabama, or any other of the great rivers which were navigable from the sea. An act of Congress was necessary, however, to extend the jurisdiction over the fresh-water lakes which were *not* navigable from the sea, Grier held, in an *obiter dictum*, because "the district courts could not assume it by virtue of this clause in the Constitutuion."[107] This conclusion, which was not in accord with the broader interpretation given by Taney in *The Genesee Chief*, derived from the confusion arising from the reference to "waters which are navigable from the sea" in Section 9 of the Judiciary Act.[108]

In agreeing with the majority of the court, Justice McLean returned to the theme first suggested by Justice Nelson in the case of *The Lexington.* "The admiralty and maritime jurisdiction is essentially a commercial power," wrote McLean, "and it is necessarily limited to the exercise of that power by Congress. Every voyage of a vessel between two or more states is subject to the admiralty jurisdiction, and not to any state regulation. A denial of this doctrine is a subversion of the commercial power of Congress, and throws us on the confederation."

One is bound to wonder sometimes whether the justices of the Supreme Court read one another's opinions or put much stock in anything to which they themselves subscribed in forming a majority, beyond the judgment itself. For here McLean, in stressing the relationship between the commerce power of Congress and the admiralty powers of the courts, seemed to be completely oblivious of Chief Justice Taney's explicit rejection of that thesis in *The Genesee Chief.*[109]

Having laid down this rule of interstate commerce, it was necessary for McLean to demonstrate that one of the two vessels involved in the collision, the steamboat *Wetumpka*, was engaged in a commercial voyage between New Orleans, in the State of Louisiana, and Montgomery, in the State of Alabama, when it was run into and sunk by the steamboat *Magnolia.* For McLean, the nature of the river on which the collision took place was of no importance; it was the nature of the voyage of the steamboat which was decisive.[110]

To the charges that the expanded admiralty jurisdiction was contrary to the wishes and interests of the state, McLean replied that the exercise of that jurisdiction to date "has not been found dangerous or inconvenient. If this jurisdiction has been found salutary in that part of our country which is most commercial, it cannot be injurious or dangerous in those parts which are less commercial."

Pointing out that the recent acts of Parliament had restored to the English admiralty virtually the same jurisdiction as was now exercised in the United States, McLean observed: "It is singular that while the English admiralty, by its extension, has been placed substantially upon the same basis as our own, ours should be denounced as having a dangerous tendency upon our interests and institutions, and a desire expressed to abandon the enlightened rules of civil law, and follow the misconstrued statutes of Richard II."

McLean concluded with these philosophical and revealing remarks: "Antiquity has its charms, as it is rarely found in the common walks of professional life; but it may be doubted whether wisdom is not more frequently found in experience and the gradual progress of human affairs, and this is especially the case in all systems of jurisprudence which are matured by the progress of human knowledge. Whether it be common, chancery, or admiralty law, we should be more instructed by studying its present adaptations to human concerns, than to trace it back to its beginnings. Everyone is more interested and delighted to look upon the majestic and flowing river, than by following its current upwards until it becomes lost in its mountain rivulets."[111]

Antiquity has its charms and Justice Daniel had his pen. Recognizing that his remonstrances so far had been to no avail, Daniel still felt obligated to protest the "still wider departures from restrictions previously recognized, until in the cases before us every limit upon power, save those which judicial discretion or the propensity of the court may think proper to impose is now cast aside. . .I cannot, without a sense of delinquency, omit any occasion of protesting against what to my mind is an abuse of the greatest magnitude, and one which, hopeless as at present the prospect of remedy may appear, it would seem could require nothing but attention to its character and tendencies to insure a corrective. It must of necessity be resisted in practice, as wholly irreconcilable with every guarantee of the rights of person or property, or with the power of internal police in the states."

The conclusion which Daniel drew from the 9th Section of the Judiciary Act was, "that the power thereby vested with respect to *seizures*, is not an *admiralty* power—was never conferred by the investment of admiralty power in accordance with the Constitution; but is in its character distinct therefrom, and is peculiar and limited in its extent." Thus any argument which extended the admiralty jurisdiction to waters navigable from the sea on the basis of this exceptional jurisdiction over seizures was entirely fallacious and *non sequitur.*

Daniel then turned to a review of the cases decided by the Supreme Court beginning with *The Thomas Jefferson.* Here, he contended, an opening wedge was fashioned when the court, "with that greed for power by which courts are so often impelled beyond the line of strict propriety, makes a query whether, under the show of *regulating commerce*, Congress might not assert a distinctive and original authority, *viz:* the power of the admiralty. The court, however, felt itself constrained to concede the necessity of a locality within the ebb and flow of the tide, and for want of that requisite to deny jurisdiction.

"In the case of *Peyroux v. Howard,*" Daniel continued, "the necessity for the ebb and flow of the tide to give jurisdiction is equally conceded; but the court, in order to maintain its power, deems itself authorized to appeal *virtute officii*, not to the attraction of the moon, the received philosophical explanation of this phenomenon, but to the current of the Mississippi which, in precipitating itself upon the waters of the gulf, occasions, they say, by conflict with the latter, some changes in the rise and fall of the river at New Orleans. This *judicial* theory of the tides possesses at least the characteristic of novelty. Whether it will be accepted and find a place in the annals of scientific discovery may admit of some doubt."

The case of *Steamboat New Orleans v. Phoebus* made the test of admiralty jurisdiction "whether the vessel be engaged substantially in maritime navigation, or in interior navigation and trade *not on* tidewaters." *Waring v. Clarke* and *New Jersey Steam Navigation Co. v. The Merchants' Bank* "both concur in establishing the *ebb and flow of the tide* as the test of jurisdiction in the admiralty." Although these decisions go beyond what Daniel himself was willing to concede, nevertheless, he said, they were not entirely without their value: "By the limit they prescribed to the admiralty, viz, the ebb and flow of the tide, they at least rejected the ambitious claim to undefined and undefinable judicial discretion over the Constitution and the laws." It was in the light of these rules that Congress passed the Act of 1845 *extending* the jurisdiction of the admiralty to the lakes on which there were no tides, an act which was "the exception, the solitary exception," to the rule of high seas and tidewaters as the locality of jurisdiction.

But then comes *The Genesee Chief*, a case, "to my apprehension, more remarkable and more startling as an assumption of judicial power than any which the judicial history of the country has hitherto disclosed, prior to the case now under consideration." The conclusions of that case are "the most startling and dangerous innovations. . .ever attempted upon the powers and rights of internal government appertaining to the states." The gist of Daniel's criticism of *The Genesee Chief* was that the jurisdiction had been extended to public navigable waters by an act of judicial usurpation which completely ignored and discarded the admiralty jurisdiction which existed in the United States at the time the government was formed.[112]

The present case, said Daniel, has now extended the admiralty jurisdiction to waters two hundred miles above the tide on a river which is entirely within the State of Alabama. The rule of navigable waters does not end the search for a standard, for the question naturally arises—which are navigable waters? "Will it be proper to adopt, in the interpretation of this phrase, an etymological derivation from *navis*, and to designate as navigable waters those only on whose bosom ships and navies can be floated? Shall it embrace waters on which sloops and shallops, or what are generally termed river craft, can swim; or shall it be extended to any water on which a batteau or a pirogue can be floated? These are all, at any rate, *practicable* waters, navigable in a certain sense. If any point between the two extremes just mentioned is to be taken, there is at once opened a prolific source of uncertainty, of contestation and expense. And if the last of these extremes be adopted, then there is scarcely an internal water course, whether in its natural condition, or as improved under the authority and with the resources of the states, or a canal, or a mill pond, some of which are known to cover acres of land, (and, as this court can convert rivers without tides into *seas*, may be metamorphosed into small lakes), which would not by this doctrine be brought within the grasp of the admiralty. Some of our canals are navigated by stream, and some of them by sails; some of them are adjuncts to rivers, and form continuous communications with the ocean; all of them are fed by, and therefore are made portions of, rivers. Under this new regime, the hand of federal power may be thrust into everything, even into a vegetable or fruit basket; and there is no production of a farm or orchard, or a garden, on the margin of these water courses, which is not liable to be arrested on its way to the next market town by the *high admiralty power*, with all its parade of appendages; and the simple, plain, homely countryman, who imagined he had some comprehension of a justice of the peace, or of a county court, is now, through the instrumentality of some apt fomenter of trouble, metamorphised and magnified from a country attorney into a proctor, to be confounded and put to silence by a learned display from Roccus de Navibus, Emerigon, or Pardessus, from the *Mare Clausum*, or from the Trinity Masters, or the Apostles."

This prospect was too much for the judge from Virginia. Rejecting all the advances made by the court from *Waring v. Clarke* to *The Genesee Chief*, Daniel submitted as the only true test of jurisdiction the rule of *infra corpus comitatus.*

Then, in a final observation which summed up his general philosophy as well as his interpretation of the admiralty and maritime jurisdiction, Daniel concluded:

"Few, comparitively, of the attributes of sovereignty and equality, presupposed to have existed in those by whom the federal government was created, have remained perfectly intact and exempt from aggression by their own creature; and by no conceivable agency could they be more fearfully assailed than by this indefinite and indefinable pretension to admiralty power, which, spurning the restraints prescribed to it by the wise caution of our own ancestors, challenges, as occasion suits, the opinions and practices of all nations, people, and tongues, however diverse or incongruous with the genious of our own institutions.

"Not the least curious circumstance marking this course is the assertion that it produces equality amongst all the citizens of the United States. Equality it may be, but it is equality of subjection to an unknown and unlimited discretion, in lieu of allegiance to defined and legitimate authority."[113]

Justice Daniel was not alone. Campbell, joined by Catron, filed a separate dissent. The judge from Alabama added a few historical notes to the many which had been published over the preceding forty years: one was a reminder of the protests of the citizens of Boston in 1768 and later of the First Congress of 1774 against the extension of the jurisdiction of courts of admiralty beyond their ancient limits; another was a denial of the fact that a cause of collision arising upon rivers of France above the ebb and flow of the tide was cognizable before the admiralty of France at the time the Constitution was adopted.

Looking to the intentions of the framers, Campbell cited the writings of Wilson, Hamilton, Randolph, and Jay to the effect that the admiralty clause was included to comprehend cases involving relations with foreign nations. "The collision described in the libel of the appellants occurred at a place which in 1789 formed a part of the State of Georgia. Had a similar cause then arisen, I can affirm with perfect safety that not an individual member of any convention, whether state or federal, who was concerned in the making or ratifying of the Constitution, would have admitted the existence of an admiralty jurisdiction over the case. Such being the facts, I affirm that no change in the opinion of men, nor in the condition of the country, nor any apparent expediency, can render that constitutional which those who made the Constitution did not design to be so."

Reviewing the course of decisions in the American courts, Campbell commented: "The opinion of Justice Story, in the case of *De Lovio v. Boit*, is celebrated for its research, and is remarkable in my opinion for its boldness in asserting novel conclusions, and the facility with which authentic historical evidence that contradicted them is disposed of. From the decision in *The Thomas Jefferson* in 1825, to that of the *New Jersey Steam Navigation Company* in 1848," he added, "two generations of judges have agreed to doctrines wholly irreconcilable with the judgment now given."

Conceding the logic of extending the admiralty jurisdiction to the Great Lakes, which "form an external maritime boundary of the United States, and are a commercial highway, which by treaty is common to inhabitants of the two maritime and commercial countries whose possessions border them," Campbell contended that not one of the considerations justifying jurisdiction over the Great Lakes applied to the case before the court: "The Alabama River is not an inland sea. Its navigation was not open to a single foreign vessel when the collision took place. No port had been established on it by the authority of Congress. The commerce that passes over it consists mainly of the products of the state, and the objects received in exchange, at the only seaport of the state. For its whole length, it is subject to the same state government, and its police does not involve a necessity for a navy."

Reiterating Woodbury's emphasis on the trial by jury as the medula of the question, Campbell referred to the abhorrence of the English commons to "the summary jurisdiction of the courts of civil law, their private examination of witnesses, their rejection of a jury of the vicinage, the discretion they allowed to the judge, and their foreign code. The people of the several States," he continued, "have retained the popular elements of the judicial administration of England, and the attachment of her people to the institutions of local self-government. . .In the court of admiralty the people have no place as jurors.

"I consider that the present case carries the jurisdiction to an incalculable extent beyond any other, and all others, that have heretofore been pronounced," concluded Campbell, "and that it must create a revolution in the admiralty administration of the courts of the United States; that the change will produce heart-burning and discontent, and involve collisions with state legislatures and state jurisdiction. And, finally, it is a violation of the rights reserved in the Constitution of the United States to the states and the people."[114]

While the Supreme Court was upholding the jurisdiction of the admiralty over a collision two hundred miles up the Alabama River, the District Court of Maine extended the jurisdiction to an action *in personam*, for an assault committed by two officers of a ship against a seaman while the ship was lying in harbor in the port of Mobile, at the mouth of the same river. Here the question was whether the admiralty had jurisdiction *infra corpus comitatus* over a tort of a personal nature. Judge Ware, who ten years previously had endorsed the widest possible role for the admiralty courts, held that the jurisdiction existed and that there was no way of distinguishing between a case of this kind and one of collision. Just as the general maritime law, rather than the local state law, governed the rules of navigation, so too did the maritime law determine the mutual rights of seamen and ship's officers, in matters of discipline, behavior and punishment. Such cases were to be decided by the laws of the United States, and the jurisdiction belonged to the admiralty courts of the United States.

"The maritime law follows the ship wherever she goes in the prosecution of her enterprise," declared Ware. "It throws over the crew its shield for their protection, and it upholds the officers in the exercise of all their reasonable and just authority. This law, by the force of the grant of admiralty and maritime jurisdiction, is, in my opinion, the law of the United States, may be enforced by their courts, and is not subject to alteration by the several states. . .These laws follow the ship wherever she goes and do not become inoperative, or a dead letter, in the whole or in any part of them, when the ship arrives in and is lying within the body of a county."[115] [116]

With the exception of this case, which dealt with a special problem unrelated to the recent rulings of the Supreme Court, the subsequent decisions of both the lower courts and the Supreme Court itself seemed to draw back for a time from the implications of Taney's doctrine in *The Genesee Chief*. In *Brooks v. The Petona*, the cautious Judge Miller of the District Court of Wisconsin held that the admiralty had no jurisdiction over seamen's wages, when the services of a vessel on the Lakes were exclusively within the same state.[117] In *The Ann Arbor*, Justice Nelson affirmed the decree of the District Court, dismissing for want of jurisdiction a breach of contract for the shipment of butter on a canal boat from Rome on the Erie Canal to New York City.[118]

In *Allen v. Newbury*, the Supreme Court denied jurisdiction over the shipment of goods on Lake Michigan between Milwaukee and another port in the State of Wisconsin, under the Act of 1845, because the interstate commerce condition of that act was not fulfilled.[119] Wayne, Catron and Grier dissented, without filing an opinion. Daniel concurred on the ground that the admiralty jurisdiction did not extend to the internal waters of the United States. "If there be any inefficiency in this view of the admiralty powers of the government," he said, "the fault is chargeable on the Constitution, and on the want of foresight in those who framed that instrument, and it can be legitimately remedied by an amendment of the Constitution only." These were Daniel's parting words, which succinctly summed up his philosophy of government and constitutional construction.[120]

At the same term the Supreme Court refused to take jurisdiction over a proceeding *in rem* to recover the balance of an account for coal supplied to a vessel engaged in trade on the Sacramento River, between ports and places within the State of California. Justice Nelson, in delivering the opinion of the court, resorted to his standard of interstate commerce: "There certainly can be no good reason for extending the jurisdiction of the admiralty over this commerce. From the case of *Gibbons v. Ogden*, down to the present time, it has been conceded by this court that, according to the true interpretation of the grant of the commercial power in the Constitution to Congress, it does not extend to or embrace the purely internal commerce of a state; and hence that commerce is necessarily left to the regulation under state authority. To subject it, therefore, to the jurisdiction in admiralty would be exercising the jurisdiction simply in the enforcement of the municipal laws of the state, as these laws, under the conceded limitation of the commercial power, regulate the subject as completely as

Congress does commerce 'with foreign nations, and among the several states.' We are speaking of that commerce which is completely internal, and which does not extend to or affect other states, or foreign nations."[121]

Applying the rule in this case, Justice Nelson denied jurisdiction to the district court in admiralty over a claim for materials and labor for the repair of a steamboat engaged in operating on waters wholly within the limits of the State of New York;[122] while Judge Hoffman of the District Court of California made a similar ruling concerning a contract for pilotage between two ports within the same state.[123]

In *Whitaker v. The Fred Lorents*, Judge Miller extended his restrictive reading of the Act of 1845 to apply to a case arising on the Mississippi River which was outside of that act. A passenger on board a steamboat, travelling between two ports in the same state, suffered injuries through the negligence of the officers in charge of the boat. Miller held that the admiralty had no jurisdiction over the case even though the boat itself was engaged in a trip between places in different states, because the contract of passage was between ports in the same state. The libel was dismissed in accordance with the principles laid down in *Allen v. Newbury*.[124]

And when Judge Hoffman dismissed a suit *in rem* by shipping masters, to recover money for services rendered in obtaining a crew to navigate a vessel from one port to another within the same state, he observed: "It is impossible not to recognize, in the recent decisions of the Supreme Court, a disposition to confine the admiralty jurisdiction within narrower limits, and restrict maritime liens to fewer cases than is desired by its more ardent advocates."[125]

This observation was expanded on by Judge Betts in the case of *Poag v. McDonald*, a libel arising from the loss of cargo and injury to a canal boat towed from Albany to New York City. We have noted that Judge Betts early held that, "There can be no longer a doubt that the navigation from port to port in a particular state is equally subject to the authority of the general government with that from state to state."[126] But now, after almost thirty years, in the light of the recent Supreme Court decisions in *Allen v. Newbury* and *Maguire v. Card*, the same judge reluctantly[127] held that the admiralty jurisdiction does not extend to matters of contract or tort arising in commerce wholly between ports in the same state.

Examining the latest decisions of the Supreme Court, Betts noted that the admiralty had no jurisdiction over a contract for transporting goods on the lakes or inland waters of the United States from one port to another in the same state (*Allen v. Newbury*), or over contracts of any description entered into with a vessel engaged in the business of navigation and trade in the purely internal commerce of a state (*Maguire v. Card*). In the latter case, Betts continued, the court held that the restriction of admiralty jurisdiction to interstate commerce existed independently of the Act of 1845, which statute was only declaratory of the general law. Betts pointed out that in spite of the fact that the vessel involved in *Maguire v. Card* was a foreign one and the navigation was upon tidal waters, "it is definitely pronounced by the Supreme Court that those waters are not within the admiralty and maritime jurisdiction of the courts of admiralty in respect to matters relating purely to the internal commerce of that state. This destitution of jurisdiction seems to be absolute, and independent of the ownership of the vessel, whether foreign or American. . .the judgment of the court appears to be unequivocal that the jurisdiction in both cases stands upon the same principle, and is derived from and dependent upon the power of Congress to regulate commerce with foreign nations and among the several states."

Referring to the case before the District Court, to the claim of the libellants that the present case is substantially one of tort and that the restrictions of the Supreme Court should be limited to matters of contract, Betts replied: "It must be observed that no such reserve or qualification of the doctrine is intimated by the court."

In a conclusion not without a certain amount of bitterness, Betts wrote, in dismissing the libel: "This judgment of the Supreme Court [*Maguire v. Card*] withdraws from the provision of the Constitution (Article III, subd. 2) the broad meaning imported in the grant of admiralty powers 'to all cases of admiralty and maritime jurisdiction' and restricts its operation to matters pertaining to 'commerce with foreign nations, among the several states, and with the Indian tribes.' "[128]

The dismissal of the libel was affirmed on appeal to the Circuit Court. There Justice Nelson, who first introduced the test of interstate commerce in *New Jersey Steam Navigation Co. v. Merchants' Bank*[129], stated that it was "quite immaterial whether we assume the libel to be in contract or tort. In either aspect, the court below has no jurisdiction. The foundation principle is that the state governments have exclusive cognizance of their purely internal trade and commerce, and hence that the federal government is excluded therefrom. . .The [commerce] clause, by necessary implication, fixes the line of jurisdiction in the states, as all power over the subject, outside of the grant, is left to the states and comprehends jurisdiction over all their exclusively internal trade and commerce."[130]

A corollary of this case was the Supreme Court decision in *Nelson v. Leland.* Here the court held that the admiralty had jurisdiction over a collision occurring on the Yazoo River, which was wholly within the State of Mississippi, at a place where at times the stage of the water was too low for navigation, because the boat involved in the collision was en route from a town in Mississippi to the port of New Orleans in Louisiana. Once more McLean applied the rule of interstate commerce: "A commerce carried on between two or more states is subject to the laws and regulations of Congress, and to the admiralty jurisdiction."[131]

Again, in *Carpenter v. The Emma Johnson*, Justice Clifford ruled that the admiralty had jurisdiction over a contract of freight between two ports in the same state, Boston and Chatham, because part of the voyage took place on the high seas, out of the jurisdiction of any state. It was necessary to emphasize the "out-of-state" nature of the voyage in order to distinguish the case from the circumstances in *Maguire v. Card.*[132]

Thus, as things stood, it was the Nelson-McLean test of interstate commerce rather than Taney's broader rule of navigable waters which spelled out the limits to which the federal judges were compelled to adjust themselves.

However, there were still voices within the Supreme Court

and on the lower federal benches which were not willing to equate the commerce and the admiralty powers. In *The Transportation Co. v. Fitzhugh*, Justice Clifford held that it was not essential to the jurisdiction of the district courts of admiralty, in cases of collision, that either vessel should be engaged in foreign commerce or in commerce between the states. Admiralty jurisdiction, said Clifford, was conferred upon the courts by the Constitution, and in cases of tort was wholly unaffected by the question of whether the ship was engaged in interstate commerce.[132] As authority, Clifford cited the opinion of the Chief Justice in *The Genesee Chief.* [133]

"It is not denied that the admiralty has jurisdiction of torts committed on such navigable waters, nor is it denied that the waters of the Hudson, where the collision in this case occurred, are within the admiralty and maritime jurisdiction of the United States," wrote Clifford; "but it is insisted that something more is wanting in order to bring the case within the cognizance of the admiralty. Our reply to that suggestion is that locality, by all the authorities, is the test, in cases of tort, by which to determine the question whether the wrongful act is one of admiralty cognizance; and if it appears, as in cases of collision, depredations upon property, illegal disposition of ships, or seizures for breaches of the revenue laws, that it was committed on navigable waters, within the admiralty and maritime jurisdiction of the United States, then the case is one properly cognizable in the admiralty."[134]

The force of this opinion, however, was tenuous, for the above remarks were *obiter dicta.* The ship involved in the collision was en route from Albany to the port of Philadelphia and evidently engaged in interstate commerce.

Even more tenuous was the *dicta* of District Judge Hall in *Western Transportation Co. v. The Great Western;* however, it was important in keeping alive the doctrine of Taney until that day when the Supreme Court could once more adopt it explicitly and authoritatively. Recognizing the paramount authority of the decisions in *Allen v. Newbury* and *Maguire v. Card*, Judge Hall, nonetheless, could not refrain from giving his own opinion on the subject:

"I confess that I am not able to perceive any solid ground for thus restricting the admiralty jurisdiction of the national courts. The constitutional grant of admiralty jurisdiction has no such limitation. It is an independent grant of judicial power or jurisdiction, unconnected with the grant of commercial power. . .It was conclusively shown in [*The Genesee Chief*] that the power of regulating commerce could not be made the foundation of jurisdiction in the courts of the United States, and I cannot satisfy myself that the courts of the Union are justified in interpolating the language or limits of the grant of the commercial power into the grant of judicial power and jurisdiction, for the purpose of restricting, any more than of enlarging, their jurisdiction. That jurisdiction must rest upon the constitutional grant of judicial power, and upon the acts of Congress passed in pursuance thereof; and, if neither the Constitution nor the acts of Congress have prescribed a particular limitation to a power conferred in unrestricted terms, such limitations should not be interposed by judicial construction."[135]

The courts had gone into great detail over a period of seventy years in an attempt to define the scope of their admiralty jurisdiction, especially with respect to its geographical limits. There was perhaps no one topic before the court during this time on which there was a greater division of opinion—not merely a polarization between two extreme positions, but a complete gamut of doctrines and rules, ranging from a strict adherence to the English common-law prohibitions glorified by Lord Coke, through the compromises of the early American judges on account of the special problems of the United States to the adoption of the maritime laws of the European continent. It is not, then, surprising that Chief Justice Taney should thus sum up the controversy in one of the last admiralty cases to come before him:

"While this court has never regarded its admiralty authority as restricted to the subjects over which the English courts of admiralty exercised jurisdiction at the time our Constitution was adopted, yet it has never claimed the full extent of admiralty power which belongs to the courts organized under, and governed altogether by, the principles of the civil law."[136]

By the end of 1864 there were still certain problems of admiralty jurisdiction for the courts to resolve, especially ones dealing with the Act of 1845, contracts, insurance and the test of interstate commerce. But insofar as geographical limits were concerned, the query: what is admiralty jurisdiction? had been finally answered, over the strong protests of a vanishing minority. The admiralty had swept into ports and harbors, rushed upstream with the tide into the interior of the states and then proceeded to preempt all navigable waters. Neither Johnson nor Baldwin nor Woodbury nor Daniel could stop this sweeping movement, yet these judges, more than any other of their day, kept alive the concepts of local government and trial by jury, which had always been so important and which were once more to become fundamental to the system of American government.

4. Epilogue: 1865-1869

The principal unsolved problem remaining after Taney's death was whether his broad rule of navigable waters laid down in *The Genesee Chief* was to be qualified by the Nelson-McLean test of interstate commerce. Chief Justice Chase did not long delay in supporting his predecessor's position. In *The Mary Washington*, decided by the Circuit Court of Maryland, Chase held that the admiralty jurisdiction conferred by the Constitution extended to all contracts of a maritime character to be performed upon navigable waters, and a contract of freight to be performed wholly between ports within the same state was not excluded from that jurisdiction.[137]

Again, in *The Sarah Jane*, Judge Lowell of the District Court of Massachusetts, declaring that there was no necessary connection between the admiralty and commerce grants, abandoned the rule of *Maguire v. Card*, in holding that the admiralty had jurisdiction of a libel by mariners for their wages against a vessel plying on navigable waters which were wholly within one state.[138] Also, Judge Blatchford of the

District Court of New York ruled that the court of admiralty had jurisdiction of a case of tort committed on navigable water, even though both vessels were navigating between ports of the same state.[139] Meanwhile, in the Northern District of New York, Judge Hall, who had deferred to the authority of *Maguire v. Card* in his *dicta* in the case of *The Western Transportation Co.*, held that the admiralty could exercise jurisdiction over a contract to carry cargo on board a vessel travelling between two ports in the same state.[140]

By this time not only the lower court judges but the members of the Supreme Court as well had swung around to the Taney doctrine, and at last were willing to abandon the short-lived test of interstate commerce. The question was finally put to rest in the case of *The Belfast* where a unanimous court, including Justice Nelson, held that a proceeding *in rem* to enforce a contract for the shipment of cotton between the town of Vienna in Alabama and Mobile, on the Tombigbee River, was within the exclusive cognizance of the admiralty court of the United States, although the contract was for transportation between ports and places within the same state and the parties were both citizens of the same state. The only condition stipulated by the court was that the transportation be upon navigable waters.

Here Justice Clifford stated: "Difficulties attend every attempt to define the exact limits of admiralty jurisdiction, but it cannot be made to depend upon the power of Congress to regulate commerce, as conferred in the Constitution. They are entirely different things, having no necessary connection with one another, and are conferred in the Constitution by separate and distinct grants."[141]

If we review the debate over the admiralty jurisdiction for the period 1789-1869 we observe that the opponents of the admiralty were forced to fall back on one defense after another: the admiralty has no business in ports or waters which are surrounded by land; the admiralty should not intrude within the body of a county; the admiralty must not pass the point at which the influence of the tide is no longer felt; the admiralty can certainly not entertain jurisdiction where commerce is entirely internal. Considering the admiralty's complete victory obtained by small stages, it is understandable why the opponents preferred not to make even the first concession. It is also easy to see why the champions of the admiralty could not rest until they had virtually lost the current of the river in its mountain rivulets for, as Justice Woodbury asked, if an admiralty jurisdiction "commensurate in length and breadth with our mighty rivers and lakes was needed. . .then why not extend it at least over all our navigable waters, and not halt short at the doubtful, and fluctuating, and pent-up limits of tidewater?"[142]

But the struggle between the two schools was not merely a dispute over geographical limits. Nor was it just a difference between those who held states' rights and the trial by jury sacrosanct and those who stubbornly insisted on more power for the admiralty. It was to an even greater extent a debate between Nationalists such as Taney, who wanted to do everything in his power to foment the commercial expansion of the growing country[143] and who were willing therefore to subordinate certain other values to this goal, and the traditionalists, such as Daniel, to whom local government, trial by jury and old-fashioned ways of doing things took precedence over progress. It is not without irony that more than one hundred years after the deaths of Taney and Daniel, the tables are turning, if not with regard to the scope of admiralty jurisdiction, at least over the basic values underlying the admiralty controversy.

CHAPTER SEVEN

Footnotes

[1] *Gibbons v. Ogden*, 9 Wheaton 1 (1824); *Cooley v. Board of Wardens*, 12 Howard 299 (1852).

[2] Article III, Section 2.

[3] Italics added.

[4] *Thompson v. The Catharina*, Case 13,949, 23 FC 1028; 1031-1032 (1795).

[5] Case 15,676, 26 FC 1088 (1806), Circuit Court, Pennsylvania.

[6] *Woodruff v. The Levi Dearborne,* Case 17,988, 30 FC 525 (1811), Circuit Court, Georgia.

[7] We shall see below, p. 314, that more than twenty years later Justice Washington himself rejected this limitation.

[8] 3 Dallas 6 (1794).

[9] 3 Dallas 297 (1796).

[10] Note to Case 6,797, 12 FC 740 (1806).

[11] Case 4,479, 8 FC 697 (1813), Circuit Court, Massachusetts.

[12] Case 13,902, 23 FC 957 (1813), Circuit Court, Maine.

[13] *The Jerusalem,* Case 7,293, 13 FC 559 (1814), Circuit Court, Massachusetts.

[14] It was not until 1871 that the Supreme Court explicitly ruled that marine insurance was subject to admiralty jurisdiction. *Insurance Company v. Dunham,* 11 Wallace 1 (1871).

[15] "The proper jurisdiction of the courts of common law is of things done within the bodies of counties," continues Story, "and its further enlargement, by means of fictions, can be considered only as ingenious subterfuges and devices, to amplify their powers."

[16] *Stevens v. The Sandwich,* Case 13,409, 23 FC 29 (1801).

[17] *De Lovio v. Boit,* Case 3,776, 7 FC 418 (1815).

[18] The common-law courts issued prohibitions to the admiralty courts on the basis of their interpretation of the statutes of Richard II.

[19] *The Jerusalem,* Case 7,294, 13 FC 564; 565 (1815).

[20] Case 14,589, 24 FC 1138 (1816). Compare the similar case of *United States v. Hamilton,* Case 15,290, 26 FC 93 (1816), where Story denied jurisdiction over an indictment for larceny aboard a ship which was within the low-water mark in the habor of Le Havre. Where, however, a crime was comitted aboard ship outside of the Newburyport harbor but within three miles of the shore, Story had no difficulty in sustaining the jurisdiction. *United States v. Smith,* Case 16,337, 27 FC 1166 (1816).

[21] *United States v. Bevans,* 3 Wheaton 336 (1818). Marshall did not

deny to Congress the power to punish crimes committed aboard a ship of war, wherever the ship might lie; he merely ruled that the power had not yet been exercised.

[22] Case 9,187, 16 FC 938 (1824), Circuit Court, Connecticut.

[23] Case 18,201, 30 FC 909 (1824), Circuit Court, E.D. Pennsylvania.

[24] 10 Wheaton 428; 429 (1825).

[25] Suits in admiralty were of two kinds: *in personam*, a suit against another party; and *in rem*, in which the suit was against the ship itself, that is, the ship was made to respond.

[26] 4 Wheaton 438 (1819).

[27] *Clinton v. The Hannah*, Case 2,898, 5 FC 1056 (1781), Admiralty Court of Pennsylvania, Hopkinson; *Shrewsbury v. The Two Friends*, Case 12,819, 22 FC 42 (1786), Admiralty Court of South Carolina, Drayton.

[28] Concurring opinion of Johnson, *Ramsay v. Allegre*, 12 Wheaton 611 (1827).

[29] Case 11,233, 19 FC 891 (1827), Circuit Court, Maine. The case itself was dismissed for want of jurisdiction.

[30] *Drinkwater v. The Spartan*, Case 3,650, 7 FC 166 (1828).

[31] *Davis v. The Seneca*, Case 3,650, 7 FC 166 (1828).

[32] *United States v. McGill*, see above, p. 301.

[33] *The Seneca*, Case 12,670, 21 FC 1081 (1829), Circuit Court, E.D. Pennsylvania.

[34] Case 12,735, 21 FC 1218 (1829), District Court, W.D. Pennsylvania.

[35] Case 13,090, 22 FC 620 (1831), Hopkinson.

[36] See below, pp. 346 ff.

[37] *Martin v. Acker*, Case 9,155, 16 FC 884 (1831).

[38] Case 17,297, 29 FC 453 (1831), District Court, S.D. New York. Betts devotes a large portion of his opinion to tracing the English admiralty courts from their origins as "instruments of the royal prerogative" in relation to matters outside the kingdom, to their

enlarged and strengthened role over matters occurring within the kingdom, through the statutes of Richard II and the subsequent conflict between the admiralty and common-law courts. Betts concludes that resort to the British admiralty jurisdiction as the criterion for jurisdiction in this country still leaves unanswered the question: to what period in the history of the English jurisdiction are we to resort?

[39] *The Wave v. Hyer,* Case 17,300, 29 FC 464 (1831), Circuit Court, S.D. New York. In *Hobart v. Drogan,* 10 Peters 108, decided five years later, the Supreme Court upheld the thesis of Betts, that such suits were within the admiralty jurisdiction.

[40] *Bains v. The James and Catherine,* Case 756, 2 FC 410 (1832), Circuit Court, Pennsylvania.

[41] Case 16,991, 28 FC 1260 (1834), Circuit Court, Massachusetts.

[42] 7 Peters 324 (1833).

[43] While this case was being decided, Judge Betts commented in *The Perseverance,* Case 11,017, 19 FC 307 (1833), District Court, S.D. New York: "Although it is difficult to discern any principle which distinguishes one kind of water, adapted to general navigation, from another, yet the adjudged cases and elementary writers regard the particular of tidewater as an essential element to the jurisdiction of the admiralty."

[44] *Wilson v. The Ohio,* Case 17,825, 30 FC 149 (1834).

[45] *Thackarey v. The Farmer of Salem,* Case 13,853, 23 FC 877 (1835).

[46] The same court in 1806 held that physicians could not sue in admiralty for wages due on a voyage: *Gardner v. The New Jersey,* Case 5,233, 9 FC 1192; however, in *The Farmer of Salem,* above, Hopkinson acknowledged that the admiralty did have jurisdiction over surgeons, carpenters and stewards. Other rulings of Hopkinson were that a seaman whose wages had been paid up to the termination of a voyage, but who afterwards remained on board the vessel, moored at the wharf, as a watchman, had no claim for services enforceable in an admiralty court: *Phillips v. The Thomas Scattergood,* Case 11,106, 19 FC 523 (1828); and that the admiralty had no jurisdiction over a suit for musicians' wages on a vessel navigating tidal waters: *Trainer v. The Superior,* Case 14,136, 24 FC 130 (1834). In the latter case it was held that to justify a person employed on board a vessel in suing in the admiralty for his wages, the services rendered must contribute to the preservation of the vessel, or of those employed in her navigation. These cases were cited to demonstrate the difficulty which arises when

a judge has to draw a line without any outside guidance.

[47] Beveridge, *Life of John Marshall,* Vol. IV, p. 119.

[48] *Steamboat Orleans v. Phoebus,* 11 Peters 175; 182-184 (1837).

[49] *Boon v. The Hornet,* Case 1,640, 3 FC 876 (1841).

[50] *McLelland v. The Robert Morris,* Case 8,896, 16 FC 293 (1842), Circuit Court, E.D. Pennsylvania.

[51] *Davis v. The Enterprise,* Case 3,632, 7 FC 120 (1842).

[52] *Pierce v. The Victory,* Case 11,149a, 19 FC 646 (1844).

[53] *The D.C. Salisbury,* Case 3,694, 7 FC 279 (1844).

[54] *Peyroux v. Howard,* above.

[55] *The Perseverance,* above.

[56] *Bulloch v. The Lamar,* Case 2,129, 4 FC 654 (1844), Circuit Court, Georgia.

[57] *United States v. The James Morrison,* Case 15,465, 26 FC 579 (1846).

[58] *Van Santwood v. The John B. Cole,* Case 16,875, 28 FC 1075 (1846).

[59] Case 10,652, 18 FC 958 (1846). (Italics added.) Woodbury excluded from admiralty coverage: carpenters; pilots when not on the high seas; and physicians. This exclusion was in the form of a *dictum* and was not accepted by the other federal judges of the time.

[60] Six years later, Judge Sprague of the District Court of Massachusetts held in a similar case that seamen on board a small vessel employed in collecting and taking paving stones from two Massachusetts beaches into Boston Harbor could sue *in rem* in the admiralty for their wages. Here it was held that the navigation was the principal activity of the seamen, the loading and unloading of stone secondary. *The Mary,* Case 9,190, 16 FC 945 (1852).

[61] Case 8,582, 15 FC 1051 (1847), Kane.

[62] Details of case unreported.

[63] "We think in the controversy between the courts of admiralty and common law, upon the subject of jurisdiction, that the former have the

best of the argument; that they maintain the jurisdiction for which they contend with more learning, more directness of purpose, and without any of that verbal subtlety which is found in the arguments of their adversaries. The conclusions of the admiralty, too, are more congenial with our geographical condition."

[64] *Waring v. Clarke,* 5 Howard 441; 452-465 (1847).

[65] *Idem,* concurring opinion of Catron, 5 Howard 467.

[66] Idem, dissent of Woodbury, 5 Howard 467-503.

[67] 6 Howard 344 (1847).

[68] See below, p. 347 for the reaction of Chief Justice Taney to this concept.

[69] *Idem,* dissent of Daniel, 6 Howard 395-418. For Daniel's reaction to a judicially inspired expansion of the constitutional grant, See Chapter Two, pp. 90-91.

[70] *United States v. New Bedford Bridge,* Case 15,867, 27 FC 91 (1847).

[71] Compare Daniel's criticism of the assumption, "that the term 'maritime' implied more than the word 'admiralty,' when unassociated with it, and that this was so understood by the framers of the Constitution, who designed it as an enlargement of the admiralty power." *New Jersey Steam Navigation v. Merchants' Bank,* above. See also Woodbury's comment in the *New Bedford Bridge* case: "And though some have supposed that the word 'maritime', added in the Constitution after the word 'admiralty' might be construed as extending the present meaning of the word 'admiralty,' yet it would seem to me to raise an implication that it was restrictive, and if any thing had got into admiralty which was not strictly maritime, or happening on the seas (*mare*), it was not to be embraced, as the cases must be as admiralty and maritime jurisdiction, that is, of both, must be of things on the sea maritime as well as called admiralty. At the utmost, 'maritime' and 'admiralty' courts are treated as the same, and the expression a pleonasm."

[72] Note to *The Huntress,* Case 6,914, 12 FC 984 (1848).

[73] *Cutler v. Rae,* 7 Howard 729 (1849).

[74] *Idem,* dissent of Wayne, 7 Howard 733-737.

[75] *Ludington v. The Nucleus,* Case 8,598, 15 FC 1094 (1850). Jurisdiction was denied in this case because the conditions of the Act of 1845 were not fulfilled.

[76] 10 Howard 586 (1851). At the same time, Daniel also dissented from taking jurisdiction in the case of a collision on Long Island Sound. *St. John v. Paine*, 10 Howard 557.

[77] 12 Howard 443 (1852).

[78] 12 Howard 466 (1852).

[79] The opinion of the court in *Fretz v. Bull* was given by Justice Wayne on the authority of *The Genesee Chief*, just decided.

[80] *Waring v. Clarke*, see p. 332, above.

[81] See Chapter Two, p. 73 ff. for further comment on *stare decisis* and the overruling of earlier decisions.

[82] *The Genesee Chief v. Fitzhugh*, 12 Howard 443-463 (1852).

[83] *Idem*, dissent of Daniel, 12 Howard 464. For more on Daniel's critique of the role of the judiciary, see Chapter Two, pp. 73-74.

[84] See pp. 361-365, below.

[85] *Steamboat New World v. King*, 16 Howard 469 (1854).

[86] *Idem*, dissent of Daniel, 16 Howard 478-479.

[87] Case 14,083, 24 FC 18 (1853). Nonetheless, the disposition of the case was not consistent with the ruling. The Circuit Court refused to annul a decree of the District Court ordering the lumber from the rafts to be restored to the owners because "it would be unreasonable and unjust to deprive the owner of the possession he has obtained, merely to subject him to the necessity of recovering it in a new suit, in a court of common law."

[88] Case 407, 1 FC 945 (1854). "If such a canal boat as this, while on the Erie Canal, up in Oneida County, can enter into and bind itself by a contract so as to come within the control of a court of admiralty," said the court, "I do not see but that any vessel or thing capable of containing freight, built and designed to make headway on the New York Central Railroad by means of the wheels of the railroad cars, can in the same county enter into and bind itself by a maritime contract and come under the control of a court of admiralty, provided it is so constructed that when it arrives at Albany it can be launched from the wheels of the railroad carriage into tidewater and be towed by a steamboat to New York."

[89] Case 17,110, 29 FC 95 (1856).

[90] Case 4,878, 9 FC 291 (1853).

[91] "In order to show the jurisdiction of the district courts of the United States in 'matters of contract and tort' arising on the lakes and *other navigable rivers,* the libellant should aver and prove the facts and conditions stated in the Act of Congress of 26th of February, 1845."

[92] Case 7,458, 13 FC 950 (1855), overruling decree of District Court and dismissing case for want of jurisdiction.

[93] *Wolverton v. Lacey,* Case 17,932, 30 FC 417 (1856).

[94] Case 16,731, 28 FC 718 (1856).

[95] See pp. 338-339, above.

[96] 18 Howard 231 (1856).

[97] Dissent of Daniel, *Durant v. Rea,* 18 Howard 223 (1856).

[98] *The Tilton,* Case 14,054, 23 FC 1277 (1830), Circuit Court, Massachusetts.

[99] Here Daniel took a shot at Story's decision in *De Lovio v. Boit,* extending admiralty jurisdiction to policies of insurance.

[100] Dissent of Daniel, *Ward v. Peck,* 18 Howard 269-271 (1856).

[101] *Kynoch v. The S.C. Ives,* Case 7,958, 14 FC 888 (1856).

[102] *Parmlee v. The Charles Mears,* Case 10,766, 18 FC 1220 (1856). Willson follows the rule laid down by Judge Hopkinson in *Davis v. New Brig,* Case 3,643, 7 FC 144 (1834), District Court, E.D. Pennsylvania, and the *dicta* of Justice Story in *De Lovio v. Boit* and *The Jerusalem,* Cases 7,293 and 7,294, 13 FC 559 and 564 (1815), Circuit Court, Massachusetts.

[103] 20 Howard 393 (1858).

[104] See Chapter Four, pp. 163-164, above.

[105] 20 Howard 583 (1858).

[106] Dissent of Taney, 20 Howard 600-617 (1858).

[107] *Jackson v. James,* ("The Magnolia"), 20 Howard 296 (1858).

[108] Grier's reasoning is doubly fallacious: first, he assumes that the admiralty is given jurisdiction over "waters which are navigable from the sea" from Section 9, whereas, in fact, the phrase is limited to seizures and does not refer to civil causes of admiralty and maritime jurisdiction in general; second, he concludes that additional legislation was necessary to extend jurisdiction to the lakes because Section 9 does not refer to waters *not* navigable from the sea. The truth is that the reference in Section 9 to "all civil causes of admiralty and maritime

jurisdiction" without any specification of waters was sufficient for the district courts to take jurisdiction over the lakes without further legislation, once the constitutional grant was interpreted to include all navigable waters.

[109] See p. 368 ff., below, for further discussion of this issue.

[110] The *Magnolia* was engaged in commerce strictly within the State. The implication of McLean's opinion is that had the *Wetumpka* also been restricted to local commerce, the admiralty would not have cognizance of the case. This doctrine is by no means that of Taney or the majority in this case. McLean also fell into the error of claiming that Section 9 of the Act of 1789 extended the admiralty jurisdiction to rivers navigable from the sea by vessels of ten tons burden and upwards.

[111] *Idem,* concurring opinion of McLean, 20 Howard 303-307.

[112] For more on the role of the judiciary in this matter, see Chapter Two pp. 90-92.

[113] Dissent of Daniel, *Jackson v. James,* 20 Howard 307-321.

[114] *Idem,* dissent of Campbell, 20 Howard 322-343.

[115] *Roberts v. Skolfield,* Case 11,917, 20 FC 932 (1858). This case may be distinguished from that of *U.S. v. Bevans* (see page 309, above) in that the earlier was a criminal indictment presented by the United States government in accordance with a statute law, the later a case of private tort arising under the general maritime law.

[116] Here we have a perfect example of the situation against which Woodbury and Daniel were fighting: an incident arising in the port of Mobile, Alabama, being resolved by a judge, without the assistance of iurors, in the City of Portland, Maine.

[117] Case 1959, 4 FC 297 (1858).

[118] Case 408, 1 FC 946 (1858), Circuit Court, S.D. New York.

[119] 21 Howard 244 (1859).

[120] 21 Howard 248.

[121] *Maguire v. Card,* 21 Howard 248 (1859). Wayne dissented without filing an opinion.

[122] *The Troy,* Case 14,192, 24 FC 220 (1859), Circuit Court, S.D. New York.

[123] *Harrison v. The Anna Kimball,* Case 6,132, 11 FC 646 (1859).

[124] Case 17,527, 29 FC 954 (1859), District Court Wisconsin.

[125] *Scott v. The Morning Glory,* Case 12,542, 21 FC 845 (1859), District Court, N.D. California.

[126] *Martin v. Acker,* see p. 316, above.

[127] "I think the safe course with the inferior court will always be to accept the plain assertion of the Supreme Court as the highest evidence of the fact of jurisdiction, and to avoid all scrutiny into the *justness of the conclusion,* and much more into the *consistency* with its own antecedent action in that high tribunal in making it. . .I shall not entertain any inquiry whether prior rulings of the court have been made *inconsistent with that doctrine;* and more particularly, I shall decline all consideration of the *varying reasonings, if there be such,* upon which the court, at the one time or the other, may have motivated its decision." (Italics added.)

[128] *Poag v. The McDonald,* Case 11,238, 19 FC 901 (1859), District Court, S.D. New York.

[129] See p. 335, above.

[130] *Poag v. The McDonald,* Case 11,239, 19 FC 903 (1860), Circuit Court, S.D. New York.

[131] 22 Howard 48 (1860).

[132] Case 2,430, 5 FC 109 (1861), Circuit Court, Massachusetts.

[133] This same point was made by Judge Willson of the District Court of Ohio in *The Isabella,* Case 7,100, 13 FC 158 (1860).

[134] 1 Black 574 (1862).

[135] Case 17,443, 29 FC 777 (1862), District Court, N.D. New York.

[136] *Sears v. Wills,* 1 Black 108 (1862).

[137] Case 9,229, 16 FC 1006 (1865).

[138] Case 12,349, 21 FC 456 (1868).

[139] *The Brooklyn,* Case 1,938, 4 FC 238 (1868).

[140] *The Leonard,* Case 8,256, 15 FC 333 (1869).

[141] *The Belfast,* 7 Wallace 624 (1869). Clifford makes no reference to the case of *Maguire v. Card.* In a companion case, *The Eagle,* it was held that the admiralty jurisdiction on the lakes and connecting waters was not limited by the Act of 1845 but was as wide as the original constitutional grant and the 9th Section of the Judiciary Act. The only clause of the Act of 1845 which was still operative was that giving to either party the right of trial by jury. 8 Wallace 15 (1869).

[142] Dissent of Woodbury, *Waring v. Clarke,* 5 Howard 467 ff.

[143] See his position in *The Charles River Bridge* case and *Pennsylvania v. The Wheeling Bridge Co.,* in both of which he takes a position destined to encourage progress.

CHAPTER EIGHT:

RULES OF CONSTRUCTION

The Supreme Court, early in its history, decided that it could exercise no power or jurisdiction which had not been granted to it by the Constitution or the laws of Congress. However, as we have seen in an earlier chapter, the court determined by a process of deduction that it did possess the very important unwritten power of passing on the constitutionality of laws. Of equal importance, the court established itself as the final arbiter of the *meaning* of the Constitution. The assumption of this power, unsupported by any explicit mandate, is particularly noteworthy when it is considered that nowhere are any guidelines or criteria given to the justices of the Supreme Court to assist them in ascertaining that meaning.

In a certain sense, however, the Supreme Court had inherited a body of rules of construction from the mother country, just as the various states had acquired the unwritten common law. But these rules by themselves were not enough, because the internal structure and the historical background of the new government differed so greatly from that of England. Furthermore, the American judges had a written Constitution before them, one whose survival and vitality was to depend on them as much as on any other branch of government or segment of society.

" 'When I use a word,' Humpty Dumpty said, in rather a scornful tone, 'it means just what I choose it to mean—neither more nor less.'

" 'The question is,' said Alice, 'whether you can make words mean so many different things.'

" 'The question is,' said Humpty Dumpty, 'which is to be master—that's all.' " [1]

"We have here a few examples of the mischiefs incident to the doctrine which first interpolates into the Constitution the term 'intercourse' in lieu of the word 'commerce' contained in that instrument, and which then, by an arbitrary acceptation given to this term, claims for Congress whatsoever it may be thought desirable to comprise within its meaning. By permitting such an abuse, every limit may be removed from the power of the federal government, and no engine of usurpation could be more conveniently devised than the introduction of a favorite word which the interpolator would surely have as much right to interpret as to introduce. This would be fulfilling almost to the letter the account in the 'Tale of a Tub,' of Jack, Peter and Martin engaged in the interpretation of their father's will."[2]

Broadly speaking, jurists are said to belong to one of two schools of construction: that of *literal* construction and that of *liberal* construction. The first confines itself to the words of the text, relying, at most, on the aid of a dictionary; the second goes beyond the test itself and takes into account numerous other considerations. These schools should not be confused with the concepts *narrow* and *broad*, as applied, for example, to the powers of Congress, except to the extent that narrow and broad interpretations both fall within the school of liberal construction, which, like Procrustes, stretches or cuts down the guest to fit the bed. Thus, to take a *narrow* view of a word or phrase in the Constitution partakes as much of liberal construction as to insist on a broad or enlarged interpretation.[3]

The justices of the court themselves, when they conceived

of literal construction, had in mind what they called "the natural sense of words." Thus Justice Story writes: "The words are to be taken in their natural and obvious sense, and not in a sense unreasonably restricted or enlarged."[4] Justice Chase declared: "When we collect the intention from the words only, as they lie in the writing before us, it is a literal interpretation; and indeed if the words and the construction of a writing are clear and precise, we can scarce call it interpretation to collect the intention of the writer from thence. The principal rule to be observed, in literal interpretation, is to follow that sense, in respect both of the words and the construction, which is agreeable to common use."[5]

Justice Daniel, for his part, asserted that the Constitution was to be interpreted, "not by indirect or ingenious or forced constructions, or by remote implications, but by the plain and commonsense import of its language, a language familiar to the common and general understanding."[6]

Related to this concept of the common sense meaning of words was the opposition to interpolation or enlarging the meaning of words. In addition to Daniel's previously cited remarks on the subject,[7] we quote this passage from an opinion of Justice Wayne: "It not unfrequently happens in discussions upon the Constitution that an involuntary change is made in the words of it, or in their order, from which, as they are used, there may be a logical conclusion, though it be different from what the Constitution is in fact. And even though the change may appear to be equivalent, it will be found upon reflection not to convey the full meaning of the words used in the Constitution."[8]

Similarly, protests were raised against the attempts made to interpret the Constitutuion by rearranging the order of words or phrases. In discussing the contract clause, Justice Washington expressed his opinion that the rearrangement of words or sentences was "a very hazardous rule to adopt in the construction of an instrument so maturely considered as this Constitution was by the enlightened statesmen who framed it." The safest course, he continued, was "to construe this clause of the section according to the arrangement which the convention had thought proper to make of its different provisions. To insist upon a transposition, with a view to warrant one construction rather than the other, falls little short, in my opinion, of a begging of the whole question in controversy."[9]

One corollary to the doctrine of literal construction was an adversion to external sources of interpretation as acceptable authority. This "xenophobia," if the term may be used, was most strongly expressed by Justice Baldwin, who objected to the frequent practice of citing opinions which originated outside the court: "We can thus expound the Constitution without a reference to the definitions of a state or nation by any foreign writer, hypothetical reasoning, or the dissertations of the Federalist. This would be substituting individual authority in place of the declared will of the sovereign power of the Union, in a written fundamental law. . .Where its terms are plain I should, as a dissenting judge, deem it judicial sacrilege to put my hands on any of its provisions, and arrange or construe them according to any fancied use, object, purpose or motive which, by any ingenious train of reasoning, I might bring my mind to believe was the reason for its adoption by the sovereign power, from whose hands it comes to me as the rule and guide to my faith, my reason, and judicial oath. In taking out, putting in, or varying the plain meaning of a word or expression to meet the results of my poor judgment as to the meaning and intention of the great charter, which alone imparts to me my power to act as a judge of its supreme injunctions, I should feel myself acting upon it by judicial amendments, and not as one of its executors. I will not add unto these things; I will not impair the force or obligation of its enactments, plain and unqualified in its terms, by resorting to the authority of names, the decisions of foreign courts, or a reference to books or writers. The plain ordinances are a safe guide to my judgment."[10]

Consonant with the doctrine of literal construction was the rule that exceptions are not to be made to general terms. Chief Justice Marshall treated this subject on various occasions, especially in connection with the interpretation of the contract clause: "Although the spirit of an instrument, especially of a constitution, is to be respected not less than its letter, yet the spirit is to be collected chiefly from its words. It would be dangerous in the extreme to infer from extrinsic circumstances that a case for which the words of an instrument expressly provide, shall be exempted from its operation. Where words conflict with each other, where the different clauses of an instrument bear upon each other, and would be inconsistent unless the natural and common import of words be varied, construction becomes necessary, and a departure from the obvious meaning of words is justifiable. But if, in any case, the plain meaning of a provision, not contradicted by any other provision in the same instrument, is to be disregarded because we believe the framers of that instrument could not intend what they say, it must be one in which the absurdity and injustice of applying the provision to the case would be so monstrous that all mankind would, without hesitation, unite in rejecting the application."[11]

A perfect example of the doctrine of literal construction can be found in Marshall's success in bringing the *Dartmouth College* case under the operation of the contract clause. Acknowledging that such a case was probably not contemplated by the framers of the Constitution, he proceeded: "But although a particular and rare case may not in itself be of sufficient magnitude to induce a rule, yet it must be governed by the rule, when established, unless some plain and strong reason for excluding it can be given. It is not enough to say that this particular case was not in the mind of the convention when the article was framed, nor of the American people when it was adopted. It is necessary to go further and to say that had this particular case been suggested, the language would have been so varied as to exclude it, or it would have been made a special exception. *The case being within the words of the rule, must be within its operation likewise*, unless there be something in the literal construction so obviously absurd or mischievous, as to justify those who expound the Constitution in making an exception."[12]

Once again, in *Ogden v. Saunders*, Marshall attempted to

demonstrate that qualifications should not be read into general terms. Insisting that the prohibition on laws impairing the obligation of contracts comprehended the prospective as well as the retrospective operation of such laws, the Chief Justice declared that, "the words of the clause in the Constitution, which we are considering, *taken in their natural and obvious sense*, admit of a prospective as well as of a retrospective operation. If the mind of the convention, in framing this prohibition," he continued, "had been directed, not generally to the operation of laws upon the obligation of contracts, but particularly to their retrospective operation, it is scarcely conceivable that some word would not have been used indicating this idea. In instruments prepared on great consideration, general terms comprehending a whole subject are seldom employed to designate a particular, we might say a minute portion of that subject."[13]

This idea is picked up again by Justice Baldwin, in *Rhode Island v. Massachusetts*, when he wrote: "This court, in construing the Constitution as to the grants of powers to the United States, and the restrictions upon the states, has ever held that an exception of any particular case presupposes that those which are not excepted are embraced within the grant or prohibition, and have laid it down as a general rule that where no exception is made in terms, none will be made by mere implication or construction."[14]

These citations by no means exhaust the criticisms which were made against the doctrine of liberal construction. When confronted with the anomalous situation wherein the 11th Amendment prohibited suits in law or equity against any of the states without referring to suits in admiralty, Justice Washington rejected the suggestion that the court supply the words which were necessary to extend the prohibition to cases of admiralty and maritime jurisdiction. "Would we be justified by any rule of law in admitting such an interpolation, even if a reason could not be assigned for the omission of those words in the amendment itself?" he asked. "I think not. In our various struggles to get at the spirit and intention of the framers of the Constitution, I fear that this invariable charter of our rights would, in a very little time, be entirely construed away, and become at length so disfigured that its founders would recollect very few of its original features."[15]

Again, in *Martin v. Hunter's Lessee*, Justice Story, insisting that the appellate jurisdiction of the Supreme Court extended to "all other cases before mentioned," contended that the Constitution could not be construed in order to make an exception to cases arising in the state tribunals. "It is incumbent," he declared, "upon those who assert such a qualification to show its existence by necessary implication. If the text be clear and distinct, no restriction upon its plain and obvious import ought to be admitted, unless the inference be irresistible."[16]

This position was echoed by Marshall a few years later when he stated: "The jurisdiction of the court, then, being extended by the letter of the Constitution to all cases arising under it, or under the laws of the United States, it follows that those who would withdraw any case of this description from that jurisdiction must sustain the exemption they claim on the spirit and true meaning of the Constitution, which spirit and true meaning must be so apparent as to overrule the words which its framers have employed."[17]

It can readily be seen from the above excerpts that in defending the doctrine of literal construction an alternative approach is clearly acknowledged. Such phrases as "construction becomes necessary," "unless the inference be irresistible," "the spirit and true meaning of the Constitution," take us beyond the text, establishing the jurist rather than the word as the master.[18]

However, when we begin to explore the various avenues of free, liberal or loose construction, we find ourselves in a maze and at times wonder whether Justice Daniel's admonition should not have been taken more to heart. It is true that no judge has ever been known to follow Peter's example and pick out and reconstruct letters found in the text of the Constitution in order to cite authority for his opinion, but it is not difficult to find examples of other methods of free interpretation employed by the three brothers in Swift's tale: thus, in the *Passenger Cases*, the majority determined that the power to regulate commerce comprehended the power to regulate passenger travel. From 1844 on the court, with Daniel dissenting, decided that the word "citizen" as used in Article III included corporations, regardless of its meaning in other parts of the Constitution; and, in more recent times, the court has ruled that the constitutional prohibition on abridging the freedom of speech covers virtually all forms of self-expression.

In order to manipulate, interpolate or construe the textual words of the Constitution it is necessary to introduce certain interpretative concepts, chief among which are: historical considerations, intent, and consequences, not to mention that immanent being, the spirit of the Constitution.

Turning to the opinions of the court we find numerous examples of these concepts. Thus, in *Martin v. Hunter's Lessee*, in the same paragraph in which Justice Story warns against taking words "in a sense unreasonably restricted or enlarged," he refers to the powers of the government as those which are expressly given "or given by necessary implication."[19] It was by virtue of this concept, indeed, that the court was able to assume the power to pass on the constitutionality of laws, for nowhere is that power expressly given.

An even broader statement of this idea was given by Chief Justice Marshall[20] in *McCulloch v. Maryland:* "Among the enumerated powers we do not find that of establishing a bank or creating a corporation. But there is no phrase in the instrument which, like the articles of confederation, excludes incidental or implied powers; and which requires that everything granted shall be expressly and minutely described."

In justification of his position, Marshall went on to deliver what may be considered the fundamental gospel of liberal construction: "A constitution, to contain an accurate detail of all the subdivisions of which its great powers will admit, and of all the means by which they may be carried into execution, would partake of the prolixity of a legal code, and could scarcely be embraced by the human mind. It would probably never be understood by the public. Its nature, therefore, requires that only its great outlines should be marked, its important objects designated, and the minor ingredients which compose those objects *be deduced from the nature* of the objects themselves. . .In considering this question, then, we must never forget that it is a constitution we are expounding."[21] [22]

Pursuing this line of thought further, in *Gibbons v. Ogden* Marshall proceeded to declare: "This instrument contains an enumeration of powers expressly granted to their government. It has been said that these powers ought to be construed strictly. But why ought they to be so construed? Is there one sentence in the Constitution which gives countenance to this rule? In the last one of the enumerated powers, that which grants, expressly, the means for carrying all others into execution, Congress is authorized 'to make all laws which shall be necessary and proper' for the purpose. But this limitation on the means which may be used is not extended to the powers which are conferred; nor is there one sentence in the Constitution which has been pointed out by the gentlemen of the bar, or which we have been able to discern, that prescribes this rule. We do not, therefore, think ourselves justified in adopting it. What do gentlemen mean by a strict construction? If they contend only against that enlarged construction, which would extend words beyond their natural and obvious import, we might question the application of the term, but should not controvert the principle. If they contend for that narrow construction which, in support of some theory not to be found in the Constitution, would deny to the government those powers which the words of the grant, as usually understood, import, and which are consistent with the general views and objects of the instrument; for that narrow construction, which would cripple the government, and render it unequal to the objects for which it is declared to be instituted, and to which the powers given, as fairly understood, render it competent: then we cannot perceive the propriety of this strict construction, nor adopt it as the rule by which the Constitution is to be expounded."[23]

In *Brown v. Maryland*, Marshall had still another opportunity for suggesting guidelines for the interpretation of the Constitution: "In performing the delicate and important duty of construing clauses in the Constitution of our country, which involve conflicting powers of the government of the Union and of the respective states, it is proper to take a view of the literal meaning of the words to be expounded, of their connection with other words, and of the general objects to be accomplished by the prohibitory clause, or by the grant of power."[24]

One of the primary standards employed in arriving at the meaning of the Constitution was the principle of historical interpretation, that is, an attempt to ascertain the circumstances and conditions existing at the time the Constitution was framed. This approach took the form, in the first instance, of deferring to the judgment of the First Congress, on the ground that many of those who enacted the first laws had also served in the creation and ratification of the Constitution itself. Thus, from the very beginning, we may note Justice Chase's observation that, "The deliberate decision of the national legislature (who did not consider a tax on carriages a direct tax, but thought it was within the description of a duty) would determine me, if the case was doubtful, to receive the construction of the legislature."[25]

The same attitude was adopted on more than one occasion by other members of the court. In 1838, discussing the constitutionality of Section 9 of the Judiciary Act, giving non-exclusive jurisdiction to the Supreme Court in cases affecting consuls, Taney wrote: "Independently, however, of any judicial authority, the conclusions of my own mind must have been very clear and free from doubt, before I should have felt myself justified in pronouncing an act of Congress passed in 1789 a violation of the Constitution. It was the first Congress that met under the Constitution, and in it were many men who had taken a prominent and leading part in framing and supporting that instrument, and who certainly well understood the meaning of the words they used. The fact that the law in question was passed by such a body, is strong evidence that the words of the Constitution were not intended to forbid its passage."[26]

The second theorem of historical interpretation was the doctrine of acquiescence. With the passage of time this doctrine became of greater importance. Confronted in 1842 with a challenge to the constitutionality of the Act of 1793 concerning fugitive slaves, Justice Story argued that the very acquiescence of the highest state functionaries "is a most decisive proof of the universality of the opinion that the act is founded in a just construction of the Constitution, independent of the vast influence which it ought to have as a contemporaneous exposition of the provisions by those who were its immediate framers, or intimately connected with its adoption. . .Under such circumstances, if the question were one of doubtful construction, such long acquiescence in it, such contemporaneous exposition of it, and such extensive and uniform recognition of its validity would, in our judgment, entitle the question to be considered at rest; unless, indeed, the interpretation of the Constitution is to be delivered over to interminable doubt throughout the whole progress of legislation and of national operations."[27]

Justice Catron took a similar stand in regard to the meaning of the commerce clause. Pointing out that for sixty years Congress had permitted the states to regulate local commerce at ports of entry, he pointed out the imprudence of overthrowing this state of affairs at such a late date: "If long usage, general acquiescence, and the absence of complaint can settle the interpretation of the clause in question, then it should be deemed as settled in conformity to the usage by the courts."[28]

Again Justice McLean, upholding the power of Congress to govern the territories, said: "What do the lessons of wisdom and experience teach, under such circumstances, if the new light, which has so suddenly and unexpectedly burst upon us, be true? Acquiescence; acquiescence under a settled construction for sixty years, *though it may be erroneous*, which has secured to the country an advancement and prosperity beyond the power of computation. . .If the great and fundamental principles of our government are never to be settled, there can be no lasting prosperity. The Constitution will become a floating waif on the billows of popular excitement."[29]

The most common mode of historical interpretation of the Constitution was, in the words of Justice Livingston, "to recur to the situation and history of the country at the time, to its contemporaneous exposition, if it has received any; and to the general understanding of the community, especially if such understanding shall have been long acquiesced by all the states, and all the courts of the Union."[30]

Justice Story followed this rule in his dissent in *Briscoe v. Bank of Kentucky*. "It appears to me," he wrote, "that the true nature and objects of the prohibition, as well as its language, can properly be ascertained only by a reference to history; to the mischief existing, and which had existed when the Constitution was formed; and to the meaning then attached to the phrase 'bills of credit,' by the people of the United States. . .I mean to insist that the history of the colonies, before and during the Revolution, and down to the very time of the adoption of the Constitution, constitutes the highest and most authentic evidence to which we can resort, to interpret this clause of the instrument."[31]

Again, Justice Baldwin, in *Rhode Island v. Massachusetts*, declared: "In the construction of the Constitution, we must look to the history of the times, and examine the state of things existing when it was framed and adopted, to ascertain the old law, the mischief and the remedy."[32]

Recourse to this historical approach became even more frequent as problems relating to Negroes and slavery came before the court. For Justice Wayne, "The Constitution is to be interpreted by what was the condition of the parties to it when it was framed, by their object and purpose in framing it, and by the actual recognition in it of the dissimilar institutions of the states."[33]

Upholding the constitutionality of that portion of the Fugitive Slave Act which permitted fugitive slaves to be returned without benefit of trial by jury, District Judge Sprague of Massachusetts insisted that it was the intention of those who adopted the Constitution which must govern: "It is their views which we are endeavoring to ascertain, and to that end what can be more satisfactory than such contemporaneous exposition, such practice and acquiescence of the fathers of the Constitution, and all those who participated in its adoption, and their succesors for more than half a century? Those who, impressed only with the feelings of the present time, find it difficult to believe that our fathers in the North could have intended to render persons of color liable to be carried out of the state as slaves without trial by jury, and with a hearing only before a magistrate, will find it useful to go back to the period when the Constitution was established, and see the actual condition of things at that time.

"Verily, since the year 1788, when the Constitution was adopted," Sprague continued, "we of Massachusetts and the North have undergone a change, but this cannot alter pre-existing facts. If from the progress of benevolence we have acquired a stronger sympathy for the African, a more zealous desire to aid and protect him, *our change cannot retroact so as to change the views and intentions which actually existed at the time the Constitution was adopted.*"[34]

It is difficult to imagine a more conservative approach to the Constitution; nonetheless, we discover its equal in the *Dred Scott* case. Here Chief Justice Taney contributed the following observations to the theory of constitutional construction: "No one, we presume, supposes that any change in public opinion or feeling, in relation to this unfortunate race, in the civilized nations of Europe or in this country, should induce the court to give to the words of the Constitution a more liberal construction in their favor than they were intended to bear when the instrument was framed and adopted. Such an argument would be altogether inadmissible in any tribunal called on to interpret it. If any of its provisions are deemed unjust, there is a mode prescribed in the instrument itself by which it may be amended; but while it remains unaltered, *it must be construed now as it was understood at the time of its adoption.* It is not only the same in words, but the same in meaning, and delegates the same powers to the government, and reserves and secures the same rights and privileges to the citizen; and as long as it continues to exist in its present form, it speaks not only in the same words, but with the same meaning and intent with which it spoke when it came from the hands of its framers, and was voted on and adopted by the people of the United States. And any other rule of construction would abrogate the judicial character of this court, and make it the mere reflex of the popular opinion or passion of the day."[35]

Independent of the question of whether Taney's rule was valid or not, there was a great flaw in his position. Not only did he form a part of the same court which managed to find no difficulty in attributing constitutional citizenship to corporations, a concept most probably not contemplated by the framers and most certainly rejected by the Marshall Court early in the century, thus necessitating a reversal of earlier opinions, but Taney himself was the author of the opinion in *The Genesee Chief*, considered by many to be the most radical step taken by the pre-war court. In this latter case he not only reversed the rule of *The Thomas Jefferson*, which had limited admiralty jurisdiction to the ebb and flow of the tide, but had gone far beyond the most advanced positions of the admiralty's foremost advocate, Justice Story, *a fortiori*, beyond the understanding of the framers of the Constitution. Here the Chief Justice completely ignored the historical interpretation on which he relied in the *Dred Scott* case, and examined the Constitution in regard to the changing circumstances of the day. The decision in *The Thomas Jefferson*, he said, "was made in 1825 when the commerce on the rivers of the West and on the lakes was in its infancy, and of little importance, and but little regarded compared with that of the present day."[36]

If we can fault Taney for inconsistency in his use of rules of construction, classifying him as a political conservative on the issue of Negro rights rather than as a true judicial conservative, we must give credit to both Justices Daniel and Campbell for their consistency in following the rule of historical interpretation. Daniel's position has been cited throughout the previous chapters. Suffice it to say that both of these judges, up to the eve of the Civil War, continued to regard the Constitution through the eyes of the framers, holding that neither corporations nor Negroes were citizens and that admiralty and maritime jurisdiction remained what it was in the beginning.

Their position was best expressed by Justice Campbell in his dissent in the case of *The Magnolia*. "The collision described in the libel of the appellants," he wrote, "occurred at a place which in 1789 formed a part of the State of Georgia. Had a similar cause then arisen, I can affirm with perfect safety that not an individual member of any convention, whether state or federal, who was concerned in the making or the ratifying of the Constitution, would have admitted the existence of an admiralty jurisdiction over the case. Such being the facts, I affirm that no change in the opinion of men, nor in the condition of the country, nor any apparent expediency, can render that constitutional which those who made the Constitution did not design to be so."[37]

If historical interpretation, though by no means a branch of literal construction, was basically, at times painfully conservative, another approach to the Constitution—the search for intent—permitted more room for interpretation. These two methods, at first sight virtually identical, differ in that historical interpretation is a backward-looking process, based on the assumption that the framers had nothing in mind except the conditions and problems of their day; whereas intent is forward-looking as well and attributes the framers with foresight, as did Marshall in *McCulloch v. Maryland.*

The first references to be found in the opinions of the court to the problem of intent are concerned with the interpretation of laws. In *Pennington v. Coxe*, Chief Justice Marshall clearly stated: "It is the duty of the court to discover the intention of the legislature, and to respect that intention."[38]

Justice Washington expressed himself in a similar vein: "Where a law is plain and unambiguous, whether it be expressed in general or limited terms, the legislature shall be intended to mean what they have plainly expressed and, consequently, no room is left for construction. But if, from a view of the whole law, or from other laws in *pari materia*, the evident intention is different from the literal import of the terms employed to express it in a particular part of the law, that intention should prevail, for that in fact is the will of the legislature."[39]

Again, Marshall wrote: "The spirit as well as the letter of a statute must be respected, and where the whole context of the law demonstrates a particular intent in the legislature to effect a certain object, some degree of implication may be called in to aid that intent."[40]

But intent is a weapon which cuts both ways, as exemplified by the conflicting positions taken in the case of *United States v. Palmer.* Section 8 of the Act of April 30, 1790, provided the death penalty for any person who "shall commit, upon the high seas. . .murder or robbery, or any other offence *which*, if committed within the body of a county would, by the laws of the United States, be punishable with death." The Chief Justice interpreted this section to mean that Congress had specified three categories of crimes committed on the high seas which were punishable by death: murder, robbery, and "any other offence which, etc." In defense of his position, Marshall wrote: "If it be answered that although this opinion was entertained, yet, if the legislature was mistaken, those whose duty it is to construe the law must not yield to that mistake; we say that when the legislature manifests *this clear understanding of its own intention*, which intention consists with its words, courts are bound by it."[41]

Justice Johnson took sharp exception to this clear understanding and declared that the phrase should be read as though the relative clause, beginning with "which," qualified "murder" and "robbery" as well as "any other offence." Thus "robbery on the high seas" would be punishable by death only if that same crime was punishable by death within the body of a county. Johnson contended that the intent of Congress was to produce a uniformity in punishment. "In my opinion," he wrote, "this intent ought to govern the grammatical construction."[42] [43]

We have previously noted Marshall's criticism of strict construction in *Gibbons v. Ogden.*[44] As an alternative, he contended that whenever there should exist a serious doubt respecting the extent of any given power, "it is a well-settled rule that the objects for which it was given, especially when those objects are expressed in the instrument itself, should have great influence in the construction."[45] Again in *Postmaster General v. Early*, he reiterated: "There is always difficulty in extending the operation of words beyond their plain import; but the cardinal rule of construction is that where any doubt exists, the intent of the legislature, if it can be plainly perceived, ought to be pursued."[46]

Craig v. Missouri presents one more example of the difficulties involved in approaching the Constitution by the rule of intent. Acknowledging that it was, perhaps, too much to understand the term "bills of credit" in its literal sense, and that "the language of the Constitution itself, and the mischief to be prevented, which we know from the history of our country, equally limit the interpretation of the terms," Chief Justice Marshall, nonetheless, held that "The prohibition is general. It extends to all bills of credit, not to bills of credit of a particular description."[48]

Justice Thompson dissented, admitting that "the language of the Constitution may, perhaps, be too broad to admit of [a] restricted application," but insisting that it was necessary to keep in mind only the purpose for which the clause was included in the text: "The great evil that existed was that creditors were compelled to take such a depreciated currency, and articles in payment of their debts. This being the mischief, is it an unfair construction of the Constitution to restrict the intended remedy to the acknowledged and real mischief?"[49]

In a separate dissent, Justice McLean added: "If the term be susceptible of a broader signification, it would not be safe so to construe it, as it would extend the provision beyond the evil intended to be prevented, and instead of operating as a salutary restraint, might be productive of serious mischief. The words of the Constitution must always be construed according to their plain import, looking at their connection and the object in view."[50]

Notwithstanding the difficulties arising out of the doctrine of intent, the Court continued to employ it. Thus Justice Nelson, in construing the Patent Act of 1836, wrote: "It is not to be denied that, upon any view that has been taken, or that may be taken of the clause, its true meaning and legal effect cannot be asserted with entire confidence; and, after all, must depend upon such construction as the court can best give to doubtful phraseology and obscure legislation, having a due regard to the great object and intent of Congress, as collected from the context and general provisions and policy of the patent rule. The rule is familiar and well settled, that, in case of obscure and doubtful words or phraseology, the intention of the lawmakers is to be resorted to, if discoverable from the context, in order to fix and control their meaning, so as to reconcile it, if possible, with the general policy of the law."[51]

A few years later, District Judge Sprague asserted: "Let us next consider what is the force of the contemporaneous construction of the Constitution. Here we must remember that in construing the fundamental, as well as any other law, the sole inquiry is, What was the intention of those who established it? If in sixty years language has been deflected or acquired new shades of meaning, still our inquiry is, What was the sense in which it was originally used? How did those who adopted the Constitution understand its language and provisions?. . .The intention of those who adopted the Constitution must govern."[52]

If it was generally and frequently proclaimed that the intention should prevail, few general remarks can be found on how to determine the intention. Referring to the interpretation of the treaty of peace with Great Britain, Justice Chase wrote: "The intention. . .must be collected from a view of the whole instrument, and from the words made use of by them to express their intention, or from probable or rational conjectures. If the words express the meaning of the parties plainly, distinctly, and perfectly, there ought to be no other means of interpretation; but if the words are obscure, or ambiguous, or imperfect, recourse must be had to other means of interpretation, and in those three cases, we must collect the meaning from the words or from probable or rational conjectures, or from both."[53]

Marshall also pointed out that, "It is undoubtedly a well-established principle in the exposition of statutes that every part is to considered, and the intention of the legislature is to be extracted from the whole."[54]

An entirely different approach to constitutional and legal interpretation was that based on considerations of convenience and consequences. Both Marshall and Washington, on opposite sides of the case just cited, had recourse to this method. In Marshall's words, "where great inconvenience will result from a particular construction, that construction is to be avoided, unless the meaning of the legislature be plain; in which case, it must be obeyed. . .That the consequences are to be considered in expounding laws, where the intent is doubtful, is a principle not to be controverted; but it is also true that it is a principle which must be applied with caution, and has a degree of influence dependent on the nature of the case to which it is applied."[55]

Washington, however, stressed the inconveniences arising from the majority's interpretation, claiming that, "if the literal expressions of the law would lead to absurd, unjust or inconvenient consequences, such a construction should be given as to avoid such consequences if, from the whole purview of the law, and giving effect to the words used, it may fairly be done."[56]

Considering the potential number of cases in which arguments of convenience or consequences might have been employed in reaching decisions, it is surprising how rarely this doctrine was employed. Justice Thompson twice had recourse to it, once in *Ogden v. Saunders*, concerning the contract clause, and again in *Craig v. Missouri*, where bills of credit were involved. In the first case, he wrote: "If the letter of the Constitution does not imperiously demand a construction which denies to the states the power of passing insolvent laws like the one in question, policy and expediency require a contrary construction."[57] In the second instance, he rejected the majority's ruling that the certificates of the State of Missouri were bills of credit in the sense used in the Constitution, as "a construction of that instrument which will lead to serious embarrassment with state legislation, as existing in almost every member of the Union."[58]

In this latter case, Justice McLean went even further. "It is admitted," he wrote, "that the expediency or inexpediency of a measure cannot be considered in giving a construction to the Constitution. But when, in giving a construction to that instrument, it becomes necessary, as it does in some instances, to look into the mischiefs provided against, and the application becomes, to some extent a matter of inference, the question of expediency must be considered."

Then, in an extraordinary act of begging the question, he added: "If the act of Missouri *conferred benefits* upon the people of the state, and was so guarded in its provisions as to protect them from all possible evil, no court would feel inclined to declare it to be unconstitutional and void, unless it was directly opposed to the letter and spirit of the Constitution."[59]

Another example of this method of arguing from consequences can be found in Chief Justice Taney's opinion in the *Dred Scott* case, where he contended that members of the African race were not contemplated as citizens of a state, in the sense in which that term was used in the Constitution. His reasoning was that a citizen of a state was entitled to all the privileges and immunities of citizens in every other state; that they were guaranteed rights which a state could not withhold from them; and that "those rights are of a character and would lead to consequences which make it absolutely certain that the African race were not included under the name of citizens of a state, and were not in the contemplation of the framers of the Constitution when those privileges and immunities were provided for the protection of the citizens of other States."[60] [61]

A number of other rules were laid down from time to time. Justice Story believed that the Court should not construe an act of Congress in such a way as to make it unconstitutional, unless the terms of the act necessitated such a construction.[62] If an act admits of two interpretations, he said, "one of which brings it within, and the other presses it beyond the constitutional authority of Congress, it will become our duty to adopt the former construction, because a presumption never ought to be indulged that Congress meant to exercise or usurp any unconstitutional authority, unless that conclusion is forced upon the court by language altogether unambiguous."[63] [64]

A less logical generalization, to be found apparently in only one instance, is Taney's observation in the case of *Aldridge v. Williams.* There the Chief Justice contended: "In expounding this law the judgment of the court cannot, in any degree, be influenced by the construction placed upon it by individual members of Congress in the debate which took place on its passage, nor by the motives or reasons assigned by them for supporting or opposing amendments that were offered. The law, as it passed, is the will of the majority of both houses, and the only mode in which that will is spoken is in the act itself."[65]

Another proposition, which has previously been referred to in Chapter Two, is that the judiciary should not set aside as unconstitutional legislation of the states under a doubtful construction of the Constitution. "Doubts should lead to an acquiescence in the act," wrote Justice McLean. "The power which declares it null and void should be exercised only where the right to do so is perfectly clear."[66]

Of an entirely different nature were the remarks made by both Chief Justices on the validity of *dicta*. Marshall, who probably sprinkled his opinions with as much *dicta* as any justice of the court, warned that, "It is extremely dangerous to take general *dicta* upon supposed cases, not considered in all their bearings, and at best, inexplicitly stated, as establishing important law principles."[67]

In *Cohens v. Virginia* he was faced with the problem of getting around *dicta* of his own in the earlier case of *Marbury v. Madison*. "It is a maxim not to be disregarded," he wrote, "that general expressions, in every opinion, are to be taken in connection with the case in which those expressions are used. If they go beyond the case they may be respected, but ought not to control the judgment in a subsequent suit when the very point is presented for decision. The reason of this maxim is obvious. The question actually before the court is investigated with care, and considered in its full extent. Other principles which may serve to illustrate it are considered in their relation to the case decided, but their possible bearing on all other cases is seldom completely investigated."[68]

Midway through his term on the Court, Taney repeated the warning of his predecessor. "It is not my purpose to enter into a particular examination of the various passages in different opinions of the court, or of some of its members, in former cases, which have been referred to by counsel, and relied upon as supporting the construction of the Constitution for which they are respectively contending. And

I am less inclined to do so, because I think these controversies often arise from looking to detached passages in the opinions, where general expressions are sometimes used which, taken by themselves, are susceptible of a construction that the court never intended should be given to them and which, in some instances, would render different portions of the opinion inconsistent with each other. It is only by looking to the case under consideration at the time, and taking the whole opinion together, in all its bearings, that we can correctly understand the judgment of the court."[69]

Dictum has been defined as "a judicial opinion on a point other than the precise issue involved in determining a case."[70] Strictly speaking, the greater part of any opinion (and of any critical work on constitutional law) is nothing more than *dictum.* Generalizations, rules of construction—virtually everything which goes beyond the immediate point at hand are comprehended under this heading. Thus an indictment of *dicta* is, to a certain extent, a criticism of judicial opinions in general. Virtually every case can be condensed to a statement of facts and a brief paragraph declaring the law with, perhaps, a few footnotes for support. However, the judicial mind, particularly but not exclusively in Anglo-Saxon countries, chose to include in the opinions handed down not only the results of its reasoning but the details of the reasoning process itself. Since the judicial mind has a weakness for generalizations, the opinions are what they are: decisions surrounded by *dicta.* We have become so used to this practice—which is mandated by neither the Constitution nor the law—that we consider that there is something lacking when a court confines itself to a simple "Yes" or "No." For it is the general reasoning, after all, rather than the *ad hoc* decision itself, which most interests all parties except the plaintiff and the defendant.

We began this chapter with a discussion of literal construction; that is, the concept that words speak for themselves. A few final remarks should be made about the negative connotations of positive words. In *Marbury v. Madison*, Marshall stated: "Affirmative words are often, in their operation, negative of other objects than those affirmed; and in this case, a negative or exclusive sense must be given to them, or they have no operation at all."[71] Again, in *Dorousseau v. United States*, Marshall concluded that the affirmative description of the appellate power of the Supreme Court "has been understood to imply a negative on the exercise of such appellate power as is not comprehended within it."[72]

It is surprising, then, to find, only a few years later, the same Chief Justice stating, "affirmative words ought not to be construed negatively."[73] It was in order to escape from the bind of his earlier remarks that Marshall found it necessary to undermine the validity of *dicta*. This inconsistency has no great importance in itself, except as a warning against overly facile generalizations.

We have previously stated that liberal construction, as opposed to literal construction, may as readily result in a strict as an enlarged reading of the Constitution. There are two particularly interesting examples of this process which have seldom been mentioned but are worth examining.

Perhaps the most important generalization made by the Supreme Court during the pre-war period was that the application of the Bill of Rights was to be limited to the exercise of power by the government of the United States. In one sweeping decision, *Barron v. Baltimore*,[74] handed down at the relatively late hour of 1833, the court construed the original amendments in such a way as to exempt the states from their operation. Certainly the First Amendment explicitly referred to prohibitions on the power of Congress, but no such express limitation was included in the Second through Eighth Amendments. Under a literal interpretation of these articles, it would have been equally possible for the Court to have extended these prohibitions to the states or to have refrained from doing so. But the Chief Justice, supported by a unanimous court and confirmed by a series of subsequent decisions during the Taney period,[75] applying the rule of historical interpretation—a restrictive rule, as we have seen—held that the exclusive purpose of the amendments was to guard against abuse of powers by the new government and that since they contained "no expression indicating an intention to apply them to the state governments," the court could supply no such expression.

In support of his argument, Marshall contended that the limitations of the tenth section of Article I on the exercise of powers by the states "generally restrain state legislation on subjects instrusted to the general government." This, of course, was an inadequate summary of the tenth section, for laws impairing the obligation of contracts as well as *ex post facto* laws did not fall into such a category. Of more importance, there was no intrinsic reason why the restrictions of the power of government could not be construed to have a general application. The fact that some restrictions had already been incorporated in the original text of the Constitution, on both the power of the general and the state governments, makes tenable the assertion that by means of amendment the people could have placed additional restrictions on the power of both governments. That the Bill of Rights obviously placed limits on the power of the general government did not exclude the construction that those amendments were intended, or could be interpreted, equally to apply to the states.

This decision is cited not only to demonstrate the application of rules of construction, but as an admonition to those who would attempt to classify judges in terms of their philosophy of construction. Taking this case along with those previously cited, we can safely say only that Marshall's approach partakes of literal construction (contract clause, bills of credit), narrow construction *(Barron v. Baltimore)* and broad construction (the powers of Congress, the powers of the Supreme Court).

One other striking example of the reasoning process employed in constitutional construction may be found on the district court level in a decision by District Judge Wells of Missouri. The question before him was whether the Congress had the constitutional power to discharge debtors from debts contracted before the passage of the Bankrupt Act of 1841. The Constitution says nothing on this subject as far as the power of Congress is concerned. However, Wells determined that it was necessary to read between the lines and his reading produced the following conclusion: Congress can exercise no power that is not granted in the Constitution; Congress is not granted the power to impair contracts;

therefore Congress is prohibited from impairing contracts even though no express prohibition is included in the Constitution.[76] At first sight, there is something marvellously simple about this reasoning process. If the Congress possesses only powers which are expressly granted in the Constitution, there is no need to ground limitations on their powers in express constitutional prohibitions. But as Justice Wayne said, "The exercise of constitutional power by the United States, or the consequences of its exercise, are not to be concluded by the summary logic of ifs and syllogisms."[77] For syllogisms cut both ways, and taking into consideration the great number of explicit prohibitions on the powers of Congress, both in the original text and the Bill of Rights, it would have been equally possible to reason: Congress can exercise no power where prohibitions on its action have been expressly stated; Congress is not expressly prohibited from impairing contracts; therefore, Congress may impair contracts even though the express power to do so is not given. Thus we become aware of the fragility of rules of construction.

This struggle to establish rules of construction is inherent in the process of constitutional exegesis. In fact, it is of such great importance that to a great extent a jurist's judicial philosophy is made to depend on his position in this continuing debate. Does he read the Constitution literally or with a degree of liberality? We have seen, however, that rules of construction as well as their application are secondary to other considerations, and it is for that reason that we find an apparent inconsistency when examining the opinions of any one judge. The concepts of literal, liberal, strict and broad are interwoven and continually create new combinations, so that we are as likely to associate "broad" with "literal" as "strict" with "liberal." Further, each jurist, in the last resort, must follow the example of Humpty Dumpty and make the word mean just what he chooses it to mean, whether he resort to a "common-sense" definition or whether he make use of every possibility to be found in the *Oxford Dictionary*.

It is not possible to attribute a superior validity to any one approach to construction any more than it is to presume that there is only one interpretation of the Constitution. If any generalization may be made, however, it is that the rules employed, consciously or unconsciously, by the justices of the Supreme Court, possess as their common denominator a high degree of rationalism. Perhaps they partake of the nature of *dicta* and seldom form a part of the decision itself, yet their rational foundations serve as guarantees of the final result. We may quarrel with the premises assumed by the judge just as the justices may dissent from one another, but we respect their opinions, even to the point of admiring philosophies contrary to our own.

CHAPTER EIGHT

Footnotes

[1] Lewis Carroll, *Through the Looking Glass,* Chapter VI.

[2] Justice Daniel, dissenting, in *Passenger Cases,* 7 Howard 517-518 (1849). The reference is to Chapter Two of Jonathan Swift's story: the three brothers begin by picking out letters of the will to spell out the word "S H O U L D E R K N O T S" where they can find neither the syllables or words to justify their use of that ornament on their coats; they next refer to tradition and hearsay where in the text there is only "*altum silentium*"; their third effort is to add a codicil; in the fourth place, they interpret a word as meaningless in order to rid themselves of an explicit prohibition; next they assert that the "rigorous Clauses in the Will did therefore require some Allowance, and a favourable interpretation, and ought to be understood *cum grano salis*"; and finally they agree "to lock up their Father's Will in a Strong-Box and trouble themselves no farther to examine it, but only refer to its Authority whenever they thought fit."

[3] The word *liberal* is employed in the sense of *loose* and as opposed to *literal.* Despite its connotations, it has no necessary relation to the term *liberal* as opposed to *conservative.*

[4] *Martin v. Hunter's Lessee,* 1 Wheaton 326 (1816).

[5] *Ware v. Hylton,* 3 Dallas 240 (1796).

[6] *Northern Indiana Railroad v. Michigan Central Railroad,* 15 Howard 251 (1854), dissent.

[7] See above, p. 387.

[8] *Ex parte Wells,* 18 Howard 314 (1856).

[9] *Ogden v. Saunders,* 12 Wheaton 267-268 (1827).

[10] Concurring opinion, *Cherokee Nation v. Georgia,* 5 Peters 40-41 (1831).

[11] *Sturges v. Crowninshield,* 4 Wheaton 202-203 (1819).

[12] *Trustees of Dartmouth College v. Woodward,* 4 Wheaton 644-645 (1819). (Italics added.)

[13] Dissent, *Ogden v. Saunders,* 12 Wheaton 354; 356-357 (1827). (Italics added.)

[14] 12 Peters 722 (1838).

[15] *U.S. v. Bright,* Case 14,647, 24 FC 1236 (1809), Circuit Court Pennsylvania.

[16] 1 Wheaton 338-339 (1816).

[17] *Cohens v. Virginia,* 6 Wheaton 379-380 (1821).

[18] Even in literal construction the judge is not completely passive, but, in a relative sense, it may be said that the words are allowed to speak for themselves.

[19] 1 Wheaton 326 (1816).

[20] It is characteristic of "liberal constructionists" to insist on "literal construction" when it is of use to them. It is rare to find a jurist whose overriding approach to the Constitution is based on rules of construction.

[21] *McCulloch v. Maryland,* 4 Wheaton 406-407 (1819).

[22] One has the impression that Justice Daniel, on the other hand, would have preferred to have had incorporated into the Constitution of the United States some such phrase as found in the Constitution of Chile: "No official, no person, no group of persons may attribute to itself, not even under extraordinary circumstances, any authority or right other than those which have been *expressly* conferred on them by the laws. Any act in contravention of this article is null." Article 4, Constitution of the Republic of Chile. (Italics added.) ("Laws" as used here comprehends the Constitution, which is considered "the fundamental law".)

[23] 9 Wheaton 187-189 (1824). In a concurring opinion, Justice

Johnson remarked: "In attempts to construe the Constitution, I have never found much benefit resulting from the inquiry whether the whole, or any part of it, is to be construed strictly or literally. The simple, classical, precise, yet comprehensive language in which it is couched leaves, at most, but very little latitude for construction; and when its intent and meaning is discovered, nothing remains but to execute the will of those who made it, in the best manner to effect the purposes intended." 9 Wheaton 223. Johnson apparently failed to see that the discovery of the *intent* and *meaning* was no small task.

[24] 12 Wheaton 437 (1827).

[25] *Hylton v. United States,* 3 Dallas 173 (1796).

[26] *Gittings v. Crawford,* Case 5,465, 10 FC 450 (1838), Circuit Court Maryland.

[27] *Prigg v. Pennsylvania,* 16 Peters 620-621 (1842).

[28] Opinion of Catron, *License Cases,* 5 Howard 606-607 (1847).

[29] Dissent, *Dred Scott* case, 19 Howard 546 (1857). (Italics added.)

[30] *Adams v. Storey,* Case 66, 1 FC 145 (1817), Circuit Court New York.

[31] 11 Peters 330; 332 (1837).

[32] 12 Peters 723 (1838).

[33] Concurring opinion, *Passenger Cases,* 7 Howard 428-429 (1849).

[34] *United States v. Scott,* Case 16,240b, 27 FC 994; 995 (1851).

[35] *Dred Scott v. Sandford,* 19 Howard 426 (1857). (Italics added.)

[36] *The Genesee Chief v. Fitzhugh,* 12 Howard 443 (1852). See Chapter Seven, p. 349.

[37] Dissent, *Jackson v. James,* 20 Howard 334 (1858).

[38] 2 Cranch 59 (1804).

[39] Dissent, *United States v. Fisher,* 2 Cranch 399 (1804).

[40] *Durousseau v. United States,* 6 Cranch 314-315 (1810).

[41] 3 Wheaton 610; 630 (1818). (Italics added.)

[42] Dissent of Johnson, *op. cit.*, p. 636-637. "Singular as it may

appear," he added, "it really is the fact in this case, that these men's lives may depend upon a comma, more or less, or upon the question whether a relative, which may take three antecedents, just as well as one, shall be confined to one alone. Upon such a question I here solemnly declare that I never will consent to take the life of any man in obedience to any court; and if ever forced to choose between obeying this court on such a point or resigning my commission, I would not hesitate adopting the latter alternative."

[43] The prisoners were acquitted because the crime was committed aboard a foreign ship by men who were not Americans. The interpretation of Marshall, however, stood. Johnson objected to the "sanguinary character" given to the law by the court's interpretation. "For it is literally true," he said, "that under it a whole ship's crew may be consigned to the gallows for robbing a vessel of a single chicken." (p. 639).

[44] See p. 394, above.

[45] *Gibbons v. Ogden,* 9 Wheaton 189 (1824).

[46] 12 Wheaton 147 (1827).

[47] The doctrine of intent was even applied to the construction of penal laws. In *American Fur Company v. United States,* Justice Washington declared: "Even penal laws which, it is said, should be strictly construed, ought not to be construed so strictly as to defeat the obvious intention of the legislature." 2 Peters 367 (1829).

[48] 4 Peters 433-434 (1830).

[49] *Op. cit.,* p. 448-449.

[50] *Op. cit.,* p. 454.

[51] *Wilson v. Rousseau,* 4 Howard 677 (1846).

[52] *United States v. Scott,* Case 16,240b, 27 FC 993-994 (1851). Here there is an obvious merging of the concepts of historical interpretation and intent.

[53] *Ware v. Hylton,* 3 Dallas 239-240 (1796).

[54] *United States v. Fisher,* 2 Cranch 386 (1804).

[55] *Op. cit.,* 2 Cranch 386; 389 (1804). Marshall held that the inconvenience which arose in this case had been contemplated by Congress and was probably overbalanced by other advantages. The court interpreted the Bankrupt Act of 1800 in such a way as to give

priority to the United States government over private creditors.

[56] *Op. cit.*, dissent, 2 Cranch 399-400.

[57] 12 Wheaton 310 (1827).

[58] 4 Peters 448-449 (1830), dissent.

[59] *Op. cit.*, dissent, 4 Peters 457. (Italics added.)

[60] *Dred Scott v. Sandford*, 19 Howard 422-423 (1857).

[61] Taney frequently contemplated the practical consequences in coming to a decision. In the *Charles River Bridge* case he was particularly anxious not to permit the contract clause to be used as a restraint on progress. 11 Peters 547-548 (1837). His dissent in *Pennsylvania v. Wheeling Bridge Co.* was motivated in great part by his reluctance to see dismantled "a structure which promotes the convenience of the public." 13 Howard 591-592 (1852). And in reversing *The Thomas Jefferson*, he asserted that the former decision, if not corrected, "must produce serious public as well as private inconvenience." *Genesee Chief v. Fitzhugh*, 12 Howard 459 (1852).

[62] *Parsons v. Bedford*, 3 Peters 448-449 (1830).

[63] *United States v. Coombs*, 12 Peters 76 (1838). Indeed, the court found only two laws of Congress unconstitutional during the period under study.

[64] This rule can be found echoed in the opinion of District Judge Jones of the District Court of Alabama. In *United States v. Gould*, Case 15,239, 25 FC 1376 (1860), he stated as a rule of construction, "never to give a statute such a construction as would render it unconstitutional, if it will possibly admit of any other construction which would make it consistent with the Constitution."

[65] 3 Howard 24 (1844). The paragraph continues: "and we must gather their intention from the language there used, comparing it, when any ambiguity exists, with the laws upon the same subject, and looking, if necessary, to the public history of the times in which it was passed."

[66] Dissent, *Craig v. Missouri*, 4 Peters 459 (1830).

[67] *Alexander v. Baltimore Insurance Co.*, 4 Cranch 379 (1808).

[68] *Cohens v. Virginia*, 6 Wheaton 399-400 (1821).

[69] Opinion of Taney, *License Cases*, 5 Howard 573 (1847).

[70] Webster's Seventh New Collegiate Dictionary, p. 231.

[71] 1 Cranch 174 (1803).

[72] 6 Cranch 314 (1810).

[73] *Cohens v. Virginia,* 6 Wheaton 394-395 (1821).

[74] 7 Peters 243 (1833).

[75] *Charles River Bridge* case, 11 Peters 578 (1837); *Holmes v. Jennison,* 14 Peters 582; 587-588 (1840); *Permoli v. First Municipality of New Orleans,* 3 Howard 609 (1848); *Fox v. Ohio,* 5 Howard 434-435 (1847); *West River Bridge v. Dix,* 6 Howard 538 (1848); *Smith v. Maryland,* 18 Howard 76 (1856); *Withers v. Buckley,* 20 Howard 89-90 (1858).

[76] *In re Klein,* Case 7,866, 14 FC 719; 723-725 (1843), District Court Missouri. The Circuit Court reversed the judgment and upheld the constitutionality of the act, even if the obligation of contracts was impaired. *In re Klein,* Case 7,865, 14 FC 716 (1843).

[77] Concurring opinion, *Passenger Cases,* 7 Howard 429 (1849).

INDEX OF JUDGES

[Dates refer to period during which Justice served on the Supreme Court. (D.C.) following name designates judge of a District Court.]

INDEX OF PRINCIPAL CASES